A Passage to China

Colin Campbell's Diary
of the First Swedish East India Company
Expedition to Canton, 1732–33

Colin Campbell (1686–1757). Painting by J.J. Streng. Gothenburg City Museum.
(Photo: Håkan Berg.)

ACTA

REGIAE SOCIETATIS SCIENTIARUM ET LITTERARUM
GOTHOBURGENSIS

Humaniora

37

A Passage to China

Colin Campbell's Diary
of the First Swedish East India Company
Expedition to Canton, 1732–33

Edited by

Paul Hallberg and Christian Koninckx

Royal Society of Arts and Sciences

in Göteborg

Communicated December 12, 1994

Distr.:
Kungl. Vetenskaps- och Vitterhets-Samhället i Göteborg
(Royal Society of Arts and Sciences in Göteborg)
c/o Göteborgs universitetsbibliotek
P.O. Box 5096 – S-402 22 GÖTEBORG – Sweden

ISBN 91-85252-55-7
ISSN 0347-4917

Rundqvists Boktryckeri, Göteborg 1996

"Comme j'ay demeuré quelques annees aux Indes orientales & y ay fait des voyages d'un Coté a l'autre Je pretends de Scavoir un peu de ce Commerce, Et que mon honneur et mon Interet est si considerablement engagé a present dans cette Compagnie, Je Suis resolu aussi d'y risquer ma Personne & d'y aller avec le Vaisseau qui va partir cette Annee, a fin de faire un Commencement, & de montrer aux autres un Chemin assez Inconnu dans ce Païs ci ..."

("Having stayed for some years in the East and having travelled there from one coast to the other I think I can say that I understand something of this trade. My honour and my interest are now so committed to this Company that I am determined even to risk my life and embark on the ship going out this year, in order to make a start and show others a way unknown in this country...")

Colin Campbell in a letter dated 9 November 1731 to Joachim Fredrik Preis, Swedish envoy in The Hague (RAS. Hollandica 793)

v

Contents

Acknowledgments

The present edition has been in preparation for much longer than originally foreseen by its editors. The reason, of course, is that the work has had to be done in our spare time, a commodity which seems to have become increasingly scarce in the lives of research library administrators.

Now that the text of Colin Campbell's journal of the first Swedish East India Company expedition is finally presented to the scholarly world, it is our pleasant duty to acknowledge with gratitude our indebtedness to a large number of persons and institutions for invaluable assistance in various ways. They are far too numerous to be listed here by name, and so we shall have to be restrictive. In particular we should like to express our thanks to Dr. *Erik Malmsten*, donator of the foundation *Rådmannen Sven Nordqvists Minnesfond*, whose generosity made it possible to save the manuscript for preservation in Gothenburg; former Directors of the Gothenburg Historical Museum (now City Museum) Dr. *Christian Axel-Nilsson* and Dr. *Henrik Ahnlund* for their active interest and practical help in the project; Dr. *Ronald Paul* of the English Department, University of Göteborg, for preparing the first working transcription of the manuscript and for revising our English; Professor *Göran Kjellmer* of the same Department for valuable advice on a number of linguistic and editorial points; Mr. *Lars Olof Lööf*, Keeper at the Gothenburg City Museum, for assistance with the illustrations; Mr. *Patrick Vanouplines* of the University Library, Free University of Brussels, for successful cooperation on the problem of the comet observed by Campbell; and Mr. *Minhai Gui*, student at the University of Göteborg, for placing at our disposal part of his doctoral thesis still in preparation.

We also most gratefully acknowledge the kind and efficient help rendered over the years by the staffs of the *Gothenburg City Museum*; the *Gothenburg Maritime Museum*; and the *Röhss Museum of Arts, Crafts and Design*, Gothenburg; the *National Library of Scotland*, Edinburgh; the *James Ford Bell Library, University of Minnesota*, Minneapolis; and last but not least, those of our own institutions, viz. *Göteborg University Library* and the *University Library of the Free University of Brussels*.

It only remains for us to express our warm thanks for generous grants received from two Gothenburg funds, *Grén Brobergs Museistiftelse* and *Fru Mary von Sydows, f. Wijk Fond*, and from the *Royal Society of Arts and Sciences in Göteborg* to cover the printing costs, as well as for the permission of the *Royal Society* to have the edition appear in their *Acta* series.

Gothenburg and Brussels, June 1996.

Paul Hallberg   *Christian Koninckx*

Introduction

Discovery and provenance of the manuscript

In September 1986 the attention of Göteborg University Library was drawn to an item in a catalogue from the well-known antiquarian bookseller H.P. Kraus in New York. It consisted of two manuscripts which seemed to be of particular Gothenburg interest and which were described as follows:

> CAMPBELL, COLIN, Autograph Journals of three voyages to China of the *Fredericus Rex Sueciae*. 1732–33, 1735–36, 1738–39.
>   Gothenburg, Cadiz, Canton, at sea, 1733–39.
> Folio and large folio. 287 (including 2 blank) pp.; 75 pp. (including 1 blank). Contemporary vellum with ties; contemporary stencilled wrappers.
>
> Colin Campbell (1686–1757), the first director of the Swedish East India Company, also acted as minister plenipotentiary from the King of Sweden to the Chinese emperor. Campbell's account of the first voyage to China in the *Fredericus Rex Sueciae* was thought to be lost because when the Dutch attacked the ship in the Straits of Sunda as it returned from China, Campbell ordered all the ships' journals destroyed so that the Dutch would learn nothing of the Company's affairs.
>   Upon his return to Gothenburg, he reconstructed his journal of the first voyage (here bound in vellum), of which 118 pp. concern the eventful voyage to Canton, including adverse conditions allegedly caused by the captain's dilatoriness and incompetence; 71 pp. are concerned with commercial transactions in Canton, including prices and availability of teas, silks, and porcelains; 80 pp. cover conflicts with the Dutch at Batavia; 18 pp. describe other events.
>   Of the fifteen extant ships' journals listed by Koninckx in his book on the Swedish East India Company, there is no record of the 1735–36 voyage and the only record of the 1738–39 voyage is that compiled by the second supercargo. The volume here in wrappers contains Campbell's journal of these two voyages, recorded in his own hand. These journals focus on navigational conditions, weather and sightings at sea and the 1736 contains colorful descriptions of flora and fauna on Princes Island and criticism of Europeans who mistreat natives in the East Indies.
>   These unique and apparently unknown journals are a valuable addition to knowledge of maritime, economic, and social history during an important period of European-Asian contact.

The University Library, whose Manuscript Department contains a large part of the extant archival material from the Swedish East India Company, was naturally extremely anxious to acquire Campbell's journals and tried to raise the considerable sum required for the purpose. When this proved impossible at such short notice, the Gothenburg Historical Museum (now City Museum) was fortunately able to intervene and purchase the two manuscripts with the help of a grant from the *Rådmannen Sven Nordqvists Minnesfond*. After having been presented at a press conference in the Museum, Campbell's journals were placed on permanent deposit in the Department of Manuscripts at Göteborg University Library.

It is the full text of the former and undoubtedly more interesting of these two manuscripts, i.e. the journal of the first expedition of the Swedish East India Company to China in 1732–33, that is here being published in an annotated edition.

As it turned out, the Campbell journals had been purchased by H.P. Kraus as part of a collection of Swedish East India Company archival material from the collection of Charles

Irvine, important shareholder in the Company, supercargo on several of its voyages and a close friend of Campbell's. Like Campbell, Irvine became a Swedish subject, but unlike him he returned to his native Scotland around 1760 and died in Aberdeen in 1771. He belonged to a well-known and reputed Scottish family, the Irvines of Drum in Aberdeenshire; his eldest brother was the 16th Laird of Drum. On his return to Scotland Charles Irvine brought with him a large collection of papers and letters, mostly his private incoming correspondence but also some other material related to the activities of the Swedish East India Company, including the Campbell journals.[1] Apparently the Irvine papers rested in peace in Drum Castle for two centuries, until they were sold by Irvine's descendants and eventually bought by H.P. Kraus in New York.

The bulk of the Irvine papers (some 2,700 items of correspondence, accounts, and other business documents), including all the material relating to the Swedish East India Company except Campbell's journals, was purchased in 1985 by the James Ford Bell Library of the University of Minnesota, USA.

The first expedition

The sailing of the *Fredericus Rex Sueciæ* from Gothenburg on 7 March 1732 must have represented a milestone in the history of that seaport, if not for Sweden as a whole. The departure of the *Fredericus R.S.*, the first vessel manned and armed by the newly established Swedish East India Company, represented the start of an enterprise that was ultimately to send more than 130 ships to the Far East, establishing for the first time regular relations between Sweden and India and more particularly China.

In fact, when the *Fredericus R.S.* left Gothenburg, it was the first substantial action concretizing the trading privileges that King Fredrik I had granted to Henrik König and his associates on 14 June 1731 (Old Style; 25 June according to the new calendar). König, a broker from Stockholm, had applied to the Board of Trade for sea passes for two ships. His application stated that he and his partners wished to conduct trade with India and jointly see what opportunities existed for establishing Swedish trade links with Madagascar and other places where other powers did not have any firm footing. König was given the sea passes he had asked for, and his plans received the assent of both the Board of Trade and the Chancellery. He put faith in his own boldness and went a step further, however, letting it be known that his partners would venture neither ship nor crew upon a mere couple of passports. He therefore requested a formal charter. For this purpose he appended a draft of the desired charter document to his application. As the privileges of the East India companies existing abroad always did, König's draft of privileges drew on earlier models. Even in Sweden, König's project was not an isolated initiative. During the 17th and very early 18th centuries many projects for establishing East India companies were submitted, too numer-

---

[1] Irvine also brought back with him from Sweden a portrait of Colin Campbell. In the course of time the Irvine family lost track of its identity, knowing it only as "Fishface", and it had been relegated to the attic of Drum Castle when discovered and identified by A.A. Cormack, through whose agency it was donated in 1953 to the Gothenburg Historical Museum (Cormack 1967/68, p. 45). It is reproduced in the frontispiece of the present edition. A duplicate of the portrait is preserved in the Castle of Gripsholm in Sweden.

ous to be cited here, but they remained unsuccessful.[1] But, even though efforts to create a company of this kind were without success, initiatives had become so numerous that people with similar ambitions were, at the same time, brought closer together. However, the final scheme accepted was that of König's.

The privileges granted to König authorized his ships to sail to the East Indies and to conduct trade there. The term East Indies was understood to embrace all harbours, places and rivers east of the Cape of Good Hope where other nations conducted trade. Trade was not to be extended to places under the jurisdiction of other powers except with the consent of the power concerned. The privileges were to run for 15 years.[2]

During these 15 years, out of the 25 ships sailing, 22 went to Canton in China, and only three to the actual East Indies. Nevertheless, in contemporary terms the company could still be considered as trading with the East Indies. The label East Indies had a wider connotation at that time than it has nowadays. Implying all ports and places east of the Cape of Good Hope, the East Indies must be conceived of in a very broad sense. It included the east coast of Africa with Sofala and Mozambique, the territories on both shores of the Red Sea, Persia and all ports and coastal tracts under the jurisdiction of the Grand Mogul, such as Malabar, Coromandel and Bengal, and also the kingdoms of Pegu, Siam, Cochin-China, Cambodia and China; finally there were the *Terra incognita australis*, New Guinea, and all the islands of the Indian Ocean, including Madagascar, the Maldives, Sumatra, Java, Borneo, and even Japan. The Company Board of Trade did not actually interpret it as widely, however. The three isolated voyages to India testify to this; although there were contacts at this time with Bengal, especially in Banquibazar, an abandoned Ostend Company loge, then still under the control of its lonely governor, François de Schonamille, no autonomous factory was ever set up there.

During the second charter, granting almost the same privileges for a period of 20 years, the Swedes tried to conduct trade in Surat and Malacca, but these efforts were also limited to three expeditions. During the next charter, from 1766 to 1786, ships only went to China, as the majority of the vessels dispatched did, although commerce was confined to the port of Canton.

In actual fact, the Swedish East India Company was never to become the instrument of a colonizing power. The Company limited itself to trading activities. Even though "colonization" was one of the main points in the granting or renewal of privileges in the 17th century, such Swedish ambitions were never successful, however, as the emphasis in the 18th century was more on trade. This evolution of ideas is closely related to the shift of political currents in Sweden. Gustav II Adolf enjoyed wider powers in the 17th century than did his successors in the 18th century. What could be effected through the influence of the King, buttressed then by all his financial and military weaponry, was later out of the question in the "Age of Freedom". In this new epoch, power rested with the estates, who were forced to take account of the opposition in the increasingly party-dominated Swedish polity outside the *Riksdag*.

---

[1] Koninckx (1980b), pp. 31–39.
[2] *Utdrag utur alle ... publique handlingar ...* 2 (1746), p. 853 (art. 1).

The charter of 1731

The *Riksdag* signed the approval of König's project through the Secret Trade Commission in April 1731. This was only a few months before the formal ratification by the Crown. On 14 June 1731 (Old Style) the Swedish King, Fredrik I, granted König and his associates trading privileges.

They were authorized to sail to the East Indies and to conduct trade there for a period of 15 years. It was laid down that the Company's ships should always depart from and return to Gothenburg, where cargoes were to be discharged and sold at public auctions. Limiting shipping to Gothenburg was apparently a measure aimed at facilitating supervision of the Company's activities and making smuggling difficult. A tax of one hundred silver dollars per *läst* was to be charged on every ship dispatched that returned with a cargo, payable six months after the ship's arrival. Therefore the ships had to be measured prior to their departure from Gothenburg. In the case of a vessel of 200 *läster*, this tax thus amounted to 20,000 silver dollars, calculated on the cargo capacity. While this tax may be considered as a levy for the Crown, a sort of municipal tax was also imposed on East Indian goods imported, at the rate of two dollars per *läst*. The Company was exempted from all other fiscal imposts, however, whether on imports or re-exports of goods. Merchandise re-exported abroad had only to pay *1/8% recognition,* whereas when intended to stay in the country, thus actually imported, it might be transported about the kingdom without let or hindrance, once the Crown levy had been paid in accordance with the aforementioned duties. Swedish goods destined for shipment to the Indies were subject to the ordinary customs tariff, as well as to municipal tax.

These arrangements regarding sales and the costs associated with them, as defined in the charter, were not the end of the matter, however. At the front of the printed sales catalogues are to be found the regulations of sale, laying down in detail the procedures for auctions. Linked with the regulations in the charter, there was a stipulation that any buyer of Company goods intending to re-export them could request a certificate showing the purchase price of the goods. This certificate had to be produced to the customs for calculation of the *1/8% recognition.* It was of course the buyer who had to pay this duty, and the regulations of the sales catalogues did not fail to stress this. Purchasers were liable for a further 0.1% for the poor.

The Company might send out as many ships as it deemed necessary. Nevertheless it had to take care when building, purchasing or fitting out vessels to give preference to Swedish materials. Even so the Company might also look abroad if circumstances required. The Company's ships were to fly the Swedish merchant flag and to be furnished with a sea pass signed by the King himself, and with an Algerian one as well[1]. It was left to the Company itself to decide what capital it saw necessary for undertaking the enterprise. The funds were to be raised by subscription in any case. The actual payment had to be demanded immediately upon subscription, although for settlement at a time determined by the Company.

---

[1] See *Diary,* p. 9, note 25.

Artillery and other war *matériel* could be loaded on board the vessels. It was also permitted to carry any minted currency or none, with the exception of Swedish coins bearing the national or royal coat of arms. Once ready for sea, in the event of a Company ship calling at or passing a Swedish port, whether on departure or return, she was not to be hindered by any authority, magistrate, or customs official. Timber and other materials carried from one Swedish port to another, or even from abroad, for construction or repair of the Company's vessels, were exempt from all import duties. This applied likewise to munitions, victuals and goods conveyed from one Swedish port to another or from abroad, in so far as they did not form the object of the Company's proper trade. They were to be declared to the customs, stored in the Company's warehouse and kept sealed until shipment, when a *recognition* of 1/8% only was to be paid.

With regard to the maintenance of discipline among crew and soldiers, the same powers were granted to ship's captains or masters as to naval officers, but as in the case of the supercargoes and other Company employees, they had to comply with the guidelines laid down by the directors in everything that concerned navigation and trade, in so far as it was not in conflict with the charter.

Guidelines were issued to the supercargoes by the Board before departure, but in the case of the first expedition no such document has been preserved. Perhaps some information can be gleaned from the instructions of the second expedition. Since the *Drottning Ulrica Eleonora,* the second vessel dispatched, left Gothenburg before the *Fredericus R.S.* was back in Sweden, it is to be assumed that the guidelines of the former were about the same as those of the latter; they could hardly have been improved under the influence of what happened during the first voyage.

Indeed, the instructions to Peter von Utfall, commander of the second expedition, stress the importance of consensus between the supercargoes and the captain.[1]

Even though the charter does mention the term "soldiers", none were ever recruited. Very probably the charter was modelled on foreign examples. Since most of the East India companies were involved in colonization, it is quite understandable that there was a need of soldiers in order to man factories or fortresses. In the case of the Swedish Company, although attempts were made, it never succeeded in establishing firm settlements needing to be manned by soldiers.

In actual fact, according to the charter, sailors (and soldiers) in the Company's service were discharged from military obligations and could not be conscripted. The Company, in any case, was forbidden to recruit deserters. This provision was aimed at defectors from the Army and Navy. At the same time, the Company was granted the right to detain and imprison deserters from its own service, when the offence took place prior to expiry of the contract of service with the Company and against the will of the ship's master. The latter enjoyed the support of the Government in the enforcement of these articles.

Strangely enough, while any Company director had to take an oath of allegiance to the King, profess the Protestant faith and be a native or naturalized Swede, residing in Sweden, nothing of this kind was required in order to be appointed as supercargo, captain, officer or

---

[1] Cordier (1889), p. 317 ff.

seaman. It will be noted that a fairly considerable contingent of aliens were recruited, not only in the case of the first expedition. It seems, however, that the regulation of 8 August 1731 concerning the merchant fleet, which stipulated that the ship's master, the mate and the major part of the crew had to be Swedes, was respected, although not at all stressed in any Company document.[1]

With regard to the recruitment of foreigners, on the other hand, the charter granted extensive privileges. The Company was authorized to employ foreigners, to whom the same rights were guaranteed as to Swedes. This even applied to investors, who were permitted to establish themselves in Sweden without their financial assets being seized. These foreigners could lodge an application for naturalization according to their rank and status.

The Company was empowered to protect itself against attack and to resist any enemy. The wording of the charter was clear: force must be met with force. This executive legal power was again expressly proclaimed in the sea passes. In the event of violence against the Company, the King promised his protection and appropriate retaliatory measures in so far as injury had been sustained and the Company had not infringed what was stipulated regarding places and areas where it was allowed to trade.

Finally, the charter confirmed the Company's monopoly of the East Indies navigation and trade for the duration of the concession. Contraventions were to be punished by confiscation, to say nothing of the disgrace.

The framing of the privileges was based on two principles, the first of which was the establishment of a company to operate ships in the trade with the East Indies, to which the King and the Government gave not merely their assent but also their active support, as evidenced by the special arrangement for the levying of duties. The second principle was a guarantee of the protection of indigenous crafts and industries in Sweden.

The Swedish Company versus the great powers

The protection promised by the Swedish monarch to the Company included in fact no extra-ordinary elements.[2] As certain writers were justly to point out, the so-called "privileges" were "des Droits communs de La nature & des Gens"[3], which no one would have refused the Company. König and his associates nevertheless attached importance to it being made officially known abroad that the Swedish East India Company had been established, in order to enforce recognition of the new Company by the other powers. To this end a memorandum was lodged with the Board of Trade for submission to the King. The King in turn dispatched the necessary directives to his envoys.[4] Consent was wanted for Swedish ships to gain free access to the harbours of the French and Danish East Indies for purchasing stocks of victuals and reserves of water. It was made known to the Government in The Hague that

---

[1] Börjeson (1932), p. 264. This regulation was in fact introduced for shipowners interested in enjoying exemption from taxation.

[2] In the event of violence against the Company, the King promised his protection and appropriate retaliatory measures in so far as injury had been sustained and the Company had not infringed art. 1 (art. 17).

[3] RAS. H & S 52. *Lettre d'un Suédois à un Amy à Stockholme, ce 11 d'aout 1731.*

[4] RAS. KKH. *Note de König & Compagnie* (s.d.).

any exclusion of the Swedish Company would be resisted by the King. While this foreign recognition was of immediate practical importance, it also had in view the indirect protection of the foreign investors. Without this assurance, the risk for foreign shareholders in the Swedish enterprise was too great. Thus there was no intention of conducting trade in the factories or settlements of other European powers.

No documents have been found establishing the official recognition of the Swedish Company by foreign courts. In fact, it is not a matter for a court to recognize a foreign private company. However, it may be of interest to know what they thought about the prime existence of the Swedish Company. One can guess the position of France, Holland and Great Britain from remarks in their dossiers on the Batavia and Porto Novo incidents. The former happened to the *Fredericus R.S.* during her maiden voyage in the Swedish Company's service (see further below p. xxiv ff.); the latter incident involved the *Drottning Ulrica Eleonora*, the second ship armed by the Company.[1] Indeed, in a letter he wrote to the Governor-General and members of the Council of the Indies in Batavia, Campbell says that the United Provinces "avait déjà avoué en Europe le Droit de la Compagnie".[2] In the same letter, Campbell also referred to the apparent concurrence of France and Great Britain. France, too, in her negotiations with Sweden over the Porto Novo incident, confirmed that she was not opposed to the Swedish Company. Matters were otherwise with England. Sparre, the Swedish envoy in London, apprised the English court of the establishment of the Swedish Company, according to König's request to the King of Sweden mentioned above, but although no official disapproval ensued here either[3], British diplomatic correspondence betrays a tendency in that direction. The correspondence between William Stanhope, the English Secretary of State, and Edward Finch, the envoy in Stockholm, reveals that the British government was flatly against the new company.[4] As a matter of fact English efforts to undermine the Swedish Company led to the Porto Novo incident already mentioned.

Unlike England, the Dutch and French governments were not opposed to the Swedish initiative, but they did not react officially to the acknowledgment of the Swedish Company being established. This initial neutrality did inspire certain fears, since their silence could very well mask some reservation. In fact, the reactions of the Dutch and the French afterwards shed more light on the opposition of the Dutch and the French East India Company employees against the newcomers than did the reluctance of their respective governments at home.

Thus it was mainly out of caution, bearing in mind what befell the Ostend Company, that Sweden had made plans for her own East India Company known to the European courts of the maritime powers of that time. Unbound by any single treaty to a foreign country, there was no need for Sweden to seek assent in order to conduct trade with the Far East. The fact

---

[1] Koninckx (1980b), pp. 75–107.

[2] RAS. H & S 52. *Ce 28 Janvier S.V. 1733.*

[3] RAS. H & S 56. *Detail circonstancié de la violence commise à Porto Novo. A Londres ce 9. de Janvier 1734/5.* "Il y a quelque temps que sa Majesté suédoise fit notifier a la Cour Britannique, qu'Elle avait une Compangnie & accordé un Octroy pour le commerce aux Indes Orientales, dans des tels lieux & places, ou, quelque autre Puissance n'avoit point d'établissement ou de droit exclusif." – *Ibid., Extrait d'une Lettre de Mr. Wassenberg datée Londres le 15 Décembre 1738.* "… que l'Octroy a été communiqué a la Cour d'Angleterre, qui là dessus n'a fait aucunes remontrances."

[4] *British Diplomatic Instructions. 1688–1789.* 5 (1928), pp. 18, 19, 22, 25 and 26.

is that the silence of some foreign governments was not to be considered a very favourable sign but merely reflected their adoption of a wait-and-see attitude, since they expected to see the Ostend Company looming up again at any moment.

Indeed, in 1727 the General Imperial and Royal India Company established in the Austrian Netherlands, better known as the Ostend Company, had been suspended under pressure from the Great Powers. Since they could not suffer the successes achieved by the Ostend Company in the East Indies, the great East India companies had urged their governments to bring about the suppression of the unwelcome competitor. This they did by threatening the Emperor Charles VI not to recognize his daughter Maria Theresia as his legitimate heir, if he did not dissolve the Ostend Company. The Emperor had been forced to suspend the successful enterprise, no doubt against his will, and even more against that of the entrepeneurial merchants of Flanders and Brabant involved in it. Knowing their spirit, the great East Indian companies were justified in fearing that the Ostenders would turn up elsewhere. This explains why they scrutinized any suspected attempt to restore the Ostend Company abroad under another label.

On these grounds suspicion hovered over the Swedish Company from its very beginning. Bearing in mind that the *Fredericus R.S.* left Gothenburg in March 1732, a little earlier than the *Hertogh van Lorreynen* and the *Concordia*, the two so-called "permission ships" sailing out of the harbour of Ostend, in the eyes of the competitors some collusion between all these ventures was perhaps not out of the question. Although the "permission ships" may be considered the last convulsions of a dying East India company, the suspicion of a connection could not be excluded. Various plans were devised for fanning the Ostend Company back into life or for absorbing it into already existing enterprises. Denmark and Sweden were involved in these designs. The Danish East India Company, established already in the 17th century, found itself in dire straits at the beginning of the 18th century. Its directors were prospecting for new capital in order to help the enterprise avert bankruptcy. It was at this point that the adventurer Josias van Asperen, an Amsterdam merchant, appeared on the scene, proposing to the Danes a broadening of the company statutes. King Frederik IV approved the proposal, and it was against this background that a free staple place was established in Altona, on the Elbe, in April 1728.[1] The Altona project was to function as a subsidiary of the Danish Company, although for a very short time. Matters never got as far as an official merger between the Ostend and Danish undertakings, however, for the Altona project did not meet the approval of the Austrian Board of Trade.[2] After the failure in Denmark, van Asperen tried again in Sweden, where he did manage to establish contact with Henrik König. Apparently his proposals inspired very little confidence in Stockholm, and he was compelled to leave the country. "Monsr. König n'y [sic] aucun de ses associez n'a eu la moindre correspondance avec Monsr. van Asperen depuis son départ, & qu'ils sont même resolus de n'en jamais avoir."[3]

How far van Asperen had progressed with the elaboration of his projects in Sweden is not known. He does seem to have submitted a plan. He even received a letter from a certain

[1] Huisman (1902), pp. 457–458.
[2] Baels (1972), p. 140. – Huisman (1902), p. 458 ff. – Glamann (1970), p. 474.
[3] RAS. H & S 52. *Lettre d'un Suédois à un Amy …*

Louis Couturier asking him for a job in the company he intended to establish.[1] According to his own account, Couturier had served for seven years in the *Bureau Général de la Compagnie Impériale d'Ostende*. Couturier was never recruited for service in Sweden, but other former employees of the Ostend Company were. The most notable case was Campbell himself, but he did not enter into Swedish service as an official representative of the suspended Ostend Company, which by the time Campbell transferred had not yet been wound up. He came as a private individual, as did the others who voluntarily switched over to the Swedish undertaking. When the Swedish Company started, there was little sign of any massive investment of Ostend Company funds in the Swedish Company, as has been alleged. On the contrary, in 1731 an agent of the Swedish Company prospected among Antwerp bankers and business directors for anybody willing to invest capital in Sweden. It was a fruitless journey, for the agent could find no one willing to run that risk.[2] In addition to the so-called "permission ships", "Ostenders" had sent out vessels under foreign flags (Polish and Prussian), which involved sufficient hazard for the moment, for it was vital that these expeditions were not unmasked by the powers which had enforced the suspension of the Ostend Company.[3] Furthermore, inhabitants of the Austrian Netherlands were prohibited from conducting trade with the Far East outside the framework of the company of their own country.[4] Such a clause was to be found in the privileges of nearly all East India companies, although frequently violated all over the world. Although the Ostend Company had just been abolished in 1731, while it did not immediately go into liquidation, loyalty towards one's own company and respect of the interdiction for "Austrians" to trade with the East Indies could thus have been obstacles to joining the Swedish Company.

At all events, Campbell's move from Ostend to Sweden alarmed the English. The Swedish initiative was much canvassed in English diplomatic circles, and there was some concern to discover whether the Swedish enterprise was an indirect continuation of the Ostend Company or not. Whitehall regarded Campbell as an official "Ostend" agent. William Stanhope, Secretary of State, wrote quite clearly to Edward Finch, the English envoy in Stockholm: "… I have been informed that one Colin Campbel is now at Stockholm, and very busy in forming schemes for a trade to the East Indies. He was employed in the service of the Ostend Company, and according to the advices I have had acts now by direction from them …".[5] The fact that the Swedish government had assured London that the Swedish Company "shall not be made a cloak for encouraging an indirect trade of the Ostenders"[6] seems not to have alleviated British suspicions regarding the Swedish undertaking. They could not refrain from trying to put a spoke in the wheel by arguing that Sweden would have little advantage to gain from the expeditions, because the profits would go to the Flemish and other foreigners.[7] The expedition of the *Drottning Ulrica Eleonora*, the second ship dispatched

[1] RAS. H & S 52. *Copie de la lettre écrite par Louis Couturier de la haute-porte à Josias von Aspern à Stockholm, d'Anvers, février 1730* (damaged).

[2] Glamann (1953–54), p. 41.

[3] Baels (1972), pp. 146–148.

[4] Huisman (1902), p. 254.

[5] *British Diplomatic Instructions. 1688–1789.* 5 (1928), p. 18. Whitehall, 18 Decr 1730.

[6] *Ibid.*, p. 25.

[7] *Ibid.*, p. 19.

by the new company, was to be harassed by England, as the Dutch were to do during the expedition of the *Fredericus R.S.*, with which the present journal is concerned.

Nevertheless there were links with the Ostend Company, even if not of the massive official nature trumpeted about by the polemicists.[1] Thus it was not easy for the champions of the Swedish initiative to counter the heated attacks of the "Ignorants & Esprits malins [qui] voudroient donc insinuer, que ce sera toujours la Compagnie d'Ostende sous un autre nom".[2] What happened to the *Fredericus R.S.* in the Sunda Strait is a typical example of the prevalent attitude in those days to newcomers. No wonder, then, that historians also have adopted the idea of the continuation of the Ostend Company by the Swedish, or have sometimes considered the Swedish East India Company as an illicit auxiliary to the English one. The interpretation of customs figures shows that such suppositions are not in accordance with facts.[3]

The promoters of the Company

The privileges which the King bestowed on Henrik König actually state that they were granted to König and his associates, but the names of these partners are not specified anywhere. König seems to have taken the initiative in submitting the project to the Board of Trade in 1729, but he appears to have been acting in concert with Colin Campbell, Volrath Tham, Niclas Sahlgren and certain other people, who were proposed as co-directors of the Company with him. The actual directors from the very beginning were Henrik König (1686–1736), Colin Campbell (1686–1757) and François Bedoire (1690–1742). As early as 1732 Bedoire left the Board and was replaced by Volrath Tham (1687–1737). In 1733 Tham in his turn left the Board, which was then joined by Niclas Sahlgren (1701–76). Even though König died in 1736, it is worth noting that both Campbell and Sahlgren were to keep their tenures until the end of the first charter, and during the second charter as well.

As already mentioned, König was a Stockholm broker engaged in the import and export business. Born in 1686 and married to Petronella Schaeij in 1716, he had a brother called Christian (1678-1762), who was secretary to the Chancellery Cabinet *(Kanslikollegium)*.[4] His father, who as the son of a rich landowner emigrated to Sweden from the duchy of Bremen in the first half of the 17th century in order to become a merchant, later settled again in Hamburg as commissioner for Swedish trade. In all evidence Henrik König was not of Flemish origin, as was once alleged.[5] He had his own firm in Sweden, and it is possible that it was in this way that he came into contact with Campbell and Sahlgren. His brother's function in a state office must have been of some help in getting the privileges through the administration. Perhaps this is the main reason why König was involved in the Company project. However, König was not to enjoy the success of the enterprise, since he died as early as 1736.

---

[1] Koninckx (1978a), pp. 295–329.
[2] RAS. H & S 52. *Lettre d'un Suédois à un Amy …*
[3] Kent (1973), p. 120.
[4] *Svenska män och kvinnor* (1942–55). 4, p. 391.
[5] Picard, Kerneis & Bruneau (1966), p. 141.

Both François Bedoire and Niclas Sahlgren were Swedish. Living in Stockholm, Bedoire was a wholesale dealer, who together with other merchants was to build up Sweden's first marine insurance company in 1739.[1] Sahlgren was sent to Holland at the age of sixteen and remained there for six years, being employed for most of that period in the office of Tietzen & Schröder.[2] Tietzen & Schröder was a well-renowned company, not least in Sweden. In the very beginning of the 18th century they were acting on behalf of the Swedish legacy secretary Joachim Fredrik Preis, who in turn was acting on the orders of King Charles XII, for the recruitment of Dutch shipwrights for the benefit of the Admiralty shipyard in Karlskrona.[3] In Holland Sahlgren also studied the activities of the V.O.C., the Dutch East India Company.[4] He travelled to Germany in 1723, visiting Hamburg and Stralsund. Returning to Sweden, he moved about the country for two years, studying mining, forestry and trade. At the end of 1726 he went to England, visiting London and other cities. In late 1727 he went on to France and visited Paris, Lyons, Marseilles, Toulon and other places. Back in Sweden, he founded the Swedish West India Company with Jonas Alströmer, who was subsequently to play a role in the East India Company. The West India Company was founded for trade with South America. In the context of this enterprise, the possibility of colonization on the Barima was envisaged. The West India Company was short-lived, however, and Sahlgren switched over to working for the expansion of the East India Company. He had in fact made contact with Sparre and supported the plan devised by the latter in 1728.[5]

Colin Campbell had also ranged himself with the adherents of Sparre's plan.[6] Although Sahlgren did not immediately become a director of the East India Company, he was still a central figure, being consulted for his commercial knowledge by Colin Campbell, the promoter from the very outset.

The story has it that Niclas Sahlgren invited Colin Campbell to Gothenburg. Campbell, of Scottish descent, had been involved in the "South Sea Bubble" (1720–23) in London and had thereby contracted a lot of debts. According to his own statement, it was Campbell's intention, by means of the profits he accumulated from foreign companies, to repay everyone to whom he had occasioned loss through the "South Sea Bubble". This in fact was done when he died in 1757.[7] In order to escape prison for debt Campbell fled to the Austrian Netherlands, where he joined the Ostend Company as a junior or assistant supercargo. He served there from 1723 to 1730, mostly as supercargo, thus gaining his experience of trade in the Far East, being there several times.[8] It must have been in Ostend that he met Sahl-

---

[1] Bedoire (1963), p. 90.

[2] Gezelius (1941), p. 15.

[3] Koninckx (1990b), pp. 127–140.

[4] Du Val-Pyrau [1777], p. 33.

[5] Carl G. Sparre was Swedish envoy in London. Although he was broaching a project for a company, the scheme was devised and drawn up by an Englishman named Rogger, formerly governor of the Bahamas. The project assumed that Gothenburg would not only serve as the company's staple place but would be designated a free port. Madagascar was involved in the scheme, and so was the slave trade. Sparre submitted the plan in March 1728, but the Chancellery and the Board of Trade rejected it, justifying their disapproval by pointing to the hazardous character of such a venture, not to mention the inevitable reaction of the Great Powers. – Hellstenius (1860), p. 3.

[6] Hellstenius (1870), p. 32.

[7] Campbell (1960).

[8] Cormack (1975), p. 25. There is, however, no evidence in the Ostend Company's records of Campbell's joining or serving that Company.

gren, who asked him to accompany him to Sweden.[1] After settling in Gothenburg he applied for Swedish citizenship in 1731. He may have done so as a measure of safety for himself, in order to be in Swedish Company service in case of capture by a British vessel. In practice, however, once a British subject, naturalization elsewhere could not wipe out British nationality. British subjects were and still are, according to a common law still valid, *glebae adscripti*. This was to be the case with many Englishmen or Scots in Swedish service. Furthermore their dual nationality deprived them of the right to seek Swedish protection for wrongs perpetrated against English law. In British eyes, this happened when taking service abroad to sail to the East Indies. It has already been mentioned that a clause in the privileges of East India companies generally laid this down. When the *Drottning Ulrica Eleonora* encountered difficulties in Porto Novo, this was one of the arguments on which the British intervention was legally based.[2] However, Campbell acquired Swedish nationality and was raised to the nobility on 14 June 1731, although not introduced in the House of the Nobility *(Riddarhuset)*. On 15 November of the same year he was appointed a minister plenipotentiary of the Swedish King. He was made first supercargo on board of the *Fredericus R.S.* In Campbell's passport for that voyage, his status as minister plenipotentiary to the Emperor of China, the Grand Mogul and other Asiatic princes was affirmed.[3]

The journal

According to Campbell's own definition, his diary is the "Journal of Sundry Transactions pass'd Aboard the Ship Fredericus Rex Sueciæ". Since Campbell found it necessary to destroy all papers or writings that might give "the least handle or pretext to People, that seem'd to bear no Good will to us", everything recorded in the *Diary*, as he asserts, was based on memory and on some loose papers he had preserved. Campbell is very conscious that this may have caused "the omission of some passages that happen'd, as well as want of exactness in the Dates", but stresses that his journal is "solely design'd for the service of the Company (and many things thereof in particular for such of the Gentlemen Directors as are not so well acquainted with such voyages) for Time to come as well as for the present".

Compared to the documents later held on board other Swedish East Indiamen, Campbell's journal must be regarded as being of a very special kind. It appears that no other ship's document of this first expedition with the *Fredericus R.S.* has been preserved. Nevertheless we must assume that there were others. A ship's log was generally kept up to date by the officer of the watch. It contained useful navigational data such as latitude, longitude, course, wind, depth of water, and mileage covered. Sometimes the number of the sick was given, as well as deaths, remarks concerning diet and consumption, etc. A ship's log was and still is used as a day-to-day working document.

While there was only one log, several ship's journals were kept for one and the same voyage. The orders and instructions for Captain Mathias Holmers, dated 6 December 1766,

---

[1] Indebetou (1908), p. 127. At first he settled in Stockholm for some time.
[2] Koninckx (1980b), pp. 98–101.
[3] RAS. H & S 52.

stipulate that the captain and the first and second mates were each to maintain a ship's journal to be submitted in fair copy to the Company directors after the voyage.[1] Whether these instructions were in force as early as 1732 is uncertain. However, in view of the variety of ship's documents (logs, journals, diaries, etc.) preserved from the earliest period of the Company, it is to be assumed that this practice must have been very common even then, although no clear instructions may have been issued. In principle, ship's journals record the same data as the log, but in greater detail and very often with the addition of the keeper's personal opinion. Both logs and ship's journals were kept by officers, although in the case of journals the task of entering them up may have been delegated by one of the mates or by the captain himself to younger members of the crew.

Supercargoes were also expected to submit certain documents on their return, mainly books recording commercial transactions in the East Indies. First among them was the *Diarium* or *Journal*, in which supercargoes had to make a daily report of all their actions.[2] They record daily business transactions and generally do not contain navigational data. They should not be confused with ship's journals, although they do furnish supplementary information. Campbell's *Diary* must be considered as belonging to this category. Since many documents were destroyed in connection with the incident at the Sunda, and since the facts were recorded from memory, any analysis of the events will have to proceed with great caution. Corroboration by means of other documents concerning this first voyage is quite impossible, since very few indeed have survived.

Some data can be collected from a general inventory showing an overview of all ships dispatched during the first and second charters.[3] This survey is undated, but since it records the return of the last expedition of the *Stockholms Slott*, calling back in Gothenburg in August 1767, it must have been written up after that date. Several surveys of this kind exist, with only slight variations.

Some significance may be attached to a document kept in Uppsala University Library, which summarizes twenty voyages, based on the contents of twenty ships' logs, including that of the *Fredericus R.S.*[4] Apparently this material was collected in order to study compass deviation. The existence of this document proves that the log of the *Fredericus R.S.* did reach Sweden and was used at least once. Some further information may be gleaned from documents established afterwards, e.g. Campbell's *Relation abrégée du Voyage du Vaisseau Fredericus Rex Sueciæ et particulièrement de son* [sic] *Rencontre avec l'Escadre Hollandoise auprez du Detroit de Sunda* and the diplomatic correspondence already used by A. van Dissel.[5] In addition, the correspondence of the Dutch East Indian Company concerning the incident should not

---

[1] Hammar (1931), p. 99 (§ 63).

[2] UUB. L 186, 13. *1º Diarium eller Journal öfver alla deras förrättningar* [1760].

[3] GUB. Ligg.fol. H 22:1. *Förteckning över kompaniets skepp under 1. och 2. oktrojerna.*

[4] UUB. L 183. *Utdrag af 20 loggböcker för att visa kompassens missvisning med dess ändringar. Förteckning på Svenska Ostindiska kompaniets skepp 1732–1765, deras afgångs- och hemkomsttid samt officere.* The figures and data concerning the first voyage of the *Fredericus R.S.* recorded in this manuscript appear to have been borrowed from Captain Trolle himself.

[5] RAS. H & S 52. – Dissel (1987), pp. 124–137. – Archives kept in The Hague General State Archives: *Archief legatie Zweden,* and in Stockholm State Archives: *Hollandica,* 374.

be overlooked.[1] There is also a sales catalogue recording the return cargo, to which we shall return later on.[2]

A large number of travel narratives concerning many other voyages of Swedish East Indiamen have survived. Unlike logs and journals such narratives were evidently written for the private purposes of their authors. By and large they contain much useful material, but they are unsatisfactory with regard to navigational data and reliable information. Travel narratives were often written during leisure time by those who were able to write, such as ship's chaplains, officers and supercargoes. They mostly deal with all kinds of observations, not least in the field of so-called natural history. Paying much attention to the countries visited and to fauna and flora etc., they are of great interest for 18th century natural science, then in full development. In the case of the first voyage of the *Fredericus R.S.*, however, no travel narrative appears to exist.

The voyage

Although Campbell started his journal on 24 February 1732, the *Fredericus R.S.* had to wait for favourable winds until the 25th. This is according to the old calendar; the reformed Gregorian calendar was not introduced in Sweden until 1753, when 17 February was followed immediately by 1 March. Prior to this reform both old and new styles were often noted side by side in ships' documents. This was probably done for practical reasons, because ships were regularly calling at ports where the new calendar had been in use for a long time. Thus the *Fredericus R.S.* left Gothenburg on 7 March 1732 (New Style).

Because of the wind, the ship was carried into Homborsund on the coast of Norway, where she was moored until 14 March to wait for better winds. She then sailed through the Channel and reached Cádiz in Spain in 34 days. The voyage was resumed after a delay of 15 days and after a cargo of silver piastres had been loaded. In Spain some seamen and supercargoes joined the crew as well. From Cádiz the course was set for the Cape of Good Hope on the southern tip of Africa, whence the ship headed for St. Paul. From St. Paul, the *Fredericus R.S.* went on to the Straits of Sunda. She anchored in the Canton roads in China on 19 September 1732, having thus reached the Far East in 6 1/2 months.

After a sojourn of four months in China, the *Fredericus R.S.* set off to return home. In the vicinity of the Straits of Sunda her passage was blocked by seven ships. The *Fredericus R.S.* announced her identity by hoisting the Swedish flag; the foreign ships responded by displaying the Dutch flag. Failing to break through the blockade, the Swedish ship anchored. This happened on 3 February 1733. The Dutch ships attempted to approach the *Fredericus R.S.* After nightfall, however, the strong current in the narrows formed an obstacle. Bremer, the mate, was sent to the Dutch squadron with the sloop next day to find out the reasons for this odd behaviour. He took with him copies of the ship's sea passes, together with a copy of Campbell's passport, in which his status was affirmed as minister plenipotentiary to the Emperor of China, the Grand Mogul and other Asiatic princes. All the documents were issued in Dutch. Bremer and the sailors accompanying him were all seized by the Dutch.

---

[1] Dissel (1985) mentions a number of sources of the V.O.C.
[2] RAS. KKA (1). *Verkauffungs Conditionen der völligen Ladung …*

Journey of the *Fredericus Rex Sueciae* (1732–1733)

	New style	Sailing-days	Days stayed
Departure from Gothenburg*	7 March 1732		
	33 sailing-days	33	
Arrival in Cádiz	9 April		
Departure from Cádiz	24 April		15
	60 sailing-days	60	
Passage of the Cape	23 June		
	48 sailing-days	48	
Arrival in the Sunda	10 August		
	40 sailing-days	40	
Arrival in Canton	19 September 1732		
Stay in Canton	120 days stayed		120
Departure from Canton	16 January 1733		
	19 sailing-days	19	
Arrival in the Sunda	3 February		
Blockade and stay in Batavia**	40 days stayed		40
Departure from the Sunda	15 March		
	56 sailing-days	56	
Passage of the Cape	11 May		
	39 sailing-days	39	
Arrival at Fernando de Noroñha	19 June		
	6 days stayed		6
Departure from Fernando de Noroñha	25 June		
	68 sailing-days	68	
Stop in Norway	6 days stayed		6
Arrival in Gothenburg***	7 September 1733		
Total days stayed			187
Total sailing-days		363	
Total duration	550 days		

Data according to *UUB L183*, showing very slight differences with Campbell's *Diary.*
*   Channel route taken
** Including short stops at North and Princes (Panaitan)
*** Round-Scotland route taken

On the morning of 5 February, Captain Trolle was preparing to take the original sea passes to the commander of the Dutch squadron, Herman de Vrij. At that moment the sloop returned, but manned by a Dutch officer and crew. The officer requested Captain Trolle to come over to de Vrij with his sea passes. Trolle complied at once. After examination of the documents, the Dutch held a consultation and decided to evacuate the *Fredericus R.S.* and to transfer the Swedish crew to the Dutch vessels. 56 Dutch sailors took over the *Fredericus R.S.,* which was also occupied by 36 soldiers, a number of petty officers and an ensign.

Only Campbell, the captain, four servants and a few petty officers of the original Swedish crew were left on board. Campbell himself was invited by the Dutch commander to partake of refreshments, but he declined the invitation, submitting instead a written protest declaring himself to be a minister of the Swedish King and demanding the immediate release of the prisoners. The protest seems to have made an impression on the Dutch commander, for the Swedes were sent back to their own vessel that evening, while Trolle was commanded to hoist the Swedish flag again.

English homeward-bound vessels appeared in the Straits of Sunda on 6 February. Campbell handed their captain dispatches addressed to the Company directors in Sweden and giving his account of the course of events. Next day Trolle was ordered to make for Batavia. The *Fredericus R.S.* sailed under escort, arriving there on 8 February. Campbell went ashore and was received in audience by the Governor-General, Dirk van Cloon, who requested information concerning the nature and value of the goods carried by the *Fredericus R.S.*[1] Campbell replied in general terms and declined to furnish details of the values. The ship's documents were again perused, and after a meeting of the local Dutch Government on 9 February, apologies were tendered to the Swedes for the unfortunate incident.

The origins of the incident were unravelled in 1987 by a young Dutch scholar, Anita van Dissel, in a paper dealing with this voyage of the *Fredericus R.S.,* based upon Dutch sources.[2] Dissel's account is in fact fully corroborated by what can be distilled from the present journal kept by Campbell and what was already known from his *Relation abrégée.*[3]

Jan Schull[4], first supercargo of a V.O.C. ship moored at Canton, had tried to find out if the Swedish newcomers should be considered impostors sent out by the banned Ostend Company. In actual fact, a Swedish officer of the *Fredericus R.S.* acted as a helping hand in spreading such rumours. In any case Schull wrote a letter to this effect to van Cloon. The Governor took it very seriously, because a couple of years earlier a genuine Ostend East Indiaman, the *Apollo,* had escaped being captured in India. He was therefore firmly determined to intercept the suspected Swedish vessel and dispatched a small squadron for this purpose.

Van Cloon evidently realized the falsity of the allegations, for he tried to undo the error as far as he could. The captain and the supercargoes of the *Fredericus R.S.* were invited by him to take their leave on the friendliest possible terms. The Governor-General once more expressed his regrets over the incident, but Campbell did not withdraw his protest against

---

[1] Cloon (1684–1735) was Governor-General from 1732 until his death.
[2] Dissel (1987).
[3] RAS. H & S 52. *Relation abrégée du Voyage du Vaisseau Fridericus Rex Sueciae et particulièrement de son* [sic] *Rencontre avec l'Escadre Hollandoise auprez du Detroit de Sunda.* – Koninckx (1980b), pp. 69–75.
[4] Campbell always spells the name "Schultz".

the insult made to the King of Sweden and the prejudice of the Company. At his request the captured vessel was made seaworthy. The Swedes were supplied with drinking water, victuals, firewood and anchor. The *Fredericus R.S.* was then again escorted from Batavia to Bantam, where she had been seized.

The *Fredericus R.S.* parted from her escort on 26 February, after the supercargoes had signed a receipt for the provisions and equipment received. The Swedes were not required to pay for them. The Swedish ship then headed back towards Europe. She passed the Cape of Good Hope on 11 May and called at the island of Fernando de Noroñha in the Atlantic Ocean off the coast of Brazil, in order to replenish supplies and allow recuperation of those stricken by scurvy. This disease appears to have broken out on a considerable scale. The shortage of manpower forced the vessel to anchor once more in Norway, but this time for signing on twenty more seamen. On 7 September 1733 the *Fredericus R.S.* was back in Gothenburg. She had been away for only just over 18 months, despite having been delayed. From a purely maritime point of view this remained one of the Company's shortest voyages.

Once ashore, Colin Campbell made a detailed report of events, accusing the Dutch of:
- loss of time amounting to at least two months because the winds and ocean currents were on the turn during the hold-up. The Swedes had encountered unbelievable difficulty – at least Campbell reported as much – in reaching Sunda from Batavia. Furthermore, Campbell asserted, they experienced still more delay in rounding the Cape of Good Hope because of the bad season;
- the poor accommodation on board the Dutch ships in which the Swedish crew was confined. Campbell stressed that these bad conditions, together with the alleged long duration of the voyage, contributed to the general spread of scurvy;
- finally, causing injury to the Company itself through the late arrival of the ship in Gothenburg, which meant a postponement of the public sale of the cargo.

Whether these arguments were strong enough to substantiate the protest may be doubted, particularly when we know that the voyage – and particularly the homeward run – had in fact been quite speedy.

The essential point, however, was the violation of the right of free commerce and the law of the sea. This had already been made plain by Campbell to Dirk van Cloon in Batavia. Campbell explained that it was the Swedish *Riksdag* that had examined Henrik König's proposals and put them into effect. Campbell also pointed out that approval had been voiced by the foreign courts of France and Great Britain and by the *Staten-Generaal* of the United Provinces with regard to the establishment of the Swedish East India Company.[1]

Nevertheless the *Bewindhebbers* of the V.O.C., its Board of Trade, sent instructions dated 4 March 1732 to the local board in Batavia not to help the Swedes under any circumstances whatsoever by providing them with victuals, drinking water, equipment, firewood or anything else.[2] In fact, after realizing their mistake the Dutch in Batavia did help the Swedes, thus in a sense disobeying these orders. Since it was a mistake, and since Campbell's protest addressed to van Cloon had very likely made some impression on the latter, the Dutch of Batavia found it quite in order to provide compensation.

---

[1] RAS. KKH.
[2] Dissel (1987), p. 125.

An exchange of diplomatic correspondence began at once between The Hague and Stockholm with the object of settling the dispute. The response of the Dutch government was conciliatory, and the incident was closed in the autumn of 1733.[1]

When the Dutch captured the vessel, they did not disturb her cargo. When they came aboard the *Fredericus R.S.* and seized the Swedish sailors, the hatches of the hold were sealed forthwith and remained so until Campbell was received in audience by the Governor-General. The public sale began as early as 26 October, realizing at the auction a total sum of about 900,000 silver dollars.[2]

One may wonder with reason whether this newly-founded company had really sustained any financial loss worth mentioning through the delay at the Sunda, for a first dividend of 25% of the amount of the shares was distributed to the shareholders, and a second one of 50%.[3]

The crew

During her first voyage in the Company's service the *Fredericus R.S.* was commanded by Captain Georg Herman Trolle (1680–1765), who had already made one voyage to China in 1706, although in foreign service.[4] He grew up in Amsterdam, but went to sea when he was ten years old. He was third mate on a merchantman sailing to Archangel and the West Indies and took service for the English, French, Dutch and Danish admiralties, before he became privateer captain for the Dutch city of Middelburg. In 1714 Trolle was appointed captain in the Swedish navy, and when he joined the Company's service he held the rank of Captain Lieutenant of the Admiralty. Trolle was promoted Admiralty Captain in 1741 and Rear-Admiral in 1758 and in the same year was raised to the nobility, hence called *af Trolle*.

If these data seem to reflect a successful career and to indicate how very experienced Trolle must have been, a totally different view of the man emerges from a reading of Campbell's journal. If we are to believe Campbell, Trolle was anything but an experienced sailor or affable gentleman but rather seems to conform to the stereotyped picture of a coarse sailor of those days: rough if not brutal, a shameless liar and a notorious drunkard. In addition Campbell even depicts him as being disloyal to Sweden: "... which with many other Signs I have had makes me assurd that he is no Swede at least in his heart which is all for Denmark where he Servd at Sea in the late war against Sweden, though he pretends to be born in Sweden".[5] Campbell had quite a lot of difficulty with Trolle from the beginning of the voyage until the bitter end. We shall not go into the details of the many conflicts between the first supercargo and the captain, since these aspects form part of the suspense of the story and will no doubt keep the reader of the present diary awake. This is one of the most fascinating ingredients of the story which Campbell tells us, but at the same time rather boring, since the quarrels very often concerned the same kind of matters. In view of all this

---

[1] Dissel (1987), p. 133.
[2] RAS. KKA (1). *Verkauffungs Conditionen der völligen Ladung ...*
[3] GUB. Ligg.fol. H 22:1. *Förteckning över kompaniets skepp under 1. och 2. oktrojerna. – Götheborgska Magasinet n:o 11, den 12. Martii 1759*, p. 85. – LAG. Öst. A 152–51/8.
[4] Horn (1937), pp. 487–489. – Börjeson (1942), pp. 198–199.
[5] *Diary*, p. 279.

the final pages of the *Diary* will come as a surprise to the reader. Soon after his arrival in Gothenburg Campbell sent a short account of the voyage and the conduct of the captain and other members of the crew to König in Stockholm. The contents of this letter reached the King's ears, who was all the more dissatisfied as the captain was one of His Majesty's officers. The King was pleased to ask Campbell about him, but Campbell was not willing to ruin Trolle and subsequently declined to make any complaints. Strangely enough, "now the voyage was over", Campbell wrote, "I had nothing to Say against any Body".[1] The King was resolved to elucidate the whole affair, since it was reported that Lieutenant Lund and the priest had conducted themselves badly too. The King sent orders to the Governor and Rear Admiral in Gothenburg to examine their cases in the presence of Campbell. Campbell then related his complaints against them and recorded in his *Diary*: "though I was not ill pleasd that some notice might be taken of their bad conduct, to prevent others doing the like another time, yet I did not care to expose them too much to the Kings resentment, So that I Sav'd the Captain as well as I could & desird the Governour to make a Report as little to his prejudice as he could consistent with truth Since the Captain had ownd himself in the wrong which is all I wanted."[2]

Campbell's continual disputes with Captain Trolle cannot always simply be imputed to the bad drinking habits of the latter. In all probability part of the dissensions must be ascribed to the lack of a clear delimitation of the tasks and responsibilities of each of them. The supercargoes, mostly four in a Company's ship, represented a hierarchy from the first and highest in rank to the fourth and lowest. They were the Company's commercial travellers and the immediate representatives of the Company directors on board. The supercargo was in effect responsible for the real business of the Company, which in specific terms meant the safeguarding of the cargo (hence the term), but he had an important say in other areas as well, and his authority was far-reaching. When a Company ship put in at a port, its cargo was sold by the owners or their representatives. The special nature of the trade with the Far East obliged the Company to engage persons skilled in the conduct of colonial trade, i.e. supercargoes. Considering that Sweden had not acquired any fund of experience of long voyages, let alone of China and India navigations, the Company directors were virtually forced to employ foreigners. This explains why foreign supercargoes were strongly represented. Of the 30 first supercargoes during the first and second charters, 13 were English, filling the function of first supercargo 24 times (out of 61 voyages).

The English were not the only foreign nationality represented. There were also French, Germans, Dutch and even Italians. There were people from the Austrian Netherlands as well.[3] During the first concession (1731–1746) it was mostly foreigners who performed the duties of supercargoes. The foreign representation was to dwindle in the course of time, but never vanished entirely.

In matters to which the authority of the supercargoes did not strictly extend, such as putting into port to take on victuals or water, or seeking a port of refuge, the commander of the vessel could give no orders without the consent of the supercargoes. In actual fact

---

[1] *Diary*, p. 294.
[2] *Diary*, pp. 294–295.
[3] Koninckx (1980b), pp. 335–336.

responsibility for the financial success of every expedition rested to a large degree upon their shoulders.

While these reflections are based upon the traditions existing in other companies and developing in the course of years within the Swedish Company, it is not improbable that responsibilities were not clearly defined, at least not in the case of the first expedition. If they were not unknown to Campbell, they may well have been to Trolle. It is true that the division of authority was clearly outlined in the charter of the Company. Since everyone on board was subordinate to the Company directors, and since the supercargoes were the representatives of the latter at sea and abroad, the position of the supercargoes was preeminent. Furthermore, since Campbell was not only first supercargo on board the *Fredericus R.S.*, but also director of the Company, Trolle should have been able to understand where his place was. Given his naval career, however, perhaps Trolle had some difficulty in confining himself in subordination, not being very well acquainted with this new condition. On the other hand, it emerges from the same paragraph of the privileges that the captain was the representative of justice on board; this reflects an even older tradition. The terms in which authority was granted must nevertheless be correctly interpreted. The supercargoes laid down the guidelines, but the execution of the orders in practice always depended upon the experience and knowledge of the officers.

Precisely at this point, there is an argument against Trolle's misbehaviour. Trolle was assisted by a second captain, George Kitchin. Kitchin, a Briton, had sailed to China in 1726 aboard the Ostend Company ship *Leeuw,* although he certainly made three voyages in that Company's service: at least once as second mate and twice as second captain.[1] On every ship sent out during the first charter, a "second captain" was appointed to assist the captain. This function was abolished before the commencement of the second charter in 1746. All first captains but two during the first charter were Swedes, while all second captains but four were foreigners. The addition of a foreign second captain – as well as of other foreign officers – was intended to offset the lack of experience of the Swedes in long voyages. It may be asked why the Company directors did not appoint only experienced foreign captains, instead of duplicating the function. Such a solution would of course have been less expensive. Because the Swedish Company, being a new shipowner in 1731, had no tradition to draw upon, it is understandable that experience and knowledge had to be recruited from elsewhere. Like Trolle, a dozen of the captains in the period 1731–66 had previously been in the service of the Royal Swedish Navy. Being recruited from the Navy for the Company's service was not always to be regarded as an asset, however. Lack of training was a frequent cause for complaint in the Navy, so that the merchant service was actually more of a nursery for the Navy than the other way round.[2] Even though Trolle did not take service again after the first voyage of the *Fredericus R.S.* and left the Company, understandably after all that had occurred between him and Campbell, in later years many officers left the Navy to join the Company for good. In fact there were two career systems. One was that of the officer or even seaman on leave of absence, who rejoined the ranks of the Navy upon returning from a voyage to the East Indies. Leave of absence could be applied for several times –

---

[1] Degryse & Parmentier (1995), pp. 192–193.
[2] *Svenska flottans historia* (1942–45). 2, p. 259.

subject to permission of their superiors in the Navy – so that such persons could pursue a double career, one in the Company and one in the Navy, receiving promotion in both. The second system involved a simple switch-over from the Navy to the Company, in which a definitive career then began.[1]

No doubt Trolle adopted the first system, partly under compulsion. This was also the case with Lars Lund, appointed third mate on the *Fredericus R.S.* He was lieutenant in the Swedish Navy. Lund was one of the crew with whom Campbell fell out, mainly because of his drinking habits and misbehaviour. As recorded above, Lund was mentioned in Campbell's report when back in Gothenburg. He wrote at the end of his *Diary:* "Lieotennant Lunds case was the most difficult to manage so as to save him from ruin, for I having proofs enough to produce of his mutiny & disobedience, had it come to a tryal it might have cost him his Life, I therefore consulted the Judge of the Admiralty who is Judge Advocat in such Cases, and showd him my Case, who told me if he was brought to a Courtmartial he must be condemnd to dye, This I being resolv'd to prevent got people underhand to hint to Lund that if he would confess his fault to the Company & ask pardon of me & his superiour officers that he had disobeyd that they believd I would be satisfyd & would clear him without bringing him to a tryal."[2] Lund was reluctant, however, and said he would stand his trial. As a consequence, Lund was sentenced by the Company to forfeit his wages for the time that Campbell had suspended him during the voyage.

Campbell's *Diary* allows us to reconstruct part of the muster roll of the *Fredericus R.S.,* as shown below.

Georg Herman Trolle	Captain	
George Kitchin	2nd captain	
– Baron	Chief mate	
Hindric Bremer	2nd mate	
Lars Lund	3rd mate	
– Muder	Doctor	
– Jacobson	Doctor's mate	
Tynis Kupens	Boatswain	† 12 April 1732 from high fever
Jacob Anderson	Boatswain's mate	
Olof Rasmuson Humbla	Boatswain's mate, later boatswain	
– Brown	Chief carpenter	
Lars Roos	Carpenter	† 23 July 1732 from scurvy
Jonas (?) Almroth	Steward (butler)	

---

[1] Koninckx (1980b), pp. 307–310.
[2] *Diary,* p. 295.

–	Eklund	Quartermaster	
–	Ekström	Quartermaster, coxswain	
–	Hultin	Quartermaster	
Olof Rudbeck		Quartermaster	

| George Kitchin | Midshipman | |
| James Maule | Midshipman | |

Anders Ambiormsen	Seaman	† 25 July 1733 from scurvy
Jonas Andersson	Seaman	† 29 Oct. 1732
Swen Andersson	Seaman	† 23 June 1733
Peter Bartz or Berts	Seaman	† 22 May 1733 fell overboard
Nils Fahlberg	Seaman	† 19 April 1732 fell overboard
– Nyman (Neuman)		
Tore Ostanson	Seaman	† 5 June 1733 from scurvy
Swen Nilson	Seaman	† 1 Aug. 1733 from scurvy
– Skarpe	Seaman, later cook	† ?

| Jack – | Ship's boy | |

Daniel Campbell	Writer/assistant supercargo	
James Moir	Writer/assistant supercargo	
Gustaf Ross	Writer/assistant supercargo, purser	

| Simon – | Supercargo's servant | |
| Morgan – | Supercargo's servant | |

Colin Campbell	1st supercargo	
– Graham	2nd supercargo	also called Brown
Charles Morford	3rd supercargo	
John Pike	4th supercargo	

Since no muster roll of the first expedition has been preserved, Campbell's Diary is one of the very few documents to inform us about the crew. The above list must represent about one third of the crew, in view of the ship's tonnage and of her complement during other voyages. According to Swedish sources the complement during her third (1737), fourth (1740) and fifth (1744) voyage in the Company's service amounts to 91, 122 and 116 hands respectively.[1] *The Chronicles of the East India Company* report that the Swedish vessel *King Fredrik* – no doubt the *Fredericus R.S.* – moored at Whampoa in 1731 had a crew of 96 men.[2] Apart from the supercargoes, very few of the persons listed have been traced in connection with subsequent expeditions. It should be remembered, however, that the spelling of family

---

[1] Koninckx (1980b), pp. 444–445.
[2] Morse (1966–69), 1, p. 212.

names, or even Christian names, was not very stable in the 18th century. Even in Campbell's journal the name of one and the same person may vary.

What is certain is that Kitchin, the second captain, sailed out another four times in the Company's service, always in the same function. His son George was appointed midshipman by Campbell at his own father's request.[1] Another midshipman called Maul is very probably James Maule, who was appointed third mate during the second voyage of the *Fredericus R.S.* and was second captain twice on the *Götheborg* and at least captain on the *Prins Gustaf.* In fact midshipmen were the same as cadets. The Swedish Company initially called them midshipmen, since they were foreigners recruited from abroad. In 1748 King Adolf Fredrik had established a cadet corps for the Navy, reserved for the education of young noblemen. The Government set up a school for cadets in 1756 as a reaction against this privilege.[2] Like others, cadets on leave of absence could take service in the Company as well. The young men had to become acquainted with all the work on board. The intention was that the cadets should eventually become officers. They made one or two voyages as cadets and could then become trainees or probationer mates.

Second mate Henrik Bremer was to be appointed captain on the *Fredericus R.S.* twice during later voyages.

Generally speaking, the careers of officers are more easily traceable than those of other crew members, particularly when some of the muster rolls are not available.

It has already been observed that at least the second captain, the chief mate, the second mate, and two midshipmen were foreigners. While there were good reasons why they were enrolled, their presence on board was liable to cause some friction, since the Swedish crew – or part of it – found it difficult to suffer the Britons. The fact that the four supercargoes were also British subjects certainly did not make things easier.

Sources of the Swedish Company mention Graham as second supercargo, but according to Campbell a certain Brown was appointed second supercargo. However, on p. 227 of the *Diary* Campbell mentions a *Mr Graham* as one of the supercargos and officers, and from then on the two names seem to alternate, with a predominance of Graham. It must be concluded that Brown was a pseudonym, used to hide Graham's real identity.[3] Neither Graham nor Brown accomplished any other voyage in Swedish service, unless under a third name. Charles Morford and John Pike, third and fourth supercargoes, were to make other voyages, Morford four times (twice as second and twice as first supercargo), and Pike three times as second supercargo.[4] Morford had travelled twice as assistant and twice as third supercargo for the Ostend Company.[5] Even Daniel Campbell and James Moir, both assistant supercargoes, appointed as writers, were British. Moir was later on to become fourth, second and first supercargo, making four voyages in all in the Swedish Company's service.[6]

---

[1] *Diary*, p. 28.
[2] *Svenska flottans historia* (1942–45). 2, p. 259.
[3] In the receipt for provisions and equipment which the supercargoes signed when parting from the Dutch escort off Bantam on 26 February 1733, the name appears as *Alexander Brown* (Koninckx 1980b, p. 73, note 13). *Alexander* was probably part of the pseudonym. Kjellberg (1974), pp. 44, 177, 203, gives Graham's first name as *Charles*, without mentioning his source.
[4] Kjellberg (1974), pp. 204–205.
[5] Gill (1961), p. 106 f. – Koninckx (1987), p. 51.
[6] Kjellberg (1974), p. 204.

So much for the people on board the *Fredericus R.S.* during the Company's first expedition. Without a muster roll it is difficult to find out more about possible later voyages of the crew members. Normally common sailors are mentioned only when involved in special circumstances, or when dying during the journey.

The ship

The *Fredericus Rex Sueciæ* was of only two hundred *läster,* giving a cargo capacity of 489.6 tons. She was the very first ship sent out by the Company, but her year of construction was actually 1725. Her previous name had been *Terra Nova,* built at the shipyard of the same name in Stockholm.[1] Contrary to what is usually alleged, with only two exceptions all Swedish Company ships were built at Swedish yards.[2] The *Drottning Ulrica Eleonora,* the vessel involved in the Porto Novo episode, had previously been in service with the English East India Company under the name of *Heathcote.* After being repaired and inspected at the shipyard of Bronsdon & Wells at Deptford, she was bought by Hugh Campbell on behalf of the Swedes.[3] The *Tre Cronor* was none other than the former *Apollo* of the Ostend Company, which had made a single voyage under the imperial flag in 1730; she was purchased in Hamburg in 1735 by Johan Friedrich König, the Swedish Company's commissioner in that city.[4] The *Ulrica Eleonora* and the *Tre Cronor* both measured 225 *läster.* Together with the *Fredericus R.S.* they had the lowest *läst* figures. After the *Tre Cronor* had been brought into service in 1736, no other ship with a cargo capacity below 620 metric tons was put into the Far East navigation, neither do the sources give evidence of any other ships having been purchased abroad during the first and second charters. In fact, the charter deeds urge the directors to order their ships from Sweden in the first instance, or to buy them from the Swedish Navy rather than get them from abroad.[5] The Company should have recourse to foreign sources only in extreme necessity, and in such cases the Government was to be informed. This rule was obviously intended to safeguard the interests of Swedish shipyards. That the rule was observed is strikingly illustrated by the fact that 19 vessels out of 22 came off the stocks of Swedish yards in the period 1731–1766. Most of the East Indiamen thus made their maiden trips for the Swedish Company, although not all of them were originally launched for the Company. Some ships first went into service for other companies, in which case a longer time elapsed between the year of building and the first voyage to the Far East. Consequently the design and cargo capacity evolved quickly to meet the requirements of the Company traffic. The *läst* figure doubled in ten years, for in 1741 building began on the *Drottningen af Swerige* with a cargo capacity of 387 *läster* or 947 metric tons. The index figure rose from 60.79 for the *Fredericus R.S.* in 1732 to 117.68 in 1742 for the *Drottningen af Swerige.* Within a period of less than 20 years the size of Swedish Company ships increased by a factor of 2.3.

---

[1] Göt. Sjö. Mus. 15:4–5.
[2] Koninckx (1980b), p. 156 ff. – Zethelius (1955-56), pp. 57–102.
[3] Gill (1958), p. 50. – Gill (1961), p. 103.
[4] RAS. KKH.
[5] *Utdrag utur alle … publique handlingar …* 2 (1746), p. 853, art. 4; 3 (1749), p. 2323 f., art. 4.

The lower *läst* figure of the *Fredericus R.S.* may mean that she was a flute. The flute or pink was a ship with a very flat first futtock and sharply rounded off at stem and stern. It could be of 150 to 200 *läster,* and by definition was intended for long-distance navigation.[1]

The problem of ship type is not too easy to resolve, especially in the 18th century, when the various categories overlapped each other. The frigate, for instance, was originally designed for operations of war. During the 17th century it developed into a full-rigger, i.e. a vessel with three complete masts, each consisting of three sections and carrying square sails. After 1756, this type of line-of-battle ship was the backbone of the naval fleet. In outward appearance the frigate was a smaller version of the line-of-battle ship, approximate to the French *vaisseau,* the type termed a "ship" in those days. Of course all Swedish Company ships are referred to as *skepp* in ship's journals and other official documents. This corresponds to the French term *vaisseau,* which is used in the Swedish archives compiled in French. Thus it is clear that the *Fredericus R.S.* passed as a *vaisseau.*[2] It is quite possible that the terms "frigate" and "ship" referred to the military classification and were applied to merchantmen as well during the period of the East India companies because of the resemblance.[3]

The East Indiaman in fact represented the emergence of the great ocean-going mercantile three-master upon the scene. Its resemblance to a vessel of war was only superficial, for the constructional requirements of a ship of the line were fundamentally different from those of an East Indiaman. A naval vessel needed more streamlining below the waterline, which meant narrower quickworks. This streamlining, which increased the ship's speed, had to be foregone when building a merchantman. A broad-beamed quickwork created more cargo-space, although it did nothing to assist rapid manoeuvring.[4]

While the naval vessel possessed as many gun-levels as decks, the first deck – the lowest – of an East Indiaman was always taken up by cargo holds. If gunports did exist on the first deck, as sketches and drawings sometimes indicate, then in practice they were kept tightly caulked-to and were not used as anything more than cargo doors or ventilation ducts.

All Company ships were equipped with cannon, but the number did not only vary roughly according to the size of the vessel, but also from one voyage to another of one and the same ship. We do not know how many guns the *Fredericus R.S.* carried on her first expedition. During her third voyage (1737) the *Fredericus R.S.* carried 26 guns, while Morse reports that she was equipped with 28 guns in 1732.[5] In 1740 and 1744, however, the *Fredericus R.S.* carried twenty guns.[6] Even during the voyage on the high sea, the guns were kept below deck.[7] They also often played a role in keeping the ship in balance. Even in the 18th century there was still reason to fear pirates. Company ships, loaded with thousands of silver piastres or with rich cargoes of Oriental products, formed a tempting prey. Thus

---

[1] [Aubin] (1736), pp. 482–485. – Zethelius (1955–56), p. 96, mentions that the *Fredericus R.S.* was registered as a "pink" when built in Stockholm, 121 Sw. feet long, 28.5 large (1 Sw. foot = 0.297 m; thus 36 m and 8.5 m respectively).
[2] RAS. H & S 52.
[3] Röding (1794–98), 1, p. 610.
[4] Hammar (1931), p. 19.
[5] Koninckx (1980b), pp. 444–445. – Morse (1966–69), 1, p. 212.
[6] RUG. FHH. Mss. 1929 & 1930.
[7] *Diary*, p. 262.

there is no doubt that guns were carried not merely for maritime purposes, as ballast or as fog and convoy signals, or for firing salutes to supercargoes, harbour authorities or other vessels encountered at sea.

The battleworthiness of even the best-equipped East Indiaman should not be overestimated. Her clumsiness and her sail-plan as well as her smaller crew made rapid manoeuvring difficult. Although a medium-sized Company ship could overmaster a brig of war or a corvette, she was no match for a larger frigate, so that it could be difficult to withdraw from battle. Her ordnance served more for keeping opponents at a distance than for engaging in battle. This is strikingly illustrated by the manoeuvres carried out by the *Ulrica Eleonora* against the English men-of-war in front of Porto Novo in 1733. After all, Company ships were merchant ships, not warships. Sketches and drawings can be misleading, even when made in conjunction with the building of Company ships, because they often show more gunports than were effectively in use. This was almost normal practice in the late 18th century. It is true that merchant ships were incorporated in the navy in time of war. Consequently gunports were provided beforehand. As already mentioned, on normal mercantile voyages the redundant gunports were often used for ventilation.

There is still something more to be said about the career of the *Fredericus R.S.* Being the oldest of the Company's vessels, her performance was a remarkable one. Coming off the stocks in 1725, she had sailed under the name of *Terra Nova* until 1731. She made no fewer than five voyages for the Swedish East India Company, all of them successful. When taken out of service in 1745 she was already 20 years old. This is remarkable when it is also borne in mind that the *Fredericus R.S.* was at the same time the smallest vessel in the Company's fleet until 1799, when the *Westergöthland,* of 162 *läster,* was sent out under the fourth charter.[1] Thus the *Fredericus R.S.* was an old ship, and it was probably with great relief that A.J. Flanderin, 2nd supercargo during a voyage in the 1740's, wrote in his journal, after a typhoon had abated: "Ons oudt Ship gedroegh hem ten uyttersten wel" (Our old ship did endure it [the typhoon] quite well until the end).

Whether the ship continued sailing after 1745 is not known for certain. The ship was sold by auction in November 1745 and is very probably identical with the *Fredericus* which the French ambassador to Sweden intended to buy for transporting auxiliary troops of Jacobites to help Prince Charles Edward Stuart against the English Crown. As it turned out, she never sailed for Scotland but instead left Gothenburg for Ostend in May 1746 with soldiers recruited in Sweden to go into armed service in France.[2]

Apart from this veteran, only the largest ships in the Company fleet sailed six or seven times, attaining in that case a maximum of 16, 17 and even 30 years of service. A cargo of 1,000 tons thus represents the lower limit of profitability.

The return cargo

Only fragmentary information, to be gleaned from Campell's *Diary,* is available about the outgoing cargo. Concerning the return cargo we are better informed.

[1] Hammar (1931), p. 23.
[2] Behre (1972), pp. 11, 15 f.

As soon as an East Indiaman had moored at its home port, the supercargoes hastened to submit an inventory of the return cargo to the directors. On the basis of this information, cargo lists or sales catalogues *(försäljningsböcker)* were printed and distributed to merchants, who could use them as a practical aid at the public sale. The sales catalogue was prefaced with a summary description of the cargo and a statement of the conditions of sale. Then followed the actual list of East Indian products. The goods were grouped into types and specified in selling lots. A blank space followed after every item for filling in the auction price and the name of the purchaser. Except for these blanks, sales catalogues do not differ in essence from the auction catalogues we know today.

From the first voyage of the *Fredericus R.S.* such a sales catalogue has been preserved, although, strangely enough at first sight, in German.[1] This is an indication that merchants from Germany must have shown interest in the East Indian goods unloaded in Gothenburg. Probably many of them were expected to come over in order to attend the public auction.

As has already been pointed out, goods destined for re-export were subject to 1/8% *recognition*. It was the buyers' duty to pay 10% of the auction price in cash not later than eight days after the public sale of the goods in question. A public sale generally went on for several days. It was often split into two sessions.

The goods had to be weighed by authorized weighers in Gothenburg weight units. A "turn of the scale" allowance of 1% was deducted from the weight of the goods. It was a proportionate discount allowed by the wholesaler as compensation for the overweight which had to be given in the retail trade. The purchaser had to take delivery of his goods within three months at the latest. If he paid cash within the first month, he got a 2% discount. If he paid during the second or third month, the discount was 1% and 1/2% respectively, but after the end of the third month there was no deduction. Goods not paid for or not collected were re-offered for sale at the next auction. Payment could be effected in Swedish currency or *Stockholms Banco-Transport-Sedlar.*[2]

Summarizing the items mentioned in the sales catalogue, a survey of the return cargo may be shown as follows:

Porcelain	499,061 pieces	2) Congou	66 chests
	12 table-sets (with an		100 half-chests
	unknown number of		24 canisters
	pieces), all in 151		8 baskets
	chests and 1,801 tubes	3) Souchong	562 chests
			15 baskets
Tea		4) Pekoe	43 chests
Black teas			105 chests
1) Bohea	627 chests		

[1] RAS. KKA (1). *Verkauffungs Conditionen der völligen Ladung des den 27 Augusti 1733 in dem Hafen zu Gothenburg, vor Rechnung der Schwedischen privilegirten Ost-Indischen Compagnie, von Canton in China angekommen Schiffes, Fredericus Rex Sueciæ benandt, welche am bevorstehenden 15/26 October jetzlauffenden Jahres, und darauf folgende Tage, in beregter Stadt Gothenburg, an den Meistbiethenden öffentlich verkauffet werden soll, als folget.*

[2] The *Riksens ständers bank* gave paper notes against deposits received, *banco transportsedlar,* as they were called. The note served as proof of the deposit; it was assignable and could be used as liquid cash by the bearer.

Green teas			Fans	5,173 pieces
1) Singlo	551 chests		Mother-of-pearl	150 boxes
2) Hyson	27 chests			2,000,000 pieces
	46 tubes		Wallpapers	2,293 pieces
	(and 9.750 kg)		Tablecloths	24 pieces
3) Bing	198 chests		Stone bottles	30 pieces
			Buttons	300 pairs
Others[1]			Rattan cord	76 bundles
1) Kilon	3 chests		Knee-bands	1,817 pieces
2) Linchi-sind	1 chest		Cinnabar	5.386 kg
	(and 4.235 kg)		Varnished furniture	7 lots
3) Kawang	110 pots		Tutenag	1,698 pieces
	6 small chests		China root	45 bags
4) Unspecified	288 boxes			1 small chest
Silk	23,355 pieces		Galingale	33 bags
	168.933 kg		Sago	3.485 kg
Cotton	633 pieces		Arrack	11 leggers

Although we have already mentioned the profits of the public auction, it is difficult to calculate the tonnage of imported goods. A wide variety of chests were used for packing tea. Even if we know the tares for the different kinds of chests (they are in fact mentioned in the sales catalogue), it still remains impossible to quantify the tea cargo. We are confronted with the same problem of quantification when it comes to porcelain, silk, cotton, tutenag, etc., all of these items being recorded in number of pieces. Conversions remain hazardous, even when having recourse to a hypothetic conversion table for two important commodities, viz. porcelain and fabrics, which anyway cannot be overlooked when trying to work out estimates.

If it is assumed that 1,000 pieces of porcelain are equivalent to about 88 kg, while 100 pieces of fabric correspond to about 71 kg, the main commodities except tea represent the following weights:[2]

$$\text{porcelain: } 499.061 \times 88 \text{ kg} = \qquad\qquad 43,917 \text{ kg}$$

$$\text{silk: } \qquad 233.55 \times 71 \text{ kg} = 16,582.05 \;\; \text{kg}$$
$$168.933 \text{ kg}$$

$$\text{cotton: } \qquad 6.33 \times 71 \text{ kg} \qquad 449.43 \;\; \text{kg} \quad \underline{17,200 \text{ kg}}$$
$$61,117 \text{ kg}$$

---

[1] These varieties can be classed as neither green nor black teas; moreover, it concerns *pacotille,* and the quantities involved were not substantial. These unimportant varieties dwindled away during the second charter.
[2] Koninckx (1980b), p. 269. These equivalents are of course to be applied with considerable reservations.

These 61.1 tons represent about 12.4% of the total cargo capacity of the *Fredericus R.S.*, since she measured 200 *svåra läster* or 489.6 metric tons.

Conversion of the tea is very hazardous. The variety of chests is too great for an estimate to be made. The term "bundle" with regard to rattan cord is too vague a concept, as is the term "piece" concerning tutenag. When attempting to calculate the cargo, tea and tutenag certainly cannot be overlooked, since the quantities of these commodities were very important.

In fact quantification of the whole cargo seems to be possible only from 1739 onwards because of lack of adequate sources until then. On the basis of our analysis of the measurable cargoes for the ships coming back between 1739 and 1742, however, we may perhaps assume that the cargo of tea, porcelain, metals, drugs and spices – it should be noted that fabrics are excluded – amounts to about 90% of the ship's capacity.[1] Once again it must be remembered that this is only an estimate.

Description of the manuscript and editorial principles

Colin Campbell's autograph journal of the first Swedish Company expedition to China is a volume bound in contemporary vellum with ties, measuring $32.7 \times 20.5 \times 4$ cm and containing 173 leaves of good, sturdy paper. The manuscript is on the whole in very good condition and does not seem to have been much read or handled since it was written; in fact some of the sand used by Campbell for blotting can still be traced.

Each page has a left-hand margin of 1–2 cm, usually marked with a line and containing dates and (pp. 1–225) pagination. Campbell's numbering of pages is occasionally erratic, some numbers occurring twice and others not at all. Thus, he uses the page nos. 9, 35, 56, 175, 195, and 228 twice, while nos. 57, 82, 174, and 194 have been omitted. The pages which according to Campbell's own pagination should have borne nos. 176, 204, 226, 296 and 297 are unpaged. Pp. 209–220 are blank except for pagination; p. [296] and the last 47 pages are completely blank.

The present edition aims to reproduce the complete text of the journal as faithfully as possible within reasonable limits. Campbell's pagination is printed in bold face as it appears, in parentheses or not, in the left-hand margin or centrally, as the case may be. When a page number is missing in the manuscript, it is supplied within square brackets (which are used throughout the text for any editorial insertions). When Campbell uses the same pagination on two consecutive pages, the second instance is marked '[bis]', unless it is a mistake for another page number, in which case the correct number is given in a footnote.

It should be noted that all page references to Campbell's *Diary* in the introduction as well as in the footnotes to the text are to Campbell's original page numbers and *not* to the modern pagination of the present volume. On the other hand, for technical reasons page numbers in the indexes refer to the modern pagination.

No attempt has been made to preserve the original lineation or to indicate word divisions at line ends.

---

[1] Koninckx (1980b), p. 271.

The volume is entirely in Colin Campbell's own hand, which is normally quite clear and easy to read (cf. facsimile on p. 2). There are nevertheless quite a few words and passages which present some difficulty of interpretation, particularly when Campbell has changed his text by writing something across the original word or letter, or by crossing it out and adding the emendation above the line. In such cases the emended text is normally rendered without any notice of Campbell's correction. Similarly, interlineations (with or without carets) are not marked but simply printed in the line. The few instances of words which we have failed to decipher are indicated thus: '*[illegible]*'.

Letters or words inadvertently omitted in the original are supplied in square brackets, e.g. 'not to incour[a]ge drinking' (p. 41); 'I went aboard with our Supercargos [in] the sloop' (p. 235). Instances of missing auxiliaries are not infrequent with Campbell: 'we should [have] had time enough to write' (p. 136); 'they would [have] given us a whole broadside' (p. 249). In a few cases the context makes it clear that a negation has been left out, e.g. 'He ownd that he did [not] believe drams were fit for them all, but that they were all usd to it' (p. 279).

On the other hand Campbell often fails to delete words, phrases or punctuation marks which have been made redundant by his changing his mind while writing, or he may unintentionally repeat them. Such words etc. are put in braces, e.g. '& in all other things {& in all other things}' (p. 55); 'I therefore expected of them that they would {have} in every thing bear a true regard to the service of the Company' (p. 89).

Sometimes Campbell leaves a space, apparently because he does not remember a name, figure or page reference at the time of writing and has forgotten to fill it in later. In one or two cases he possibly did not wish to take the risk of putting a certain name on paper. Such spaces are reproduced in the way they appear in the manuscript, either with a blank space or with a row of dots or hyphens.

Campbell's punctuation is faithfully reproduced in the present edition, which means that a full stop will often be found to be lacking at the end of a sentence.

Some further possibilities of misinterpretation of Campbell's handwriting deserve special mention. Occasionally it is very hard to distinguish carelessly written *o* from *e*. A carelessly looped *a* may look like *u*, and *s* and *f* are sometimes liable to confusion, as are *l* and *t*, while a casually written *b* may degenerate into an *l*. Majuscule *I* and *J* are normally indistinguishable. Such cases as these can generally be easily interpreted from the context, but for instance when they occur in proper names not found elsewhere, they may present problems.

Majuscules are as a rule easily distinguishable from minuscules. The exceptions are the letters *m, n, o, s, u, v,* and *w*. Here the majuscule is no more than an enlarged or elaborated minuscule, so that there is no fixed borderline between the two, and it is often quite impossible to determine which is intended. Thus it is inevitable that the editors cannot pretend to have achieved any high degree of consistency. In doubtful cases where Campbell's general spelling habits would seem to favour capital letters, they are printed in upper-case.

There are four instances of what appears to be Campbell's rendering of Swedish *ö* and Norwegian *ø*: he writes *´o, ó* or *o´*, which are here printed as *ó* (*Diary* p. 227: *Kónig*; p. 281: *Swin óe*; p. 287: *Wingó*; ibid.: *Wargehóla*).

Bibliographical Essay

Publishing Colin Campbell's *Diary* means adding a new testimony to those already published. Journals and diaries kept by the Swedish East India Company's employees as well as scientific descriptions and dissertations dealing with natural history and written by seafarers or scholars must have contributed greatly to the widening of knowledge about the Far East in Sweden. They certainly did when printed and published even in the Company's lifetime.

Some travel reports in fact appeared in the 18th century, although the reception of that kind of literature must not be exaggerated, even when foreign authors were translated into Swedish.

If we limit ourselves to genuine Swedish authors in the service of the Swedish East India Company, or otherwise closely related to it, it is worth noting that Campbell's *Diary* is now the oldest testimony published. On the other hand this is not really surprising, since it concerns the very first voyage.[1]

It is not our intention to list here all journals and diaries of the Swedish Company's voyages still extant in Swedish and foreign archives. The manuscripts would hardly be of very great interest to the average reader, while access to them will probably remain restricted to those being able to view the archives.[2] Suffice to mention that at least half a dozen records of this kind have been published so far. Some of them appeared shortly after the completion of the expedition on which they report, while others were not printed until the first half of this century.

The first diary to appear in print was kept by Pehr Osbeck and is entitled *Dagbok öfwer en Ostindisk resa åren 1750. 1751. 1752. Med anmärckningar uti naturkunnigheten, främmande folkslags språk, seder, hushållning, m.m. Jämte 12 tabeller och afledne skepps-predikanten Toréns bref.* Stockholm 1757. A facsimile reprint appeared in Stockholm in 1969 as vol. 5 in the series *Suecica rediviva*, and it was also translated into English and German. Osbeck has given us an extensive account of the voyage of the *Prins Carl* (1750–52), but he supplies only a few nautical data. His account is neither a ship's journal nor a ship's log, but rather a travel narrative. Although it is no doubt of considerable interest from the point of view of cultural history, the anonymous but more complete ship's journal kept in Göteborg University Library is of greater importance for a nautical approach. This journal has not been published, however.[3] On the other hand, to a common reader Osbeck's narrative is likely to appear more attractive than the anonymous journal, which no doubt explains why it was printed. Osbeck was one of Linné's disciples. The treasure of information which he gathered was of very great scientific importance, especially for natural scientists.

---

[1] Before the Swedish East India Company was established there were Swedes who took service in foreign companies and visited the Far East. One of them, Olof Eriksson Willman, in the service of the Dutch East India Company, participated in a diplomatic mission to Nagasaki in 1651–52 and left a travel narrative: *En kort beskrivning på en resa till Ostindien och Japan den en svensk man och skeppskapiten … gjort haver* (published in 1992 by J. Bernström and T. Wretö).

[2] See "Sources and literature" in Koninckx (1980b), pp. 507–513.

[3] GUB. H 22:4 A. *Journal hållen uppå Respective Swänska Ost-Indiska Compagniets Skiepp Printz Carl ifrån Giötheborg, destinerad till Canton uti China. Första Resan Annis 1750. 51. 52.*

As indicated on the title-page, the volume in which Osbeck's narrative was published in 1757 also contains letters written by Olof Torén, another of Linné's disciples. The subtitle runs as follows: *En Ostindisk resa til Suratta, China &c. från 1750 April 1. til 1752 Jun. 26.* The letters were reprinted in 1969 along with Osbeck's journal. A separate, annotated edition of Torén's letters was published in Stockholm in 1961 in the series *Tidens svenska klassiker*.[1] For scientific purposes Torén's letters also have to be considered as a travel narrative, dealing mostly with natural history.

Torén embarked upon the *Götha Leijon* (1750–52) as ship's chaplain, just as Osbeck did on the *Prins Carl*, although the former made a combined voyage, the first destination of which was Surat and the second one Canton in China. To some extent Torén's notes supplement the journals of C.H. Braad, the ship's writer, and of George Elphinstone, first mate.[2] Their journals were never published.

In 1758 the travel narrative of Johan Brelin was published under the title *Beskrifning öfver en äfventyrlig resa til och ifrån Ost-Indien, Södra America, och en del af Europa, åren 1755, 56 och 57.* Upsala 1758. A reprint appeared in Stockholm in 1973 as volume 39 of the series *Suecica rediviva*. Brelin's narrative is a short and incomplete account. As a cadet on board the *Prinsessan Sophia Albertina* (1755–56), he was left behind, by an oversight, on Ascension Island during the homeward journey from China. This adventure explains why Brelin's report of the expedition is incomplete, although it contributed to making the author a kind of Swedish Robinson Crusoe.

In 1773 Carl Gustaf Ekeberg's narrative was published in the form of letters addressed to the Secretary of the Royal Academy of Sciences, under the title *Capitaine Carl Gustaf Ekebergs Ostindiska resa, åren 1770 och 1771. Beskrefven uti bref til Kongl. Svenska Vet. Academiens secreterare.*

Ekeberg had a long career in the Company's service. He made six voyages in command. Although Ekeberg was captain on board the *Finland*, whose voyage to China in 1770–71 he himself narrated, his account cannot be considered a diary. To a much higher degree this is true of Jacob Wallenberg's *Min son på galejan, eller en ostindisk resa innehållande allahanda bläckhornskram, samlade på skeppet Finland, som afseglade ifrån Götheborg i Decemb. 1769, och återkom dersammastädes i Jun. 1771,* published for the first time in Stockholm in 1781. Wallenberg's story, which relates to the same ship and voyage as Ekeberg's, should perhaps be regarded as trivial literature. Even though Wallenberg gives evidence of a wide knowledge, a cultural background and a sharp pen, what he reports must be taken with caution. His book was undeniably a great success, however, with several later editions being published, including one as vol. 1 in the series *Svenska klassiker* with an introductory essay by Oscar Levertin (1904).

As already pointed out, all of the accounts mentioned above are travel narratives, even though some of them are entitled 'diary'. The first proper diary, kept day by day, was printed in Helsinki in 1939 and edited by Birgit Lunelund. Its title is *Journal hållen på resan till*

---

[1] Torén (1961). Strangely enough this is the only edition recorded in the *Svensk historisk bibliografi* (Swedish Historical Bibliography) of all items discussed in the present essay.
[2] GUB. H 22:3 D. *Sjö Journal öfwer Skeppet Götha Leijons Resa till Ost Indien. Åren 1750. 51. och 52.* – KVBS. *Kort Dag Bok öfver en Resa med Skeppet Götha Leyon hållen af George Elphinston.*

Canton i China med Höglofl. Ostindiska Comp$\underline{ts}$ Skiepp Cronprintzen Adolph Friedrich … (Skrifter utg. av Svenska Litteratursällskapet i Finland. Vol. 273). It is a record of a China voyage in 1745–48 written by the brothers Johan and Israel Reinius, both of whom were appointed cadets or midshipmen. It is the first instance of special attention being paid to nautical aspects.[1]

Colin Campbell's journal, which is published here, is of a third kind: it is the very first journal known to have been kept by a supercargo in the Swedish Company's service.

Confining ourselves to the ship *Fredericus Rex Sueciae,* journals of later voyages have also survived, besides some commercial documents. They deal with the voyages to China in 1737–39, to Bengal in 1740–42, and again to China in 1744–45.[2] These three complete diaries were all compiled by the Ostender André Jacques Flanderin, supercargo in Swedish service on board. Although kept by a supercargo, they are ship's journals and may be compared with the Reinius record rather than with that of Campbell. Flanderin's journals were written in Dutch. None of them has so far been published.[3]

This is not the place to enumerate all the printed journals, diaries and travel narratives relating to the foreign East India companies in France, England or the Dutch Republic. Reference can be made to the series edited by, for instance, the Hakluyt Society or the Linschooten Vereeniging. Some attention should, however, be paid to accounts by Swedes in foreign service. Two cases will be mentioned here, viz. that of another Linné disciple, C.P. Thunberg, who was enrolled by the Dutch, and that of the surgeon Anders Sparrman, who made a voyage under Ekeberg's command but later on had the opportunity of accompanying James Cook during his second expedition.[4]

Compared to ship's journals or logs, travel narratives are not usually boring. Since the authors were the very first Swedish eyewitnesses to report about the Far East, their stories must have exerted an attraction for their countrymen.[5] Exoticism, unknown countries, unexplored regions, foreign peoples, adventurous experiences are good and profitable ingredients for literary success. Even when the authors are occasional writers, the information recorded is not phantasmic at all. Indeed, some narratives were merely for leisure, but most of them result from assignments of the Swedish Royal Academy of Sciences, located in Stockholm. Young scholars, often enrolled as ship's chaplains or trainees, were commissioned to report about the voyage. Some of them made the trip to the Far East several times.

In actual fact, the records are not strictly limited to the voyage at sea but, in a broader sense, deal with history, geography, ethnography and economics as well. It has already been pointed out how they contributed to the widening of scientific knowledge in those days, especially in the field of *natural history*, as it was then called. This characterizes precisely 18th-century voyage literature in comparison with that of earlier times. Moreover, any genuine Swedish literature of that kind is rather scanty in the period preceding the East India Company era.

---

[1] A large part of the original nautical data were not published in Lunelund's edition, however.

[2] RUG. FHH. Mss. 1928, 1929 & 1930.

[3] Other records concerning the voyages of the *Fredericus R.S.* in 1735–36 and 1738–39 have been preserved. Although entitled "journals" they deal only with the commercial transactions. They are neither actual ship's journals nor travel narratives, but provide useful information about the East Indian trade.

[4] Thunberg (1788–93). – Sparrman (1783).

[5] Holmberg (1988), pp. 39–47.

Ship's journals or logs must have been much more numerous, because, as we have seen, they were always kept by order for the management of the Company's business. The contents were primarily confined to nautical data and could hardly be adapted to make them attractive publications for a broader public. This explains the lack of printed material of that kind. It has to be borne in mind that they were written for an immediate practical purpose.

The narratives were not without value to the Company itself, certainly not when dealing with geography, oceanography, trading or economics. From their records travellers also derived short essays and dissertations. One of the most active in that field was Captain Ekeberg himself[1], but Osbeck and Reinius should be mentioned here once again, as well as Grill.[2]

As evidence of the Company's existence all this printed literature, in its turn, contributed to a vivid debate in Sweden focusing on the usefulness of the Company itself, its profits, the harms it inflicted upon Swedish industry and trade, etc., and resulting in a great many 18th century lampoons and pamphlets[3].

Fiction too followed in the Company's wake. The above-mentioned narrative of Wallenberg, and even that of Brelin, are borderline cases between fiction and objective report. The same can be said of *Kort utdrag af Ostindiske journalen, som fördes under resan med skeppet Prints Carl och Capitainen, Herr Johan Rundsten, i wers författad af Jonas Greggelund, som på samma resa war förhyrd för matros, med omberörde skepp och Capitain* (Gefle 1794). Greggelund was not afraid of versifying the story of his voyage, which took place in 1763–64.

As far as we have been able to ascertain, the first real novel is that of Sam Ritzler (pseud. of Olof Traung, 1935), while the latest, in fact a trilogy, was written by Evert Lundström (1978; 1979; 1980). The tragic story of the *Götheborg* has even been adapted for youngsters in a picture-book by Anita Steiner with text by Evert Lundström (Steiner 1994).

In a comprehensive survey of 18th-century printed material on the history of the Swedish Company, one cannot overlook contemporary newspapers, from which some information can also be gleaned.[4]

Coming finally to scholarly literature, the first serious students of the Company's history were J.A.C. Hellstenius (1850) and J.F. Nyström (1882). It may be noted that this was in the second half of the 19th century. However, special tribute must be paid to Eskil Olán, a journalist of Gothenburg, who acquainted a larger reading public with the Swedish East India Company by his thorough, popular science work printed in 1920. After that more than fifty years elapsed before the publication of the synthesizing studies of S.T. Kjellberg (1974) and C. Koninckx (1975, 1980b).[5]

---

[1] Ekeberg (1756; 1757; 1768).
[2] Osbeck (1758). – Reinius (1749). – Grill (1774; 1775).
[3] See the items listed in Koninckx (1980b), pp. 514–515, to which must be added David Davidson Roukonen (1765; *ibid.*, p. 517), all the other pamphlets remaining anonymous. Although a dissertation, Christiernin (1768) may also be cited here.
[4] See Koninckx (1980b), p. 515.
[5] It should be noted, however, that Koninckx's original doctoral dissertation, of which *The First and Second Charters of the Swedish East India Company …* is an adapted version in English, was written in Dutch. M. Åberg's unpublished licentiate thesis (1988) could also be cited here.

Probably a new breakthrough is on its way because of the renewal of interest during the 1980's in the wreck of the *Götheborg,* which sank near the Nya Älvsborg fortress in 1745 on her arrival from China. In the first place, reference should be made to the reports of the team engaged in rediscovering the wreck.[1] The book published in 1990 by B. Wästfelt, B. Gyllensvärd and J. Weibull concerns the actual results of the *Götheborg* diving programme and may be considered the most recent monograph published on the Company's history, although in this case limited to the tragic fate of one particular ship.[2]

---

[1] Olsvik, Johansson & Wästfelt (1986). – *Ostindiefararen Götheborg. Rapport om 1986 års undersökning* (1987).
[2] Wästfelt, Gyllensvärd & Weibull (1990).

Bibliography

In addition to manuscript sources used for the present edition, this bibliography is intended to cover all relevant monographs and journal articles published. Notices in general biographical reference works and articles published in newspapers have been excluded.[1]

A. Manuscript sources

Abbreviations

FHH	Fonds Hye Hoys
Göt.Sjö.Mus.	Göteborgs sjöfartsmuseum (Gothenburg Maritime Museum)
GUB	Göteborgs universitetsbibliotek (Göteborg University Library)
H & S	Handel & Sjöfart (Trade & Maritime Affairs)
KBS	Kungl. biblioteket (Royal Library, Stockholm)
KKA	Kommerskollegium. Arkivet (Board of Trade. Records)
KKH	Kommerskollegium. Huvudarkivet (Board of Trade. Main Records)
KVBS	Kungl. Vetenskapsakademiens bibliotek (Library of the Royal Academy of Sciences, in Stockholm University Library)
LAG	Landsarkivet i Göteborg (County Record Office in Gothenburg)
Öst.	Östadsarkivet (Östad Records)
RAS	Riksarkivet (National Record Office, Stockholm)
RUG	Rijksuniversiteit Gent (Ghent University Library)
UUB	Uppsala universitetsbibliotek (Uppsala University Library)

Braad, C.H., *Berättelse om Resan med Skeppet Hoppet ... från Götheborg till Canton i China, ifrån d: 26 Ian: 1748, till d: 11 Iulii 1749.* UUB. X.389.

–, *Sjö Journal öfwer Skeppet Götha Leijons Resa till Ost Indien. Åren 1750. 51 och 52.* In: Id., *Beskrifning på Skeppet Götha Leijons Resa till Surat och åtsillige* [sic] *andre Indianske Orter.* GUB. H 22:3 D.

Campbell, C., *The Diary or Journal of Sundry Transactions pass'd Aboard the Ship Fredericus Rex Sueciæ in her Voyage from Kensie Sund (near Gottenburg) to the Port of Canton in China, & from Canton back to Gottenburg in Sweden Annis 1732 & 1733.* GUB. Ligg.fol. H 22:3 B.

–, *Journal or Diary of Transactions aboard the Ship Fredericus Rex Sueciæ bound from Gottenburg in Sweden To Canton in China beginning 15th february 1735. – Journal of the Voyage of the Ship Fredericus Rex Sueciæ homeward bound from Canton ... to Gottenburg ... beginning 28th January 1736 ... – Journal or Diary of Transactions aboard the Ship Stockholm (in Company with the Fredericus Rex Sueciæ) bound from Gottenburg ... to Canton ... Annis 1737 & 1738. – Journal of the Voyage of the Ships Stockholm & King Frederick from Canton to Gottenburg A⁰· 1739 Aboard the Stockholm.* GUB. Ligg.fol. H 22:3 C.

–, *Relation abrégée du Voyage du Vaisseau Fridericus Rex Sueciae et particulièrement de son* [sic] *Rencontre avec l'Escadre Hollandoise auprez du Detroit de Sunda.* RAS. H & S 52.

Dalman, J.F., *Dagbok Uppå Kongli Vetenskaps Academiens befalning Hållen ... Under Resan från Giötheborg til Canton och Hem som börjades År 1748 d. 19 Febr. och slutades År 1749 d. 11 Julii.* KVBS. Ms. Dalman, J.F.

---

[1] For a brief and incomplete bibliography of 18th century newspapers and pamphlets, see Koninckx (1980b), pp. 541–542.

Ekeberg, C.G., *DageBok under Resan till och ifrån Canton uti China Åhren 1746.47.48.49. med Skeppet Götha Leyon.* KVBS. Ms. Ekeberg, C.G.

Elphinstone, G., *Kort Dag Bok öfver en Resa med Skeppet Götha Leyon.* KVBS.

Flanderin, A.-J., *Journal gehouden op het schip de Coninck Frederick gecommandeert door Capiteÿn Hendrick Bremer gemonteert met 26 stukken Canon, in Compagnie van het Schip de Stockholm, Capiteÿn Comte Dederÿck Taube gedestineert naer Canton in China, voor Rekeninge der Sweetsche Indische Compagnie. Anno 1738.* RUG. FHH. Ms. 1928.

–, *Journal gehouden op het schip genaemt Fredericus Rex Suesiae gedestineert naer Canton in China gemonteert met 20 stukken canon gecommandeert door de Capiteyn Benjamin Swanson vertrokken van Gottenburg 5/16 april anno 1740.* RUG. FHH. Ms. 1929.

–, *Journal gehouden op het schip Fredericus Rex Suesiae gedestineert naer Canton in China gemonteert met 20 stukken Canon gecommandeert door den Capiteyne James Maule vertrokken van Wariholle 1/12 January 1744.* RUG. FHH. Ms. 1930.

Förteckning över kompaniets skepp under 1. och 2. oktrojerna. GUB. Ligg.fol. H 22:1.

Gethe, C.J., *Dagbok Hållen På Resan till Ost Indien Begynt den 18 octobr: 1746 och Slutad den 20 Iuni 1779.* KBS. M.280.

Journal hållen uppå Respective Swänska Ost-Indiska Compagniets Skiepp Printz Carl ifrån Giötheborg, destinerad till Canton uti China. Första Resan Annis 1750. 51. 52. GUB. Ligg.fol. H 22:4 A.

Utdrag af 20 loggböcker för att visa kompassens missvisning med dess ändringar. Förteckning på Svenska Ostindiska kompaniets skepp 1732–1765, deras afgångs- och hemkomsttid samt officere. UUB. L 183.

Verkauffungs Conditionen der völligen Ladung des den 27 Augusti 1733 in dem Hafen zu Gothenburg, vor Rechnung der Schwedischen privilegirten Ost-Indischen Compagnie, von Canton in China angekommen Schiffes, Fredericus Rex Sueciæ benandt, welche am bevorstehenden 15/26 October jetzlauffenden Jahres, und darauf folgende Tage, in beregter Stadt Gothenburg, an den Meistbiethenden öffentlich verkauffet werden soll, als folget. RAS. KKA (1).

1° *Diarium eller Journal öfver alla deras förrätningar* [1760]. UUB. L 186, 13.

B. Printed primary and secondary sources

Åberg, M. (1988). *Svensk handelskapitalism – ett dynamiskt element i frihetstidens samhälle? En fallstudie av delägarna i Ostindiska kompaniets 3:e oktroj 1766–1786.* Göteborg. Unpubl. licentiate thesis. (Historiska institutionen, Göteborgs universitet.)

– (1990). "The Swedish East India Company 1731–66. Business Strategy and Foreign Influence in a Perspective of Change." *Scandinavian Journal of History* 15, pp. 97–108.

Allison, R.S. (1943). *Sea Diseases. The Story of a Great Natural Experiment in Preventive Medicine in the Royal Navy.* London.

Andersson, B. (1988). "Den ostindiska bubblan." In: Andersson, B., *Göteborgs handlande borgerskap 1750–1805.* Göteborg, pp. 103-126. (Rapporter från Göteborgsprojektet vid Göteborgs universitet. 7.)

Après de Mannevillette, N.D. d' (1775). *Le Neptune oriental ...* Paris & Brest.

Arne, T.J. (1953–54). "Svensk sjöfart och handel med Kina under 1800-talets förra hälft." *Sjöhistorisk årsbok,* pp. 49–65.

– (1960). "En svensk Kinaresenär och hans signatur." *Unda maris,* pp. 5–10.

Attman, A. (1960). "Travellers i Göteborg under Ostindiska kompaniets dagar." *Unda maris,* pp. 11–21.

– (1987). "John Hall & Co:s konkurs." In: *Historia kring Göteborg.* Red. av H. Andersson ... Stockholm, pp. 121–131.

[Aubin, N.] (1736). *Dictionnaire de marine contenant les termes de la navigation et de l'architecture navale ...* Seconde éd., revue, corr. et augm. Amsterdam.

Baeckström, A. (1948). "Några notiser rörande William Chambers." *Rig* 31, pp. 25–29.

Baels, E.J. (1972). *"De Generale Keizerlijke en Koninklijke Indische Compagnie gevestigd in de Oostenrijkse Nederlanden", genaamd de Oostendse Compagnie.* Oostende.

Bedoire, F. (1963). "Släkten Bedoire." *Personhistorisk tidskrift* 61, pp. 65–92.

– (1966). "Tillägg till släkten Bedoires genealogi." *Personhistorisk tidskrift* 64, pp. 49–53.

Behre, G. (1966). "Ostindiska kompaniet och hattarna. En storpolitisk episod 1742." *Historisk tidskrift* 86, pp. 31–46.

– (1972). "Göteborg och upproret i Skottland 1745–1746." *Göteborg förr och nu. Göteborgs hembygdsförbunds skriftserie. 7.* Göteborg, pp. 5–35.

Belfrage, E. (1992). "Chinese Watercolours from the 18th Century Illustrating Porcelain Manufacture." In: International Association of Bibliophiles, *Transactions [of the] 15th Congress, Copenhagen, 20–26 September 1987.* Ed. by P.A. Christensen. Copenhagen, pp. 124–131.

Berg, J., & Lagercrantz, B. (1962). *Scots in Sweden.* Stockholm.

Berg, W. (1879). *Om införseln till Sverige af kinesiskt porslin under Svenska ostindiska kompaniets tredje oktroj åren 1766–1786. En keramisk studie.* Göteborg.

Beurdeley, M. (1956). "La Suède grand importeur de porcelaines au XVIIIème siècle." *Bulletin de la Société des études indochinoises* 31, pp. 263–269.

Börjeson, D.Hj.T. (1932). *Stockholms segelsjöfart. Anteckningar om huvudstadens kofferdiflotta och dess män. Med en översikt av stadens och rikets sjöfartsförhållanden från äldsta tid intill våra dagar. Minnesskrift 1732–1932.* Stockholm.

Börjeson, Hj. (1942). *Biografiska anteckningar om örlogsflottans officerare 1700–1799.* Stockholm.

Brelin, J. (1758). *Beskrifning öfver en äfventyrlig resa til och ifrån Ost-Indien, Södra America, och en del af Europa, åren 1755, 56 och 57.* Upsala. – Repr. Stockholm 1973. (Suecica rediviva. 39.)

British Diplomatic Instructions. 1688–1789. 5: Sweden, 1727–1789 (1928). Ed. by J.F. Chance. London.

Brorsson, H. (1990). *Handelsrelationer och vetenskap under 1700-talet med anknytning till Svenska ostindiska kompaniet.* Stockholm. (University of Stockholm. Center for Pacific Asia Studies. Working paper. 16.)

Campbell, C. (1960). *Colin Campbell 1686–1757. Merchant, Gothenburg, Sweden. His Will. Annotated [by] A.A. Cormack. A Scoto-Swedish Study.* Peterculter.

Cheong, W.E. (1991). "The Age of Suqua, 1720–1759: the Early Hong Merchants." In: *Asian Trade Routes.* Ed. by K.R. Haellquist. London, pp. 217–230.

Christiernin, P.N. (1768). *Academiskt försök, om Sveriges nytta af handelen och segelfarten på Ost-Indien.* Uppsala.

Constant, C. de (1964). *Les mémoires de Charles de Constant sur le commerce à la Chine.* [Publ. par] L. Dermigny. Paris. (École pratique des hautes études. Sect. 6. Centre de recherches historiques.) (Ports, routes, trafics. 16.)

Cordier, H. (1889). "Les Débuts de la Compagnie royale de Suède dans l'Extrême Orient au XVIIIe siècle." In: *Recueil de textes et de traductions publié par les professeurs de l'Ecole des langues orientales vivantes à l'occasion du VIIIe Congrès international des orientalistes tenu à Stockholm en 1889.* Paris, pp. 301–343. (Publications de l'Ecole des langues orientales vivantes. Sér. 3:6.)

Cormack, A.A. (1967/68). "Scots in the Swedish East-India Company. Passports in Drum Castle for 1730–1760." *Aberdeen University Review* 42, pp. 38–47.

– (1975). *Scotsmen in the First Swedish East India Company 1731–1745.* Repr. from Banffshire Journal Annual 1975. Banff.

Degryse, K. (1974). "De Oostendse Chinahandel (1718–1735)." *Revue belge de philologie et d'histoire* 52, pp. 306–347.

– (1988). "Sociale en sexuele spanningen aan boord van de Oostendse Oost-Indiëvaarders (1715–1734)." *Bijdragen tot de internationale maritieme geschiedenis.* Brussels, pp. 69–79. (Collectanea maritima. 4.)

Degryse, K., & Parmentier, J. (1993). "Maritime Aspects of the Ostend Trade to Mocha, India and China (1715–1732)." In: *Ships, Sailors and Spices ...* Ed. by J.R. Bruijn and F.S. Gaastra. Amsterdam, pp. 139–175.

– (1995). "Kooplieden en kapiteins. Een prosopografische studie van de kooplieden, supercargo's en scheepsofficieren van de Oostendse handel op Oost-Indië en Guinea (1716–1732)." In: *Vlamingen overzee. Flamands en outre-mer. Flemings overseas.* C. Koninckx (ed.). Brussels, pp. 119–240. (Collectanea maritima. 6.)

Dermigny, L. (1964). *La Chine et l'Occident. Le commerce à Canton au XVIIIe siècle, 1719–1833.* 1–3 +

Album. Paris. (École pratique des hautes études. Sect. 6. Centre de recherches historiques.) (Ports, routes, trafics. 18.)

Dickson, P.G.M. (1967). *The Financial Revolution in England. A Study in the Development of Public Credit 1688–1756*. London.

Dictionnaire du Citoyen ou Abrégé théorique et pratique du commerce (1761). 1–2. Paris.

Dissel, A. van (1985). *De oprichting van de Zweedse Oost-Indische Compagnie: reacties in de Republiek en Indië 1731–1735*. Leiden. Unpubl. thesis.

– (1987). "Het Batavia-incident: de reactie van de VOC op de komst van de Fredericus Rex Sueciae in Aziatische wateren (1732–1733)." *Tijdschrift voor zeegeschiedenis* 6, pp. 124–137.

Doursther, H. (1965). *Dictionnaire universel des poids et mesures anciennes et modernes. Contenant des tables de monnaies de tous les pays*. Amsterdam.

Dutch-Asiatic Shipping in the 17th and 18th Centuries (1979–87). Ed. by J.R. Bruijn, F.S. Gaastra and I. Schöffer. 1–3. The Hague. (Rijks Geschiedkundige Publicatiën. Grote serie. 165–167.)

Du Val-Pyrau, L'Abbé [1777]. *Eloge de Nicolas Sahlgren, Commandeur de l'ordre de Wasa et Directeur de la Compagnie des Indes &c.* [Frankfurt a.M.]

Ekeberg, C.G. (1756). "Underrättelse om Tutanego." *Kongl. Svenska Vetenskaps Academiens handlingar*. 17. Stockholm, pp. 316–317.

[–] (1757). *Kort berättelse om den Chinesiska landt-hushåldningen*. Af C.G.E.B. Stockholm. (Published as an appendix to Osbeck (1757).) – English transl.: see under Osbeck (1757). French transl. by D. de Blackford: *Précis historique de l'économie rurale des Chinois*. Milan 1771.

– (1768). *Tal om hafvets strömar; hållet för Kongl. Vetensk. Academien, vid Præsidii afläggande den 26 Octob. 1768*. Stockholm.

– (1773). *Capitaine Carl Gustaf Ekebergs Ostindiska resa, åren 1770 och 1771. Beskrefven uti bref til Kongl. Svenska Vet. Academiens secreterare*. Stockholm.

Flückiger, F.A., & Hanbury, D. (1878). *Histoire des drogues d'origine végétale*. Trad. de l'ouvrage anglais "Pharmacographia" … par J.L. de Lanessan. 1–2. Paris.

Forsberg, K. (1951). "Claes Grill, en frihetstidens mecenat och handelsfurste." *Fataburen. Nordiska museets och Skansens årsbok*, pp. 119–128.

Forsstrand, C. (1928). "Carl Gustav Ekeberg, hans färder till Ostindien och Kina, naturvetenskapliga intressen och förbindelser med Linné." *Svenska Linné-sällskapets årsskrift* 11, pp. 147–161.

Förtekning öfver Framledne Commercie Rådets, Directeurens vid Svenska Ost-Indiska Compagniet samt Riddarens af Kongl. Maj:ts Nordstjerne Orden Välborne Herr Colin Campbells Bok-Samling, som den 27 Februari 1758 och följande dagar … genom offentelig Auction kommer att försäljas (1758). Götheborg.

Frängsmyr, T. (1976). *Ostindiska kompaniet. Människorna, äventyret och den ekonomiska drömmen*. Stockholm.

Gezelius, K.J. (1941). *Släkten Sahlgren från Göteborg. En personhistorisk utredning*. Göteborg.

Gill, C. (1958). "The Affair of Porto Novo: an Incident in Anglo-Swedish Relations." *The English Historical Review* 73, pp. 47–65.

– (1961). *Merchants and Mariners of the Eighteenth Century*. London.

Glamann, K. (1953–54). "En ostindisk rejse eller Thomas Thomson på Galejen. Bidrag til det svenska Ostindiska Kompagniets tidligste historie." *Sjöhistorisk årsbok*, pp. 13–47.

– (1958). *Dutch Asiatic Trade 1620–1740*. Copenhagen & The Hague. (Diss. Copenhagen.)

– (1970). "The Danish East India Company." In: *Sociétés et compagnies de commerce en Orient et dans l'Océan indien. Actes du huitiéme colloque international d'histoire maritime (Beyrouth, 5–10 septembre 1966)*. Paris, pp. 471–479.

The Golden Age of China Trade. Essays on the East India Companies' Trade with China in the 18th Century and the Swedish East Indiaman Götheborg (1992). Ed. by B. Johansson. Hong Kong.

Goubert, J.-P. (1974). *Malades et médécins en Bretagne, 1770–1790*. Rennes. (Institut armoricain de recherches historiques. Publications. 15.)

Grape, A. (1918). "Om Christopher Tärnströms resejournaler." *Svenska Linné-sällskapets årsskrift* 1, pp. 126–144.

Greggelund, J. (1794). *Kort utdrag af Ostindiska journalen, som fördes under resan med skeppet Prints Carl och Capitainen Herr Johan Rundsten, åren 1763, och 64. I wers författad af Jonas Greggelund, som på samma resa war förhyrd för matros med omberörde skepp och Capitain.* Gefle.

Grill, J.A. Abrahamson (1774). *Tal, om silfvers årliga förande til China, huruvida det är för Europa nyttigt eller skadeligt; hållet för Kongl. Vetenskaps Academien, vid præsidii nedläggande den 26 Octob. 1774.* Stockholm.

– (1775). "Berättelse om en sorts malm af tutanego, som är en naturlig flos zinci, ifrån China." *Kongl. Vetenskaps Academiens handlingar.* 36. Stockholm, pp. 77–78.

Grotefend, H. (1960). *Taschenbuch der Zeitrechnung des deutschen Mittelalters und der Neuzeit.* 10. erw. Aufl. Hrsg. von T. Ulrich. Hannover.

Gui, M. (1994). [Göteborg University doctoral dissertation on Swedish East India Company trading with China in the 18th century. In preparation.]

Gyllensvärd, B. (1985). *Kina i dröm och verklighet.* Skövde.

– (1990). *Porslinet från Kina. En tusenårig exportvara. Ur Kulturens samlingar.* Västerås.

Hahr, G. (1957). "Henrik Wilhelm Hahr d.ä. och Ostindiska kompaniet." *Forum navale* 14, pp. 30–107.

– (1966). *Hinrich Hahr. En handelsman från frihetstidens Stockholm.* Stockholm. (Stockholms stadsmuseums skrifter. 1.)

Hallerdt, B. (1994). "Ostindiefarare och skeppsbroadel." *Sankt Eriks årsbok* 1994, pp. 9–42.

Hammar, H. (1931). *Fartygstyper i Svenska ost-indiska compagniets flotta.* Göteborg.

Heckscher, E.F. (1944). "Sveriges framgångsrikaste handelsföretag. Ostindiska kompaniet." In: Heckscher, E.F., *Historieuppfattning. Materialistisk och annan. Uppsatser.* Stockholm, pp. 199–230.

Hellstenius, J.A.C. (1860). *Bidrag till Svenska ost-indiska compagniets historia 1731–1766.* Upsala. Diss.

– (1870). *Några blad ur Göteborgs historia.* Stockholm.

Henau, B.P.F. (1986). *Charles Irvine (1693–1771) and the Swedish East India Company 1732–1743.* Minneapolis. (University of Minnesota, Minneapolis. History Department. Unpublished.)

Herlitz, N. (1936). *Grunddragen av det svenska statsskickets historia.* 2. uppl. Stockholm.

Holmberg, Å. (1988). *Världen bortom västerlandet. Svensk syn på fjärran länder och folk från 1700-talet till första världskriget.* Göteborg. (Acta Regiae Societatis scientiarum et litterarum Gothoburgensis. Humaniora. 28.)

Horn, L.L. von (1937). *Biografiska anteckningar. 2. Officerare, som tjenat vid örlogsflottan åren 1721–1824.* Örebro.

Hornstedt, C.F. (1888). *Anteckningar under en resa till Ostindien åren 1782–1786.* Helsingfors. (Skrifter utg. af Svenska litteratursällskapet i Finland. 10.)

Horst, W.A. (1942). "De peperhandel van de Vereenigde Oost-Indische Compagnie." *Bijdragen voor vaderlandsche geschiedenis en oudheidkunde.* Reeks 8. 3, pp. 95–103.

Huisman, M. (1902). *La Belgique commerciale sous l'empereur Charles VI. La Compagnie d'Ostende. Étude historique de politique commerciale et coloniale.* Bruxelles & Paris.

Indebetou, G. (1908). "De svenska grenarna af skottska ätterna Campbell." *Personhistorisk tidskrift* 10, pp. 109–128.

Jägerstad, H. (1964). *Sveriges historia i årtal.* 2., omarb. uppl. Stockholm.

Jansson, E.A. (1964). "v. Kantzow. En adlig köpmanssläkt." *Forum navale* 19/20, pp. 43–59.

Johansson, B. (1992). The Diary of Colin Campbell – the World's First China Trade Handbook." In: *The Golden Age of China Trade. …* Ed. by B. Johansson. Hong Kong, pp. 59–66.

Kent, H.S.K. (1973). *War and Trade in Northern Seas. Anglo-Scandinavian Economic Relations in the Mid-Eighteenth Century.* Cambridge.

Kjellberg, S.T. (1930). "Svenska Ostindiska Compagniet." In: *Svenska kulturbilder.* Under red. av S. Erixon och S. Wallin. 2. Stockholm, pp. 67–94.

– (1931). "Till Svenska Ostindiska Compagniets 200-årsminne." *Ord och bild* 40, pp. 465–481.

– (1938). "Svenska Ostindiska Compagniet." In: *Svenska folket genom tiderna. Vårt lands kulturhistoria i skildringar och bilder.* Red. av E. Wrangel … 7: *Frihetstidens kultur.* Malmö, pp. 179–194.

– (1974). *Svenska ostindiska compagnierna 1731–1813. Kryddor, te, porslin, siden.* Malmö.

Klein, E. (1931). "Matts Holmers, fiskardräng – 'ostindisk capitain' – godsägare i Roslagen." In: *Svenska kulturbilder.* Under red. av S. Erixon och S. Wallin. 4. Stockholm, pp. 65–90.

Klerck, E.S. de (1938). *History of the Netherlands East Indies.* 1–2. Rotterdam.

1

Koninckx, C. (1971–72). "Drie reizen van de Zweedse Oost-Indiëvaarder 'Fredericus Rex Sueciae'." *Mededelingen van de Marine Academie* 22, pp. 77–98.

– (1972). "Cargaisons chinoises et indiennes au XVIIIᵉ siècle. Le vaisseau 'Fredericus' de la Compagnie suédoise des Indes orientales." *Revue du Nord* 54, pp. 195–202.

– (1973). "Andreas Jacobus Flanderin. Een achttiende eeuwse middelgrote koopman." *Bijdragen tot de geschiedenis* 56, pp. 243–290.

– (1973–75). "Het Scheepstype in de Zweedse Oost-Indische Compagnie tijdens het eerste en tweede octrooi (1731–1766)." *Mededelingen van de Marine Academie* 23, pp. 63–94.

– (1977). "Zuidnederlandse deelname in de Zweedse Oost-Indische Compagnie 1731–1766." *Handelingen van de Koninklijke Zuidnederlandse Maatschappij* 31, pp. 121–136.

– (1978a). "La Compagnie suédoise des Indes orientales et les Pays-Bas autrichiens. Esquisse succincte d'une participation 'belge' à l'étranger au dix-huitième siècle." *Bulletin de l'Académie royale des sciences d'outremer*, pp. 295–329.

– (1978b). "The Maritime Routes of the Swedish East India Company during its First and Second Charter (1731–1766)." *The Scandinavian Economic History Review* 26, pp. 36–65.

– (1978–79). "Voeding op zee in de 18de eeuw. Een kwantitatief en vergelijkend onderzoek." *Mededelingen van de Marine Academie* 25, pp. 1–32.

– (1980a). "L'Alimentation en mer au 18ème siècle. Comparaison entre les régimes alimentaires européens." In: *Seamen in Society – Gens de mer en société. Rapports de la Commission internationale d'histoire maritime.* 2. Perthes, pp. 119–133.

– (1980b). *The First and Second Charters of the Swedish East India Company (1731–1766). A Contribution to the Maritime, Economic and Social History of North-Western Europe in its Relationships with the Far East.* Kortrijk.

– (1980–82). "Ziekten op zee. Pathologie van de ziekten in de grote vaart in de achttiende eeuw." *Mededelingen van de Marine Academie* 26, pp. 33–54.

– (1983). "L'Alimentation et la pathologie des déficiences alimentaires dans la navigation au long cours au XVIIIème siècle." *Revue d'histoire moderne et contemporaine* 30, pp. 109–138.

– (1985). Les Iles atlantiques comme relais au long cours pour l'Extrême-Orient." In: *Coloquio de historia canario-americana (1982). Coloquio internacional de historia marítima.* 4. Geografia e historia. Madrid, pp. 337–358.

– (1986). "Navires et équipages au long cours au XVIIIème siècle. Les Compagnies des Indes orientales scandinaves, prussiennes et ostendaise." In: *Les Hommes et la mer dans l'Europe du Nord-Ouest de l'antiquité à nos jours. Actes du Colloque de Boulogne-sur-Mer* 1984. Villeneuve d'Ascq, pp. 369–383. (Revue du Nord. Numéro 1 spécial hors série. Coll. Histoire.)

– (1987). "Zuidnederlanders in vreemde dienst buitengaats. Een schakel in de overdracht van nautische kennis in de 18de eeuw." In: *Nautische en hydrografische kennis in België en Zaïre. Historische bijdragen.* Brussel, pp. 39–71. (Collectanea maritima. 3.)

– (1988). "Ownership in East India Company Shipping: Prussia, Scandinavia and the Austrian Netherlands in the 18th Century." *Collectanea maritima* 4, pp. 33–42.

– (1990a). "Marginal but Profitable Foodstuffs: Drugs and Spices. Swedish East Indian Trade in the Eighteenthth Century (1731–1766)." In: *El comercio y transporte maritimo mundial de alimentos. Congreso internacional quinquenal de historia maritima.* Brussels, pp. 215–236. – Also publ. in: *Maritime Food Transport.* Ed. by K. Friedland in assoc. with C. Koninckx … Köln … 1994, pp. 465–482. (Quellen und Darstellungen zur hansischen Geschichte. N.F. 40.)

– (1990b). "Recruitment of Dutch Shipwrights for the Benefit of the Royal Shipyard of the Admiralty at Karlskrona [Sweden] in 1718." In: *Baltic Affairs. Relations between the Netherlands and North-Eastern Europe, 1500–1800. Essays.* Ed. by J.Ph.S. Lemmink, J.S.A.M. van Koningsbrugge. Nijmegen, pp. 127–140. (Baltic Studies. 1.)

– (1993a). "Les Compagnies des Indes orientales, vecteurs dans les circuits et placements d'argent belgo-suédois au XVIIIème siècle." In: *A Special Brew… Essays in Honour of Kristof Glamann.* Odense, pp. 293–313. (Odense University Studies in History and Social Sciences. 165.)

– (1993b). "The Swedish East India Company (1731–1807)." In: *Ships, Sailors and Spices …* Ed. by J.R. Bruijn and F.S. Gaastra. Amsterdam, pp. 121–138.

Koninckx, C., & Vanouplines, P. (1994). "Natuurwetenschappelijke observaties op zee tijdens achttiende eeuw. De scheepvaart in dienst van de wetenshap." In: *Een kompas met vele streken." Studies over Antwerpen, scheepvaart en archivistiek aangeboden aan dr. Gustaaf Asaert ter gelegenheid van zijn 65ste verjaardag.* Onder red. van G. Maréchal. Antwerpen, pp. 110–126. (Archiefkunde. Verhandelingen aansluitend bij Bibliotheek- & archiefgids. 5.)

– (1995). "De Zweeds-Belgische komeet C/1733 K1." *Heelal* 40:3, pp. 64–70.

Koninckx, C., Vanouplines, P., & Marsden, B.G. (1995). "Comet C/1733 K1 – Discovery and Rediscovery." *Vistas in Astronomy* 39, pp. 323–334.

Lagerberg, C. (1907). "Svenska ostindiska compagnierna." *Vårt fosterland och dess försvar* 14, pp. 10–12.

Lagercrantz, B. (1951). "Släkten Grills vapenporslin." *Fataburen. Nordiska museets och Skansens årsbok,* pp. 87–110.

– (1956). "I Ostindiska kompaniets tjänst." *Fataburen. Nordiska museets och Skansens årsbok* 1956, pp. 137–152.

Lewis, I. (1991). *Sahibs, Nabobs and Boxwallahs. A Dictionary of the Words of Anglo-India.* Bombay & Oxford.

Ljungstedt, A. (1992). *An Historical Sketch of the Portuguese Settlements in China; and of the Roman Catholic Church and Mission in China. A supplementary chapter: Description of the City of Canton.* Hong Kong. (Repr. of 2nd, rev. ed. 1836.)

Lundström, E. (1978). *Ostindiefararna.* Stockholm.

– (1979). *Indialand. Andra berättelsen om ostindiefararna.* Stockholm.

– (1980). *Kinaland. Tredje berättelsen om ostindiefararna.* Stockholm.

Lunelund, B. (1939). "Peter Johan Bladh och Svenska ostindiska compagniet åren 1766–84." In: *Historiska och litteraturhistoriska studier. 15.* Helsingfors, pp. 298–341. (Skrifter utg. av Svenska litteratursällskapet i Finland. 275.)

Lunelund-Grönroos, B. (1944). "Peter Johan Bladhs 'Räkning öfwer böcker til 1771. års slut'. En bokförteckning från Svenska ostindiska companiets tid." In: *Miscellanea bibliographica. 4.* Helsingfors, pp. 85–100. (Helsingfors universitetsbiblioteks skrifter. 19.)

Marchander, E. (1961–62). "Resan till Kanton. Red.: O. Ekström." *Sjöhistorisk årsbok,* pp. 58–77.

Metcalf, M. (1988). *Goods, Ideas, and Values: the East Indies Trade as an Agent of Change in Eighteenth-Century Sweden.* Minneapolis. (The James Ford Bell Lectures. 25.)

Morse, H.B. (1966–69). *The Chronicles of the East India Company Trading to China 1635–1834. 1–5.* Repr. Taipei.

Nyström, J.F. (1883). *De svenska ostindiska kompanierna. Historisk-statistisk framställning.* Göteborg. (Göteborgs Kongl. Vetenskaps- och Vitterhets-Samhälles handlingar. 18.)

Olán, E. (1921). *Sjörövarna på Medelhavet och Levantinska Compagniet. Historien om Sveriges gamla handel med Orienten.* Stockholm.

– (1923). *Ostindiska Compagniets saga. Historien om Sveriges märkligaste handelsföretag. 2. uppl.* Göteborg.

Olsvik, A., Johansson, I., & Wästfelt, A. (1986). *Berättelsen om Svenska Ostindiska Compagniet och skeppet Götheborg.* Göteborg. (Also publ. as: *Meddelanden från Marinarkeologiska sällskapet. 8:4.* Stockholm 1985.)

Osbeck, P. (1757). *Dagbok öfwer en Ostindisk resa åren 1750. 1751. 1752. Med anmärkningar uti naturkunnigheten, främmande folkslags språk, seder, hushållning, m.m. Jämte 12 tabeller och afledne skeppspredikanten Toréns bref.* Stockholm. – Repr. Stockholm 1969. (Suecica rediviva. 5.) – English transl. from the German version of the Swedish by J.R. Forster: *A Voyage to China and the East-Indies … Together with a Voyage to Suratte by O. Torén … and an Account of the Chinese Husbandry by C.G. Eckeberg* [sic]. 1–2. London 1771.

– (1758). *Anledningar til nyttig upmärksamhet under Chinesiska resor, upgifne i Kongl. Vet. Academien, uti et inträdes-tal, den 25 Februarii, 1758.* Stockholm.

– (1960). *Pehr Osbecks självbiografier.* Jämte inledning och kommentarer av A. Ejwertz. Halmstad. (Halland och hallänningar. Årsbok. 7.)

Ostindiefararen Götheborg. Berättelsen om den sista resan, silvret, porslinslasten och utgrävningen (1992). [Av] J.E. Nilsson … Göteborg.

Ostindiefararen Götheborg. Rapport om 1986 års undersökning (1987). Göteborg.

The Oxford Companion to Ships & the Sea (1976). Ed. by P. Kemp. London, New York & Melbourne.

Palm, L. (1946). "Skeppet Finlands ostindiska resa åren 1769–1771." *Segel och motor,* pp. 622–627.

Pédelaborde, P. (1970). *Les moussons.* Nouv. éd., entièrement ref. et mise à jour. Paris.

Peterson, K. (1948). "Ostindiska compagniet. Sveriges märkligaste handelsföretag." *Hällungen,* pp. 6–9.

Petterson, G., & Petterson, B. (1967). "En reseberättelse av prosten Pehr Osbeck år 1776." *Varbergs museums årsbok* 17, pp. 97–116.

Picard, R., Kerneis, J.-P., & Bruneau, Y. (1966). *Les Compagnies des Indes. Route de la porcelaine.* Paris.

Pleijel, H. (1965). "En småländsk skeppspräst på Gustav den tredjes tid. [Sven Thunborg.]" *Militärhemmet* 27, pp. 19-25.

[Prévost, A.F.] (1753). *Histoire générale des voyages, ou Nouvelle collection de toutes les relations de voyages ...* Nouv. éd. ... 10. La Haye.

Pritchard, E.H. (1929). *Anglo-Chinese Relations during the Seventeenth and Eighteenth Centuries.* Urbana. (University of Illinois Studies in the Social Sciences. 17:1–2.)

Rasmusson, N.L. (1959). "'Piasterns klang är vår musik.' Till de interkontinentala ädelmetallströmmarnas historia." In: *Septentrionalia et orientalia. Studia Bernhardo Karlgren A.D. III Non. Oct. anno MCMLIX dedicata.* Stockholm, pp. 343–356. (Kungl. Vitterhets Historie och Antikvitets Akademiens handlingar. 91.)

Reinius, I. (1749). *Anmärckningar samlade under en resa til China och med wederbörandes tilstädielse under Professorens i naturkunnigheten och Kungl. Vet. Acad. ledamots herr Carl Fridric Mennanders inseende som et academiskt prof, framgifne i Åbo den 12 Decembr.* 1749. Åbo.

Reinius, I., & Reinius, H.J. (1939). *Journal hållen på resan till Canton i China med Höglofl. Ostindiska Compts Skiepp Cronprintzen Adolph Friedrich ...* Utg. ... av Birgit Lunelund. Helsingfors. (Skrifter utg. av Svenska Littcrursällskapet i Finland. 273.)

Ritzler, S. [pseud. of O. Traung] (1935). *Med styrman Gathenhielm till Canton uti China.* Göteborg.

Röding, J.H. (1794–98). *Allgemeines Wörterbuch der Marine in allen europæischen Seesprachen nebst vollstændigen Erklærungen.* 1–4. Hamburg & Leipzig.

Rollof, Y. (1958). "Fredric Henric af Chapman." *Tidskrift i sjöväsendet* 121, pp. 457–577.

Rosman, H., & Munthe, A. (1945). *Släkten Arfwedson. Bilder ur Stockholms handelshistoria under tre århundraden.* Stockholm.

Roth, S. (1949–50). "Ostindiskt vapenporslin. Evert Strokirks samling i Göteborgs museum." *Göteborgs museum. Årstryck,* pp. 193–206.

– (1965). *Chinese Porcelain Imported by the Swedish East India Company.* Göteborg.

Roukonen, D. Davidson (1765). *Oförgripliga tankar öfwer den ost-indiska handelens nytta uti Swea rike.* Stockholm.

Savary des Bruslons, J. (1759–65). *Dictionnaire universel de commerce, d'histoire naturelle, & des arts & métiers.* Nouv. éd. ... 1–5. Copenhague.

Ships, Sailors and Spices. East India Companies and their Shipping in the 16th, 17th and 18th Centuries (1993). Ed. by J.R. Bruijn and F.S. Gaastra. Amsterdam. (NEHA-series. 3.)

Sinclair, G.A. (1928). "The Scottish Trader in Sweden." *The Scottish Historical Review* 25, pp. 289–299.

Sparrman, A. (1783). *Resa till Goda Hopps-udden, södra polkretsen och omkring jordklotet, samt till hottentott- och caffer-landen, åren 1772–76.* Stockholm. – German transl.: *Reise nach dem Vorgebirge der Guten Hoffnung, den südlichen Polarländern und um die Welt ...* Berlin 1784. English transl.: *A Voyage to the Cape of Good Hope, towards the Antarctic Polar Circle, and around the World ...* London 1785. French transl.: *Voyage au Cap de Bonne Espérance et autour du monde, avec le Capitaine Cook ...* Paris 1787. – Vol. 2 of Sparrman's account was published much later in two parts (1802 and 1818).

Spens, E. (1931). "Från Svenska ostindiska kompaniets dagar. En återblick med anledning av 200-årsjubileet." *Vår flotta* 27, pp. 140–142.

Stackell, L. (1931). "Ostindiska kompaniets minnesutställning i Göteborg." *Nautisk tidskrift* 24, pp. 294–300.

Steiner, A. (1994). *Jacob seglar till Kina. Ostindiefararen Götheborgs resa 1743–1745. Historisk bildberättelse för barn och ungdom.* Text: E. Lundström. Göteborg.

Strindberg, A. (1884). *Notice sur les relations de la Suède avec la Chine et les pays tartares, depuis le milieu du XVIIe siècle jusqu'à nos jours.* Paris.

Strödda anteckningar om Compagniet och sjöfarten under senaste 200 åren jämte meddelanden om utställ-ningsföremålen (1931). Red. av O. Traung. Göteborg. (Ostindiska Compagniets minnesutställning, Lisebergs kongresshall, Göteborg, 15 aug. – 15 sept. 1931.)

Svenska flottans historia. Örlogsflottan i ord och bild från dess grundläggning under Gustav Vasa fram till våra dagar (1942–45). 1–3. Malmö.

Svenska män och kvinnor. Biografisk uppslagsbok (1942–55). 1–8. Stockholm.

Svenskt skeppsbyggeri. En översikt av utvecklingen genom tiderna (1963). Huvudred.: G. Halldin. Malmö.

Thulin, O. (1934). "Från Ostindiska kompaniets dagar. En auktion på 1700-talets mitt." *Tidskrift för Göteborgs stads tjänstemän* 16, pp. 159–163.

Thunberg, C.P. (1788–93). *Resa uti Europa, Africa, Asia, förättad åren 1770–1779.* 1–4. Upsala.

Torén, O. (1757). *En Ostindisk resa til Suratte, China &c. från 1750 April 1. til 1752 Jun. 26. Uti bref öfwersänd til Archiat. Linnæus.* In: Osbeck (1757), pp. 313–376. – Repr. Stockholm 1969 (see Osbeck 1757).

– (1961). *En ostindisk resa.* Stockholm. (Tidens svenska klassiker. [2.])

Traung, O. (1931). "En färd till Ostindien med skeppet Cron Printcessan Lovisa Ulrica. En glimt från den blivande Ostindiska minnesutställningen." *Nautisk tidskrift* 24, pp. 231–235.

Tullberg, A. (1995). "En svensk-belgisk komet." *Bladet. Medlemsbrev för Svenska klubben* 1995:6, pp. 23–27.

Utdrag utur alle … publique handlingar, placater, förordningar, resolutioner och publicationer, som Riksens styrsel … angå … 2–3 (1746–49). [Utg. af R.G. Modée.] Stockholm.

Wallenberg, J. (1781). *Min son på galejan, eller en ostindisk resa innehållande allahanda bläckhornskram, samlade på skeppet Finland, som afseglade ifrån Götheborg i Decemb. 1769, och återkom dersammastädes i Jun. 1771.* Stockholm. – Several later editions, e.g. Stockholm 1904 (with an introd. essay by O. Levertin). (Svenska klassiker. 1.) – Stockholm 1928–40, in: *Samlade skrifter av Jacob Wallenberg.* Utg. av N. Afzelius. 1, pp. 153–334 [text]; 2, pp. 263–378 [commentary]. (Svenska författare utg. av Svenska Vitterhetssamfundet. 13.)

Wassén, T. (1967). "Två elever från 1700-talet. [Johan Gothenius, Pehr Osbeck.]" *Gamla latinares årsbok,* pp. 39–44.

Wästfelt, B., Gyllensvärd, B., & Weibull, J. (1990). *Ostindiefararen Götheborgs porslinslast.* Höganäs.

Wikström, T. (1931). "Svenska Ostindiska Compagniet. Några anteckningar om dess historia i anledning av tvåhundraårsjubileet." *Nautisk tidskrift* 24, pp. 193–199.

Willman, O.E. (1992). *En kort beskrivning på en resa till Ostindien och Japan den en svensk man och skeppskapten, Olof Eriksson Willman benämnd, gjort haver.* Utg. … med red. och kommentarer av J. Bernström och T. Wretö. Stockholm. (Orig. publ. Wisingsborg 1667.)

Wright, H.G. (1935). "Scots in Sweden." *The Anglo-Swedish Review,* pp. 322–324.

Zethelius, G.A. (1955/56). "Stockholms-varven under 1700-talet." *Sjöhistorisk årsbok,* pp. 57–102.

The Diary

The Diary
or
*Journal of Sundry Transactions pass'd
Aboard the Ship Fredericus Rex Sueciæ
in her Voyage from Kensie Sund (near
Gottenburg) to the Port of Canton
in China, & from Canton back to
Gottenburg in Sweden*
Annis 1732 & 1733

The Introduction

Being very uncertain, when the Dutch Ships
stopp'd us at the Entrance of the Straits of Sunda, what
they intended to do with us, It was thought necessary to
destroy all Papers or Writings that might give the least
handle, or pretext to People, that seem'd to bear no Good
will to us, to do us or the Company any wrong or Prejudice;
I therefore, for my part judg'd it the Safest Course, to clear
my Self of every Paper or Writing that might (in case of
being seiz'd as I apprehended) afford them the least light
in the Company's Affairs, or in any thing that regarded the
present Voyage, and amongst other Papers destroy'd on
that Occasion was a Journal I had kept from my going
on board Ship in Kensie Sund of our Daily Transactions.
This will occasion probably the omission of some passages that
happen'd, as well as want of exactness in the Dates, having

The first page of Campbell's *Diary*.

The Diary

or
Journal of Sundry Transactions pass'd
Aboard the Ship Fredericus Rex Sueciæ
in her Voyage from Kensie Sund[1] (near
Gottenburg) to the Port of Canton
in China, & from Canton back to
Gottenburg in Sweden
Annis 1732 & 1733

The Introduction

Being very uncertain, when the Dutch Ships stopp'd us at the Entrance of the Straits of Sunda[2], what they intended to do with us, It was thought necessary to destroy all Papers or Writings that might give the least handle or pretext to People, that seem'd to bear no Good will to us, to do us or the Company any wrong or Prejudice, I therefore for my part judg'd it the safest Course to clear myself of every Paper or Writing that might (in case of being seiz'd as I apprehended) afford them the least light in the Companys Affairs, or in any thing that regarded the present voyage, and amongst other Papers destroy'd on that Occasion was a Journal I had kept from my going on board ship in Kensie Sund of our Daily Transactions. This will occasion probably the omission of some passages that happen'd, as well as want of exactness in the Dates, having

now no other way to furnish an Account of what is past (before we were stopt by the Dutch) but by memory, & some loose papers I have yet preserv'd, But I hope I shall be able to recollect all that was material, and even some things which though at first view may appear Triffling yet in my humble opinion may be of some use & for the Companys service on another Occasion, as they may help them to some Knowledge of the manners & ways of People at sea and in particular of those that have been imploy'd this Voyage, and thereby to see who are the fittest People to be imploy'd another time and what Instructions & orders may be found the most Necessary to give them that are Imploy'd.

---

[1] *Känsö Sound* (Swedish *sund*), outside Gothenburg.

[2] *Straits of Sunda*, channel between Java and Sumatra. European East Indiamen directly bound for China had to pass through the Straits of Sunda. It often offered the opportunity of regrouping the ships of a dislocated convoy after crossing the Atlantic and the Indian Ocean. Sometimes it was the first place for taking in fresh supplies, after having left Spain or the Canaries. On the way back to Europe, East Indiamen coming from China stopped in the vicinity of Sunda to take in fresh drinking water, before crossing the Indian and Atlantic Ocean again.

As this Journal is solely design'd for the service of the Company (and many things thereof in particular for such of the Gentlemen Directors as are not so well acquainted with such voyages) for Time to come as well as for the present, I am in hopes that if any Mistakes happen in this Account through Inadvertency or haste, they will meet with a ready Excuse. For one thing I solemnly assure them that though perhaps Exactness may be sometimes wanting, yet another, no less Essential, quality never shall, (to the best of my Knowledge,) I mean Truth.

Anno 1732

on board the Ship Fredericus Rex Sueciæ
in Kensie Sund

Feb^{ry} I had not been long Aboard before I perceiv'd that I should have Trouble enough
with the Captain whom our bad fortune had found out for us, But my principal
business being to get the ship to sea assoon as possible, I was firmly resolv'd to
bear with all his ridiculous humours & avoid having any disputes with him or of
giving him any manner of provocation that might discourage him from doing his
Duty or hindring the Companys service, I therefore sooth'd & carry'd as fair &
Civil with him as I could in order to make him come in the more readily to the
measures I had form'd to my self for the Companys Interest, at least to give him
no handle to cross them which he had too much in his power as well as in his will
to do. What chiefly troubled me was an extreme dilatoriness he show'd in every
thing he set about or in what was propos'd to him or even purpos'd by himself,
It being his Constant Rule to put off till another time or till to morrow, (and that
morrow did not appear sometimes for some months) And though the season was
already too far advanc'd for our voyage, yet I could not perswade him of the
necessity of putting to sea with the first Air of wind that could carry us out of the
vile Hole where we lay, It was in vain to talk to him of proper seasons or a Good
or bad time of year for a voyage to India, or of Trade winds or such like; He
either did or would not know any thing of the matter, his whole view being, as
far as I could see, to ly here till the beginning of summer or that fine weather came
or that the Easterly winds, or just such winds as he lik'd should be well set in.
This made me take

(4) such measures as I could to disappoint his scheme, by sending every day for the
Pilotes[3] to know if they could carry the ship out if but so far as Marstrand[4] where
I knew we would ly more Ready for many fair winds which we could not get out
with from the Creek where we were in at present, but the winds having prov'd
long Contrary made my design impracticable till the 25th.

Feb^{ry}
24th
O.S.[5]

On the 24th at Night, Though he saw my daily impatience to put to sea, yet he had
resolv'd (as I was inform'd) to go for Gottenburg next morning, for no other reason
but to quarrell with our Secretary for some Truths which he had wrote to him

---

[3] Swedish ships of a bigger size used to rely on pilots to cross the dangerous waters outside of
Gothenburg. 'Pilot' is also used as a term for mates or wheelmen, however.
[4] A port on the west coast of Sweden, somewhat north of Gothenburg, one of Sweden's staple towns.
In the 18th century Marstrand was known as a harbour for smugglers trying to import goods into
Sweden without paying taxes.
[5] *Old Style*, the former method of reckoning dates using the Julian calendar. The Gregorian reform of

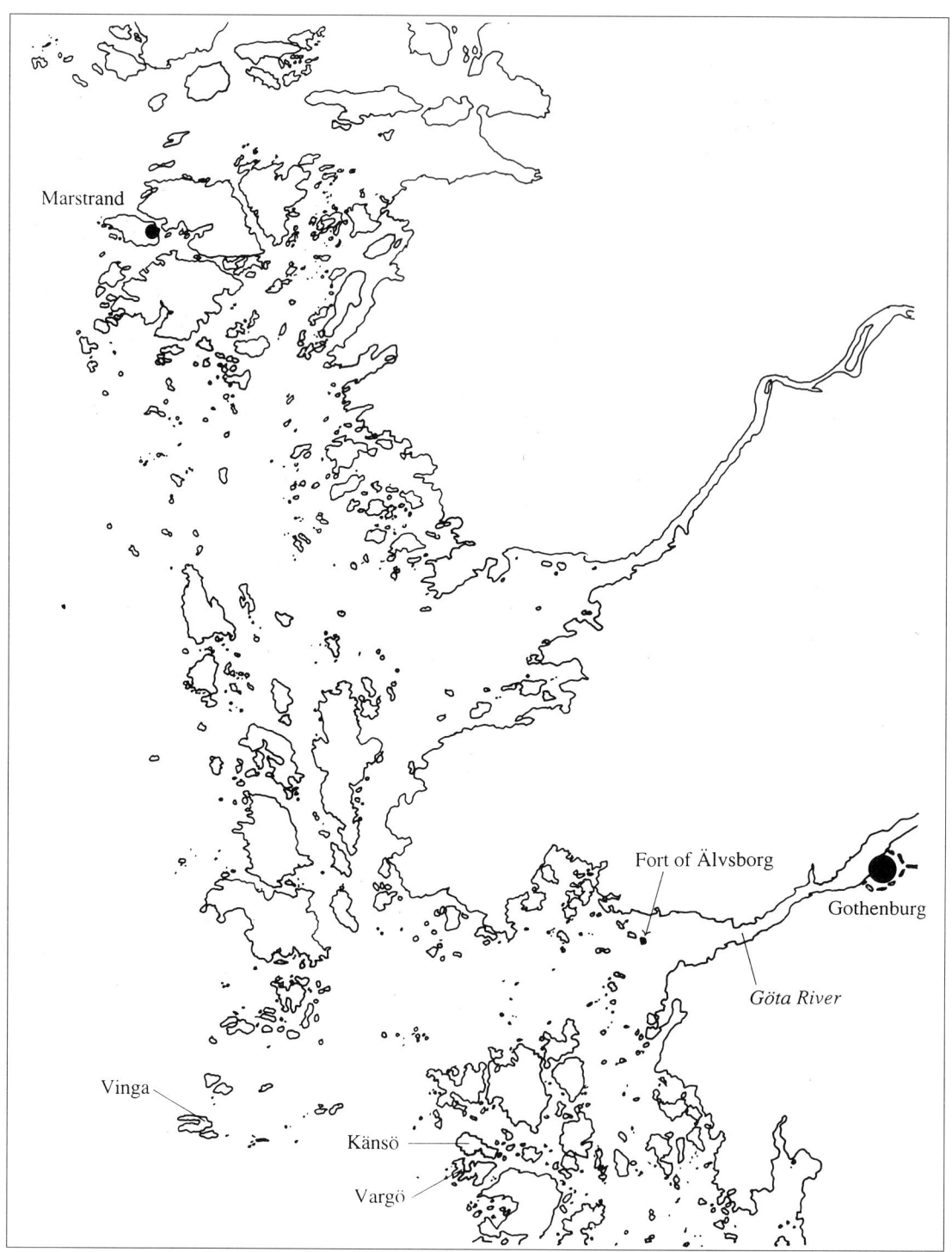

Marstrand

Fort of Älvsborg

Gothenburg

Göta River

Vinga

Känsö

Vargö

The Gothenburg archipelago.

6

some days before which were not at all grateful to a Gentleman of his Temper. As He had not sayd anything to me of this his worthy resolution, I took no notice that I knew any thing of it, but before I went to Bed order'd him to be sure to have a Gun fir'd by 4 a clock next morning to warn the Pilotes to come Aboard for I was in great hopes of having a good wind next morning. He promis'd to do as I desir'd, but not trusting much to his promises I resolv'd to get up Early & see it done myself, Accordingly waking about 4 a clock I call'd to know if they were making ready to fire, and was uneasy to find he thought nothing of it, I soon got upon Deck where I stay'd till I saw the signal made. He told me it was to no purpose it being impossible to go out with the wind we had, I bid him have patience, and that I hop'd it would be better by the time the Pilotes should come on board. About 7 a clock in the morning The Pilotes came, but before I could see them he took care to discourse them & concert with them that they could not venture to take the ship out with the present wind, Hearing they were on board I sent for them to come down into the Cabbin, where they came with the Captain at their head,

(5)   As I saw the wind to the Eastward of the South I told them it was my opinion we could put to sea very well, The Captain immediately open'd & sayd that they could not carry the ship out with the wind we had[6], and was back'd by the Pilotes who unanimously aggree'd with him that they could not, Nettled at this Answer

---

the calendar was not introduced in Sweden until 1753, when the 'old style' was replaced by the 'new'. 17 February 1753 was followed immediately by 1 March. Prior to this reform the old and the new styles were often footnoted side by side in ship's documents. This was probably done for practical reasons, because ships were regularly calling at ports where the new calendar had been in use for a long time. (Jägerstad 1964, p. 82; Grotefend 1960, pp. 27–28.) On board Swedish East Indiamen the English method of sea style was adopted, according to which the day began at noon (instead of midnight), since the sun determining the position of the ship is then culminating. Thus, when recorded in logbooks and ship's journals, 1st January p.m. in fact meant the afternoon of 31st December (to which of course 11 days had to be added). In other words the date of a day started 12 hours earlier than on shore. It is not always clear whether Campbell is following the sea style when recording dates. On p. 21 of the *Diary*, however, he is explicit in this respect.

[6] For sailing ships, the problem of favourable winds presented itself from the very outset. The monsoon winds of the Indian Ocean and China Sea were important factors to be considered by East Indiamen. Since they fluctuated periodically, they determined the time of departure from Sweden. Therefore the Swedes had to leave Gothenburg in winter. This meant waiting for an off-shore east wind. At that season of the year, an east wind often brings frost with it. If the fairway froze up, this could immobilize an East Indiaman for an indeterminate period. If the ice was not too thick, the ship could be freed by sawing through the surrounding ice. In order to avoid being frozen in, Company ships were sailed down the Göta River to Vargö in the Gothenburg archipelago as soon as the portents of frosty weather were observed. Nevertheless the sudden onset of sustained winter weather inevitably caused delays. In November and December, the winds were mostly SSW, SW, W or NW, none of them favourable for getting out of the roadstead. The winds might veer NE, E or SE during these months, but not usually for more than a day or two at a time. These were almost the only opportunities, however precarious, of getting out of the Kattegat. January and February offered more favourable conditions, with winds from NE, E and SE, and not only at the mouth of the Göta River but over all of the Kattegat. The predominant NE and SE winds also bring the hardest frost in these months. Notwithstanding the risk, this was the preferred time for setting off. (Pédelaborde 1970, p. 103 ff.; Koninckx 1980b, p. 120 ff.)

I told the Captain that I did not ask his opinion but that of the Pilotes whose business it was, and being persuaded he had oblig'd them to speak as they did to please him, I resolv'd to try if I could not make them change their mind, I then call'd for Mr Ross[7] to bring Pen & Ink & Paper and write down the opinion of the Pilotes about not being able to go out &c And told them at the same time I would send it to the Admiralty[8] at Gottenburg that moment who would punish them if they told me a Lie or refus'd to do their Duty when it was in their power to do it, upon this They consulted together & answer'd they believ'd they could venture to take the ship out but could not go far with this wind & that she would have enough ado to get to Marstrand with it, I told them that was all I wanted and therefore order'd them & the Captain to get up our Anchor & set about sailing immediately, which was done before noon. We got soon out of our Creek, & soon after the Pilotes left us, by whom I wrote to the Directors. In the Afternoon the wind not being so favourable as we could wish the Captain had a great mind to make for some Port, but I begg'd him to have patience & keep the sea that night & that perhaps next morning we might find the winds more favourable, having very little inclination my self to put in any where but Cadiz[9].

Febr 26 & 27 The winds continuing unfavourable, and perceiving we

(6) did not advance in our way by our frequent tacking, and that the Captain was very pressing to put in to Norway, I consulted Styrman[10] Breemer, who was the only officer I could trust, who was also of opinion that we could not keep the sea any longer with such a wind & so bad weather, I was oblig'd to aggree to put into the first Good Harbour in Norway, & thither we steer'd our Course.

Feb^r 28 Early in the morning there came off the Pilotes who carry'd the ship into Hamer-

---

[7] *Gustaf Ross* was appointed ship's purser by Campbell (*Diary* p. 25). He was later to sail as 3rd, 2nd and 1st supercargo on three subsequent voyages with the Swedish Company to Canton (Kjellberg 1974, pp. 177, 205).

[8] Representative of the Navy's central authority, which moved from Stockholm to Karlskrona in 1680. In 1634, after the death of Gustav II Adolf, it was established as one of Sweden's five leading state offices, also called "amiralitetskollegium". The Admiralty did exist earlier but functioned as a corporation without a clearly organized structure. From 1634 on, it became a well-established part of the country's centralized administration. (Herlitz 1936, pp. 106, 108.)

[9] In the 18th century, the Spanish piastre was the hard currency in China because of its high and dependable silver content. Like the other nations engaged in the China navigation, Sweden had to supply herself with silver piastres in Spain. This in fact was the significance of the call paid by sailing-vessels to Cádiz. Spain was inundated with silver from the Mexican and Peruvian mines. The great silver fleets collected their cargoes from Latin America and carried them to Cádiz. Thus Swedish vessels bound for China moored in Cádiz and picked up a considerable quantity of piastres. An alternative was to sail to Madeira in order to pick up a silver cargo there. Only three Swedish vessels stopped at Funchal for this purpose; they were in fact bound for Surat. (Dermigny 1964, 2, p. 726; Doursther 1965, p. 324; *Dictionnaire du Citoyen* 1761, 2, p. 234.)

[10] *Styrman*, Swedish for 'mate'.

sund[11] and moor'd us at the very bottom of the Harbour making us fast to the Rocks of both sides to two Iron Rings plac'd it seems there for that purpose, The Port is narrow in the Entrance, with some small Islands lying in the fair way, I was inclin'd to think that the Captain had chose this place on purpose, to make it more difficult for us to get to sea again

– 29   The Captain pretending he wanted Beer and wood for firing which he could purchase here cheap, I order'd him to provide them assoon as possible, because my resolution was to leave this place with the first spurt of fair wind.

As I was very desirous to let the Directors know what had become of us, I inquir'd if there was any place near where I could put in a Letter for Gottenburg, Arent-dahl[12] (to the Eastward of where we were about 2 Swedish miles)[13] happening to be the nearest I hir'd a Boat to carry me there, where we arriv'd before dinner, after about 3 hours Rowing, Here I bought some few Provisions for the ships Company, put my Letters for Gottenburg into the Posthouse, & return'd to the ship at night. While I was here I found they had got the news of our ship being in Hamersund, which they gave out to be a large ship of 40 Guns, & suppos'd it must have been the same that they heard some time ago had been ready at Gottenburg to sail for India.

While we lay in Hamersund, considering that the way of Dieting sailors aboard of Swedish ships would never do in so long a voyage

(7)   as ours was, by reason of the extravagant Consumption of water[14] occasioned by boiling victuals 3 times a day constantly, I thought the sooner I chang'd this method the better, and having often mention'd it to the Captain I at last perswaded him to leave off boiling in the morning & give them for Breakfast (instead of Grout[15]) a little Cheese[16] & Bread, which was accordingly put in Execution, to my great satisfaction but to the no small discontent of our Gottenburg sailors. The winds blowing contrary for some days I was very uneasy, but luckily on the 3[d] of March

---

[11] *Homborsund*, pilot station on the south coast of Norway.

[12] *Arendal*, town and port on the south coast of Norway in the Skagerrak.

[13] A Swedish mile at this time = 18,000 Swedish ells = 10,688.5 metres.

[14] Although varying from one voyage to another as well as during one and the same voyage, Swedish water rations averaged c. 3.4 litres a man a day (Koninckx 1983, p. 130 f.). This figure is based on computations of the daily consumption of drinking water on board several Swedish East Indiamen, but includes water consumed in preparing some dishes (such as groat) and very probably the existence of the "public barrel" where anybody could drink water at any time.

[15] *Groat* (Swedish *gröt*), or porridge, was one of the main items of ship's diet, being served every day in considerable quantities. It was usually made from hulled barley, oats or buckwheat. Rice might also be used, especially on Christmas and New Year's Eve, as is still the Swedish tradition *(risgrynsgröt)*. (Koninckx 1978–79; *id.* 1980a; *id.* 1983.)

[16] Cheese seems not to have been very common on board Swedish ships, at least as a daily foodstuff, compared to the practice in other East India companies (Koninckx 1983, p. 117 f.).

March 3d	As I got up in the morning I saw the weather much alter'd and a fine breeze at North East so told the Captain to get ready to sail immediately, I found he had no great mind to it, He say'd it was better to wait till the wind was settled, &c However finding that I insisted on going, He pretended he had order'd some Beer to be brew'd which was not yet ready,[17] I told him to go immediately & fetch aboard what was already brewd for I would not wait a moment for that or any-thing, At his going ashore I recommended to him Dispatch & to bring the Pilote along with him assoon as possible, His tarrying so long made me very Impatient, & having got all our Boats ashore I could not send to hasten him, so that I did not see him nor the Pilote till Dinner time. After having check'd him a little for stay-ing so long, I order'd him to weigh Anchor & immediately put to sea, According to his constant Custom he was for delaying till next day pretending we would be then more sure of the wind, and that his Beer would be all ready &c But finding me positive for sailing immediately, He had the Impudence to tell me that though the wind appear'd fair here in the Harbour, yet it was quite otherwise out at sea & bid me ask the Pilote if it was not so. However as I was well acquainted with his Tricks, & not doubting but he had prepar'd the Pilote to say what he had a mind to, I was resolv'd not to be so impos'd upon, However I ask'd the Pilote who very gravely repeated the same Lie that the Captain had done & pretended that the wind
(8)	without was quite Contrary to what it was here in the Harbour as he saw by the ships at sea passing by, I had enough to do to keep my temper at seeing such a piece of Roguery carry'd on between them, and told them both with some warmth not to trouble me more with such nonsense, but to weigh Anchor & set sail immediately, & that would be the best way to know whether the wind at sea was different from that in the Harbour. The Captain perceiving his Tricks would not do, thought best to follow orders, & we Accordingly weigh'd & got out to sea in the Afternoon with a fair wind.
March 3d	I gave the Pilote Letters for the Directors at Gottenburg and gave him money to make him carry them to the first Post house, which he faithfully promis'd to do assoon as he should get ashore. The wind continued very Good all night & part of next Day & carry'd us a Good way off the Coast.
– 4th	The wind coming about to the Southward delay'd us very much, And it continuing so several days made me think of going North about between Orkney & Shet-land[18], which was the only Course left us if the wind had not shifted, which it

---

17 Considering what Campbell has just told us about the consumption of water, the captain's ordering of an additional stock of beer was not a bad measure at all. Although beer could not be preserved for a long time but only during the first stage of the voyage, it contained more calories than water and thus came in handy at the beginning of the journey, when the cold climate required a diet of higher caloric value.

18 Past the Naze of Norway the route of Swedish East Indiamen lay NW to latitude 60° N. They

– 9th   luckily did when we most wanted it on the 9th in the Evening just as we were in sight of the Downs[19], when springing up Easterly It gave us the favourable opportunity of passing in the night the narrow Pass between Dover & Calais.

From Hamersund nothing remarkable happen'd, but our having fallen the same day too near the Banks off Gravelines[20], & to get clear of them run into another danger by going too far over on the other side towards the Goodwin Sands[21] which Styrman Breemer told me was owing to the Captains obstinacy who would not be perswaded to keep off till it was very near too late, though he had warn'd him of it several times to no purpose. But this is one of his delightfull qualities to like no mans opinion but his own & to act in downright contradiction to every other Persons sentiments for this only reason

(9)   because they don't come first from himself. This made me begin to apprehend that he was Ignorant as well as obstinate, and I had but too many strong Evidences to confirm my suspicion in the sequel of this voyage, We saw no ships in the Downs, nor met with any in our passing down the Channell.

March 11th   We pass'd the Isles of Ornay[22] & Kiscas[23] very near about a Couple of English miles to windward of them only which I doubt was too near, for what reason I can't tell, but he seem'd all the way to Cadiz to keep as near the Land as he could.

We had frequent Alarms between the Channell & Cadiz, particularly off the Portugal & Spanish Coasts, from some ships that seem'd to look narrowly after us, & whom we took to be Salley Privateers[24] (or rather Salley Pirates) they not being so large as the Algerine ships[25] generally are, There were two vessells in

---

    generally sailed between the Orkneys and the Shetland Islands, Fair and Foula Isles often serving as points of reference. Some ships set a more northerly course towards the Faeroes. Although this northern route was longer than through the Channel, because the wind patterns in the North Sea are generally distinctly unfavourable to a north-south passage through it, the sailing time was very much shorter, certainly during the winter months.

[19] Anchorage on the east coast of England inside the Goodwin Sands, between North and South Foreland.

[20] Town close to the coastline of French Flanders.

[21] A large bank of shoal sands, partially exposed at low water, lying about 6 miles east off the coast of Kent near the entrance to the English Channel from the North Sea. Because of their shifting habit the sands are particularly dangerous to shipping.

[22] Probably *Alderney* (French *Aurigny*), the northernmost of the larger Channel Islands.

[23] Probably identical with *(Les) Casquets*, notoriously dangerous rocks to the west of Alderney.

[24] The Sallee pirates were Mediterranean corsairs, operating from the port of Salli or Sallee, in Morocco. They harassed Christian trade from about the beginning of the 16th to the end of the 19th century. (*The Oxford Companion to Ships & the Sea*, 1976, p. 746; Olán 1921, p. 49 ff.)

[25] Algerine pirates owed allegiance to the Dey of Algiers and operated from that port in the 14th to 19th centuries. In 1729 Sweden signed a treaty with the Dey; by paying a yearly tribute, she obtained for her merchantmen the privilege of avoiding privateering. Therefore, Swedish authorities delivered an Algerine pass for ships having to cross the area where the corsairs were operating. This pass had to be shown when the ship was hailed. (Olán 1921, p. 50 ff.; *The Oxford Companion to Ships & the Sea*, 1976, p. 16.)

particular that were Consorts that watch'd us two days the largest to windward seem'd to be a ship of about 18 Guns & a small vessell or sloop[26] in shore, for we see them often get together and sometimes the larger would make off & come up with us pretty near then go a head & out of sight & some hours afterwards we saw here on the other side to Larboard[27] by the small one. Upon such occasions I order'd always English Colours to be hoisted (those of Salley being at Peace with England) which with the make of the ship I was in hopes would deceive them & make them take her for English. What gave us the greatest grounds to suspect them was their bearing down upon us in the night (& once very near before we discover'd them) with an intent no doubt to surprize us, we soon got our selves in a posture of fighting, and assoon as they discover'd we were upon our Guard by seeing our Lights & Lantherns between

(9)
[bis]
Decks[28], they immediately tack'd about & left us. Some of these Privateers show'd no Colours, others did, but we could not well discern what they were.

As we had the Good fortune after having got clear of the Channell to have very fine weather and fair winds, I was surpriz'd to find he us'd no top gallant sails[29], & talk'd to the Captain about it, which I repeated at the sight of every ship we met who all had them out, All I could preach to him was in vain, He pretended it was hazardous and bad weather might come &c I represented to him the lateness of the season for our voyage, which oblig'd us not to lose one moment, and the Example of all the ships we met But all to no purpose, for he had neither top Gallant yards nor sails up nor ready to put up even at Cadiz & very likely would never have put them up if our English officers & English Carpenter[30] had not come, Assoon as they went on board they took care to get them up.

I found it necessary during my voyage to Cadiz to prepare the Captain & all the ships Company for a scheme I had resolved to execute very soon, viz of taking the power out of his hands since I saw he made a very bad use of it, For this reason I drew out some Articles of the Octroy[31], which show'd the dependance

---

[26] *Sloop*, older navy class of ships during the 17th, 18th and 19th centuries, used mainly for auxiliary naval duties. Until the late 18th century the term was used somewhat indiscriminately to cover any of the small naval ships that did not fit specifically into a recognized class of minor warships. (*The Oxford Companion to Ships & the Sea*, 1976, p. 809 f.)

[27] The old term for the left-hand side of the ship when facing forward. To avoid confusion with the similar-sounding *starboard*, *larboard* was officially changed to *port* in 1844. (*The Oxford Companion to Ships and the Sea*, 1976, p. 466.)

[28] This seems to imply that the gunports were open, showing the crew manoeuvring at the guns.

[29] The sail set on the topgallant yard, next above the topsail, and normally the third sail in ascending order from the deck.

[30] Generally there were four carpenters, of the first to the fourth grade. Their functions were to keep the vessel watertight, maintain the decks, repair the timbers, and construct bulkheads. A joiner was also frequently taken aboard to handle finished woodwork. (Koninckx 1980b, p. 318.)

[31] *Octroi*, a charter or privilege granted by the King, especially a commercial privilege, as an exclusive

the Captain & Officers & all the ships Company had upon the Directors & the obligation they were [under] to comply punctually with their orders in every thing, These I order'd our Priest[32] one Sunday after Sermon to read to all the people as also Her Majestys order[33] for the Captain Officers & every Body to obey my orders during the voyage. I had I confess too long delay'd letting them know this, out of meer regard to the Captain, and in the hopes he would grow better, and indeed as I was not acquainted with sailing of a ship & other sea affairs, had he behav'd & done his Duty as he ought I had never taken the Command upon me, But as I found he grew every day more Impertinent & negligent, making it a constant rule never to follow my advice or opinion in any

(10)   thing, but rather if possible to act quite Contrary to it, I found it high time to let him & them all see that I was not come aboard to be an Idle Spectator (as he would have me to be) but that I would take upon me to give orders and have them obey'd. Though for want of persons about me capable and willing to advise me I was oblig'd to arm my self with patience & bear many of his Ridiculous humours till I got our Gentlemen[34] & officers aboard whom I expected at Cadiz some of whom I knew to be men of Capacity and Probity by whose asistance I did not doubt to be able to set all things to rights for the Good of the voyage & for the Companys Interest. I well foresaw this would bring me a great deal of trouble, as it did in the Course of our voyage much more than I could have ever imagin'd. For in fine it was a daily struggle all the out voyage (at least) whether He or I should govern.

---

right of trade (now obsolete in this sense). Campbell is referring to the Company's charter (see Introduction p. xiv ff.).

[32] In all East India companies, there was a ship's chaplain or priest on board every ship. Such was the case in the Swedish Company too, where he was sometimes called *magister*. Under the terms of the charter, the Company directors were permitted to select the chaplains. These had to be "devout, learned and capable persons", who were to preach the pure Evangelical Lutheran doctrine and furnish the crew with the means of salvation. In practical terms duties consisted of leading morning and evening prayer and of conducting religious services on Sundays and holy days. The liturgy was not very longwinded: the main feature was the Sunday sermon, which might or might not be followed by communion. Weather conditions often interfered with pastoral work at sea. The chaplain also provided religious instruction for the cadets and ship's boys, and saw the deceased to their last resting place. The great contribution of the chaplains lay in the scientific domain, i.e. in the study of the natural sciences, a pursuit unrelated to their office but to which they had almost sole access by virtue of their learning and their leisure. Some of them became great contributors to science, such as Christopher Ternström, Pehr Osbeck, and Olof Torén. David Pontin and Jacob Wallenberg were remarkable too by virtue of their writings while in the Company's service. (Koninckx 1980b, p. 315.)

[33] Here and elsewhere (cf. *Diary* pp. 32, 46, 58, and 75) Campbell refers to a royal commission giving him unrestricted authority over everybody on board including the captain (cf. also Kjellberg 1974, p. 43). No such document, mentioning both Campbell's and Trolle's names (p. 58), seems to have survived. In a memorial dated 9 December 1731 (RAS. KKH. E XVII a:I) there is mention of an application to the King for a special commission for Campbell, which may well be the document in question.

    Why Campbell alternately mentions it as having been issued by "Her" and "His Majesty" remains unclear. Since the commission was probably in French, it is just possible that he was occasionally misled by the feminine form *Sa Majesté*.

[34] I.e. the supercargoes; see below note 35.

For other matters I refer to Letters I wrote from Cadiz to the Directors.

March 28

By 8 a clock in the morning we got to Anchor in Cadiz Bay, Coming in I found the Captain knew not well where he was going, which oblig'd him to follow Breemers advice (which he never lik'd to do) about our getting in to the Bay. As they were handing down their sails on coming to an Anchor, the foreyard split, which I was told was occasion'd by wrong management.

As I was preparing to go ashore, there came aboard in a Spanish Boat two of our SuperCargos[35], Mr Brown[36] & Mr Pike[37] with some others, They inform'd me that there was a strict Imbargo lay'd upon all merchant ships by orders of the Court and that they were forc'd in to their service for carrying on a secret Expedition they design'd up the Mediterranean, As such an Accident (if not prevented) would have ruin'd our voyage, we concluded there was no other way to prevent it but

(11)

by passing for a man of war bound up the straights &c I therefore immediately order'd the Captain to hoist a man of war's Pendant, & desir'd him to pass always for a Captain of one of the Kings ships & to suffer no Spanish Boats to come on board of him on pretence of asking to see their health brief[38] or Bill of Product[39] (as is customary with all merchant ships) nor to let any of our people go ashoar for fear of their chattering & discovering what we were & whither bound &c For the greater privacy I went ashoar with our SuperCargos in the same Boat that brought them aboard, which we did with some difficulty, it blowing very hard, I got into Town without being question'd at the Gate, & went directly to Lodgings which Mr Brown had provided for me at a friends house. From

---

[35] Supercargoes were the Company's commercial travellers and the immediate representatives of the Company directors on board. They were in effect responsible for the real business of the Company, which in specific terms meant the safeguarding of the cargo – hence the term. In addition to general instructions concerning route and destination, the supercargoes received from the directors shortly before departure special secret orders. They frequently demarcated the respective spheres of authority of the captain, second captains and supercargoes. The directors desired the supercargoes to prick out the sea route, but to take account of the knowledge and views of the second captain, who had more experience of the East Indies navigation. The position of the supercargoes was pre-eminent. They laid down the guidelines, but the execution of the orders in practice always depended upon the experience and knowledge of the officers. There were generally four supercargoes, aided by assistant supercargoes, on board every Swedish East Indiaman. They were ordered as a hierarchy, as were the ship's crew proper. When deaths occurred among the supercargoes, they succeeded one another upwards in order. Because of the lack of experience among the Swedes, a great many foreigners were appointed as supercargoes, at least in the beginning of the Company.

[36] For *Brown* alias *Graham*, see Introduction p. xxxiii and note 291 below.

[37] For *John Pike*, see Introduction p. xxxiii.

[38] *Health brief*, contamination of the English term *bill of health* and the Dutch *Gezondheidsbrief*; 'brief' means letter or bill. However, it was a certificate properly authenticated by a consul or other recognized port authority certifying that the ship came from a place where there was no contagious disease, and that none of her crew, at the time of her departure, was infected with such a disease.

[39] Bill of loading, by which the master of a ship acknowledged the receipt of goods specified on the bill (see *Diary* p. 18).

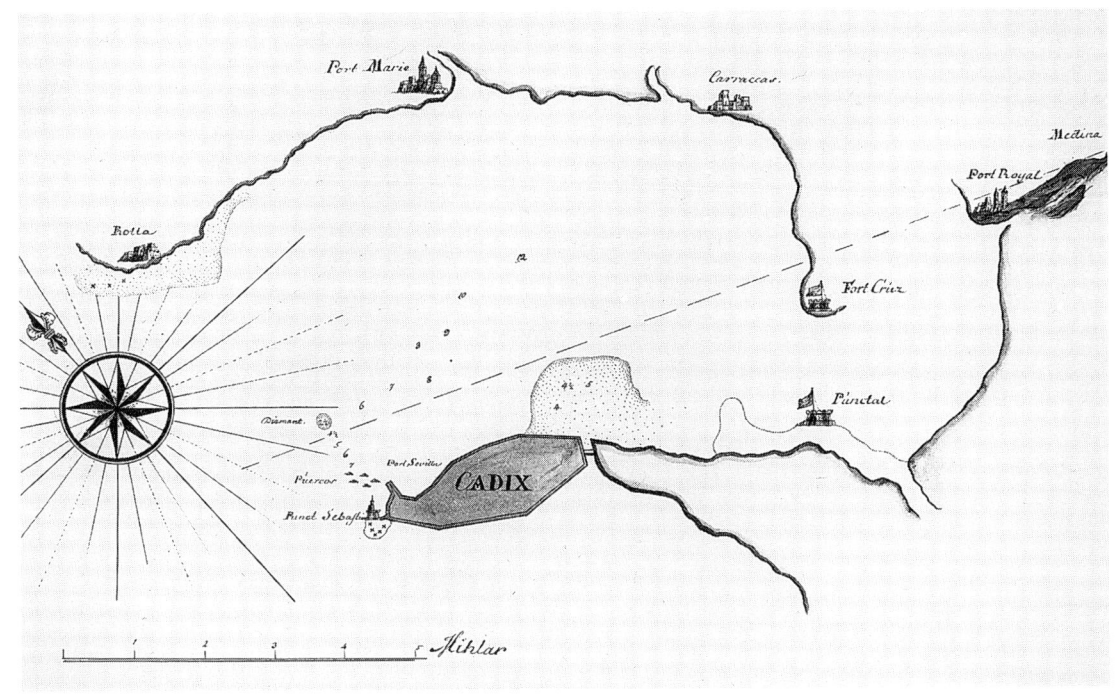

Map of Cádiz. From C.G. Ekeberg, *DageBok under Resan till och ifrån Canton uti China Åhren 1746.47.48.49 med Skeppet Götha Leyon.* (KVBS. Ms. Ekeberg, C.G.)

View of Cádiz. From C.H. Braad, *Berättelse om Resan med Skeppet Hoppet … från Götheborg till Canton i China … 1748–49.* (UUB. X.389.)

thence we went directly to our merchant from whom I receiv'd sundry Letters that had been waiting me there some time from some friends. The merchants having the money[40] all ready, the first thing we set about was to see it weigh'd, which we did immediately & press'd them to get it shipp'd assoon as possible, because we intended to stay but a few days, next thing was to get sundry provisions ready which I desir'd Mr Gough[41] & others to help us to, There was some Sherry or Xeres wine bought by the SuperCargos before I arriv'd, which was very necessary having so small a quantity on Board. As we had a great deal to do here with the ship (she having been put in a very poor order by the Captain who knew very little of such affairs) and we had not a moment to spare, I sent for our 2^d Captain Capt Kitching[42] & Chief mate Mr Baron & the English Carpenter & Caulker who had been all waiting at Cadiz for about 3 weeks, I order'd them immediately aboard ship where their presence was much wanted & recommended them to work night & day to get the ship ready for sailing, And indeed they soon put the ship in another condition than she had been in before, there not being one person on board from Sweden that knew any thing of fitting the ship as it ought to be for such a voyage.

As there were some Goods which the Company had order'd

(12)   from England for our out Cargo aboard of the Hannibal (Capt Morgan Master) now lying in the Bay, I concerted with him to get them aboard our ship from his (without the Charge & trouble of bringing them ashore) as privately as he could which he readily undertook to do, for which reason As our ship lay far out in the Bay I wrote to the Captain to weigh & come further in & as near the Hannibal as he could, which he was not able to do for some days by reason of very blowing weather, And when they weigh'd they were oblig'd to leave an Anchor behind, by reason of the winlace's[43] breaking.

When I sent the 2^d Captain & other English officers aboard I wrote by them to the Captain recommending them to him as Persons imploy'd by the Company and very Capable to asist him & the People in putting the ship in good order & fit for

---

[40] Silver piastres; other terms commonly used are *Mexican peso, Mexico dollar*, or *Peso duro*, less frequently *Mexicans* and *Pesoforte*. They do not all signify one and the same coin. The true piastre, the *peso fuerto* or *peso duro*, was designated *stuck van achten* ('piece of eight') by the Dutch, *Reales de a Ocho* by the Spaniards, while the Portuguese used the term *pataques*. The chests in which the piastres were carried did not take up much room in the ship's hold. There seems not to have been a standard chest. Silver consignments were also shipped in bags (see *Diary* p. 21; Campbell stated that all silver came on board in bags and that four bags of 1,000 *dollars* each were put in a small chest, thus making 4,000 *dollars* a chest).

[41] *James Gough & Co.*, brokers established in Cádiz, had already helped the ships of the Ostend Company dispatched to Spain to collect a cargo of piastres (Dermigny 1964, 1, p. 192). Edward Gough, Jr. was a shareholder in the Ostend Company and associated with Jacomo de Pret, one of the directors of that company.

[42] The 2nd captain's name was *George Kitchin*; see Introduction pp. xxx, xxxiii; Gill (1961), p. 106.

[43] *Windlass*.

the long voyage we were going upon &c But this was not sufficient to prevent him from flying out into his Ill humours, He could not bear the thoughts of any body being imploy'd (tho' capable to serve the Company) but himself, or that we should want any Bodys asistance but his own tho' he was utterly incapable of performing such a voyage himself, But he had other views (not much I believe for the Companys Interest) and was not very desirous to have any person on board to be witnesses or who were able to give me any advice about sea Affairs, In fine the 2^d Captain wrote to me from the ship to let me know that he could do nothing on board for the Captain would give him no help nor order the men to go about any work in the ship which he requir'd & found necessary &c This gave me an opportunity to begin to exert the Authority I had always resolv'd, when the Good of the voyage requir'd it, so wrote to him pretty seriously to let him know that as the Company was very sensible that neither He nor any Body that we had ingag'd in Sweden

(13)   understood much what related to a voyage to the East Indies they had taken the necessary precautions to imploy some English Officers who had made many such voyages, and who knew perfectly what was fit to be done to ships imploy'd in such service, & would be able to put our people in the right method, and therefore I wonder'd at his not giving them all the necessary asistance to inable them to perform the Companys service as they were ready to do, that I must now assure him that for the future I would suffer no shuffling or putting off things or neglecting my orders which I would have punctually obey'd & the moment I should give him them, that therefore I order'd him immediately to give the proper orders to all the officers & sailors aboard to act & do whatever work Capt Kitching & Mr Baron should require to be done from time to time, and to let them all know what stations they were in & the Command they had under him &c

Having made the ship pass for a man of war or Kings ship, It was necessary some Body should appear that had Command of the ship & wait upon the Governour as a man of war Captain (as is usual with them) And as it was not very proper for me to appear here much myself, I order'd the Captain to put on his best Cloaths & come ashore in his Pinnace[44] & bring his Commission he had from his late Majesty[45], in order to wait upon the Governour &c All this was necessary in order to carry on the farce the better, and it took extremely well, As I much dreaded the Captain's committing some blunders in Conversation with the Governour, I press'd Mr Gough to go along with him (which he had no great mind to) & to answer for him all Questions the Governour should ask, & to tell him that the ship was bound up the Mediterranean & he did not know what he was to do till

---

[44] *Pinnace*, a ship's boat, rowed with eight oars, but later increased in length to accommodate 16 oars. The larger variety was capable of stepping a mast when required (see *Diary* p. 16). (*The Oxford Companion to Ships & the Sea*, 1976, p. 649.)
[45] I.e. *King Charles (Karl) XII of Sweden* (1682–1718).

he got there where he was to open his Majestys orders &c They accordingly went to the Governour & were well receiv'd, He ask'd whither he was bound and for what service &c And Mr Gough made the proper Answers.

Now the Captain was ashore I took the opportunity to explain my

(14)   mind very freely to him, repeating what I had wrote to him the day before (to which Letter I refer in case the Captain has it yet by him) As he has always a good knack at lying & dissembling he did not fail to make use of it on this Occasion by pretending to be very ready to obey my orders, & to give all necessary asistance to the officers I had sent aboard, &c

When the Captain went on board again he thought fit to alter his former method, and suffer the English officers to put the ship in a proper condition for the voyage, and as the utmost dispatch was necessary, they took care to work night & day, This was a subject of Complaint from the Captain who wrote to me that the People were quite spent with working night and day & would not be able to hold it out, &c As I knew well his temper & design in hindring the people from working & setting them against every officer that press'd them on to their Duty, I little regarded his Complaints but wrote to him that their working hard at present was absolutely necessary, that it would not last long &c and to support them the better I sent aboard almost every day fresh meat, Greens & Bread &c A propos as to the Captain's always incouraging the People in Idleness, of which I had too many Instances afterwards during the whole voyage, his Rule was to make the People believe that he was the only Person that had any Regard for them, & that the officers who were for making them work & do their Duty had a mind to kill them &c This method he had too successfully put in practice against Styrman Breemer, who was the only Brisk Swedish Officer we had and was always ready to make the People do their Duty, which brought upon him their Ill will as well as his, The Captain was so open & barefac'd in brow beating & discouraging Breemer on all Occasions that he could not help doing it sometimes before my face, so that once overhearing

(15)   him abusing Breemer on the Quarter Deck[46] before the People, I could not refrain reprimanding him, & letting him know that Breemer was in the right & that instead of discouraging him, as he did from using an Authority over the People he ought to support him in it & every officer that was under him, without which there would be no Command nor nothing done to purpose in the ship. I believe

---

[46] *Quarterdeck*, part of the ship from which she was commanded by the captain, or by the officer of the watch. Traditionally it was also the part of the ship where the captain used to walk and from which the navigator took his sights when determining the ship's position. According to custom officers only were supposed to use the quarterdeck. The boatswain, the carpenter, and other warrant officers or seamen were called to the quarterdeck to receive orders and announcements. (*The Oxford Companion to Ships & the Sea*, 1976, p. 679.)

another Cause of his hating Breemer was that he knew some Gentlemen of the Company had an esteem for him as well as I, & that he found he could not draw him into his schemes as he was able to do some others who had not that regard to the Companys Interest as Bremer had.

As to sailors the Captain Imploy'd at Stockholm, there were but the Boatswain & his Mate{'s} & half a dozen more that deserv'd the name of sea men, the rest being all Boys[47] many of whom knew very little of the business of a sailor & some not so much as the names of the Ropes of the ship, And when I spoke to the Captain about them he sayd he took such people on purpose Boys being the easiest to manage and whom he could breed up as he pleas'd, I told him I thought at the same time he had done very well to have hir'd a few Able experienc'd sailors at least to teach his Boys &c However to do them Justice though they are Ignorant enough yet they are willing enough to do what they are order'd, and I believe there are no sailors in the world more tractable or easier govern'd,& had they a Good brisk Captain & officers, no doubt they are Capable of proving as good seamen as any whatsoever, But that is what they want at present (at least as to a Captain) to whom I impute intirely the laziness & Indolence of our People. But the very worst men we have are those of the Kings People ingag'd at Gottenburg who (except a very few) are a parcel of stupid Boors, who have never been at sea, & know nothing & I believe never will learn, and yet these fellows are always the first to grumble & dispos'd to mutiny on any Occasion. But had they a Captain that knew

(16) how to carry command and would take any pains about them it would be an Easy matter to check all the mischief they are capable of, & even to make them Good for something, But they will never be so under such a one as they have at present.

Notwithstanding of my orders, on my Arrival here, to the Captain to let none of our people come ashore but such as row'd the Pinnace, yet I saw Nyman & some others ashore, which the Captain pretended was without his knowledge (which I think could not well be) Amongst the rest that came ashore was the Parson to Christen it seems a Protestant's Child by which means he might have brought himself into great trouble, had the Priests of the Country got notice of it, In that case there would have been no redeeming him from the Inquis[i]tion at least; when he went back to the ship, The Captain told me he was very drunk, and made great noise & disturbance in the ship, It is likely he had been too free with the favours shown him ashore especially at the Christning where he might think he had some privilege to break through ordinary Rules.

Being oblig'd to fetch sundry of our Provisions from Port St Mary[48] on the other

---

[47] Generally there was a complement of young boys aboard, employed for lighter tasks. They were of the lowest rank of the crew.
[48] *El Puerto de Santa Maria*, Spanish port on the Bay of Cádiz.

side of the Bay, we were hinderd some days by it, for the Spanish men of war lying in the Bay stopp'd all Spanish Boats & forcd the men out to imploy them on their present Expedition, As they did the same by some Boats bringing our Provisions to the ship they were oblig'd to put back again, to wait for another opportunity to come aboard. To make the greater dispatch I order'd our own Boats to asist in fetching the water.

April Having now got our money Goods & Provisions aboard, it was time to prepare for our departure, And as there lay at the Entrance of the Bay a Spanish man of war that stopt all ships going

(17) out, It was necessary to take all precautions to prevent such an Accident, and therefore it was thought advisable for the Captain to wait upon the Admiral ashore to let him know of his going to sail & to desire there might be orders to the Guard ship to give us no hindrance, The Captain accordingly waited on the Admiral (in Company with Mr Gough) who receiv'd them civilly and assurd them we should meet with no stop or hindrance. I then order'd him to go on board & weigh Anchor & take the ship out to the Entrance of the Bay to be ready to sail assoon as I & the rest of the Gentlemen should come on board, which he did & Anchor'd close by the Spanish Guard ship.

I ingag'd here one Mr Maul[49] as a midshipman[50], a Person who had been very serviceable to us here in providing sundry necessaries for the ship, which would not have been so easy for us to do for want of the Language & Knowledge of the place, He had been once a voyage to India and as he was recommended to me as a good man I was the more inclin'd to ingage him, not knowing what use we might have on occasion for such a Person in case of the death of any of our officers, And he prov'd an honest diligent man.

As I had brought no Cook from Sweden for the Cabbin, and all my passage from thence to Cadiz had none but the ships Cook, who was the worst that ever pretended to that Trade, though I had accustom'd my self to the Captains way (who was indeed the Chief Cook[51] & a sad one) yet I was very sensible that the

---

[49] *James Maule* is listed in 1740 among English mates and cadets in the service of the Swedish East India Company (Kjellberg 1974, p. 128) and was later captain of two voyages to China (*ibid.* pp. 177 f., 206).

[50] Synonym for *cadet*. Cadets or midshipmen were young men seeking to become acquainted with all the work on board. To that end the boatswain and gunner gave them instruction in all aspects of tackle, timber, sails and ordnance, storage, navigation, command, and even trade. Religious education was included in the programme as well. Theoretically, they were not allowed to perform any heavy work aboard ship. They could even be called upon to replace officers. The intention was that the cadets should eventually become officers. They made one or two voyages as cadets and could then become a trainees or probationer mates. (Koninckx 1980b, p. 312 ff.)

[51] On board a Company ship, meals were taken in three or four separate groups. The "top table" was reserved for the supercargoes. Also seated there were the captain, mates, ship's chaplain, first surgeon and assistant supercargoes. The cabin cook prepared the meals for that table, while the

English SuperCargos & officers could not easily come in to a way of Eating they were not us'd to (& which indeed was none of the best) I desird them to look out amongst the English ships in the Bay for a Good Cook, And Mr Morford found one an Italian whom I ingag'd for the voyage.

Besides the SuperCargos & officers that were imploy'd

18)   and had been here some time waiting for our Arrival, I found here also Mr Moir[52] & Daniel Campbell, who were recommended by some of the Companys Good Friends in England, and whom I intended to imploy as writers[53] to the Super-Cargos.

The Captain complaining here that we wanted planks & Deals (though he had bought some in Norway, and as I found afterwards, we had a great deal more than we had Occasion for) I hear'd of one Selander master of a Swedish ship belonging to Director Tham[54], that had some, I took some of him, leaving the price to be settled between Mr Tham & the other Gentlemen at Gottenburg. The Captain being very desirous to have things to buy, though not wanted, in order to have the pleasure of making out an Account, And I having reason not to like his Accounts, from what I had seen of them already in Sweden, I was resolv'd to prevent his making up any more Accounts, and therefore would not suffer him to buy anything for the ship, More during this voyage, thinking it more for the Companys Interest to take that trouble my self,than to run the hazard of being impos'd upon by him, as I much dreaded.

---

steward served it. At the "second table" sat the ship's writer, the probationer mates, the purser and the second surgeon. The difference between this and the top table lay not only in the hierarchy but also in the beverages served. Wine and other alcoholic drinks were allowed to be dispensed only occasionally at the second table. There did exist a "third table", although it was not described as such; it was merely prescribed that the gunner, the steward and the cadets should eat together. The diet was probably identical with that of the fourth group, comprising the remainder of the ship's company. The ship's cook, probably the same as the chief cook, prepared the meals for the crew and presumably also for the "second" and "third" tables. (Koninckx 1978a; *id*. 1980a.)

[52] *James Moir* or *More* (1713–84), laird of Stoneywood, Aberdeen, was to complete three expeditions as supercargo in the Swedish Company between 1737 and 1745. After taking part in the unsuccessful rebellion of Prince Charles in Scotland he lived as a refugee in Gothenburg until 1763, when he returned once more to Scotland. (Campbell 1960, pp. 21, 41 f.)

[53] As already mentioned in the Introduction (p. xviii), the captain and the first and second mates were each to maintain a ship's journal to be submitted in fair copy to the Company directors after the voyage. On their return supercargoes were also expected to submit a journal with daily reports of all their actions. Other documents had to be written as well, however. The task of entering up the journal could be delegated by the captain, the mates or the supercargoes to younger members of the crew. Mostly the supercargoes appointed an assistant supercargo for that job, but the ship's writer was in duty of administrative services. Usually they were one or two per ship, compiling the muster and pay rolls and the ship's journal for the captain. Not infrequently younger ship's personnel such as cadets were appointed. In the case of this particular voyage it is clear that Moir and Daniel Campbell were employed, not as ship's writers, but as writers serving the supercargoes (see *Diary* p. 25 for the Swedish term *skrivare*). (Koninckx 1980b, p. 112 ff.)

[54] *Volrath Tham*, Gothenburg merchant; see further note 408.

As it was very proper that the Captain should have sign'd here a Bill of Lading for the money & Goods belonging to the Company shipp'd here, of which I should have sent one to the Directors, when he was last ashoar I desir'd him to do it as being always the form for all masters of ships &c But all I could say could not overcome his Obstinacy & Ignorance, And all I could prevail upon him to do with the utmost difficulty was to get him to sign a bill of Lading for only part of the stock belonging to our friends in Sweden

(19)   which was not yet insurd, and which I was to insure from this place, and necessary to have a Bill of Lading sent to England to prove (in case of any Accident to the ship) the having such a Concern in the ship, which having at last obtain from him I sent to London.

April 11   I desir'd all our People that were ashoar to go aboard in the morning, intending to follow them the same day assoon as our Accounts with the merchants were finish'd, It being post day I was oblig'd to stay till the Post was over, which made us lose the opportunity of going aboard that night as we intended, for as we were come to the Gates they were shutting them & would not let us pass. I wrote the same day to the Directors but had not time to send them Copies of our merchants Accounts as I intended to have done, but desir'd the merchants to send Copies to them which they promis'd & no doubt did.

Apr. 12   In the morning Early Mr Brown & Mr Pike & I got ready to go aboard. Hearing there was an opportunity to send Letters to Sevil[55] which would overtake the Post of the day before, I stay'd a little while to write to some friends what I had forgot the day before, which Letters I hope they Receiv'd. We got safe aboard before noon, & set about immediately taking up the Anchor that was left at the ships first Birth, which was accordingly done & brought aboard.

Having no place to lodge our SuperCargos & Officers as I wish'd I knew no other way but to order Cabbins to be made in the steerige[56], for the SuperCargos, and a Round house[57] on the After part of the Quarter Deck for the Captain & Officers, I thought to have had them all done long before this time, having often spoke to the Captain about it in the passage to Cadiz but according to his constant dilatory way it was neglected, & for ought I know it had never been done had it not been for our English Carpenter & his son who finish'd

---

[55] *Seville*, chief city of Andalusia and a seaport of Spain, on the left bank of the Guadalquivir River, about 54 miles from the Atlantic Ocean. The discovery of America by Columbus in 1492 brought the growth of Seville as a seaport, where many expeditions for colonizing America started. Since then and for along time Seville was the heartbeat of the East and West Indian trade.

[56] *Steerage*, a large space below deck, next below the quarterdeck and immediately before the bulkhead of the great cabin. (*The Oxford Companion to Ships & the Sea*, 1976, p. 831.)

[57] *Round house*, square or rectangular cabins built on the quarterdeck, called 'round' because one could walk round them. (*The Oxford Companion to Ships & the Sea*, 1976, p. 724.)

(20)　the Round house while we lay here. The Captain had ingag'd a great many fellows as Carpenters at Stockholm (and some we had I believe from the Admiralty there) but all so bad, that they were capable of nothing, and I must say it was very well for us we had an English one on board who was a diligent Careful man & a Good workman, And had we met with any Accident at sea as springing a Leak or such like, there was not one of them capable of helping us, This ought to be well consider'd by the Company in all their voyages, for there is no Officer more neccessary in such voyages as a Good Carpenter, especially that we have not Ports to put into upon any Accident to get asistance as ships can do near Homo. In fine by making the Round house the Captain & 2^d Captain & Chief mate got pretty good Accomodations, and indeed better than our Super-Cargos two of whom were oblig'd to take up with two small Cabbins in the steerige (or near it) and Mr Brown could find no place but the Cabbin to place a Cott in.

When I came aboard I found Styrman Lund in Arrest, It seems he had got drunk aboard a Swedish ship in the Bay, & made some noise when he came back to the ship which drew upon him a Quarrell with his Good friend the Captain, who found no better way to settle his Impertinence than by confining him to his Cabbin, which as I was inform'd, he well deserv'd. However as his fault was committed in Liquour & he was become submissive, and that [we] were now beginning our voyage as it were, I spoke to the Captain to release him, which he did, and I sent for him and gave him a Reprimand, & advis'd him to keep a due respect for the Captain & his superiour officers, He promis'd to behave well for the time to come, & so I made them good friends again And indeed they

(21)　soon prov'd too Good friends to my Cost as appear'd in a short time afterwards. But they were not the only Instances of Ingratitude that I met with this voyage.

While we were getting under sail, as we lay very close to the Spanish Guard ship, she fir'd 2 or 3 shot very near us, which alarm'd the Captain & some of our officers not a little tho' without much reason, However It was thought proper to send aboard & ask the meaning of it, Mr Maul (who understood the Spanish Language) went aboard of him, The Commanding Officer excus'd him self, that he intended us no harm, but that he had fir'd at some Spanish Boats that were crossing the Bay, whom he had a mind to stop, which we soon perceiv'd to be true, For we saw his Pinnace Arm'd stopping all the Boats that pass'd.

April 13th (or to write in the sea stile[58]) April 14th Post meridiem, In the Evening we weigh'd & got under sail, we follow'd the Advice of some of the knowing people at Cadiz to keep over for Cape Cantin[59] on the Coast of Barbary where we might

_____

[58] At sea the day began at noon, because the position of the ship was determined when the sun was culminating (see note 5 above).
[59] *Cape Cantin* is situated on the coast of Morocco, south of Casablanca.

23

expect to meet with Easterly winds, which we did, & found them so.

– 14   As our Treasure had come all on board in Bags, we had got small Chests to stow the Bags in, But as the Carpenter had made them too big, we order'd him to make new ones, big enough to hold four Bags only, which contain'd about a thousand Dollers each, being much more handy for moving about in case of any Accident. When we had the Chests taken up a few days afterwards, we found another fault, they had been made of Green wood, which had rolled a great many of the Bags so that the money had fallen out and lay a great part of it loose in the Chests, which made us get new Bags made, when we chang'd them to the smaller Chests, By this Accident, we could not know exactly whether at Canton the weights would come out exactly (of each bag as it weigh'd at Cadiz) which I would gladly have known.

(22)   But in the whole As I saw every Bag weigh'd my self I found our merchants at Cadiz had us'd us well, or whether it might be owing to the English scales we had & with which we weigh'd them at Canton, They generally came out better there than the weight charg'd by the merchants at Cadiz, by which the Company is a gainer, though some of the China merchants complain'd of me for it & say'd I did not give them good weight, though they were always present when their money was weigh'd to them, They pretended that the English SuperCargos & others gave them much better weight than we did.

April 18   At 2 a clock P.M we saw Cape Cantin bearing S E b E, we then steerd for the Canary Islands[60]. As for the Course & winds &c I shall seldom trouble the Company with [them], Referring them for such like matters to the Officers Journals where they will see them set down as they ought to be and much exacter than I can pretend to do.

– 20   At night we had the misfortune to lose one of our sailors, Nils Fahlberg, who through heedlessness fell over board from the forecastle & was drown'd, without a possibility of saving him it blew so fresh & the ship running at a good rate with a great sea.[61]

I have forgot to mention in its due place the Death of the Boatswain[62] Tynis

---

[60] The north-east trades and the Canaries current drove the ships from Cádiz fairly rapidly south-west towards the Canary Islands. They passed either in between them or left to the east, depending on the instructions. Generally the Swedes sighted the mountains of Tenerife and Palmas, which greatly helped the sailors to correct their computations of longitude; still many navigators made use of the prime meridian of Tenerife, at least during the first half of the 18th century. (Koninckx 1980b, p. 120 ff.)

[61] The words "without a possibility … with a great sea" were added later by Campbell, who apparently felt that some explanation and justfication would be in place.

[62] Immediately beneath the mates in the hierarchy came the boatswain, who had charge of all operations

Kupens, which happen'd April the 12th the very day I came aboard; I heard he had been sick a few days of a fever, but seeing him upon the main Deck thought he was recover'd, & asking him how he did, he answer'd me he was better, In a few hours afterwards I was surpriz'd to hear he was dead. As I was inform'd he had a high fever & had been Delirious, I ask'd the Doctor[63] if he had not blister'd[64] him, He told me no and that they seldom us'd to give Blisters but when they were very bad, that is in short past recovery, This being very contrary to the method of the Physicians in England who make no scruple to blister even Children when a disease requires it, made me begin to suspect that we had got a Doctor who

(23) did not know much of his Business (notwithstanding of the great Commendations given of him in Sweden) I was but too much confirm'd in my opinion of him afterwards, for I found him very Averse to applying of Blisters or giving vomits or even Bleeding, but when it was too late, I often talk'd to him on this subject & sometimes I got him perswaded, though with difficulty, to try each of these methods, which I may venture to say sav'd some peoples Lives. The observation our Gentlemen made of the Doctors way of treating the sick, who had been us'd with other sort of Physicians in their Country as well as on board the ships they had been in, gave them no inclination to fall sick. But to return to the Boatswain, The Captain told me that he was afraid he had been in some measure the Occasion of his Illness (which he pretended gave him great Concern) having had some dispute with him about some of the ships stores under his Care which he could not give an Account of, But he had more reason to allege another Occasion he may have been of his Death, As he is the strangest fellow in the world for pretending to be & to know every thing, he thought fit to set up for Doctor too & to know much more than Mr Muder or his mate, and upon no other foundation than Brandy & some Sprus[65] (as he calls it) or Dantzick Beer[66], which he believes to be good for all Diseases, And he thought proper to give some of this to the Boatswain, contrary to the Doctors opinion, which by the By was a very strange Remedy for a fever. As I found afterwards he would be dabbling with the sick people & ordering them some of his stuff, without having any regard to the Doctor, I fearing the dangerous consequence of his meddling in such things & that he

purely to do with working the ship. In weighing or dropping anchor, in setting or reefing sails, he was the coordinator, usually assisted by two boatswain's mates. As a general rule he had to be first into the breach and last to leave it. (Koninckx 1980b, p. 317.)

[63] Although there was no difference between the wages paid to a first surgeon and to a doctor, only a few of them were actual doctors of medicine. One may nevertheless suspect that there was a difference in the level of training. Very probably the harsh living conditions did not help to make life at sea attractive, while at the same time the wages offered were low. There was always a shortage of them, which explains why here also many foreigners were appointed in the Company's service. In fact surgeons were prohibited from practising medicine, but the force of circumstances made it necessary because of the limited availability of doctors. (Koninckx 1980b, p. 315 ff.)

[64] *To blister*, 'to raise blisters on', by the application of mustard etc.

[65] *Spruce*, 'Prussian'; *spruce beer*, an alcoholic drink made of fermented molasses flavoured with spruce twigs and cones.

[66] *Danzig beer*, a black syrupy beer made at Danzig.

might kill the People by his folly & Ignorance, was oblig'd to tell him of it, & to advise him to give

24 [the] sick nothing, but leave them to the Doctor, whose Business it was otherwise he could not answer for the Peoples health, and that if he the Captain should pretend to give them Physick[67] and they should chance to dy, People would be very apt to say that they dy'd of his Physick &c This frighten'd him a little & I believe made him more Cautious Afterwards, though he was not a little affronted that I did not take him for an Able Physician. I thought it was too much that he pretended to be Carpenter, Butcher, Smith, Cook & all Trades, as he did constantly, for there could not be a nail made or drove in any where, or a bit of wood to be cut but he must be always giving his foolish Directions, which only hinderd the Persons whose Business it was from doing things as they ought to be, But I would easier excuse his meddling with those other Trades than that of a Doctor, as being of less dangerous consequence.

The Boatswains Death occasion'd a warm dispute between me & the Captain, & gave me an opportunity to begin to exert my Authority & power I had in the ship, Assoon as the Boatswain dy'd He was pleas'd to make a Promotion of officers without acquainting me in the least with it, for he immediately appointed Olof Rasmuson Humbla (who had been mate to the former) for Boatswain, an Ignorant silly fellow, &   [68] Jacobs[69] for Boatswain's mate (who indeed is a good man) & worse than that appointed Olof Rudbeck Quartermaster[70] a meer Boy & no more fit to be a Quartermaster than I to be an Admiral, by which means he spoild a Boy that would have prov'd a good brisk seaman, from being now of almost any service to us; I had waited two or 3 days without speaking to the Captain about it in expectation that he would have come & recommended to me some proper persons to fill the vacancys according to his orders from the Company, I did not know what he had done till looking over a List he had drawn out & pasted

(25) up of the ships Company I found the Persons before mentioned promoted as I have now related, I took occasion from this to put a Check to such management for the future & ask'd if he had so soon forgot the Commission & powers I had receiv'd from his Majesty that nothing should be done in the ship contrary to my orders or without my Knowledge or Consent, as also the particular orders he had receiv'd from the Directours relating to this very point not at all to pretend to make any Changes or Promotions that being intirely left to me to do, He alleg'd

---

[67] *Physic*, a medicine or drug, especially a cathartic or purge.
[68] Campbell has left a blank.
[69] The name of the boatswain's mate is elsewhere given as *Jacob Anderson* (*Diary* p. 49) and *Jacob* (*Diary* p. 59), so *Jacobs* here is probably an error.
[70] The quartermasters were four in number, later six, but always without distinction of grade. They functioned by turns as helmsmen. (Koninckx 1980b, p. 318.)

that he had only plac'd them in those stations in the mean time to do the Duty to see if they were fit for it, I let him know that even in that Case he ought to have first spoke to me, and that his promoting those people was doing them no manner of service, for the Company would take no notice of their Advancement if not done by me, and therefore I told him I would suffer no such thing to be done for the time to come, In fine he was resolv'd to try every way he was capable of contriving to keep the power in his hands & see if I would take notice of it, And I finding him thus dispos'd took care betimes to curb him, which was no small mortification to a Person of his Pride & Insolence. This Check put a stop to such attempts afterwards, I had observ'd him very fond of the ships steward and often spoke of him to me as a very Capable Person for Accounts &c wanting to make him Purser, which title he always gave him (viz Schrivare[71]) & never Boteler[72] or Steward) & made him do all his Business for him, To prevent his troubling me upon this subject, Assoon as I came aboard from Cadiz, As the ship was not provided with a Purser, I presented Mr Ross to him, telling him that I appointed him the ships Purser, and that he was to take care of all the business in the ship that was usual for Persons in that Post; He is a Capable young man and very serviceable to me by reason of his understanding the Swedish as well as English Languages, and I had often occasion

(26) to imploy him during the voyage, particularly in turning several Orders & Instructions into the Swedish Language, which I was often forc'd to draw out for the Captain, for he had no regard to any verbal order, I gave him, But he stood a little more in aw of a written one, which I chose to give him in Swedes[73] to prevent his Excuse of not understanding any other Language I might have given them in.

The Boatswains Death occasion'd another scuffle between the Captain & the Priest, which happen'd thus, The English Carpenter had no Cabbin[74] when he came aboard, for the Boatswain had got a Cabbin in the steerige which had been Empty, As his place to ly was properly forward and that the Carpenter ought to have that Cabbin, He did accordingly give him the Key of it while he was sick with an intent to leave it to him, After his Death The Carpenter acquainted me with the Affair desiring I would let him take possession of that Cabbin having no place to lay up his Tools in &c I readily granted his request knowing the reasonableness of it, And he accordingly took possession, it serv'd both him

---

[71] Swedish *skrivare*, 'writer' (cf. note 53 above).

[72] *Butler*, the same as steward, subordinate to the cabin cook.

[73] Campbell's spelling *Swedes* for 'Swedish' (cf. *Diary* pp. 64, 71, 277 and 287 for further instances) no doubt reflects his Scottish pronunciation. The ending *-is* for *-ish* is well-known in Middle English northern dialects: *Inglis*, *Scot(i)s*, etc.

[74] The assignment of cabins to supercargoes, officers, surgeons, and chaplains always remained a matter of discussion on board, because of its implications for the opportunity of stowing away merchandise for private trade. The larger the cabin, the more it could hold.

and his son. This gave the Priest occasion of great disgust, He had plagued the Captain since ever he came aboard for a Cabbin in the steerige, who told him his place was in the Gun-Room as it really was, It seems however upon the Boatswains Death he intended to give him that Cabbin, & was very Angry when he heard it was given away; which made him come full mouth'd to me with a Complaint that the Captain had promis'd him the Cabbin that the Carpenter had got, & desir'd I would let him yet have it, I told him he apply'd too late for I had already dispos'd of it, but that if the Carpenter was willing to resign it to him I should be satisfy'd & would indeavour to find him another place and promis'd to speak to him about it which I did but the Carpenter being very unwilling to part with it and that he was a very necessary man & had a right to a Cabbin

(27) I did not care to press him much to quit it, upon which I order'd to make a Cabbin forward between Decks (the only spare room we had) large enough to hold his Bed & a Table & Chair which was presently done, The Captain told him that he must be satisfy'd with it for there was no other to give him, This fir'd the Priest who refus'd to take the Cabbin that was made for him & gave the Captain very abusive language, & for some time after refus'd to say prayers to the People, and when he was pleas'd to do it he behav'd once or twice so very irreverently that the Captain reprimanded him, This put the Priest in a great fury so that he would neither come to prayers nor to Table for some days, which made the Captain forbid carrying him any victuals. In the mean while he wrote me a Letter (to which I refer) In answer I sent Mr Ross to him to advise him to come & do his Duty as before & be reconcil'd to the Captain (against whom he complain'd heavily) and that I would provide as good a place for him as I could, upon which he thought fit to grow weary of his Retirement & to return to his Duty & take the Cabbin that was made for him. This small dispute occasion'd a great misunderstanding between the Captain & the Priest for some time, which Styrman Lund promoted as much as he could by siding with the Latter, And though the Captain knew this very well yet in a little time he and the Priest became his fast friends, and Lund his Chief Counsellour & very Instrumental (as I have reason to believe) in stirring him up against me & the English on board all the rest of the voyage; Indeed they were very fit for one another both being very silly & Ignorant & proud, strangely blown up with their high Caracter of being Kings Officers[75] which they frequently boasted of. In fine these were generally the Returns I met with from [the Captain] & his friends, when they fell a quarrelling growling at one another,

---

[75] There were always officers, even petty officers, who had been in the service of the Royal Swedish Navy. Some naval officers were allowed to sail to the Far East in the Company's service by permission of their superiors. Two career systems were possible: one was that of the seaman on leave of absence, who rejoined the ranks of the Navy at the end of a voyage to the East Indies; the second involved a simple switch over from the Navy to the Company, in which a definitive career then began. King's officers belonged to the first system, since they kept in the Company the rank and status that they had in the Navy.

I was oblig'd to take the trouble to reconcile them, & for my pains they joyn'd their Clod-pates together to make me as uneasy as they could.

Assoon as the Boatswain dy'd I sent Mr Ross with the Captain to lock up his Chest, after taking an Account of what he left, and

(28) in a few days afterwards orderd them to be sold by Auction[76] upon Deck, which the Captain took a great pleasure of doing himself, and made Mr Ross keep a regular Account of all that was sold & of the price & to whom, which method was always observ'd afterwards when any Body dy'd.

From the moment I came aboard ship, but more especially from our leaving Cadiz, did my plagues & war with the Captain begin, And were I to recount all the occurrences that happend of this sort would be to write a Diary of a continual scene of the greatest Obstinacy, folly, Disobedience, Ill nature, Drunkenness & madness that can be imagin'd, It will be sufficient for me to relate some of the most material passages, as my memory can furnish me without being able to keep exactly to the time they happen'd

The first thing to be done on our all getting aboard at Cadiz was to make some Regulations about the Diet[77] of our Gentlemen SuperCargos Officers &c & the whole ships Company, And as there were more of us than could dine at one Table we were oblig'd to have two, one in the Cabbin for the SuperCargos, the Captain, 2^d Captain, the Chief mate & my self, of which I desir'd Mr Morford to take the Trouble of ordering, I knowing him much more Capable of such an Affair than I & I believe than any of us, which he willingly undertook. For the 2^d Table which was in the steerige I appointed Mr Breemer, Styrman Lund, the Doctor, the Priest, Mr Maul midshipman & George Kitching a son of our 2^d Captain (to whom I had given the Caracter of midshipman to[78] at his Father's Request) and our Gentlemen writers & Purser.[79] I would willingly have taken Mr Breemer to

---

[76] When a member of the crew died during the voyage, his belongings were sold by auction on board at the foot of the mainmast. As soon as the news could reach Sweden, newspapers published a list of deceased seamen with the amounts of their estates. The heirs were invited to come to the Company's office to collect the proceeds of their estates. In addition, the wages of the deceased were paid to the heirs, but account was probably taken of the date of death in relation to the expedition as a whole, as was also done in the case of the so-called privilege money. The voyage was divided into sections: Gothenburg–Cádiz, Cádiz–Far East and Far East–Gothenburg. Depending on the section during which the crewman died, the heirs would receive 1/3, 1/2 or 1/1 of the pay. However, apart from a few monthly wages paid out to the crew while in the Far East, the rest was handed over only at the end of the voyage.

[77] The diet at the top table was more sumptuous than that of the ordinary crew. No fixed bill of fare was prescribed, probably because the stores themselves presented no problem. Food was simply not rationed but given out *ad libitum*. There were personal provisions to tuck into as well. Supercargoes, captains and mates, chaplains, doctors, assistants, and writers were all allowed to supplement the ship's fare by taking along their own provisions.

[78] For *too*.

[79] See note 51 above for details of how meals were taken in three or four separate groups and who was

our Table But as it was necessary to have a prudent man to be at the head of that Table where there were so many young People I had none else to trust with that care but himself, which I easily prevail'd with him to undertake, at the same time

(29) letting him know that Mr Morford would take care to give them fresh provisions as many days of the week as we could spare it. Mr Morfords having the ordering of our Table was a great mortification to the Captain for he had got it in his head that neither I nor any body else was to meddle with any thing relating to the ship but himself, He set up for a man of all Trades, Doctor Steward Carpenter Butcher & Cook &c As for the last, I had no great reason to desire his meddling more, for I had got enough of his Cookery all the way to Cadiz of which I was heartily tir'd. As to being Carpenter we could not drive a nail or make the least Alteration in the Cabbin without his coming down with his hammer & Rule to give directions to the Carpenter (and always without being desir'd) which I took care should never be follow'd but when I lik'd them; As for Butcher that he seem'd very well qualifyd for & for ought I know better than for any thing else, and I know no Body envy'd him that post, so that he continued overseer of the shambles all the rest of the voyage. To prevent all mistakes I drew out a Regulation in writing for the Diet of both Tables every day, and for the peoples Diet too, which last I consulted him about & gave him in writing sign'd in his own Language, of which I order'd him to give the ships steward a Copy.

Another matter necessary to look after was to see how the ships stores were dispos'd of, for I found them daily cutting up sail-Cloth &c so in order to keep him within bounds & to make him take care how he squander'd such things I order'd all the Officers as Gunner[80], Carpenter, Sailmaker, Boatswain &c to bring me their Accounts of all that was made use of since they were in the ship, which being brought me I confess I could make little use of them, being such terms & names as I knew little about, & those of our People on board that

30 understood them in English names, could make as little use of them as I in the Swedish terms, so After a few days I return'd them to the Captain & never ask'd more for them, except the weekly Consumption of the ships Provisions from the steward which I order'd to be brought me regularly once a week, But as he concerted that always with the Captain & gave it first to him, I had enough to do to get it out of his hands, without asking for it more than once, But however I made him observe this method all the voyage by which means I had in my

---

sitting at which table, according to common practice in the Swedish Company. Since this is the story of the very first Swedish voyage, there could hardly have been a general custom before. When Campbell here mentions *the 2nd Table*, he is in fact referring not to the second table proper but, as he explains, to a second first table, merely because of lack of space. This circumstance was a helping hand to Campbell in his effort to separate some people who could not suffer each other.

[80] The gunner was responsible for the powder magazine, the dryness of which was one of his foremost anxieties, and for the care of the cannon, the cartridge bags etc.

power to curb him often when he pretended to dispose of the Provisions without my knowledge. He observing that I was beginning to look in to the minutest things, spoil'd no doubt a noble scheme he had form'd to himself of doing what he pleas'd & of disposing everything in the ship according to his own fancy, And he grew extremely sour & sullen upon it & set all his wits to work to rebel & shake off the yoke that he saw was ready to be put about his neck. The truth was, He had undertaken this voyage with a view no doubt to make the most of it, and fancy'd that the moment he was Captain of the ship that it & every thing in it was his own, and though I was present yet no doubt the Poor man flatter'd himself that I would give my self no trouble about the Affairs of the ship, but would leave that intirely to him, which hopes my bearing with him till I arriv'd at Cadiz had strongly confirm'd him in, But when he saw the Contrary He was almost craz'd & now & then would fly out into very Impertinent Airs, and amongst others of his wise speeches told me once that he was nothing at all in the ship and that it was a sin not to trust a Captain with the intire

31

management of every thing &c I thought proper to let him talk & preach as he pleas'd but never alter'd my measures one jot for it. But let us leave the Captain Growling & return to the Voyage.

April
20th

At 11. P.M. we fell in Amongst the Canary Islands, betwixt I. Lancerota & Forteventura[81] & pretty near the Latter, and pass'd through between them safely. The same night we observ'd among the Islands a great Light like fire in the sky, which I suppose must have been some burning mountain[82] on one of these Islands.

− 21

In the Morning pass'd to windward within a couple of English miles of the Grand Canary, which appear'd very high Land, I took a view of it as I did of several other places we passd for all which I refer to the End of this Diary where I intend to place them.[83]

As the Captain knew nothing of the navigation or Course that was proper for us to steer, yet would be always meddling & instead of taking advice of those English Officers that did know & were imploy'd by the Company for this purpose he on the contrary thwarted them as much as he could and constantly hinder'd Contradicted & oppos'd them in every thing they propos'd or found necessary to be done about the ship, and at the same time would do nothing himself but all he could to delay our voyage by ordering to make less sail & reefing every night (as

---

[81] *Lanzarote, Fuerteventura*, two of the Canary Islands.
[82] I.e. a volcano.
[83] If Campbell ever realized his intention, his drawings may have been destroyed together with the first version of the diary, when the *Fredericus R.S.* was captured by the Dutch in the Straits of Sunda.

he had been us'd to do in our passage to Cadiz constantly every Evening about sunset though in the finest weather & wind that we could wish for) The English officers being very uneasy with such Conduct complain'd to me that they could be of no service if the Captain would not let them steer & manage the ship as they thought

32 most for the Good of the voyage &c I was resolv'd to take this Affair intirely out of his hands & commit it to their Care who only understood it, I first try'd to gain him by fair means & told him that these officers were ingag'd by the Company as Pilotes to carry the Ship to East Indies as being Persons well acquainted with such voyages which none of us did & therefore It was not his part to meddle in such things as he was not so well acquainted with, but leave it to them who did &c But all my discoursing him signify'd nothing, but made him rather more troublesome & Impertinent, He would give himself Airs & say he had been this voyage before (which I scarce believe ever he was without it was when a Boy[84] or a Common sailor, for he knows nothing of any one part in the East Indies not even of those parts where he pretends to have been as I have discover'd on several Occasions by asking him about some places where he says he has been & which I know as having been there my self) and then would walk about like a very Great Person & clap his hand to his forehead, and say with an Emphasis I know &c This oblig'd me to take another method with him, and to take a little more trouble upon me than I wish'd to do by coming frequently upon Deck, and asking why he did not make more sail, and immediately order the reefs to be let out & to set our top-gallant-sails[85] &c when our officers told me it was proper, And I took care to stay upon Deck till I saw it done, I also told Capt Kitching & Mr Baron though I approv'd of their keeping fair & Civil with the Captain yet never to let his folly & obstinacy hinder them from doing what they thought for the Good of the voyage, & to make them more Easy I let them know the powers I had from his Majesty & the

33 Directors to command him &c of which I show'd them Copies & assur'd them that I would support them in every thing they should order as necessary for the voyage, And in case that after trying all other methods to perswade the Captain

---

[84] On board there were a number of trainee seamen (Swedish *jungmän*) and ship's boys over and above the complement of seamen. Ship's boys were employed as servants for the officers and senior petty officers, and for lighter tasks. In the course of time they became seamen. (Koninckx 1980b, p. 319.)

[85] Foremast and mainmast carried three rectangular sails. The foremast stood well forward and carried the foresail, foretopsail and fore-topgallant sail on the top. The mainmast was not positioned exactly amidships but a little further aft, at about 3/7 the distance from the sternpost. It was furnished with the mainsail, maintopsail and main-topgallant sail. Only at the end of the century was a fourth sail, the upper topgallant, added. The mizzen-mast was right at the stern. It carried a lateen sail, of which the fore-section was dispensed with, leaving only a trapezium-shaped sail. Above it there was still a small rectangular sail, the mizzen-topsail. (Koninckx 1980b, p. 175 f.; Röding 1794–98, 4, plates XIV and XVI.)

to let them take the proper measures if they found he would hinder them then to tell him roundly that they must complain to me that as they could not act as they judgd best for all our Good & safety & for the Companys service, they would desire to be excus'd from doing any Duty but would leave him & me to do as we pleas'd.

As it will give some light into the Conduct of this voyage, and show the reasons I had for a great many things that I was oblig'd to do for the Companys service (at least as I thought) I will take the Liberty to give the Gentlemen Directors a sketch of the Plan I form'd to my self as necessary to make this voyage succeed. And first I must take notice of the scheme he seem'd to have lay'd & the Arts & little stratagems he us'd to bring it to bear, which will make more evidently appear what reason I had to set my self betimes to countermine him. To begin then with his Plot.

As his Design was to slight my Authority, and to cast off all regard or obedience to me, in order to Rule & Govern as he pleas'd, he imagin'd he would be Able to do it by these two ways, 1st by Getting the sailors of his side. 2^d by bringing over as many of the officers & under officers to his schemes as he could, The 1st he had pretty well succeeded in, by incouraging them in Idleness, & discouraging every officer or under officer that wanted to make them mind the ships Business and do their Duty, which he had long done by Styrman Bremer in a scandalous manner, by abusing him before them, only for calling out a little loud to them to do their work; Besides he took care to give them drams of Brandy from time to time more than the Company allow'd them, and maliciously insinuated to them, after my coming on

34 board, that I was the Cause he did not do better for them than he did which I prevented as he gave out amongst them. As for his 2^d point of gaining the officers and underofficers, he did not succeed quite so well in [it], though he did all he could by calling them in every morning to his Cabbin & giving them a Dram, and treating them with wine when he had any which was what I had allow'd him sometimes, upon those Occasions he us'd to represent what a great man he was one of the Kings Captains, and that the English aboard were a parcel of strangers that hated the Swedes and had resolv'd to treat them as ill as they could, & wear them out (to wit the sailors with working) and particularly it was my fault that they had not as much wine & other things as they wanted, which he pretended they had a Right to, This some of them listen'd to with pleasure, and it might have had worse effects had not two things contributed to hinder it viz 1st He could not bring over Breemer to approve of his madness, whom he had try'd but to no purpose, the 2^d was his own folly, For he could not keep long in good terms with any of them, one day coaxing & being very familiar with them & giving them Drams & next day perhaps using them roughly or not speaking to them, It was enough to lose his favour to speak one word in opposition to his

opinion on any subject, so that there was scarce any Body stuck fast to him (especially after he had no more wine nor Brandy to give them) but Styrman Lund & the Steward (or Boteler) Almroth[86], As for the new Boatswain whom he coax'd too he was of no Great Consequence, And the Priest was too high minded and fiery to keep right with him being almost as proud as He therefore not easily brought to submit to his opinions & Tyrranical Temper, As for the Gunner whom he thought himself sure of I believe he had no ill design seeming to be a Quiet Inoffensive man.

(35)   As I soon discoverd his drift, I set myself to work to counter plot him, which I was pretty sure of succeeding in (though Most of our Gentlemen were not a little uneasy at observing his management & Bad Temper, which I am sorry to say some of them forgot soon & I have reason to think contributed by their Imprudence to make him cast off the Respect he ow'd & had sometimes show'n me) For when I consider'd his want of sense and his Intolerable Temper I could not apprehend any very bad Effects from a Person of so low a Genius. However I thought proper to take all necessary precautions to blast his views, And as I make it always a settled Rule to indeavour to gain people by Reason & Good nature before I use force or Authority I did all I could to humour him by bearing with his nonsense Impertinence & Growling & when he behav'd a little better than ordinary, (As I found he had a strong Inclination to drink and often complain'd that he had no wine to treat Capt Kitching & Mr Baron who sometimes intertain'd him with a Bottle &c) I even indulg'd him more than he deserv'd by sending him some wine that he might be kept in Good humour & hinder'd from doing any mischief amongst the People till my Authority & Power was better known & establish'd. When I found that there was no gaining him by this method, I set about executing my Plan, which was 1st by indeavouring to bring the Officers off from him, by now & then allowing them a little wine & some small things they stood in need of, by which means I thought they would see it was their Interest to keep well with me. 2dly By bringing the sailors to know their dependance upon me & the obedience due from every Body to my orders, and showing that the Captain as well as every Person belonging to the ship was under my Command. 3dly As the British (or English) on board had no reason to like to be under his Government or Command, I thought my self pretty sure of their contributing all they could to support my Authority & Power over the Captain, which was

35
[bis]   plainly their only Interest, as well as the Good of the voyage, as they often acknowleg'd, and as they were a considerable Body in regard of their Ranks & stations, I resolv'd to live in friendship & unity with them all especially the SuperCargos, & show them & the Officers all Civility, and to make the latter

---

[86] Possibly identical with *Jonas Almroth*, who sailed with the *Riksens Ständer* in 1760-62 (Koninckx 1980b, p. 345) and as 6th supercargo with the *Stockholms Slott* in 1765–67 (Kjellberg 1974, pp. 180, 202).

to have as much Command in the ship as was necessary to counterbalance the power the Captain assum'd to himself, which they evidently saw would ruin our voyage if not taken out of his Hands. The Course of this Journal will show the several{s} methods I took to put my scheme in Execution as the Circumstances of things that happen'd requir'd it, and will also show another thing I never apprehended viz the disappointment of the asistance I expected from some of those who had the greatest reason & Interest to give it to me.

The first thing necessary was to let every Body coo what footing we were all upon, & what were the Companys orders & Instructions to us all, I therefore produc'd to the Super-Cargos the Companys orders & instructions to us from Sweden, some Letters of Advice from other Friends, And then gave them to read Copies of the Powers I had from his Majesty to command the Captain & officers &c as also from the Company, with their Instructions to the Captain to pay all regard & Obedience to me, by all which it was order'd that nothing should be done in the ship without my knowlege or consent or contrary to my orders & that in case of my Death the same power devolv'd upon them each according to his Rank, Amongst other things in discourse about the voyage I told them it was our business to live in friendship & unity, which I was resolv'd to do, and that as they saw already what a strange man the Captain he was and how he would certainly ruin the voyage (especially having the sailors & some others in his Interest) if I did

36   not take the power from him & make use of that his Maj^{ty} & the Company had honour'd me with, in order to prevent his bad designs & to put things in their proper Channell for the Companys and all our Interest, which I did not question they would concur in, & contribute as much as they were able to sustain my Authority in the ship &c This was aggreed to be all right which they promis'd to do. I also took the Liberty to advise them to be cautious in their discourse before the Captain & others of some of their friends, for I knew he would make a bad use of it &c I also warn'd them that though neither Dutch nor English had any right to molest us in our voyage, yet I was apprehensive that if it should be our misfortune to meet any Dutch ships in the East Indies that if they could privately do us an Injury or hinder our voyage they would not make much scruple of doing it, A Certain Person who had a great opinion & regard for the Dutch[87] would not believe this possible, However I told him & them all that be as it will it was none of our Business to come in their way if we could shun them which I assur'd them I was resolv'd to do to the utmost of my power, But that if such a misfortune should happen The Company in Sweden had taken all the necessary precautions to prevent the ill Consequences of such an Accident, & what was the utmost security could be given was obtaining from his Majesty for me the honour of

---

[87] Campbell is referring to John Pike, 4th supercargo; cf. *Diary* p. 74.

Envoy & Plenipotentiary to the Emperour of China[88] & other Princes in the East-Indies by which not only my Person but also all theirs would be safe as being included in my Retinue, and I therefore show'd them those Commissions & Credentials I had from his Majesty; some of them had very little regard to this and I believe thought it of no Consequence, though it afterwards happen'd the only thing to preserve the ship & voyage as well as their own Persons; But it is the nature of some People never to apprehend or foresee danger till it is come

37 upon them, and that it is too late to prevent it. At the same [time] I begg'd of them not to mention to any Body, whether Swedes or English in the ship, the last Powers I had of Envoy &c because I did not intend to make use of them, but in case of absolute necessity, and that it was not at all convenient for me to be know'n under that Caracter except when such an Extraordinary Case should happen. As for this request, I believe it was punctually observ'd (for reasons obvious enough afterwards) had they as exactly observ'd the other things I desir'd of them as this, I may venture to say I should have had much less trouble than I have met with during the voyage, and they would have much better consulted the Companys Interest & the Good of the voyage.

After having discours'd the Super-Cargos, I went to Capt Kitching & Mr Baron & repeated a great part of what I told our Super-Cargos, And to make them Easy as to the Captains Conduct I gave them to read a Copy of the Power I had over from his Majesty, which I assur'd them upon every occasion necessary I would exert & desir'd them to let me know when he pretended to hinder them in their Duty or in the management of the ship when it was their turn to watch, & that they might depend upon it I would sustain them on all such Occasions, They seem'd to be very much pleas'd with all this. Whether one of them did not change his mind soon afterwards he knows best.

As some things happen'd during the voyage betwixt me & one of the Super-Cargos which much surpriz'd me, I can't help letting know the pains I took to be in a good understanding with them. Having met them all at Cadiz we were all soon acquainted & seem'd to be very good friends, As for the 2^d SuperCargo I had never seen him before, But as he was recommended by some of the Companys

38 Good friends as a very honest man & an Experienc'd Able sea Officer, and was also considerably concern'd in the stock, I was very glad of his Company, it being his Interest in a particular manner to joyn with me in all measures for the Companys service & for the Good of the voyage, As I was to use also a Command in the ship, & was not acquainted with sea Affairs my self, I thought my self very

---

[88] Colin Campbell was affirmed as minister plenipotentiary to the Emperor of China, the Grand Mogul and other Asiatic princes by King Fredrik I of Sweden.

fortunate to have such a Person about me who could on all occasions asist me to make a proper use of my power, and to give the necessary orders about the ship when my interposing was wanting; And I have not been deceiv'd in my expectations of him, having always found him a true friend to the Companys Interest, & an honest man in all Dealings, a Diligent Expert man in sea Affairs, & thereby very serviceable to me on many Occasions in things relating to the ship, which, I must do him the Justice to say had not been so well carryd on had he not been with me. As to the other two Gentlemen, It was natural enough to suppose they might have come with some prejudice against me and not without some reason, because I had made some difficulty to approve of them as fit for the stations they were recommended to and I thought I had reasons sufficient to justify my self to any Indifferent Person that was not very much prejudic'd in their favour, and I cannot say that this voyage has given me much reason to alter my opinion in relation to them, But however as the Dispute I had with some of their friends on that score was over (at least on my side) and that I had consented to their being in the stations they are in, I was resolv'd to think no more if possible of what was past, and to make the first Advances to them in order to show them that I was very willing (now that the Company had imploy'd them) to live in Good friend-ship with them for the time to come, not doubting but that they would very readily come into the same with me, it being at least as much their Interest as mine to do so, and I had perswaded my self that their friend who is a Good friend of the Companys and for whom I have a real

39   Esteem & Regard, had given them proper Advices on this head, I therefore took the first opportunity I could at Cadiz to tell them, (and more particularly Mr Pike) that I confess'd I had some dispute with their friend upon their Account and that though I had then made some Objections against them yet as on my part I had lay'd aside all prejudice to them on that Account, I was resolv'd for the future to live in good harmony with them, and I assur'd Mr Pike a more particular manner that if it lay in my power I should be very glad of any opportunity to serve him, He did not seem to take any notice of what I sayd & made me no Answer, However this did not discourage me from repeating the same to him aboard ship some days after I left Cadiz, and told him that now we were imbark'd in the same Affair together All I desir'd was to carry on the Company's service well and I made no Question but he would joyn with me in the same design faithfully, &c He made me no Reply at all. Notwithstanding of this I was firmly resolv'd to give him no reason for keeping up his prejudice against me, & rather if occasion offer'd to do him all the service I could, which I did afterwards as far as lay in my power. I repeated much the same to Mr Morford, and plainly told him my reasons of making objections against his being imploy'd as 2^d SuperCargo, & even told him some of the Persons who (by their Account of some things that had happen'd in his Conduct) had given me some prejudice to him, He justify'd himself as well as he could, And I told him that I was satisfy'd with what he sayd in his own defence and hoped that as he was capable to serve the Company, he would do it honestly &c He receiv'd my discourse very well and promis'd all I could wish, adding that he hoped to have my friendship & words to that purpose, And to do him Justice, As to his personal behaviour towards me aboard ship, It appear'd all fair & Civil, and I had no dispute with him.

I am ohlig'd to be a little more full on this subject than I could have wish'd in order to show that I did all that could be done on my part to carry on things Amicably & Easily with every Body by making even the first Advances & by taking more

40   pains to humour & bear with some People than many in my station & power in the ship I believe would have done, But it is the nature of Many to take all such Condescensions as marks of a mans being in fear of them or that he has some design upon them instead of a sign of good will as I intended it and therefore they grow more Insolent and the more they find you dispos'd to bear the more they will make you suffer, not knowing what a generous way of acting is themselves they can have no notion that others can act so different from themselves. Of this I have met I may say with daily Instances during the whole voyage, some of which will soon appear.

Notwithstanding of my firm resolution to keep well with Mr Pike, (and chiefly upon Account of some of his friends whom I also believ'd my Good friends and had often found them so and wish'd always to continue so) it was not possible for me to do it without breaking through all Rule & order & suffering every thing to go to Confusion & to the prejudice of the Companys Interest, I found that he kept very shy of me & avoided Conversation with me which I had no reason to take ill I allow but I thought it was not my business to make further Courtship to a Person that did not seem to like it, and as I saw he was of a touchy temper & apt to take things in a wrong meaning, I judg'd the best way to live well together was to let him take his own way & not force my self into a familiarity with him. But as it was evident that he harbour'd malice in his heart against me, he could not long refrain from showing it, as will appear by what I am going to relate, and which I had never related (nor did in my Journal that I kept during the out voyage which was afterwards destroy'd) had not some things afterwards happen'd at Canton by which I was convinc'd that he was fishing to find out faults (if he could) in my Conduct in order to make his Complaints in proper time & place, This makes me now to relate the several facts that pass'd, & leave the Directours to judge whether I gave him provocation for

41   such behaviour, and whether He or I was in the wrong. The first dispute (as I remember) happend thus, As by the powers I had both from King & Company the Command of the ship was taken from the Captain (whom the Directours had no Good opinion of before his leaving Sweden) and given to me, though without the name of Commander, I therefore thought it my Duty to prevent his pretending to give orders in the ship to the Companys prejudice & particularly by giving away

& squandering the Companys stores & Provisions as he had often done without my knowlege And therefore I order'd the Carpenter Gunner Steward & some others of the Officers to make use or dispose of nothing in their Custody without first acquainting of me, As for the Boatswain Sail-Makers & others I left them to the Captain & Capt Kitching to order as they judgd necessary they knowing better than I what was fit for the ships use. Another regulation I made about the SuperCargos & my self & those that din'd at our Table, in order to keep a good Oeconomy & save the Liquours the Company had allow'd us, was not to incour[a]ge drinking after Dinner or Supper, but two or 3 glasses a piece & then break up, I would willingly have brought every Body to no drinking wine between meals but as in the out-voyage we had very hot weather I did not insist upon that but allow'd them to call for a Glass of wine & water now & then as they wanted it, But as I soon saw that there was like to be made an ill use of this Indulgence by the Captain & some others by their sending for wine & wine & water upon Deck when they pleas'd, I spoke to our Gentlemen SuperCargos and told them it would be better when they wanted a Glass of wine or of wine & water to come down for it to the Cabbin, & my reason was because though I did not grudge it them yet I was not willing the Captain should take that Liberty too often as I found he was much inclin'd to do, and which their calling for it upon Deck would incourage him to do

42   I had also observ'd for some time they us'd to send a young pert Boy a servant of Mr Baron's our Chief mate to bring them wine or wine & water upon Deck, I had appointed my servant Simon & Mr Brown's servant to take care of the Liquour and every thing that was made use of for our Table, and not to let any of the Boys whether Barons or the Captains (for he had his Boys to send for Drink when he wanted it) to meddle with the Pantry or take out any wine, but when it was wanted they to give it themselves, As I knew them to be both Careful sober fellows I knew they would give a good Account of everything, I acquainted our Super-Cargos also with this, which all approv'd of & observ'd except Mr Pike who soon afterwards sent down Barons Boy to the Pantry for wine or wine & water (which he had us'd to come for before & carry up a Bottle which I suppose always return'd Empty) As I happen'd to spy him carrying up wine I ask'd him what business he had there & told him to be gone & come near the Pantry no more that if any of the Gentlemen wanted any thing Simon or Morgan Mr Brown's servant should carry it to them, which I orderd them immediately to do, This (I found afterwards) put Mr Pike in a great wrath that the Boy he sent for a Glass of wine & water was not allow'd to bring it him, though he knew there were others order'd to do it, But that was not consistent with his scheme & other peoples who very well knew that I should know how the Liquour went from those I had appointed for the Charge of it, but could not if such Boys as they pleas'd had the disposing of it, I did not know that this had given Mr Pike any offence till a few days afterwards that another thing happen'd which oblig'd me to speak to our Gentlemen about, and then He complain'd himself of this other Affair about

Barons Boy. The Affair that happen'd which brought me discourse our SuperCargos was this, Mr Pike wanted of the Gunner or Carpenter some Glass for a window for the scuttle made in his Cabbin, They according to the orders I had before given them answer'd they must acquaint me first with it, having had orders for that Purpose &c upon this He flew out in a great passion against them before several People in the steerige, and expressd himself with great contempt of my power or Authority, part of which I heard

43   my self, (being near where I was a writing) to the Gunner to whom he spoke in Dutch, as what did he value the Directour's (as the Swedes us'd to call me) Orders, that he had as much power to order as I and that he would have what he thought proper to call for in the ship &c I took no notice that I heard (being willing to bear with him as long as I could) him, but sent for the Gunner & Carpenter & desird them immediately to let him have a Pane of Glass to put in his scuttle. But this did not satisfy him, I saw him look very sour, and as allowing things of this nature without my knowlege or so much as allowing the proper Officers to speake to me first might prove of bad consequence & bring things into disorder & Confusion in the ship by giving a handle to the Captain to take the same Liberty as other people did to which he thought he had a better right than any Body in the ship except my self, For though by our Octroy & Companys Instructions they were preferr'd to him in everything, yet he show'd no regard to that but often say'd he knew me & my power but he knew nothing of the Super-Cargos, and had the folly to threaten that if I dy'd he would order as he pleas'd & laugh at the SuperCargos orders if they should pretend to meddle with any thing, By this it was plain that he stood in some Aw of me & of no Body else & that therefore it was necessary for the Good of the voyage for every Body to joyn in sustaining my power & Aw over him, who only could keep him in order & hinder him from ruining the voyage, For this reason I thought it would be best to take this opportunity to represent the things as they were to the SuperCargos, and to convince them of their own Interest and my intention to make a due use of the power I was intrusted with for all our Good. I call'd the SuperCargos into the Cabbin, and address'd my self to Mr Pike in as calm a manner as I could, showing him that he was in the wrong to be Angry with the Gunner or Carpenter for a thing they could not be blam'd for, in following the orders I had given them, of which he knew very well the reason, And that though he had as much right as I to any thing necessary

44   for him in the ship and that he knew he might have had that or any thing else for sending the meanest Boy in the ship to me to ask for it, in case he thought too much to speak to me himself, as he saw I had order'd immediately the thing in question even without his speaking, But what right He or I had was not the point for my part I pretended to no Right to any thing of that nature more than He, And I would take nothing to my self what I would refuse any of the Super-Cargos, But that it was necessary for the Good of the voyage & for order & decency sake that

John Pike. Chinese painting on mirror glass. National Maritime
History Museum, Stockholm. (Photo: Johan Jonson.)

one Person or other among us should give the proper orders for if every Body pretended to command or order he might easily foresee the Ill Consequences and what Incouragement it would give to the Captain to assume again his power of ordering & doing as he listed, So I desir'd to know whether they would choose that the Captain or I should have the Chief Command, for one of us it must be, That I thought as being only 1st Super-Cargo it was natural enough for me to have the ordering of things, as I am sure was always practis'd in such Cases, as some of them very well knew, especially that they knew it was for a Rule to my self as well as to them, And I should take care never to desire a better share of any thing than they had, But that in the present voyage I had some more reason to pretend to order, for things relating to the ship, because the Company had thought proper not to trust the Captain with it but me, and for the better inabling me to execute their orders had obtain'd for me the same power from his Majesty &c Mr Pike not being willing to understand this, fell a complaining that he thought it very hard he should be refused any thing he wanted, and amongst other discourse mention'd as a great grievance (for that lay uppermost in his thoughts) that Boy Jack should be forbid to carry him any wine and that he did not drink more wine or wine & water than any of us (which by the by his Conscience might tell him was not true) & more to this purpose, without my having given him occasion to mention it not one of us having spoke one word about Drinking or such

45 like, Though he knew very well the reason of forbidding Jacks carrying wine up upon Deck, and that the other Gentlemen were satisfyd with the reasonableness of such an order which they never disputed, yet I was willing to clear my self from doing this with any design to affront him, not knowing who the wine was going to, & immediately ordering those who had the Charge of the Pantry to carry it to them, All this signifyd nothing He went on complaining of hardships & I don't know what, so that to prevent disputes of this kind for the future I was oblig'd to open my self a little more freely and tell them that in short since it was come to this pass to dispute without rhime or reason, I would take upon me for the time to come to make use of the Powers given me & would govern as I thought most proper for the Companys Interest, and where I did not so well understand things my self I would take the advice of them who knew them best, and I must let them know that though they were intrusted with every thing relating to the Cargo & Companys stock & things relating thereto as well as I, which I would always take care to do in Conjunction with them yet none of them had any share in the Command of the ship, that was my province alone, and a province I had very little reason to be satisfyd with for my own Account since I saw it would occasion me daily plague and uneasiness and that was all I was to get by it, that I was not at all fond of the rank or title of Commanding, else I might have been Captain of the ship as well as 1st Super-Cargo, which the Directours would have willingly made me If I had approv'd of it, but as the Power they had obtain'd for me did serve the End propos'd as well as if I had been Captain,

I should think my self very unworthy of the Charge they had trusted to me if I did not make use of it for their Interest to the utmost of my power. I had reason to put Mr Pike in mind of some other things I had cause to find fault with as saying things behind my Back not very proper especially before

46   the Captain & some others who would be glad enough to hear anything to lessen me, Nor was it very prudent for him to boast of his friends & even name them, & what great service they had done the Company, which though very true yet was better not to be publish'd amongst People that were glad to make use of any thing to hurt the Company & voyage, as the Captain & Styrman Lund who had already been a chattering & saying that the Company was all forreigners and that one SuperCargo had come from England, & Mr Pike from Holland, & another from another place all to manage their different Affairs, But to prevent any longer dispute I did not touch upon these heads with him at this time, finding him a Person above all Advice, and had begg'd of him & all of them more than once never to mention such things but to little purpose. One thing happen'd to be sayd by him in this Conversation which showd he had a Jealousy of Mr Brown and without reason, to wit that if Mr Brown had done or orderd what he had done I would not have been angry with him, I assurd him of the Contrary that I would not suffer Mr Brown nor any Body to act in Contradiction to my orders given about the ship, & that I knew nothing he had ever orderd to be done, and that I did not take him to be Capable of it being very well acquainted with the nature of a Command to be kept up in a ship ever to attempt to break through it, He then gave an Instance that Mr Brown had got the Carpenter to stop up a hole behind his Bed in the Cabbin, I could not but wonder at so ridiculous an Instance, of putting a piece of Timber in a hole that let the water come into the Cabbin. In fine as Mr Brown was the Person in the ship I may say (without prejudice to any Body) the best acquainted with shipping matters, I found him a very necessary Person to advise with on most of those Affairs and as that drew me to be pretty much in Conversation with him, I suppose occasion'd this Jealousy, Another grew as angry for my advising with Captain Kitching who is an honest diligent Good Officer & a very modest man, & whom I always advis'd with too about things relating to

47   his Business, I had show'd the same Civility to Mr Baron as to him and had try'd him by asking his opinion in somethings but soon discover'd him to be a Person not at all what he & his friends wanted to give himself out for, to wit the most knowing Person in the ship, They could not bring me into that opinion, for I could see when he committed blunders well enough though I took no notice of it to him, And his Temper is quite contrary to what I expected, Positive to a vast degree, of great Assurance, conceited, and I doubt, not very knowing in his own Affairs, so that I grew soon tir'd of being very familiar with him, or troubling my self with his opinion except in Cases of Consequence where I was willing to hear what every Body had to say. I must now return to my daily plague, the Captain.

In pursuance of the method I had resolv'd on, as before mentiond, of trying to gain the Fool by Good usage first, I even indulg'd him in his favourite Inclination of Drinking; He pretended now & then to be sick and that wine was good for him, and besides that he had no wine to take a Glass in an Evening with some of his officers, with whom he had sometimes Business, & with others who sometimes treated him, that the Directours had told him at Stockholm he had no occasion to lay in wine because there would be enough of the Companys for him & us all, I answer'd him that I thought there was enough for us all to take at our meals, but that the Directours never intended to provide any Body with wine to drink between meals, That he had as much as I had and that he very well saw that I never call'd for a bottle of wine to drink with the Super-Cargos after he left the Table, & more to this purpose, He got some others to speak for him too being Afraid of his Bad humours & that it was better break through Rules to make him Easy & prevent him from falling into wrong measures, &c In fine I was prevail'd with to send him as much Florence[89] as I thought might serve him for the whole voyage to wit 60

48

Apr. 27

small flasks or Bettys[90]. This I sent him the 27th of April, but that did not last long, not above 10 days, for he took care not to lose so good an Opportunity of getting Drunk every night & inviting his officers and others to treat them which he did very plentifully while it lasted, When he had dispatch'd the Florence wine he complain'd that the Red wine did not aggree with him and that if I would spare him a little white wine it would suit him better, As I did not know the Florence was done I was resolv'd to take back what remain'd & send him some white in the room of it, I accordingly on the 9th of May let him have 12 bottles of a sweet French white wine had been bought in the Sound, & when I came to inquire after the Florence I found it was all gone. I did not know the reason at first of some [of] our SuperCargos being so earnest to let him have a little wine from time to time which I found to proceed from their getting a share of it for he ask'd them sometimes to drink a Bottle with him. In fine in 3 months time by his frequent Importunity he prevaild with me to spare him about 3 dozen of Bottles of wine of different sorts, which was not enough however to satisfy him, for he wanted more in a few days after he had got some bottles, And as I found there was no end in supplying such a Drunkard, & that he made use of it to a very wrong purpose even to ruin us all & overset the voyage by taking the opportunity of treating his officers & caballing with them against me & the English Aboard, I alter'd my measures & flatly refusd him when he ask'd me for more, telling him I had given him more than I could answer for to the Company already, and that if he could not be content to live as I did he must get it where he could, This put him in a terrible ill humour as it help'd to deprive him of the opportunity of keeping his friends true to him, & likewise check'd him in his most favourite Inclination of

May 9th

---

[89] A kind of Tuscan wine brought from Florence.
[90] *Betty*, a pear-shaped bottle covered round with straw; also called Florence flask.

getting Drunk, so that for the time after he was oblig'd to get drunk with Brandy which he did not fail to do every day. As a proof of his wicked designs, I must relate a passage Styrman Breemer told me soon after it happen'd, one

49   Evening while he had his worthy Guests with him drinking, viz to the best of my remembrance, Lund, the Priest, the Butler & some others whom I have forgot, he call'd in Breemer to take a Glass of wine, & amongst other propositions ask'd him if he would be of his side (after having complain'd of my Ill usage of the Swedish officers & sailors) Breemer reply'd he did not know what he meant, upon that the worthy Captain told him he was of the Party of the English & more stuff of that sort which I have forgot, Breemer answerd him he knew of no party, and that if instead of English they were Turks or Heathens and imployd in the Companys service he thought we should all live well together and every one mind the Companys Interest without being of parties, This put him in a passion which brought on words between them, and Breemer being too honest to disguise his mind told him plainly that if he thought to bring him into such measures he was much mistaken for he was not a man to court any Bodys favour for the sake of a dram of Brandy as others did &c.

I found it necessary to pursue my scheme of countermining him as well as I could, and therefore to find out what pass'd amongst the sailors and to have a party amongst them, I imployd Breemer to go amongst them & find out some of the best of them & incourage them & make them his friends & to bring him Account of any thing that pass'd amongst them, and for that purpose order'd him some Brandy to give them a dram when he thought proper, which is what they like above all things, He found out some honest fellows who he was sure would not enter into any wrong measures as Peter Berts[91] & Jacob Anderson the Boatswain's mate & some others.

In order to gain the sailors & make them take a liking to the English Officers I allowd Capt Kitching & Mr Baron some Brandy to give some of the best of them a dram extraordinary upon occasion & in bad weather or when they thought

(50)   proper to all the men that were upon their respective watches.

To keep the Swedish officers from running in to the Captains mad Projects I was resolv'd also to try what I could do wit[h] them by Good usage, & not only let Breemer (who I knew to be the Companys friend) but also others whom I had no so good opinion of have some wine, Brandy, Sugar, a little Tea Coffy &c which I thought they might want, as to Styrman Lund, the Priest, the Gunner & Gunners mate (whom I take to be a harmless quiet man) & others.

---

[91] Elsewhere spelt *Bartz* (*Diary* p. 260).

45

Next in order to bring the sailors to know really who was their master, & whom they most depended upon, I orderd the Butler to give no Drams nor any thing else to the people, when the Captain or any Body order'd it but my self, And took the opportunity sometimes in rainy weather or when I thought it convenient to send for the Butler on the Quarter deck & order a dram for all the ships Company, I chose to do it in publick &.before the Captains face to let them all see that it was I that could only oblige them with what they lik'd so much, and that the Captain was a person of no Consequence further than I thought fit to allow him to be. As for the sailors I must do them the Justice to say it would be no hard matter to manage them, being an Easy tractable people, and a Good Captain at their head could make any thing of them he pleas'd, for I don't find they have any malice or mutinous disposition except a very few & fewer I believe than in any ship that ever went before to the East Indies.

Another way the Fool of a Captain had to plague me & himself, was to set spys upon me, that wherever I went or whoever I spoke to they might tell him & pick up what they could hear & make their reports to him of whatever they heard me or any of the English aboard talk about, Lund had the Impudence often on the Quarterdeck to follow me close when I was walking there with any Body & talking of common things with some one or other of our Gentlemen, But as I did not much

51   value what he heard, I for some time little regarded it, till repeating his Impudence too often I turnd about to him pretty abruptly & star'd him in the face without saying anything, enough to let him know that I observ'd his Impudence; As I know the Captain set him on I did not think worth while to speak to Lund, but spoke to the Captain & told him of what I had observ'd of Lund and that if he did so any more I would expose him upon Deck, This He soon reported to him, and from that time I was deliverd from that Fools Ill manners. The Captain indeed us'd often to do the same himself, especially if he saw me with Breemer or any of the Swedes, but not in so bare fac'd a manner as Lund did, and finding I had taken notice of the others Assurance, he thought better to set other spys upon me, & one of the most notable was young Neuman who follow'd me down often to the steerige to see if I spoke to any Body there which I little regarded till one time, going down off the Quarter Deck & instead of going into the Cabbin I turn'd towards Breemers Cabbin to speak with him, The Captain observing this immediately posted Neuman after me who came & planted himself close at my Back while I talk'd to Breemer, I looking about & seeing him so near me & knowing his Errand gave him a smart reprimand for his Impudence, by which means I was no more troubled with him. But to Come to our Voyage

May 17   We saw a sail about 3 leagues off standing to the Southward, we supposd her to be a Portugueze bearing for the Coast of Brasil. We were then in 6 degrees S. Latitude.

The Super-Cargos thinking their passage to Cadiz should be pay'd by the Company, spoke to me upon the subject, And as . . . . had charg'd the Company in his Account Current for Mr Pikes passage & some others that had come to Cadiz to go the voyage believing they would allow it but at

52   the same time wrote to me at Cadiz that he did not pretend to determine the thing but desir'd me to settle it according to the orders I might have receiv'd from the Directours about it, But as it was a thing I had not thought of I never had spoke of it to the Directors, But when I consider'd that it was allow'd the Officers that came from England (as by their aggreement) I thought it not unreasonable to aggree to their having the same Privilege, but upon this Condition that if the Directours at Home did not think fit to allow it they must pay it back again, which they consented to.

All I could do to keep well with Mr Pike was to no purpose, for unfortunately the General orders I gave, which were chiefly aim'd against the Captain & for the publick benefit happen'd to meet him in the way, The one I last related given to the Steward or Boteleer was a new Occasion of offence to him, He happen'd to pay a visit some where forward out of Curiosity and as it seems it is the Custom in ships, the sailors whose business is there ask'd him to give them some Brandy by way of penalty, He presently order'd the steward to give them a few Bottles of the Companys Brandy, which he told him he could not give without an order from me, This put him in his Airs again & prov'd another great Grievance, He had an easy remedy on such occasions which was no more than telling the steward or whatever officer he wanted things of to come to me to tell me of it, and I would not have refus'd such small matters, But even that it seems was too great a Condescension for him and did not suit with his high mind. However as he took no notice to me of it I was willing to avoid a fresh dispute with him, & therefore never mention'd it to him. But I am forc'd to return to the Captain again.

It is impossible for me to remember his daily follies, and his frequent grumblings & Ill humours, which, when no other method would take with me, made him lock himself up in his Cabbin & like a forward Child not come to Table and pretend

53   to be sick, thinking {to move me} by such a method to move me (as I suppose) to come in & comply with some of his extravagant views, At first not knowing but he might be really sick I us'd to pay him a visit on those occasions, and then he put on all his looks & Airs of a man very sick, & close his hands & cast his Eyes up to Heaven & mumble over some Prayers (as he is in all things the falsest lyingest fellow ever I knew so is he the greatest Hypocrite) and then cry out all on a sudden as being in great pain, I did not know well sometimes what to think but advis'd him to call the Doctour who I thought the only Person fit to deal with him on such Occasions, But I soon discoverd this was all Grimace for asking the Doctour what was the matter with him he would smile & tell me that is niet met

dad & dat gaat straxt over, & I also learn'd that sick as he was he did not forget his dear friend the Brandy Bottle which was a never failing Cordial to him in all his sicknesses, and I believe sometimes might help to make him really sick, omitting many such pretended fits of sickness I cannot forget one which he carry'd on several days, which happen'd about the 3^d of June.

June 3^d

He happen'd in Company with some of the Super-Cargos & Officers, & fell into some reflections against me, for not using the Gentlemen & officers of the 2^d Table well in not allowing them victuals enough for them, but that He could not help for it was my orders, some of the Gentlemen present (I believe Mr Morford) answerd that it could not be my orders for he had seen them or heard me mention them and that in the Regulation for their Allowance I had orderd, if the daily allowance was not sufficient, to let them have so much more as Breemer & the rest should judge necessary, This he denyd & to justify what he alleg'd produc'd my written Order by which they convinc'd him that He

54

was in the wrong (if it is possible to convince such an Obstinate Conceited Fool of ever being in the wrong) and that it must be their own fault if they wanted, Being inform'd of what had passd I ask'd Breemer how it came to pass that they had not enough of victuals after the orders I had given to let them have more (in case the ordinary allowance was not sufficient) when he should demand it, Mr Breemer discover'd to me the whole secret, He sayd the Allowance was very well but that sometimes the Pork being very fat did not answer for so many, and that he had according to my orders gone to the steward and demanded some more or sometimes Beef instead of it or other things, but that the steward refus'd to give him any telling him that he could not because he had the Captains Orders to the Contrary. I resolv'd not to let slip this opportunity of checking him for such an open breach of obedience & of orders given him under my hand which I had told him always to explain or give a Copy of to the steward (but which it seems he never did) so at Table I told him I wonderd how he could so mistake my orders about the Allowance of the 2^d Table & pretend to give orders to the Steward quite contrary to mine, & make him refuse Mr Breemer an Addition to their Allowance when he call'd for it, that since I found he did not think fit to let the steward know my orders I would take another method for the future and not trust to him any more but send them directly to the Steward, and I would take care he should obey them, & if he pretended to make any difficulty to do so, he should not be long Steward and I should find another that would know better how to do his Duty. This nettled him extremely, but had not a word to reply in his own defence, but however to raise his spirits & get Courage to attack me Assoon as we rose from Supper he retird to his Cabbin & apply'd to his Brandy Bottle which he was not sparing of, for soon after he came out upon Deck very drunk, & immediately accosted me in an Impudent manner

55 chattering a great deal of Impertinence, which observing him to be drunk [I] did not care to answer but desird him to let me alone & not to trouble me at present that I would settle all that next morning, But the Brandy having made him very stout he continued teazing me & prating in a bullying manner, I willing to shun talking with him left him & went to the other side of the Deck, He followd me & begun again in the same impertinent strain, So that I had enough ado to keep my Temper, However was oblig'd to tell him I was not in a humour to hear him at present and that he might say & allege what he pleas'd I would have no manner of discourse with him, & with some emotion told him to let me alone. Upon which he retir'd in great rage to his Cabbin, where he lock'd himself up for many days & acted to admiration his usual farce of being sick by sad lamentations to every body that went to see him, and by sending for the Doctor 6 or 7 times a day, and spreading abroad about the ship by his Emissaries that he was very bad & would die & that I was the Cause of it, I was resolv'd none of these little Arts should have any effect upon me more or make me alter the measures I had purpos'd to pursue for the time after with regard to him, So that during all the time of this his Retirement I never went to see him, nor took no notice that I knew of his being sick, only desir'd the servants to ask him what he wanted of victuals or Drink & to let him have it. Sick & dying as he pretended to be yet his heart was as whole & wicked as ever, for all the while he was lock'd up he had his Cabal of Fools about him as Lund, the Priest & others, where no doubt he represented to them that I would kill him by ill usage &c Being however tir'd of being sick and taking some physick (as I believe he did sometimes to carry on his farce the better) he was resolv'd to use one stratagem more with me, which was to imploy his

56 Favourite & Prime Minister Lund to talk to me & to represent his Condition as very desperate, which Commission he executed punctually, For he came to me while walking the Deck and bemoan'd the Captains terrible Condition saying he was extremely sick and he did not know what would become of him, nay that he was afraid that he would make away with himself If I did not take some notice of him & comfort him & do all I could to make him Easy, &c As I soon perceiv'd that he was imploy'd by him to talk so & by the drift of his discourse found that the sore which gave him all his pain was that I would put any Trust in any body in the ship but himself or allow any Body else to pretend to meddle with any thing but that all the management of Affairs should be committed to him solely & intirely, I well knowing that Lund would repeat every word I sayd to him was glad of the opportunity of opening my mind & showing my thoughts & opinion of him with all the freedom I could, by telling him what a bad Character I had heard of him in Sweden soon after he was ingag'd in the Companys service, & what I had seen of his Obstinacy Dilatoriness & other bad behaviour there, and how notwithstanding of all that I had supported his Character against his Enemies and even against some Insinuations of some of the Companys best friends as well as mine, always flattering my self with the hopes that the Oath he had taken

to the Company, the Directours kindness to him in Sweden, their orders & Instructions to him, the Commission I had from his Majesty of having the Chief Command, my being Directour & having a hand in imploying him in so Good a Post, and above all If he had no sense of his Duty I believ'd the sense of his own Interest would have made him complying & obedient to me especially when I requir'd nothing of him but to let me promote the Companys service to the best of my power, & in all other things {& in all other things} he was as well treated as he could wish

56[92] nay better than I or any Body in the ship was, But I knew well what put him so often in such strange humours to wit, that I should allow the officers the Company imployd to carry their ship to the East Indies to have any manner of Command in their several stations or give them leave to do their Duty or any thing relating to the ships Business, that I could not help wondring at his Assurance to let such thoughts enter into his Pate, & that he was not sensible of his own Ignorance as to the Navigation to India of which he did not know the least thing as was evident by many Instances (some of which I told him) that a man of sense & one who really regarded the Companys Interest would have been glad to have had such officers with him, who were perfectly acquainted, by long Experience, of such a Voyage, and who were ingag'd on purpose as Pilotes to show him & all our own People the Course & way how to carry on a voyage that none of them had any knowlege of, And if he were so silly as to believe I would trust him with the management of things he understood nothing of he would find himself mightily deceiv'd, for In fine I was resolv'd to command & govern the ship & every thing relating to the voyage as I thought best and most for the Companys Interest, by the advice of such people as I thought best Able to asist me, and that he ought to joyn in the same design, by aggreeing to every thing that I by the help of such Advice should think most for all our Good, that in other things he had the Chief Command of the officers & sailors, and that if he would cheerfully comply and obey & asist to see my orders obeyd, as was his Duty, I should always live friendly with him & show him all the Civility I could, and that was all the Consolation I could give him, But that I never would any more let him have it in his power to ruin the voyage by his Obstinacy Ignorance & Unaccountable humours, that

58 if he were wise he had best alter his Conduct, & then he might live as happy as he pleasd or could reasonably desire. This no doubt & other things I sayd that I have now forgot were faithfully repeated to the Captain, And he thought fit soon after to come out of his Retirement & behave very quiet for a day or two, which was a long time for him to continue in any tolerable temper.

---

[92] Error for *57*.

During this pretended fit of sickness of the Captains there happen'd an Affair which I believe was concerted by him & some of his Rascally friends, To wit about the 4th of June Mr Breemer went forward to order the people to do something about the sails, upon which the Boatswain was very insolent & told him to go about his Business for he had no Business there that being his post, & in short refus'd to do what was commanded, This put Breemer in just Anger which made him give the Boatswain some warm Language, upon which the fellow had the Impudence to fly at him & take him by the hair of the head cursing & swearing that if it were not out of regard to his own soul he would kill him &c I being soon inform'd of what had happen'd came upon the Quarter Deck & call'd for the Boatswain & ask'd him how he came to be guilty of such open mutiny & have the Impudence to touch or make use of the least bad Language to his Officer, He had little to say for himself but general stuff of Breemers using him & them all very Ill &c upon which I reprimanded him severely telling him I would take care to have him punish'd as he deserv'd, In the meantime I told him I suspended him from his Post of Boatswain, & forbid him to come upon the Quarter Deck or in my sight any more, and then, being highly provok'd, I kick'd him off the Deck. I would have punish'd him more effectually, but that I thought there was some villainous plot at bottom & that the Rascal could not [have] had so much impudence without having been push'd on to it by the Captain & Officers & people whom I knew the Captain from the beginning had stirr'd up as much as he could against Breemer, and as the Captain was now lock'd up there was no holding a Court Martial till he was pleas'd to come out, so that I did not

care to venture to stretch my Authority further at that time for fear of not being able to go through with it and of being obeyd by the officers & People (many of whom I found afterwards to be in the plot) which would have prov'd of dangerous consequence all the rest of the Voyage. However I was glad to imbrace the opportunity of turning the fellow (who was very Ignorant of his Business) out of his Post, and put a better man in it, And therefore ask'd Capt Kitching Mr Baron & Mr Breemer who they thought fittest, There were 2 or 3 nam'd as Eklund & Hultyn Quarter masters, & Jacob[93] the Boatswain's mate, each of whom I call'd upon & offer'd to advance to the post of Boatswain, which they all refus'd, saying that they did not like to take any Body's Bread from him, so that all I or the Officers could say to them could not perswade them to accept of it. Soon after this Affair showd its Authors & discover'd that my suspicions were not without ground, For notwithstanding of my orders to the Boatswain not to come upon the Quarter Deck (which I did with a view chiefly to keep him from coming near the Captain) yet I was inform'd that sometimes in the Dark & when I was not upon Deck he would sneak in to the Captain's Cabbin with several others of the Captains Council[94] who set their heads to work to destroy Breemer in my opinion & to save

June 4

59

---

[93] *Jacob Anderson* (cf. *Diary* p. 49). *Jacobs* on p. 24 is probably an error (note 69).
[94] Cf. note 95 below.

the Boatswain, These Consultations produc'd a Letter or memorial from the Boatswain directed To me & the Captain, observing the Direction I would not receive the Letter but sent it back ordering to tell him if he had any thing to write to direct it to my self for I was in no Partnership with the Captain, & that he might do what he pleasd with it. Upon this he carry'd it to the Captain, who next morning came from his Retirement down to me (putting on the Air of a very sickly person) with the Letter in his hand, and after having told me what he had receivd from the Boatswain, fell

60 a justifying the Boatswain as much as he could and blaming of Styrman Breemer, which strange conduct provok'd me very much and I told him that As for that Letter I had nothing to say to it, as not being address'd as it ought, for I was not in Company or Partnership with him, This I sayd on purpose to mortify him and then told him I could not but wonder that he could make so light of an underofficer flying in the face of his superiour & in so gross a Manner or that he could be guilty of taking the part of a Rascal that was guilty of open & direct mutiny & more to the same purpose, and that In short I would have a Court Martial call'd immediately and have him punish'd as he deserv'd, He not willing to have a Court Martial desir'd I would hear what he had to say for himself which I consented to, In the meantime he went out to bring the Articles of war[95] & whether he then spoke to Breemer to forgive him or no I can't tell, but on his return I sent to call Mr Breemer & the Boatswain in the Captains Presence, And after having perus'd the Letter & heard Breemer I ask'd the Boatswain how he came to be guilty of such Mutiny, He had nothing to say to Justify himself but he was sorry & ask'd Mr Breemer's Pardon for what he had done, I told him that was not satisfaction enough, so made the Captain read over some of the Articles of war to him & to

---

[95] *Articles of war*, disciplinary code for the Navy, but also in use in the Company. The same powers were granted to ship's captains or masters as to naval officers with regard to the maintenance of discipline among the crew. Notwithstanding the word 'war' in the title, the articles applied in peace as well as during hostilities. Instructions prescribed two kinds of ship's court: a general one and a mixed one. The former had jurisdiction over officers, petty officers, seamen and cadets. The court was convened by the captain, who acted as president *ex officio*; he was assisted by six officers. The supercargoes had no vote but might attend as observers. They could submit their observations to the Company directors in writing. However, they might urge the captain towards justice on condition of their refraining from this course. For offences committed by supercargoes, assistant supercargoes, purser and cabin cook, and also by the first supercargo's servant and by the captain himself, a mixed ship's court was assembled. This court was composed of supercargoes and their assistants together with officers, totalling seven in all. In both courts the ship's writer entered up the court minutes, and sentencing was in accordance with the Swedish Legal Code, the Directives of the Government dated 2 May 1685 and the Articles at Sea (or of War). Punishment was awarded by the court by simple majority vote. This dual system of justice arose from the fact that a Company ship was on the same footing as ships of war as far as discipline was concerned. At the same time a Company ship was a merchantman, which perhaps offered the crew some protection against a captain who was too severe. This measure was unthinkable in men of war.

It is not at all certain whether a sitting of the ship's court was held for every offence. The impression is that punishments were pronounced immediately upon detection of offences, without any formal procedure, but mostly when settling of quarrels remained in vain. (Koninckx 1980b, p. 365 ff.)

show him the greatness of his Crime which deservd no less punishment than Death, This frighten'd the poor fellow heartily, & he earnestly begg'd Pardon And Breemer who is a good natur'd man very readily came into forgiving him & ask'd me to Pardon him this time, I ask'd Breemer if that was all the satisfaction and if he would not have a Court Martial to try him, He answer'd he desir'd no other satisfaction and begg'd that I would insist upon no more, which I was prevail'd to consent to, & made the Boatswain go ask M\u02b3 Breemer Pardon for his Impudence which he did with all submission, Breemer also he ask'd he might be restor'd to his Post, which I also aggreed to, (as not knowing

61 whom to get to fill it) upon his promise of Amendment & behaving with all respect to all his superiour officers, and of being brisker & more diligent in his Duty & making the people also do theirs & the work requir'd of them &c But before I dismiss'd him I was willing to find out who had help'd him to draw up that Letter for I told him I knew very well that he could not do it himself, He confess'd that the Gunner had made the Letter and that his Boy had wrote it out fair from the Gunners Draught, I ask'd him if any Body else was asisting in it He sayd he did not know but that the Priest & steward had seen and read it over before he sent it to me. Upon this I dismiss'd the Boatswain & sent for his Boy who confirm'd what is now related. I then call'd the Gunner & told him I had expected better things of him than to incourage or take the part of an underofficer against his superiour as he had done by such a strange Letter &c He had little to allege for himself, but that Breemer had abus'd him &c However promis'd not to meddle in such things for the time to come, & that I should have no reason more to find fault with him, The cause of his malice to Breemer (as well as of all the rest) was owing to his putting them in mind of their Business now & then which the Gunner (as well as all the rest) much wanted to do{)} though a Kings Officer, for he is lazy & Indolent and no sea main[96] and knows very little how to act at sea, whatever he may be fit for ashore; As for his Indolence & neglect of the ships Business, which I have been often oblig'd to tell him of, it is chiefly owing to the Captain who is eternally imploying him about drawing of Draughts & views of Land, & other things which are of little or no service to the ship, for otherwise the man is a quiet Inoffensive Person. And to do him & the Boatswain Justice they behav'd both much better afterwards, & gave no occasion for any more disturbance. I call'd the steward also who acknowlegd he had read the Boatswain's

62 Letter but had no hand in the drawing of it, that on the Contrary he had seen another Draught, which was more abusive of Breemer, & which he advis'd them not to make use of, I reprimanded for what he had done & for meddling in Affairs that did not belong to him & advis'd him to mind his own Business well, and that would be Enough for him. I would gladly have got a sight of their first Draught mention'd by the steward, but they had destroy'd it.

---

[96] *Sic*, for "man".

Having mention'd the Gunner's being imployd by the Captain in drawing of maps &c brings me to my remembrance what the Captain has often told me to wit that he would give the Company upon his Return the finest Maps that ever were seen of the East Indies, that they would have no occasion to trust any more the Dutch Draughts or any other, for that none of them would be comparable to his, I answer'd him that I made no question of that (meaning the last part of his speech) upon which he would show me a Rough draught of what the Gunner had begun, I had enough ado to keep my Countenance especially once he show'd me some bearings he had taken of the Coast of Java as we pass'd along, He & the Captain took every point of the main Land they saw to be Islands and set them down so in this Extraordinary map, and as the Captain sayd no other map had taken notice of these Islands he would give names to them himself, I told him to go on that it would be a great Curiosity and no doubt very Acceptable to the Gentlemen of the Company as I perswade my self it will by affording them a little diversion, if ever he shows it to them. He added that he would present also one of them to his Majesty which he believ'd would be very Acceptable.

I had almost forgot to take notice of a piece of silly malice the Captain show'd against Styrman Breemer in the Affair before related, which was among other Complaints of Breemer's bein[g] in the wrong he say'd what had happend was an Affair of

63   very great Consequence, which he could not tell how to behave in with regard to Breemer who had spoke against the King of Denmark, By this he thought to frighten me from taking Breemer's part, But I having heard before the Occasion of this foolish charge, to wit that Breemer had call'd the Boatswain a Dane & no Swede but that he would let him know that he was now in the Swedes service, I ask'd him how he could imagine that those words were speaking against the King of Denmark, or how the Boatswain could be angry to be call'd what he really was born a Dane, But had he sayd much more than was alleg'd, how did that clear the Boatswain from that Act of mutiny &c

Another Circumstance that shows what a Tartuffe[97] he is (that is as far as his shallow parts inable him) when he came & brought me the Boatswains Letter he told me, that there was a Petition of the Boatswains about an Affair He knew nothing of before, though the Boatswain (as I told before) had been many times privately with him after it happen'd. But this is nothing to what he had the folly to tell me another time, As he wants much to pass for a Saint & a Person not capable of committing any fault or even mistake, & how good a Conscience he has &c He told me once very seriously, introducing his discourse with blessing

---

[97] Character in Molière's comedy of the same name (1664), hence used as the epitome of a moral and religious hypocrite. An edition of Molière's *Oeuvres* was to be found in Campbell's library, which was sold after his death (*Förtekning öfver … Colin Campbell's Bok-Samling …* 1758, p. 51).

of God, that he never had come near any woman in his Life but his own wife, I answerd him that he must be a very Extraordinary man, He reply'd with a very demure look that upon his word it was very true. Another time he with the same manner of blessing of God Almighty affirmd that he never had been drunk in his Life, though at the same moment unluckily for him he was really fuddled (as indeed he is for the most part every day & often more than once) I could not help staring him in the face & telling him that I was not blind & could easily see when People were Drunk

or when they were sober, without being told of it, This Answer struck him Dumb of a sudden, which was all I wanted, nothing being so nauseous as to hear him prate nonsense which he has ever an inclination to do while he can get any Body to hear or Answer him.

After the Affair of Breemer with the Boatswain I was in hopes that the Captain & all his friends would grow better. But I soon found that it is not possible for him ever to mend. I may with reason Compare him in his mad humours with a Tiger or some wild beast let loose, when I keep him under & at a distance he grows quiet for a day or two, But the moment I turn sociable or commonly Civil to him (which I don't know how to help being when he behaves anything tolerably) he then springs out of all bounds and returns to his former fury till I chain him up again to his Good behaviour. He not being at all satisfy'd with my having left off furnishing him with wine to gratify his debauch'd Appetite and inable him to keep up his Drunken Companions in his schemes, he was resolv'd to make one Attempt more upon that subject, and with great Assurance told me that wine & every thing on board was designd for the use of the Officers and that they ought to have it as they wanted it &c nay went further and sayd the Directors in Sweden had promis'd that the sailors should have wine & water when the Beer was out[98], This malicious Lie provok'd me & I told him I wonderd he was not ashamd to assert a thing that he knew to be false of having promisd the sailors wine & water, and how he could put such notions Either in the Officers or Peoples heads, & ask'd him if that was consulting the Companys Interest or not? That in short

---

[98] About the use of wine, water and beer Colin Campbell is telling the truth. Normally the crew had beer or water, but the beer had to be consumed first, for that beverage quickly turned sour in warmer climates. It was only after these stocks had been exhausted that the issue of drinking-water began. In actual fact, the beer was a malt-based beverage (light beer, Swedish *dricka* or *svag-dricka*) with a maximum alcohol content of 0.18%. Its ration, just the same as drinking-water, was one stoup a day per man (=1.3 litres). The beer was often mixed with other ingredients. *Flip*, for instance, was beer mixed with distilled spirits and sugar. In cold regions and in bad weather the captain supplied the entire ship's company with spirits, but in any event they would not be drunk neat but mixed with one third of water. In Cádiz, the ship's company had sherry every Sunday. Punch was served as well, but then to replace the porridge ration. Sometimes *gloria* was issued, pre-pared from boiling water, tea, sugar and spirits. As for wine, it was reserved for the top table, and occasionally for the second one. However, drinking matters appear to have caused serious problems among officers on board.

the officers had wine enough & they should have no more nor he either, and for the sailors they must be content with water now that the Beer is done, so I expected he would trouble me no more with such nonsense. Upon this he lock'd him self up sick, according to Custom for two or 3 days. I often wish'd to my self this

65   voyage that the Company had allow'd no wine to any of us neither SuperCargos nor Officers, but have been obligd to buy for ourselves that every Body might drink as they pleas'd, which would have made me much Easier than I have been, For I may venture to say that this very Article has been the Chief Cause of all the plague & Trouble I have had, & even from some people that ought to have had a better way of thinking, For had I consented to the squandering the Companys Liquours & allow'd Super-Cargos (I am asham'd to say it of some even of them) and Officers to drink as they pleas'd, I should have been enough in their Good Graces and might have acted in other things as they pleas'd without any of their growling or finding fault with me. But though some of them did not deserve it at my hands I resolv'd to take better care of them & not let them live in plenty for a month or two & starve the rest of the voyage, as I have been inform'd happen'd in a Certain voyage to India where the Chief Super-Cargo, not having resolution or power enough to keep the rest & the Captain to any order, had the mortification to see Casks of wine brought upon Deck and there remain while every one of them swill'd as much as they pleas'd out of their mugs & Kans or what they could find to Empty it in. But to leave a while such disaggreeable subjects which I am sorry I have so many to fill this Journal with, I must shift the scene & turn to something that is more diverting or rather Ludicrous, of which the Priest was the Chief Actour.

The Priest it seems is no Lover of Butter, And it happen'd one morning he ask'd of the Surgeons mate to give him something that was good, (expecting perhaps some good Cordial Dram which I suppose he has not the same Aversion to as to Butter) The Doctor's mate out of a frolick takes a bit of Bread he had then in his hands & puts a little butter upon it which he gave him saying that was something very Good, The Priest putting it in

66   his mouth soon discover'd what it was, and in a great passion bawl'd out he was poyson'd, & went directly to his Friend the Captain full of indignation to Complain that He had ask'd the Doctors mate for some Physick (being indispos'd) and he had given him Poyson, and desir'd he might be call'd to an Account for it. The Captain inquiring into the Affair found out the Truth. But this occasion'd a great Quarrell betwixt the Priest & the Doctor's mate, which the Priest could not put up, and was resolv'd to be reveng'd of Jacobson in the most publick manner, for the Sunday after, in his serom[99] he fell upon the subject of poysoning, & say'd

---

[99] Accidental misspelling of *sermon.*

that it was but too Common for wicked People when they bore malice against another to mix Poyson in their meat or Drink nay even in their Physick, (with more to that purpose) and pray'd that God Almighty might deliver them All from such vile Persons &c The Doctors mate being present & hearing himself so pointed at, thought of being reveng'd in his turn which he did by absenting from prayers & sermon, for some time, which the Priest made use of for a new cause of Complaint, and Jacobson being ask'd why he did not come to Church or to prayers, he say'd he could not come with a safe Conscience since he could [not] reap benefit either by the Prayers or sermon of such a man who rail'd at him so maliciously before all the People. If this matter had gone no further it was well enough, but it had like to have prov'd of bad Consequence for it having gone about amongst the sailors that the Surgeon's mate was a Poisoner a good many of them were afraid to take any Physick from him when they were sick. But to come to our voyage.

June 13 We found our selves to day in soundings off the Cape of Good Hope[100], as our officers expected, in 87 fathom[101] water green mud, Thus far we had a fine passage, fair winds, moderate weather, & no Calms, so that we got so far from Cadiz in about 2 months to a day. This brings to my mind a passage that happen'd to the Captains Mortification as it

67 discover'd his great Ignorance of our navigation to every Body & even to his best friends, and was the means of saving all of us from the daily plague of hearing him prate nonsense about our Course & Navigation, any more the rest of our Out-Voyage, About a fourtnight before we got so far he had been teazing the officers & every body that we would be off the Cape of Good Hope in 4 days, As the thing was impossible with the fairest wind that could blow people laugh'd at him But he insisting on it and at last telling me the same stupid story, I Ask'd him How he could think so, seeing we were so many hundred leagues from it; No matter for that He knew very well pointing his finger to his wise noddle, upon this I resolv'd to humble him by taking this opportunity to expose his Ignorance, and told him

---

[100] Generally, the Cape was not rounded within visual distance but more towards the south: it was rather the Bank of the Cape, the shallows of Cape Agulhas, that were mentioned in ship's journals, their proximity being estimated by sounding. The bank extends beyond lat. 36° S., and its depth fluctuates around 200 metres. Out in the Atlantic Ocean, the Cape and the Bank announce themselves by the pintados or Cape pigeons, albatrosses and whales, and sometimes seals. No wonder the passage of the Bank of the Cape was intensely and closely watched. It was one of the few objective points available for observation after cruising off the Canaries, for few Swedish ships actually sighted the Cape Verde Islands, and even fewer the small islands off the South American coast such as Santa Trinidad or Tristan da Cunha. There are two reasons why the Swedes did not sail within sight of the Cape. Firstly, they hoped to avoid a region of frequent storms (hence – and with good reason – the name of Cape of Storms, as it was called in earlier times). Secondly, the alternative route offered the opportunity of capitalizing upon favourable ocean currents. Before 1759 no Swedish ship stopped at the Cape; even then it happened during the voyage home. (Koninckx 1980b, p. 130.)

[101] Unit of measurement for the depths of the sea, or the lengths of rope; approximately 6 feet.

I wish'd I had a good wager on that score, He answer'd He would lay any wager I pleas'd, not being willing to deal with him my self that way I brought on the subject at Dinner telling the Captain was so sure of being off the Cape in 4 days that he offer'd to lay a wager for any sum of money with any Body that would take him up, upon which Mr Brown told him he would lay the wager with him & would be so fair as give him ten days instead of four, The Captain immediately struck & the wager was lay'd for 10 Spanish Dollers[102] that we should not be off the Cape or have the Cape of Good Hope directly North of us in 10 days, It was express'd so particularly that he might [not] have a hole to creep out at as he generally indeavourd to have when he was found out in any blunder by giving another turn quite contrary to what he had say'd before, The Gunner & others who had heard of his wager soon show'd him his mistake for he was pretty quiet afterwards upon the head, but gave it

68   just the turn we expected, to wit that he only meant we should be in the Latitude of the Cape in 4 days, notwithstanding of its being express'd as above related, However I resolvd not to lose so good a proof of his Ignorance & to bring People to have a right opinion of him as well as the other officers who know much more of their Business than he did, hinted it to severals & particularly to his Chief Counsellour Lund who own'd him in the wrong but thought to bring him off by saying he must have meant as before mention'd. However as he appear'd pretty humble upon the subject of our Course & navigation for a good while we all shun'd the putting him out of humour by putting him in mind of his wager. But one would not believe that a man that had been so long at sea could be so Ignorant of his Trade if they did not see it as we do daily, And as for an Account of the voyage he seems to keep no other than that of the Log-Book[103], (our English Officers have brought them into the method of) and by pricking down on his Chart every days Run from that, If he keeps any other Account he must be obligd to the Gunner who is constantly writing with him, But we must refer this till he returns when the Company will see what a noble Journal he has kept.

I forgot to relate that a few days before we got into soundings off the Cape, meeting with squally weather and a great sea as is usual hereabouts, the Cook could dress no victuals for the ships Company by reason of not being able to keep any fire in[104], which dispos'd some of them to mutiny[105], for in the night as C. Kitching

---

[102] See note 40 above.
[103] On board there was generally a single ship's log, kept up-to-date by the officer of the watch. Course, wind, depth of water and mileage were entered in it, and it was used as a day-to-day working document. On the other hand, more than one ship's journal or deck journal were occasionally maintained. (Koninckx 1980b, p. 112 f.)
[104] Although smoking was allowed on board, open fires were forbidden except in the galley. Fire getting out of hand was in fact the greatest danger threatening wooden sailing-ships.
[105] Mutiny was considered the heaviest crime of all, not only because of the insult to the commander but also in view of the dramatic consequences, especially during long-distance voyages.

had order'd one of them to hand the sails or do something about them one of the fellows call'd out let them work that had victuals for they would not because they had got no supper or to that Purpose, The rest joyn'd in the same discourse; And though Styrman Lund

69 was upon the main Deck and heard these mutinous words yet did not think proper to check them for it, next morning being inform'd of this Insolence & folly of the sailors without any reason, since they fard as well as any of us not having had any victuals dress'd more than they, I thought this a proper opportunity to check all such tendencies to mutiny for the time after by making an Example of the Ring-leader of them, I therefore made inquiry who began it, but Lund though he knew very well being just by them when it happend & own'd he had heard one of them express himself as above related would not discover who he was pretending he did not know, I sent for the Cook & ask'd him what he knew of the matter he sayd there were severals of them and amongst the rest nam'd one Skarpe & some others who not only then but daily were plaguing him about their victuals, and had beat & abus'd him on this occasion, I then call'd for the Captain & some others into the Cabbin to examine Skarpe who being call'd did not deny what was alleg'd against him, but say'd they were all as Guilty as He, upon this I orderd Skarpe to be put in Irons[106] & went with the Captain & others into the steerige to see it done, while they were putting the Irons upon him all the sailors came to the steerige Door pleading for Skarpe & saying that he had sayd no more than many others, & that they had great reason to complain of the Cook for he was so Nasty & dress'd their victuals so very Ill that they could not Eat them, & some of the poor fellows fell a crying when they saw their Comorad[107] in Irons, upon which I not knowing but they might have some reason for their Complaints against the Cook & mov'd by all their Concern & pleading orderd the Irons to be taken off & Skarpe to be set at Liberty, I then spoke to him & all the ships Company reproving them for their mutinous behaviour & warning them

70 to beware of such a fault for the time to come, and advising them if they had any thing to Complain of to send their Complaints to me or the Captain in a regular manner by the Boatswain & not to get into a Body & make noise or disturbance which I would not allow of & would certainly punish the first time that any of them were found Guilty, They all promis'd very fair, & so I dismiss'd them, But believing the poor fellows had some Grounds of complaint against the Cook observing him to be very dirty, & hearing he never had been a Cook before, but a poor old Invalid who had sail'd formerly with the Captain & put into this post by

---

[106] Giving orders to have a sailor put in irons was strictly speaking not within a first supercargo's competence, not even as a director of the company, since only the captain or a ship's officer had jurisdiction over the crew. In view of Trolle's general behaviour Campbell's action is understandable, but it was precisely situations such as these that served to increase the ambiguity of the first supercargo's and the captain's relative positions.

[107] *Comrade.*

him because he was not fit for a sailor having lost some of his fingers & lame in his hands, I told the Captain of it & desir'd him to see if he could get any other fit for that Post and who would be more Acceptable to the People, upon which the Captain ask'd Skarpe if he would be Cook, to which Skarpe answer'd he would provided the old Cook were taken away from the kitching[108] and that I would give him some more sailors pay, which I promis'd him, and desir'd the Captain to speak to the old Cook, which he did & was very willing to quit his Charge, aggreeing (as the Captain told me) to have so much of Cooks pay taken from him & given to him who succeeded him.[109] So we got over this Affair, the ships Company were made Easy and Skarpe prov'd a Good Cook & pleas'd them all & behav'd very well to his Death, for we had no Complaints about their Eating while he liv'd.

June 14 Sounded again in 95 fathom gravelly sand with Oase[110]. We now propose to go on our Course & make if possible St Pauls & Amsterdam[111]

Not long after this, finding that all I could say to the Captain and all that I had yet done both by fair Civil usage & by Reproof made no effect upon him longer than a day or two, still returning to his mad rebellious humour without rhime

71 or reason, & still continuing to cabal & make a Party both amongst the officers & sailors against me, of which we all apprehended the Consequences if suffer'd longer to go on as it had done, upon which I resolv'd upon one method more to show every man in the ship my superiority over him & to put it always before their Eyes that they might not forget their Duty & dependance upon me, which was, by drawing out fair a Copy of Her Majestys Commission to me to Command the Captain officers &c and that nothing should be done in the ship without my orders or Consent &c and pasting it on a piece of board & nail it to the Mizen-Mast to be in every Bodys sight & power to read, which I did without giving him any hint of what I was about, and which he knew nothing of till he saw it nail'd to the mast, which put him in great wrath & made him tell a friend of mine that

---

[108] *Kitchen.*

[109] It was quite unusual that one of the crew could enjoy a higher pay when taking over somebody else's function. Wages were normally settled once and for the whole voyage when recruitment took place before the departure from Gothenburg. This was the general rule when someone succeeded in the function of another man who died, even when it meant promotion for the successor (e.g. when a third mate became second mate, or a second surgeon became first surgeon). The same applied to supercargoes and their assistants.

[110] *Oase*, obsolete form of *ooze*.

[111] Ships bound for Bengal or China set course for *St. Paul* or *New Amsterdam*, although the latter name is hardly ever mentioned in Company documents. These two islands were of great importance, because when sighted or indicated by soundings, the ships used to change course. Their importance was equal to that of the Cape Bank. They were reference points in the ocean, in the zone of the westerlies, and also the terminus of the eastward course. Sometimes it was the first land seen after the Canary Islands.

I had done him a great Affront in exposing him to all the ships Company by putting his name in a paper upon the mast &c He was answerd he had not reason to take that as an Affront since my name was there as well as his & even her Majestys &c But not being able to bear this attempt to make him little as he thought amongst his own people (as he call'd them) he was free enough to throw some reflections upon me, and amongst other nonsense, in which he is generally very fluent, he sayd that it was an Article of the Octroy and the Companys orders that there should be no Language spoke in the ship but Swedes and that at Table I & the SuperCargos & Officers ought to speak no other Language &c I mention this as a specimen of his wonderful understanding to fancy People should speak a Language they knew not one word of or never heard spoke before. But we had often such Instances of his wisdom which gave us matter of Diversion & Contempt but more frequently matter of Anger. In fine I found he had a great mind to speak to me about this Affair often telling me what a sin it was & a hard-ship

72 to be Captain of a ship & not to be trusted with the management of Affairs,[112] especially that no man had a better Conscience than He & that all his view was to promote the Companys service & such stuff, but did not come directly to the point of the Commission I had naild up, But as I was well us'd to such Impertinence and resolv'd to keep my Temper with him (though to continue to pursue the measures I had layd down to my self) seldom made him any Answer, thinking it the more prudent way not to give him the Replys he well deserv'd but rather bear with him as much as I could and as long, so I avoided entring into the particulars of his Grievances & other nonsense for fear of being oblig'd to explain my mind too freely to him & tell him what I thought of him & his Conduct which might have brought upon me some rude Answer from him which might have got the better of all my Patience and forc'd me to an open Rupture with him, which I was willing to avoid for fear of hurting the Companys & all our Interest especially as I could not tell but we might meet Dutch ships in our Passage and still dreaded that He & some others by their malice or Imprudence might tell them Lies & stories & thereby give them some pretext to do us some prejudice or hindrance in our voyage, I say for this reason chiefly I was willing to bear with him & several others to the utmost of my power & suffer some pain & uneasiness rather than hazard the Good of the Voyage which perhaps some might not have had that regard to had I treated them with less Civility & moderation, which some too often deservd, However with regard to him All he could say, & growl & fall sick as often as he pleas'd, I went on the way I had followed for some time to order on Deck before his face & before the people a Dram Extraordinary & fresh provisions

---

[112] If Campbell could blame the captain for many grievances, at this point it was the latter who expressed the reasons for his dissatisfaction, arising from the unclear division of authority and pro-bably explaining the captain's misbehaviour, at least in part. If it was clear to Campbell, who had experience from previous voyages, to Trolle it was not.

as often as we could spare any, which was no small mortification to him as was every thing he did not do him self

73   These & Such like methods, but especially the last of nailing up a Copy of Commission, succeeded as I could wish, & brought the people by degrees to a sense of their duty & true Interest & to an Aw & respect for me and much less for him, for for several days one or other of them went to read the Commission & seem'd by their Conduct afterwards to take the True meaning of it. Yet from time to time he continued to use new stratagems to undermine my power, and cross all my Intentions & views, But not with the success he expected, for assoon as I knew what he was doing, which I was soon inform'd of I turn'd all his Batteries against himself & thereby brought him down a step lower & lower by degrees till I at last renderd him almost useless & even Contemptible to most in the ship, which his own foolish behaviour & mad Drunken humours help'd very much to bring about. But to leave him growling & fretting his ungovernable soul out, I must take notice of another merry sermon of the Priests.

Amongst other ridiculous things he sayd, that many People had the Good things of this Life who deservd it the least, & those that deservd them & work'd hardest for them had the least, & to prove it brought this fine simile, that it was just as often with the Horses They that labourd hardest & did the most work eat the least Corn, & they that work'd the least were the most pamper'd & had the best share of the Corn, He probably meant himself & some of his friends & the sailors for the Horses that work'd most & eat least and the SuperCargos & me & others for those that work'd the least & eat most; But this did not move me to give him or them one grain of Corn more.

June 25th Though I was very sensible that the Dutch had no Right nor reason to give us any hindrance or molestation in our [voyage]

74   yet As I had no great opinion of their friendship & Good will to us, I could not tell what private orders might be sent from the Dutch Company to Batavia[113] about us to play us some under hand piece of Roguery, and what made me more suspicious of their Intentions before I left Sweden was some hints I receivd from his Majestys Envoy at the Hague & his never being able to procure an Answer from that Company upon the subject though he had notifyd the Octroy to the States General by a memorial which was afterwards sent by them to the Dutch East India Directours. I say for these reasons I thought our safest way was to shun meeting them at sea or any Port where we could avoid them, which I knew there was no doing of in keeping the ordinary Course of going through the Straits of Sunda or Banca, where no doubt their ships would ly (at one or other of those

---

[113] *Jakarta* or *Djakarta* on Java, fortified in 1619 by the Dutch, who changed the name to Batavia.

places) in case they had any design to stop us, so thought the only way to shun them was to pass the Straits of Bally[114] if it was a thing our officers could undertake, I mentiond it to Mr Brown who was well acquainted with the India navigation & knew also the sentiments of some friends with relation to the Dutch, and he was intirely of my opinion, But before I would come to any Resolution I calld the SuperCargos together & layd open to them my suspicions & my reasons before them as above related, we were all of the same opinion but Mr Pike who never could believe that the Dutch could or would stop us or do us any prejudice notwithstanding of all we could allege to him, I sent then for Capt Kitching & Mr Baron & ask'd what they thought of what we had been Consulting upon, They readily approv'd of it & were willing to undertake it, believing it a safe passage as well as a means to shorten our passage to China, which considering the lateness of the season[115] we much wanted, & Mr Baron had passd that way once before in an English ship & though it was a good while yet he sayd he rememberd it & it was very safe &c especially at this season of the year. Upon which we came to a

75   Resolution of passing by the Straits of Bally which we sign'd & wrote fair in a Book I kept for setting down Resolutions of Consequence for the voyage & that requir'd a serious & joynt Consultation, which was afterwards destroyd with other Books & Papers. I then orderd the officers to take their measures & direct their Course accordingly. I did not call the Captain for two reasons 1st his not being fit to be trusted with such a thing, for as we might have occasion to make use of the same passage on our Return in case it succeeded now I was not willing the Dutch in China should know that we took that Course on purpose to shun them. My 2^d Reason was his not being capable of giving any opinion of the matter, as knowing nothing of one passage more than Another, I desird that he should not be acquainted ever with our design which as far as I can learn he never has yet been.

July 1st I must mention Mr Baron upon a small occasion which he gave me a handle for to day, As we had design'd to make S Pauls & Amsterdam in order to direct us better in our Course for Bally, this night Capt Kitching expecting to make S Pauls next day, when he went off his watch left the Course he thought most proper to

---

114 *Bali*, the island immediately to the east of Java.

115 The time of arrival in the Sunda was crucial to the further progress of the voyage. Certainly the greater part of the distance had been covered, but the most time-consuming stage of the journey was still ahead. Ships rarely fell behind schedule in the Indian Ocean because of the regular wind regime in this area. Any delay on the outward voyage occurred in the Atlantic Ocean. It did not prevent ships which were late from starting the Indian Ocean passage, but once in the Sunda Straits it was impossible for latecomers to traverse the China Sea to Canton. Wintering must then perforce be accepted as a fact. Vessels bound for China had to reach the Sunda Straits in the June–September period in order to be carried to Canton by the onshore southwesterly summer monsoon. July was the best month, but most of the Swedish vessels arrived in August. (Koninckx 1980b, p. 131.)

Mr Baron who came upon the next watch desiring him to follow it, But Mr Baron who is full of his own merit & fond of his own opinion did not approve of the Course Capt Kitching had orderd & propos'd to hold another which he thought better This occasiond some words & made Kitching retire in some Anger to his Cabbin saying he might do as he pleasd or something to that purpose. But to explain this Affair I must go a little back, & relate what I observ'd of Barons Conduct before & some of his friends. Mr Baron finding his superiour officer Capt Kitching to be a Good natur'd Easy man not positive in Opinion but too apt to be swayd by others who know much less than he does, had taken in his Head (as I presume

76   from what I observ'd of his manner of Acting) that as I was not acquainted with sea Affairs my self, that I must be advis'd by some Body in such matters as did know them, and as he believ'd himself to be much the most knowing Person aboard, and that he could manage Capt Kitching easily enough, he did not doubt to be able to make me believe himself to be the only Person fit to consult with & to leave to him the Conduct & navigation of the ship, There was one Rub in the way which he very Early thought to get Clear of, I mean Mr Brown whom he knew to be a Good sea Officer and had been one in the same ship with him when he was but a Boy & Cockswain to the Pinnace & therefore knew him perfectly well; And as he was 2^d Super-Cargo he naturally suppos'd I might often talk with him and upon sea Affairs by which means I might come at the knowlege of things I was not us'd to & was before Ignorant of, To remove this Obstacle or guard against it, He told me the first moment he came to see me at Cadiz that he hop'd Mr Brown would have nothing to do with the Affairs of the ship &c I not perceiving the drift of such a speech answerd that Mr Brown was not imploy'd to manage the Affairs of the ship but as Super-Cargo, so that passd over, But I could not help then wondring at his reason for having spoke to me to that purpose, when he knew very well what Mr Brown was imploy'd for, and that I thought He & every Body Aboard would be very glad of so good help on occasion as that of a Person universally know'n for an Experien[c]'d sea-officer, and whose Interest it was more than any of them to do his best for the Good of the voyage, But this was not what He & his Friends wanted, By that speech he was resolv'd to give me timely warning that Mr Brown was not to interfere in any thing &c & by that means he would be master of our navigation &c. To inable him to gain his point the better he brought over two of the Super-Cargos into his measures (one of whom had been long his Intimate friend & the other soon became so by being daily together over a Bottle) who upon all occasions were crying up Mr Baron, & often indeavouring to lessen Capt Kitching, and when I talk'd about the ship or

77   things relating to it, then the word was you had as good ask Mr Baron, & Mr Baron thinks so & so, & words to the same purpose which I have now forgot, In fine they had teaz'd me so often with their praises of Baron (whom I could not find out at all to be the oracle they wanted to set him up for) that one day as they

were going on in the same strain, I ask'd them why always Mr Baron,? was not Captain Kitching in the ship who was his superiour officer, and I believ'd a Good sea man as well as Mr Baron, and then would send or go & ask Capt Kitchings opinion. This did not at all suit their views, but as they very likely took me to be an Easy man fit to be made a Fool of, they resolv'd not to quit their Design, so in the Evening (after they had been in close Consultation with Mr Baron as I was well inform'd) the plot discover'd it self, Baron came down to me & sayd he wanted to speak with me I made him sit down, He begun by saying he could not tell why I was not satisfyd with his Conduct, & that he hop'd He had given me no Offence &c I answer'd that I knew no reason he had to think that I was dissatisfyd with his Conduct never having intimated any such thing to him, and assur'd him that while he minded his Business & did his Duty diligently I should never be dissatisfyd with him, This preamble being over He came to the main point which had brought him down to me, and sayd he did not know what Course to steer, for Capt Kitching when he went off the watch had spoke to him of such a Course but he knowing it to be a wrong one & not so proper to help to fetch the Island St Pauls he told him so & proposd another Course, which Captain Kitching was affronted at & went away in Anger saying he might steer what Course he pleas'd, He therefore desir'd to know of me what he was to do in this Affair? I easily perceiving his design, ask'd him what Course it was that Capt Kitching had order'd him

78   which he told me & which I have now forgot, I then ask'd him if he thought it was a wrong Course, He reply'd he could not say it was a bad Course, but that he doubted we could not steering so fetch the Island of S. Paul as we propos'd, and that the Course he had propos'd was better & he was sure to make the Island by it, upon which I thought I could not take a fairer Occasion to blast his foolish design and to tell him my sentiments freely in a Civil manner, I therefore calmly told him, That He ought to consider that Capt Kitching was his superiour officer and therefore as it was absolutely Necessary to keep up a due subordination in the ship It was his Duty to have no disputes with Capt Kitching, but if he believ'd that He was directing things wrong to propose his opinion to him honestly & with good manners, I went further & told him that if notwithstanding of his having offer'd another opinion that Capt Kitching should insist upon his in the steering or sailing of the ship or such like that then he ought to submit to it, That I knew no other Rule for him to follow, which he ought surely to know as well as I & that he had been long enough acquainted with C. Kitching to know that he was an old sea-man & far from being Ignorant of his Business, I therefore told him that he must follow all such orders as C. Kitching should give him, and as for this particular Occasion to steer the very Course that he had left in order to him when he went off Deck. This Answer destroying all his scheme confounded him & made him retire without making any Reply. But as I suspected he would follow his own humour, I went upon Deck before going to Bed to see if he steerd as C. Kitching had directed & found that he had alterd it & followd his own, upon

which I told him to steer the other Course that C. Kitching had order'd, & so went to Bed. C. Kitching when it came his Turn to watch found the Course had been alterd which he soon rectify'd & we found next day by the Event that his was the True Course (in spite of Barons positive opinion) for we made St Pauls as C. Kitching expected, as well as we could wish. Next morning

79 I ask'd Kitching if any words had passd between him & Mr Baron He ownd much the same as Baron did & as is above related, I went no further upon the subject not being willing to occasion a misunderstanding betwixt them, which could not as I thought conduce to the Good of the voyage, But I had reason to repent my moderation soon afterwards, For Baron by his positive assuming way drew C. Kitching into a Course that made us miss the Straits of Bally, as shall be related in its place. This Affair I confess gave me but an Indifferent opinion of Mr Baron, & less of his Friends who could enter into such a preposterous scheme of setting up an Inferior officer (& a young fellow that was not extraordinary either for his knowlege or Carefulness) against his superiour & a Person whom some of them know very well to be esteemd for an Experienc'd seaman & a diligent honest officer, & who had been often trusted with the Chief Command of ships as to the sailing part which Baron never had. I must have had a very mean opinion of C. Kitching indeed to have suffer'd him to be so treated, or to have introduc'd so bad an Example in the ship, for by the same Rule the next thing to do was to set up C. Trolle above me, which I believe some of them would not [have] been sorry{,} for at least in some things, to wit in the distribution of our Liquours &c I thought it very strange that Persons whose Duty it was to consult the Good of the voyage as well as me should think of destroying all order & decency & so bring us into Confusion without the least reason for it. This & such like Incidents made me often think it was happy for me & the Company too that I had so good a Man as Mr Brown with me who had always the real Good of the voyage in view without ever attempting to sacrifice it to any particular scheme or humour of his own, & who I was sure to find ready always to back what I propos'd tending to the Companys service

80 and often to give very useful Advices of his own to carry on the same Good purpose. But He was not the better lik'd for this by many of them, who have to my knowlege often show'd their malice & Ill will to him, & only because (as far as I could see) he knew more than they & that I repos'd some Trust in him.

July 1 Mr Barons saying (as above) that he hop'd I was not dissatisfy'd with him &c{)} might be owing to a thing that had happen'd some time before, As He & his two friends the Super-Cargos often went & took a glass of wine together while it was his watch, They did not take all the Caution they should have done to avoid being seen by every Body, by leaving his Cabbin Door open & being seen by the Captain & every Body upon Deck, This I had observ'd several times, without taking any notice of it to them, But being willing to save them from exposing themselves to the Captain & others who would be glad of any handle to say they were addicted to Drinking &c I spoke to Mr Morford to advise Mr Baron when he drank a glass of wine in his Cabbin to shut his Door or contrive {some} not to let the Captain & some others see him because they would be ready to lay hold of any thing to find fault with in their Conduct which I wanted to hinder his having any ground for, This no doubt he had told Mr Baron of, & He I mean M^r M[orford] sometime afterwards spoke to me in much the same strain as the other saying that he hopd I was not angry with him, I told him no, that All I pretended to desire of him was that for his own sake & the Good of the voyage he would not incourage Mr Baron to drink upon his watch, As for other times when not upon Duty I had nothing to say they might do as they pleas'd, Mr Morford took this Advice in a right manner & thank'd me for it. What made me indeed mention this to M^r M[orford], on purpose that Baron should know it, was that I was inform'd he was often drunk & asleep upon Deck when upon Duty and what I had seen some times my self, which shock'd me very much, and yet I bore with it, without speaking to him about it, only sometimes sent other people civilly to push him in order to wake him &c I was well assur'd besides he had say'd some very reflecting things of me behind my Back (I don't know for

81   what occasion) so that his own Conscience could tell him that I had reason enough not to be well satisfy'd with him, my regard to the good of the voyage and chiefly to prevent any of them from being dissatisfyd & thereby hurt us by their imprudence at Canton (or any where else where we might meet the Dutch) made me put up many things I did not approve of & hide my Resentment to the utmost of my power, hoping always to be able to reclaim them from their follies by mild usage & hints given in a Civil manner by second hands, But this I found to be the wrong way to deal with some People especially your sea faring men who require rougher treatment than it was natural for me to give them, Had I [illegible] them to huff & strut & bounce & curse & swear upon Decks as many Captains of ships do and I believe are forc'd to do I had no doubt kept them more in aw, But such a way being odious to me made them I believe (some at least) think that I stood in aw of them, till they provok'd me so long that I was oblig'd to talk to them with a more arbitrary Air than I had us'd or than I lik'd to do, which I found to be the best way to make them tame & reasonable. I had another view at first (which I did not care they should know) of indulging them a little, which was to find out their true Natural Tempers & Inclinations, For as there were several imployd this Voyage who I thought if they behav'd well would be imployd another time I was desirous to see what they were Good for by giving them a little loose, which I should never have known by huffing & scolding or even putting them in mind often of what I observ'd, By this means I am much mistaken If I am not pretty well acquainted with all their Good as well as bad Qualities & can form a tolerable Good Judgment of what they are fit for & Capable of Doing. But to come to the voyage.

July 2	Before noon we made the Island of St Pauls as we expected. The Captain who could never believe where we were going, though I had told him on leaving Cadiz that we were bound for China,
83	look'd alway[s] sour & put on very sage & fierce Airs when any of the English officers would say they hop'd to see such a place or make such Land about suchatime, he would clap his hand to his forehead (as usual) & cry Ja Ja I know better & then tell his friends that we pretended to talk of places that were not in the Route &c & as for the Island we now made he would not be perswaded there was such an Isle in the world till he saw it, which made him look very demure. Being pretty near the Land & having fine weather off it, it was proposd to put out our Boat & see to catch fish, But I considerd the weather might change & that it might occasion us a Loss of time,which we could not spare no not an hour of a Good wind, I thought better proceed our Course, not doubting we should meet with Refreshments, & fish & other things in the Straits of Bally or, if we should happen to miss them, in the Straits of Sunda
July 3^d	Being inform'd that next day was the Queens BirthDay or rather Name day (from the Saint of her Majestys name[116]) I resolv'd to pay honour to it, & with the more reason in order to let the People & every Body [know] who we belong'd to so I orderd a Couple of sheep[117] to be kill'd for the ships Company's Dinner.
– 4	orderd by sun-rise the Swedish Colours to be hoisted, and spoke to the Captain to muster the people & to prepare them for firing some musquets to her Majestys health (whom God long preserve) About 11 a clock in the fore noon, Having orderd a small Intertainment on the Quarter Deck, The Super-Cargos & I went up & when all was ready & the People under Arms I began the Queen of Sweden's health to the Captain, upon which the men that were under Arms fir'd 4 salvos, When the Hea[l]th had gone round all the SuperCargos Officers & young Gentle-men[118], I then drank a glass to the King of Sweden's health (whom God long preserve) which was also saluted with 4 salvos, This health having gone round I drank to the Prosperity of the Company & their ship the Fredericus Rex Sueciæ on which they fir'd 2 salvos, This Ceremony being over I orderd
84	a dram extraordinary for all the people to drink to the Queen's health, & to the underofficers & Quartermasters a bottle of wine a piece. About 5 a clock in the Evening, I order'd a Tub of Punch for the ships Company upon the Quarter Deck,

---

[116] Viz. *Ulrika*. Queen Ulrika Eleonora was the sister of the former King of Sweden, Charles XII, and married to the reigning King Fredrik I.

[117] Live animals were taken on board not only in Gothenburg but also in practically every port at which the vessels called. The livestock could include cows, oxen, sheep, lambs, goats, pigs, capons, chickens, geese and other poultry such as ducks, turkeys etc. The crew could obtain fresh meat when it was decided to slaughter animals.

[118] The supercargoes' assistants.

where they all were call'd up, one after another, and in a good draught drank to Her Majesty's Health. I believe they wish'd this or such like days would often come, for some of them got very merry upon it.

July 18th Another day to the Peoples great Joy, I mean his Majestys Name-day[119], which we kept in much the same manner as the Queens, with the difference only of some more firing, which the Captain is a great Lover of & wish'd our Guns had been in the way to have fir'd them, But they being stow'd below to stiffen the ship it was too troublesome to move them, And indeed had they been [on] Deck I should not have thought it proper to have fir'd them for fear of any ships in hearing as it might have happen'd and I was not very desirous of seeing any in these seas.

I ought not to forget that the Captain was pleas'd to pay me (as he thought no doubt) a great Compliment, of coming down with the Officers in the morning to wish me Joy of his Maj^{tys} Name-day, But he put on so Grim & sour a face that it was easy to see that what he did was much against the Grain, & he continued in bad humour the whole Day.

In order to execute our Design of passing the Straits of Bally, it was necessary to keep several degrees more to the Eastward than is usual for ships passing this way that design for the Straits of Sunda, and which indeed is the safest Course even to make sure of the Straits of Sunda in case we had design'd for them, Mr Brown who well knows this Navigation pressd me often to keep C. Kitching & Mr Baron in mind of it, which I did every day more than once, The former (to whom I had left the Direction of the Course) was convinc'd of the necessity of doing so, But Baron who pretended to know that passage (though it was plain that he knew very little of the matter) being extremely positive

85 & full of Assurance teazd C. Kitching so, (& sometimes in a much ruder manner than became & which few superiour would have suffer'd so long as he had done) about keeping more to the Westward, offering to lay his Head (with other foolish Assurances) that by that method & the Course he proposd he would make Bally, which in fine got the better of Capt Kitching and made him keep some degrees more to the Westward than Mr Brown had often told them they should do, so that by this Ignorance & Conceited Positiveness of Barons & by C Kitchings weakness in being misled by him, (which he confessd afterwards to me with shame) our design of passing those Straits miscarry'd as we shall see presently.

July 23 Lars Roos Carpenter dy'd of the scurvy[120], after having been long Ill.

---

[119] The King's name was *Fredrik*.
[120] *Scurvy*, a form of vitamin deficiency caused by malnutrition, more particularly lack of vitamin C in the diet, aggravated by lack of exercise and by suppressed tension. Scurvy was rife, but in many cases it was no longer a fatal disease. The ailment occurred mostly on the homeward voyage,

King Fredrik I of Sweden (1676–1751). Painting by G.E. Schröder.
Swedish Portrait Archives, National Swedish Art Museums.

– 25   We saw Land which our officers were perswaded was to the Eastward of Bally, &
so sure they were of this (owing to the same Positive Gentleman's Assurances)
that they did not think worth while to go near the Land to make it & see what it
was, which had they done at first seeing of it they perhaps might have had it in
their power not only to correct their mistake but also to pass the Straits of Bally,
But on the Contrary went on steering westerly along the Coast of Java which at
last they knew when it was too late to mend their fault. This made me not a little
uneasy (not knowing what consequence it might be of to us besides the time we
had lost in keeping more to the Eastward than we needed [to have] done had we

which is easy to understand. The stocks of victuals lost their freshness as the voyage progressed,
while scurvy is precisely attributable chiefly to a lack of fresh vegetables and fruit. As a counter-
measure lemon juice was used long before Lind's *Treatise of the Scurvy* (1753) was published. Other
juices and fruits were also effective, however, especially grapes (pumplemusses) and coconuts
(cf. *Diary* pp. 92, 275 ff. below). (Koninckx 1983.)

made for the Straits of Sunda directly) after having taken all the pains imaginable to prevent this Blunder, Besides Mr Browns often telling them of it for a long time, I had the day before making the Land at his desire (who lay then sick) spoke to them to keep more Easterly, for Mr Brown was dubious to the last that by their Course they would miss Bally, which I pressd them to take care not to do as being a matter perhaps of more Consequence than we could foresee. But all his warning of them and my keeping them in mind

86   was in vain, for there was no making Baron alter his opinion & it prevaild with C. Kiching above all we could say to him. This disappointment made me resolve to prevent if possible our falling into other such mistakes another time by the Ignorance of a Positiveness of Baron, so I spoke very seriously to Capt Kitching about it wondring he would let himself be swayd by a Person that could not know so much as himself & who never had the Direction of a Course or Voyage to India in his Life & whom he plainly saw himself commit many mistakes, and therefore desird him never to let him again pretend to rule him as he did & even drive him from his own better Judgment, C. Kitching took my Advice very well & own'd he was in the wrong to have been so overswayd as he was, which he would take care to avoid another time. I then address'd my self to Baron & ask'd him where was now the Effect of his positiveness, & Assurances & laying his heads upon things he was not capable of, & advis'd him to be more modest in his opinion another time & not so positive in things that no man could be sure of, The fine Gentleman (for he aims much to pass for that) was in no small huff, for instead of owning himself (as he ought to have done) in the wrong, he denyd that he had overperswaded C. Kitching from his opinion which we all knew to be false & which Kitching affirm'd to his face, & flew out into several expressions which show'd his Impudence & high opinion of himself, as that He was as Good a man as any Body & knew as much as any other, &c meaning I suppose chiefly Mr Brown & Capt Kitching as well as me & every one of the ship, I was not a little provok'd at a behaviour so unsuitable for a man that had just committed a Blunder he ought to have been asham'd of, But having put on a strong resolution to bear & master my Temper all this voyage, I stiffled my thoughts & such an Answer he deservd only telling him that his great opinion of himself signify'd

87   nothing at all & would not make any man of sense think the better of him, but on the Contrary the more humble & modest people were in their opinions the more they were esteemd by all men of wisdom & understanding.

What had happen'd had no effect upon this Positive Gentleman as we had many Instances of afterwards, He is something like Trolle as to this, I mean Incorrigible. I could not however omit this occasion to show some of his friends the fallibility of their mighty oracle, who had not a word to say in his defence.

Having miss'd Bally, we had nothing to do but to proceed as fast as we could for the Straits of Sunda, & having a fair wind & fine weather we run down all the South side of Java in about 5 days

July 29   We made Java head in the morning, upon reflection I can't tell but it was lucky for us that we attempted to pass the Straits of Bally, though our design miscarryd, because by that means we made sure of hitting the Straits of Sunda, by keeping so much more Easterly than we should have otherwise have done, for C Kitching own'd that he had steerd some degrees more to the Eastward than he thought of doing (being teazd with Baron's Assurances) only on Account of Mr Browns contrary opinion and pressing him to do so, so that if we had directly design'd for the Straits of Sunda we might have probably miss'd it by keeping a much more Westerly Course than we did now, which would have quite ruind our Voyage.

A few days before we made the Land of Java I consider'd that then we were approaching to places that belongd to the Dutch and where we might very likely meet Dutch ships in our Passage, And being afraid that in case of such an Accident if they should come aboard of us or that we should be obligd to send aboard of them, the Captain or some of the officers might through Indiscretion or malice let drop some of their Idle fancies to the Companys Prejudice, which might prove of fatal Consequence to us, I thought it best to give them

88   all my Advice & warning on this subject, And therefore call'd the Captain, Styrman Breemer, Styrman Lund & the Gunner, And in order to give them a greater Concern for the Affair, and show them how truly we were Swedes & how much his Majesty & the Nation had this voyage at heart, as well to strike some more Aw in them and Respect for me in order to prevent any more Caballs & Intriguing against me or attempting to throw off that Obedience they ow'd me, And having advis'd with the other Gentlemen SuperCargos about it, we judg'd it would be very proper now to discover to them the Character I had hitherto conceal'd of having the Honour to be his Majesty's Envoy sent on purpose to China to begin & settle a Trade there upon a sure & good foundation &c I therefore produc'd my Commissions & full Powers from his Majesty of Envoy, & after having warn'd them in case of meeting with the Dutch or being oblig'd to talk with them to be Cautious of saying any thing that might hurt the service & Interest of the Company, & particularly not to mention any strangers being on board, especially that as they were imployd now in the service of Sweden in this Affair they ought all to be esteem'd Good Swedes, and that his Majesty by his Octroy had promis'd them all the privileges of Swedes &c I then told them that I must let them know that I was sent to China by his Majesty in a Character I had not yet thought proper to discover which was that of Envoy & Plenipotentiary, & pointed to the Commissions lying before me, by which they might be convinc'd How much his Majesty & the nation favour'd this Affair, & that nothing could better demonstrate to all the world that we were really Swedes, & how much therefore it was incumbent upon every one of us to do our utmost to defend his Majestys honour & that of their Country, & that this also was a further Evidence of the power &

89   Authority I had in this ship, as having the honour not only to represent the Company but even his Majestys Person, that I therefore expected of them that they would {have} in every thing bear a true regard to the service of the Company which had imploy'd them & to whom they were bound by oath as well as other obligations to do their Duty to the utmost of their power, And I assurd them this would be an effectual way to recommend them to his Majestys favour (as well as to that of their Country & the Directors their masters) to whom I was oblig'd, if God should please to return me safe, to make a faithful report of all their Conduct & of all the Transactions that passd while I was aboard. This last was a little Touch I aim'd at my Kings officers, to make them stand in aw, as indeed wanting it the most. Styrman Lund, whom I most suspected, was the most hearty in his Protestations & Promises, of which I did not however believe one word, The Captain did not open his mouth but put on his Malecontent demure Look, as not being at all pleas'd at this Ceremony & Declaration. I then desird them not to mention any thing to any Body, of the Character I bore of Envoy till I thought proper to take upon me that Character, And then I dismiss'd them.

July 20   I forgot to mention this I am going now to take notice of in its due place, which happend about 30 Leagues to the Eastward of S. Pauls in Latitude d.m 15.37. South. About 11 a clock at night we were surpriz'd by an unusual phænomenon which puzzled us all, to wit the sea appeard all over as far as we could see almost as white as milk, The officers judging they must be near some Land or Bank though unknown to them, & orderd the sails to be furld and to ly by, which we did all night believing there was something extraordinary in it, no Body in the ship having ever [seen] such a thing before, I orderd to draw a Bucket of the water & found it when upon Deck to lose its white Colour & to have same taste & Colour as other sea water,

90   which made me conclude we were not near any Land or Bank that could occasion it, I then observ'd the sky the Appearance of which was a little uncommon, The moon being then up did not appear being hid by a sky all over coverd with light fair white Clouds, except just about the Horizon which was all around very dark & gloomy & black, This made me conjecture that the whiteness of the water was owing to nothing more than the Reflection of the moon Light upon it through those white Clouds, for not being able to shine through those Clouds she had thrown that whiteness upon them & they had given it to the water, And what strengthend my conjecture was that the whiteness began gradually a little after sun-set when the moon was up & pretty much the same Part of sky, And as the moon got higher & the white Clouds gatherd thicker & closer the whiteness of the water increas'd, and assoon as day light appear'd, the sea return'd to its natural Colour. Not knowing at first what to make of it, I look'd over some of my Books &

found in one of the volumes of Dampier's Voyages[121] that he had seen the same phænomenon once being in the South-Seas & without any extraordinary or uncommon Consequences following. I told this to the Captain & Officers & my Conjecture about the Cause of it, But the Captain he was not to be Comforted, He was like a man out of his senses expecting every moment immediate destruction, And then fell a demonstrating to me what would happen, Though all the night we had but little wind & no appearance in the sky of much yet he pretended to assure me that there was a terrible storm a coming & it would begin first all round the Horizon and then mount & gather just over our heads, & then all of a sudden come tumbling down directly upon us & overwhelm us & ship all in the sea, And as he observ'd [me] smile at him & bid him have a Good heart for there was nothing to fear, but the loss of

91   a nights sailing which I was sorry for, He replyd he knew better and to prove it told very gravely (which we all knew to be a lie he having sayd just before that he had never seen the like before) that he had met with just such an Appearance once off Iceland and immediately a dreadful storm insued almost in the same manner he had describ'd it & that they narrowly escapd being cast away &c This was matter of Diversion to us for we had been us'd to such proofs, for when he was at any Loss to prove what he affirm'd he then went either to Iceland or Green Land or some strange out of the way place to the Northward where he supposd none of us had ever been and therefore not so liable to contradict him, and say he had seen such things there. But still he had one sheet Ankar[122] left which was to consult the Gunner whom he took Occasions for a Conjurer & bid him consult his Books & give his opinion, & having done so returnd & sayd he could find no Account of such a thing but readily fell into the Captains sentiments that a storm was a coming, Being thus confirmd in his wild notion by so Learned a man, the poor Captain gave over all thoughts of Living till next day, I had no other way to comfort him but to call for a Glass of wine which I knew was the likeliest thing in the world to give him proper Consolation. Next morning I could not help asking him what he thought of the violent storm we had the night before, He answerd nothing but put on a very Grim Look.

---

[121] When still a boy of 18, *William Dampier* (1652–1715) was apprenticed to a ship's captain, with whom he made a voyage to the Newfoundland fisheries. He joined the English East India Company as an able seaman and sailed to Java. He was for a time enlisted in the Royal Navy, which he left invalided at the end of the Third Dutch War (1672–74). For a while employed at a sugar plantation in Jamaica, he later became a buccaneer. Then he met Captain Cook (not to be confused with the famous James Cook (1728–79)), who in 1683 set out on a piratical voyage to the South Seas, which was eventually to take Dampier round the world. During this voyage he kept a journal, later published as *A New Voyage Round the World*. It is notable not so much as an account of his voyage as for his observations on the wind and tides, and on the flora and fauna of the places visited. After many adventures, the British Admiralty appointed him as captain to make a voyage of discovery around Australia, during which he made a careful survey of much of the west coast of the continent. (*The Oxford Companion to Ships & the Sea*, 1976, p. 226 f.)

[122] *Anker*, obsolete form of *anchor* (Swedish *ankare*). *Sheet anchor*, a large strong anchor for use in emergency.

On this Occasion & many others He gave us eminent proofs of his want of Courage, for he never saw a Cloud in the Heavens rising or any thing about the horizon a little dark though we were in the Trade winds & fine weather but he always foretold a storm, & bawld to have the sails reef'd, nay his fears & Ignorance went so far that if he saw the Cat scratch a Rope he then told C. Kitching & all about that a storm was a coming, & therefore warnd

92 him to reef the sails & take in some of them, And what was more wonderful he would tell us by the Rope the Cat scratchd what sail it was necessary to lower or Reef, that is according to the sail the Rope belong'd to.

July 21 To night we had the same phænomenon as the night before though the sea not so white, with the same sort of sky & Horizon which confirmd me in my former opinion. But we did not think fit to lose one moments sailing for it any more.

– 31 Came to an Anchor in the Straits of Sunda off Angra[123] point, next morning saw a Dutch ship at an Anchor a couple of Leagues a stern of us, Here the Javans came off in their small boats with fowls Goats, Plantans[124], & Pumplemusses[125] & Guavas[126], & other fruits, (with some Curious Birds) &c which were very very acceptable to us, Especially the fruit such as the Coco nuts & Pumplemuses which recoverd the people that were sick of the scurvy to admiration in a very little time that not one of them died of it, which very likely they had done had not they met with this Refreshment, the natives would have brought us Cows too if we would have stayd a few hours, but not being willing to lose a moment for any thing Assoon as the Current permitted we got up our Anchor about 9 a clock A.M. same day & proceeded our voyage, In a little while on the Sumatra saw another Dutch ship at an Anchor, But we pass'd on without taking any notice of her or she of us,
August 1 which we were very glad of. In the night of the sea stile P.M. 10 a clock pass'd Bantam[127] point, where we saw the Lights of some Dutch ships at an Anchor, and
– 2 next day got out of the Straits of Sunda.

As the Straits of Banca[128] (which is the Common passage for China) was a likely place to meet with Dutch ships going or coming between Batavia & many parts of India, I was willing to avoid passing through them if we could find another

---

[123] Nowadays spelt *Angeri* or *Anjer* (cf. *Diary* p. 194: *Angerpoint*), on the Java side of the Sunda Straits.
[124] *Plantain*, the green-skinned banana-like fruit of *Musa paradisiaca*, eaten as a staple food in many tropical regions.
[125] *Pumplemousse* (Dutch *pompelmoes*), also called *shaddock*, the yellow grapefruit-like edible fruit of *Citrus maxima* or *C. decumana*, grown widely in many tropical countries.
[126] *Guava* or *gujave* (*Psidium guajava*), an edible fruit. (Osbeck 1757, p. 193.)
[127] *Bantam* or *Banten*, city-state on northwest Java, ruled by a Muslim king. Pepper constituted the main trade, which the Dutch tried to take over. At the outset, the Dutch East India Company (V.O.C.) had its headquarters there, guarding the Straits of Sunda, but transferred it to Batavia in 1611.
[128] Malay *Selat Bangka*, the straits between the southeast coast of Sumatra and the island of Bangka.

way And as in the maps & Accounts there is a fair passage on the outside or East side of Banca, upon which I advis'd

93

with the Super-Cargos & English officers who were of the same opinion, & though they never had pass'd that way yet believd it to be a good passage & would shorten our way upon which it was resolv'd on, But though we steer'd a good way to the Eastward of the Island Banca as it is layd down in the Draughts yet we found our selves disappointed, for when we made Land which by the maps should have been the Island Billiton[129], as we proceeded we found it was the Island Banca, & about 4 a clock P.M saw the Island Lucipara[130] off the mouth of the Straits, In the Evening we came to an Anchor not far from it, & in the night weigh'd again, but fearing the going too near the Sumatra shore we went too much the other side & got upon a Bank on the Banca side, & were obligd to drop our Anchor till we had a little more favourable wind to take us off again, so next morning or same day A.M. sea stile weigh'd & got off clear.

Aug 3ᵈ

– 4

As we pass'd along we saw off Palimban[131] Rivers mouth several Proes[132] or Boats of the Country, and one Dutch small vessell or sloop, which uses to Cruize here for to conduct their ships up this River, we saw her come off from the shore very fast & made directly for us with an intent no doubt to speak with us, & show'd her Colours, As I was not willing she should know what we were I orderd to hoist English Colours, which she perceiving made all the sail she could to come to us, But being resolv'd not to speak with her made her know as much by taking down the Colours immediately & pursuing her Course without waiting for her, or lying by as she expected (which it seems is often the Custom here, for these sloops bring off Goods to sell privately to the ships that pass) she soon understood our meaning & tack'd about & went back to her former station near the Sumatra shore. There is money to be got in China by dealing with Dutch ships that one meets in these parts by buying Pepper[133] & other Goods off them, which though a Capital Crime for the Dutch to do & strictly forbid them, yet they daily practise it, for they value no such orders that clash with their Interest & extreme desire of getting money. But I was so

---

[129] *Billiton* or *Belitung*, between Sumatra and Borneo.

[130] *Lucipara*, island covered with forests. The passage between Lucipara and Sumatra was dangerous if not impossible for larger vessels because of the insufficient depth.

[131] The river *Palembang* or *Palimbanka* (present-day *Musi*) on southern Sumatra has its estuary in the Straits of Bangka.

[132] *Proe*, proa (Malay *prau*, Dutch *prauw*), in the Malay language the term for all types of ship or vessel, from sampan to square-rigged *kapal*, but generally regarded by westerners as the vessel used by pirates in eastern waters. It carries a very large triangular, usually lateen sail and an outrigger to prevent excessive heel. (*The Oxford Companion to Ships & the Sea*, 1976, p. 671.)

[133] Pepper constituted a large share of the V.O.C.'s trade. It was obtained from the Company's own colonies, where a really large-scale pepper industry had developed. At the same time the V.O.C. tried to keep the monopoly of the pepper produced there. (Savary des Bruslons 1759–65, p. 269; Horst 1942, pp. 95–103; Glamann 1958, p. 14.)

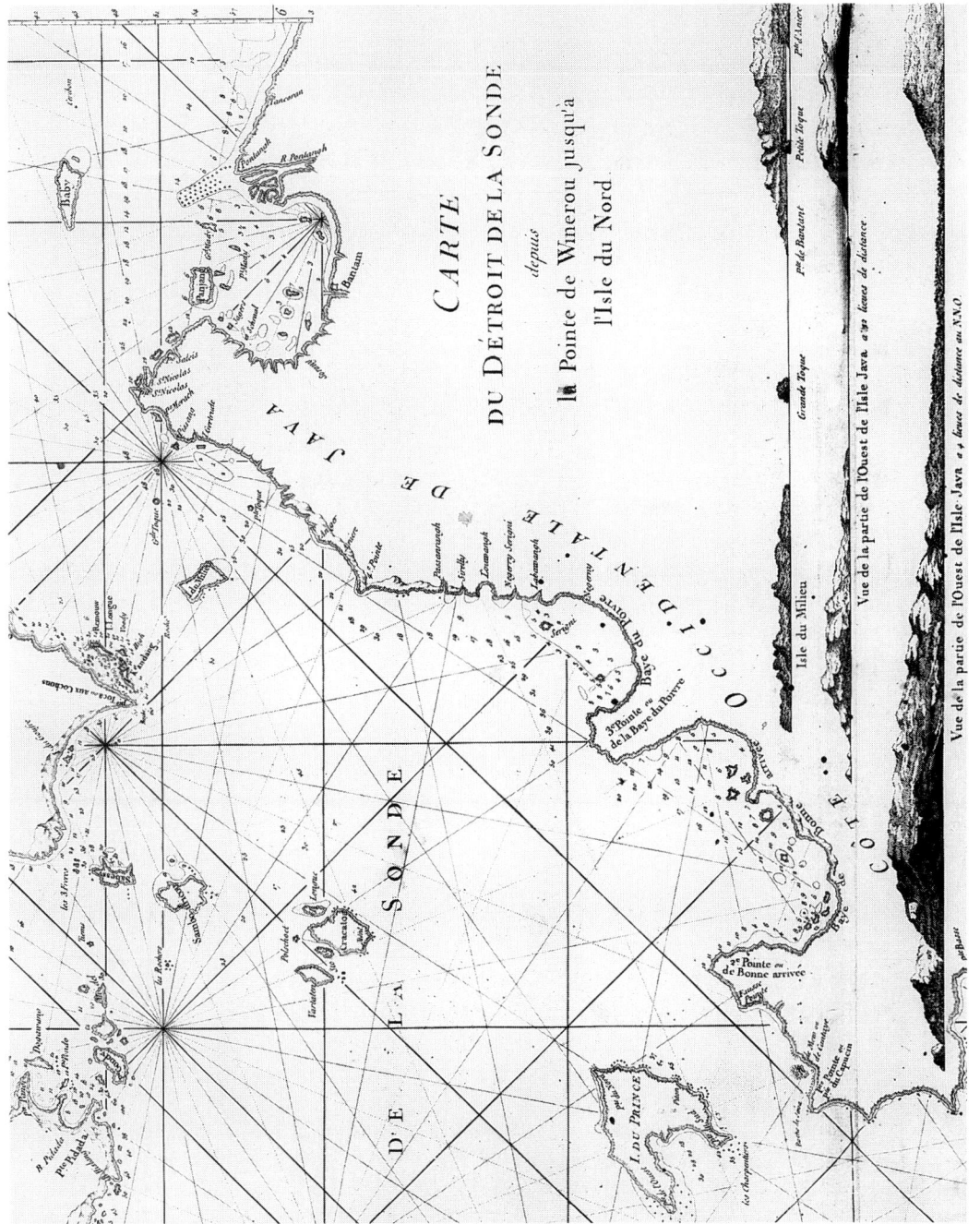

Nautical chart (detail) of the Sunda Strait. From N.D. d'Après de Mannevillette, *Le Neptune oriental* … Paris & Brest 1775.

94   Averse to all Affairs of this nature for fear of giving the Dutch any pretext to find fault with us & to pretend that we transgress'd the Conditions of our Octroy, that I would not so much as allow any Body to buy any merchandise, even of the natives of Java who came aboard while we lay near Angra point, though they offer'd to sell us both Pepper & Coffy a little of which they brought with them & would have fetch'd us more if I would have permitted it.

The Straits of Banca is a dangerous & tedious passage, we were oblig'd, by reason of contrary Currents & small winds, to come to an Anchor here 4 different times, which was not so often as many ships are oblig'd to do that pass this way.

Augt. 5   We got out of the Straits of Banca.

Since pasting up on the Mast my Commission from her Majesty (which I was resolvd to stick fast there notwithstanding of the Captain's earnest wishes to have it taken away) things are much chang'd, and especially since the last Discourse I had with him & the officers, They are a little quieter than formerly, and though the Captain puts on very sour fierce looks from time to time yet he does not pretend to meddle so much & hinder the Officers as he us'd to do in the sailing of the ship. It is not for want of Good inclination | to plague us but for fear which I resolv'd to keep him always in if possible, all other methods being ineffectual to govern such an unreasonable Creature. I may venture to say (since every Body daily sees it & all our English have own'd it many times) that nothing could have preserv'd us & the voyage from his malice & villainous designs (I can give them no better name) but that Commission impowering me to command him. A Good & Great Friend of the Companys who first gave me the hint in Sweden of this being necessary, well knew what the Kings sea Officers are & what they are Capable of, for there was nothing else that this fellow regarded but this Commission, As for the Directours orders or his dependence upon me as being one of them, all that was a Jest to him assoon as they were out of his

95   sight & his back was fairly turn'd upon Sweden, He forgot all that as well as his Oaths to the College of Commerce[134] & to the Company & to me in particular which were all Cobweb-ties upon him, & had he been able to have frighten'd or coax'd me not to make use of that power & Order, he would then have done with the ship & Cargo what he pleas'd, I often thought he had no design ever to return to his own Country or see the Directours more since he might easily perceive by such Conduct he could not be very aggreeable to them upon his Return, In short he is so Inconsistent a fellow that there is no making any Judgment of what was really his Design, God knows best what they were & his own Conscience, which

---

[134] The *Kommerskollegium* was a central Swedish government agency, established in 1651 (merged with *Kammarkollegium* in the 1680's, but reestablished in 1711 and still in existence), exercising authority and giving advice in trade matters.

he has assurance enough often to praise to me. A propos As to his Indeavours to prevent me if possible from making the proper use of my powers & exerting my Authority over him, he made use of several stratagems, (for though he is an arrant Fool in many things yet he does not want a good share of wicked Cunning & Art after his way) At first before we got the English officers on board (which he always dreaded) he would sometimes in Triffles show me some Care as he thought to please me, even as to go to the Cook-room & help to dress our victuals and thereby spoil every thing I eat which I bore for some time in order to humour him, He would then talk of his being an old experienc'd sailor & what stations he had been in at sea in different Countries, & how well he was acquainted with the navigation to the East Indies &c and sometimes slily pass some reflections upon the English way of acting in their ships by Cursing & swearing & making a noise (as he pretended) and bawling amongst the sailors to make them work &c which he very much condemn'd & sayd he knew much better, that he had always taken care to have all the sailors at his Command without such rough ways & often has made them comply with any thing even when he had Captains nay Admirals over them that could not quell their mutinous temper, And as to the ship he was now in he was so much master of the sailors & they lov'd him so much that if he spoke to any one of them to jump into the sea they would do it, that he knew the Swedes Tempers & how to

96   govern them & make them do any thing he pleas'd, and he would take care they should do their Duty, for he had the Companys Interest very much upon his Conscience & a great deal more of such Cant, which I was oblig'd often to hear except that I would have quarrell'd with him, which I did not think then proper to do. And no doubt my patience in hearing & giving him no Answer made him think that I believ'd all he say'd and that he would find it an Easy matter to make me a Tool & govern me as He pleas'd. But when he found at Cadiz after I had got the English Officers who knew the Business they came for and that I trusted them with a good part of the management, & that he saw I was resolv'd not to submit longer to his folly & Arbitrary humours but to take the Command upon my self, He grew inragd & set all his little wits to work how to prevent me, by making Parties against the English & other methods as have been before related, He also with the help of his friends aboard wanted to make the people believe the ship was a King's ship, and that I & others on board were only a parcel of merchants sent to manage the Trade when we came to our Port, and that He being the Kings Captain had an absolute Command & Power, & next to him Mr Lund who was a Kings Lieotennant & therefore far above any Body in the ship but himself, This scheme Lund help'd forward mightily & would never part with, He had even the Impudence once in the outvoyage to say something like it to me (afterwards a great deal more{)} which shall come in its place) I told him he knew very well what he was imploy'd for & that both He & the Captain were told that all Caracter & Rank they had ashore was to be layd aside aboard ship & every man to have rank & place & respect according to the post he was imploy'd in by the Company,

& that for my own part I assur'd him that I knew no Kings Captain nor no Kings Lieotennant here, that I knew one George Herman Trolle & one Lars Lund, the one imployd as Captain the other as 3ᵈ Styrman of a merchant ship belonging to the Swedish

97 East India Company who were their only masters & owners there, & that I knew my self to be here far above Capt Trolle and had the sole Charge & absolute Power in this ship, & next to my self I knew the SuperCargos, & under Capt Trolle as to the command of the People I knew Capt Kitching 2ᵈ Captain Mr Baron Chief mate & Styrman Breemer 2ᵈ mate & he Mr Lund 3ᵈ mate over whom all these officers I had nam'd had a Command Power & Rank in this ship according to their several stations, & that I would support them in it. This Answer set my Lieotennant a musing, & he turn'd it off by saying well he would take place of any of them ashore, To be sure says I when you come ashore you are there Lieotennant Lund again & every body no doubt will give you place there according to your Caracter. After this I was seldom troubled with this Fools Conversation, But that did not restrain him from talking in the same strain to other People behind my Back, and even had the Impudence once to say that Capt Trolle was Chief Commander in this ship as being Kings Captain & that he ought to have had the Great Cabbin to himself, & no Body was to take him out of it no not an Admiral if he should come on Board & make the voyage &c¹³⁵ I thought best take no notice of such things as I heard but too often till it was proper time & that I saw they had effect upon the Affair in hand, being resolv'd (and well foreseeing that a proper occasion would offer) to tame & humble him before the voyage should be over, which he gave me often room for, & oblig'd me at last on our Return to do it effectually.

Aug. 6 Came to an Anchor out of the Straits of Banca, finding the Current change, In a few hours we weigh'd again, & made the 7 Islands¹³⁶, Pulo Taya¹³⁷, & Pulo Touton¹³⁷ same day.

– 7 P.M in the Evening, saw Island Lingen¹³⁸.

– 8 Saw Pulo Panjang¹³⁹ in the Evening. & on the 9ᵗʰ in the morning

---

¹³⁵ An illustration of the problem of hierarchy between the supercargoes on the one hand and the officers on the other. Trolle seems not to have understood the difference between the hierarchy on board a merchantman and that on a man-of-war.
¹³⁶ *Seven Islands*, Malay *Pulau Tujoh* (*pulau* 'island', *tujoh* 'seven'), a group of coral islands north of Bangka.
¹³⁷ Islands in the China Sea. After the passage of the Sunda, the many islands served as observational reference points providing a step-by-step route.
¹³⁸ *Lingga*, island on the equator, "on the line", hence its name.
¹³⁹ *Pulau Panjang*, "Long Island" (Malay *panjang* 'long'), east of the larger island of Bintan, southeast of present-day Singapore.

– 9	Pulo Auroe[140], Pulo Sijang[137], & Pulo Timaon[141], all Islands in our Route, as the word Pulo in the Malay tongue signifys.
– 15	In the morning made Pulo Condore[142].
– 17	Made the Catwicks[143] & Pulo Capata[144] & the 20th sounded on the Macclesfield Sands[145]
– 23	Saw two ships bearing

98

Aug. 25   We made the Land (which were Islands off the Coast of China) and directly in our right way for Canton had we known it, But all our officers being of opinion that they were a great way to the Eastward of Canton or Macao[146] made them steer a very wrong Course & hazardous at this time of the year viz Westerly & run down several Islands as Pedra Branca[147], Asses Ears[148] &c which they knew after to be so but could not believe it then; Though I knew nothing (& had not rememberd them though I had seen them formerly) yet I could [not] help taking notice to them that these Rocks & Islands very much resembled the names they bore & look'd to be the same, But we would not trust our own Eyes but still run on to the Westward, which might have probably made us miss our Passage to China this year had we not luckily met with a China vessall or Junk[149] that set us right.

---

[140] *Pulau Aur*, "Bamboo Island" (Malay *aur* 'bamboo').

[141] *Pulau Tioman*, the northernmost of the Malay islands.

[142] *Pulau Condore*, present-day Vietnamese *Con San*, island in the South China Sea, off the Mekong delta.

[143] Rocks northwest of Pulau Sapatu.

[144] *Pulau Sapatu* or *Zapata*, "Shoe Island" (from Portuguese *sapato* 'shoe'), so named because of its shape.

[145] *Macclesfield Bank*, in the China Sea off the coast of present-day Vietnam, named after the English galley *Macclesfield*, supposed to have discovered it.

[146] Chinese city on the west banks of the Pearl River, where the Portuguese had a permanent factory, which was later to become a Portuguese colony, as it still is. Because of having this firm foothold on the Chinese continent, the Portugese seem to have gained the greatest advantage to conduct trade in the Far East, especially with China, at the most favourable juncture: when the season was over and all the European ships had left Canton, they could buy whatever they wanted at half price.

[147] Portuguese for "The White Rock", a well-known sea-mark east of present-day Hong Kong. Large crowds of sea gulls inhabited this high cliff and spoiled it with their excrements, giving it a white appearance. (Ekeberg 1773, p. 80.)

[148] English name of two islands southwest of present-day Hong Kong and southeast of the Ladrones. Their sharp pointed cliffs had the appearance of a donkey's ears, hence their name. (Ekeberg 1773, p. 80.)

[149] Native vessel common to Far Eastern seas, used by the Chinese and Javanese. Flat-bottomed, high-sterned with square bows, carrying two or three masts equipped with lugsails made of matting stiffened with horizontal batons. The largest junks were built at least to the size of a square-rigged ship of the 18th century and were ocean-going trading vessels. They were also the warships of the Chinese, being armed with guns on deck.

However I must say for their Excuse that it is no Easy matter to be exact in the remembring Rocks or Islands that one has seen before without one comes directly to the same point of view and just the same bearings & distance from them as before when they saw them, which I believe seldom happens. All that can be done in such a Case in my opinion, is when one designs for a Port and makes the land near to it to run into it as near as is safe in order to be sure of it, Had we done this we had gone directly to Canton without loss of so much time, & have sav'd our selves in all probability from a violent storm which we met with off these Islands in a few days afterwards.

- 28　　We saw a China Junk a head & steering towards us, which gave us no small satisfaction; I order'd English Colours to be hoisted (with which they are best acquainted here) to incourage them not to run from us as they are apt to do when they see unknown flags; I then order'd the Pinnace out & Mr Baron to go aboard of her to inquire where we were & how to steer our Course for Macao or Canton, He came soon back with information that were too far to the Westward & that Macao lay N.E from us. She happend to be bound for Canton & got there before us several days (passing between the Islands) & was the first that gave

99　　any notice to the people of Canton, that we were upon the Coast bound for Canton, The English there hearing of an Europe ship without, immediately con-cluded that we were from Sweden having known before they left England of my intending to come out this year for India & they supposd for China so that the China merchants expected me for some time and there were Letters from them sent down to Macao for me waiting there some time in hopes of my Arrival. The information we receiv'd from the Junk made us presently alter our Course & go back the very way we had come & so we passd by all the Islands we had made before continuing our Course Easterly a little further than was necessary till the storm came & drove us back again to the Westward.

Septr 1st　About 10 or 11 at night the storm (or Typhoon[150] as it is call'd in the China language & too common on this Coast about this time of the year & a little earlier) began, At sun-set Captain Kitching had observ'd the sun set very red with Clouds near it streak'd with various Colours, which by old observations portends a Typhoon in these seas, which made him apprehend some storm a coming & to prepare for it, It began at S.E & continued that night to blow with great violence, which made us lower our yards & top masts & run under our Courses[151], It

---

[150] Tropical storm in the western North Pacific, very intense, consisting of fairly small but deep depressions around which the wind circulates anti-clockwise in the northern hemisphere. This wind causes very heavy seas, with torrential rain and driven spray reducing visibility almost to nothing. Because of their extreme intensity, with the force of the storm concentrated in a small area, typhoons can be immensely destructive. Their season in the northern hemisphere is June–November, with maximum frequency in August and September, occurring in connection with the change of the monsoon. (Lewis 1991, p. 241.)

[151] *Course*, any of the sails on the lowest yards of a square-rigged ship.

lasted all next day with same fury but chiefly in the Afternoon or P.M. about 3 or 4 a clock, & did not give over to blow violently till the morning after about 8 a clock, still between the South & the East, we could not do nothing but run before it, and in the night found it very difficult to keep off the shore which we was in great danger of running upon had it continued longer, It was very dark & dismal all night, so that we did not see our danger till Day came, & kept off as well as we could, And assoon as the wind moderated, being heartily weary of our late bad situation, & not being Certain where we were, we thought our best way was to run in to the first place we could come at for a little shelter till we could find some Body or other to direct us where we were & help us to get to Macao, so that I order'd to make for a Bay in sight under an Island

100

which the Chinese call Tam-Cun[152], & which I thought we had great reason to call Shelter-Island, where we cast Anchor, Next morning I sent the Pinnace ashore to see

Sept[r] 3   if we could find any of the fishermen or natives thereabouts to pilote[153] up the ship to Macao, They accordingly found by the shoar two fisher Boats with Chinese in them whom they brought aboard, we wanted to know of them as well as we could, with the little Chinese Language we could muster up, amongst us, how far it was to Macao and how it lay &c But they not willing to understand us & resolv'd not to lose so good an occasion of getting a little money would give us no information of any thing, In fine I was oblig'd to give them near their own price and aggreed with them for one & fourty Spanish Dollers (which to make sure of they would not stir till I pay'd them down) to pilote us to Macao Road, so about 3 a clock A.M we weigh'd Anchor & steering W & W NW passd between a vast number of Islands (unknown to us all) and found our selves about noon in sight of the Castle of Macao, which was much nearer to the place where we had been than we could have imagin'd, Here we cast Anchor about 5 leagues off, & our fishermen Pilotes bid us fare well.

Sept[r] 4   I Sent the Pinnace ashoar to Macao to fetch a Pilote off to conduct us to Canton, & advis'd M[r] Baron not to go near the Governour except oblig'd to it nor to take any notice ashoar who we were being desirous to get to Canton before any Body there should hear of our Coming, However he was carry'd to the Governour who ask'd him a few Questions & dismiss'd him soon, Here he found a China man sent from Pinky[154] a merchant of Canton who had been waiting here some time

---

[152] *Tam Kan*, the largest of the Lema Islands south of present-day Hong Kong.

[153] In the vicinity of the Pearl River delta, a pilot was engaged to guide the ship in the appropriate channel, beyond Macao and Linting through the Strait of Bocca Tigris to Whampoa. Piloting consisted merely of an agreement between a Company ship and a junk, or even a fishing-boat, which sailed ahead and showed the way to the unwieldy European vessels. (Constant 1964, p. 382 ff.)

[154] *Pinky*, nickname for *Zhang Zhuquan* (Gui 1994), an important Hong merchant, whom Campbell had evidently got to know when he was in Canton in 1726. On p. 106 of the *Diary* he refers to Pinky as an old friend, to whom he at first intended the Swedes to go on their arrival in Canton. After Campbell had made some contracts with him for buying tea and silk and for selling him some English cloth (*Diary* pp. 116, 124), Pinky was arrested, accused of having been involved in the export of red copper, which was strictly forbidden (*Diary* pp. 127, 168). This led to great problems

for my Arrival with a Letter inviting me to his House at Canton &c But Baron having orders not to tell who we were and denying my being there prevented him from delivering his Letter, but suspecting I was there he went to Boca Tigris[155] to meet me.

101   The news reach'd at Canton before us that there was an Europe ship had arriv'd at Macao, but that they could not tell who we were, but that the officer (meaning our mate Baron) spoke English & the men wore mustachios or whiskers, which our Cocksswain Eckstrom did, The Europeans at Canton immediately guessd who we were no Europe ship being more expected there this year. About 9 a clock at night the Pinnace return'd with a Chinese Pilote to carry the ship up the River

Septr 4   of Canton. So next morning or same day A M. in the sea-stile we weigh'd Anchor
A.M   & got soon out of sight of Macao, but were oblig'd to come to an Anchor again about 11 before noon

– 5   It blowing hard from the East we were forc'd to ly at Anchor all day & next day just by a small Island or Rock call'd the Inner Ladroen[156]. We beginning to run short of water, I sent ashoar the Pinnace to the little Island to fetch us Some, And indeed we stood in great need of some Good, of which we had not one drop we could call so all our outvoyage, which was owing to the badness of the Casks bought at Stockholm, they being old Casks which had before been fill'd with Beer wine or Brandy and had given a sour Taste to the water, when I us'd to complain of this the Captain us'd to say as he had done in Sweden that the water would be the better for that and more aggreeable to the men because the water would thereby acquire a fine Taste of the Liquours that had been before in the Casks, But the sailors were not Fools enough to believe him rather than their own senses, The only way I found to correct that sour quality was to toast or burn Bisket[157] & throw some in every Jar they drank, which did very much mend it. In the Evening the Pinnace returnd with fresh water. In the Afternoon we spyd at a considerable distance a stern (at least 5 or 6 leagues off) a large ship at an Anchor, The Chinese that had seen her Colours gave a description of them as well as they could, by which we guessd she might be an Ostender, as she afterwards provd to be.[158] This news did not at all please me, supposing it might be one of the

---

for Campbell, since Pinky's son, "young Pinky", was reluctant to recognize his father's agreements (*Diary* pp. 151, 156 f., 172, 184 f.).

[155] *Bocca Tigris*: the Portuguese called the Pearl River delta "The Tiger's Mouth".

[156] *Ladrones* or *Larrones Islands* (from Latin *ladro, -onis*), the present-day Wan Shan archipelago in the estuary of the Pearl River, from which pirates operated in the China Sea; not to be confused with the Larrones or present-day Mariana Islands in the Pacific, which would seem to be too far away for pirates operating in the vicinity of Canton.

[157] *Biscuit*, made with flour, mixed with the least possible quantity of water, and thoroughly kneaded into flat cakes and slowly baked. Ship-biscuits were issued until bakeries generally began to be fitted in ships at the beginning of the 20th century and bread became available even for long voyages. It had a strong resemblance to present-day Swedish *knäckebröd*, hard rye bread which would keep for a long time provided it was kept dry.

[158] This was the *Hertogh van Lorreynen*, one of the two so-called "permission ships", having left Ostend

Pearl River delta, with entrance to the roadstead of Canton. From C.J. Gethe,
Dagbok Hållen På Resan till Ost Indien … 1746–49. (KBS. M.280.)

102   two Ostend ships that had Liberty to go this year to the East Indies by the late
Treaty of Vienna[159], And I well knew that assoon as the China merchants should
be inform'd of such a ships arrival it would be a handle to them to raise the price
of Goods upon us, as is their Custom on such Occasions, which made me very
Earnest to get to Canton & if possible make our Contacts before the merchants
should have news of the Ostenders Arrival, or at least before their Super-Cargos
should be able to get to Canton.

---

in the Austrian or Southern Netherlands in April 1732, sent out by the Ostend East India Company
by special permission, since that Company had been suspended on 31 May 1727. Cf. note 159
below and Introduction p. xviii.

[159] The Treaty of Vienna was concluded between Austria, England, Spain, and the Dutch Republic.
Besides the acceptance of the Pragmatic Sanction recognizing the female succession of the Austrian
Emperor, Charles VI, by his daughter Maria Theresia, this treaty suspended definitely the Ostend
Company. In fact, a first act was signed by Austria and England in 1731 and a second one in 1732
(hence "the late Treaty") between Austria and the Dutch Republic, accepting two ultimate Ostend
East Indiamen to be dispatched. Cf. note 158 above.

Bocca Tigris (Tiger's Mouth), the entrance to the Pearl River and Canton.
Oil painting. Gothenburg City Museum. (Photo: Håkan Berg.)

Septr 6 At 9 a clock P.M we set sail & bore for Linting[160].

– 7 At 4 a clock P.M. saw Boca-Tigris or the Entry of the River of Canton, At 7 a clock
we were oblig'd to come to an Anchor, & next morning or 7 a clock A.M weigh'd
again & between 8 & 9 passd Boca-Tigris, & about noon pass'd the first Bar where
we were oblig'd again to cast Anchor.

As I apprehended the moment I should leave the ship the Captain & his wicked
friends would begin to their old mad freaks & hinder C. Kitching & M[r] Baron
from doing the ships Business, and as we had little Time to stay there would be
a great Deal of work aboard both in unloading & reloading the ship and doing
a thousand things about her she wanted which they only understood, I had
prepar'd a Long Letter of Orders & Instructions to the Captain with regard to

---

[160] Island in the Pearl River estuary, halfway between Macao and Bocca Tigris.

86

his Conduct there & what I expected of him, to wit to keep up a Good order & Command in the ship & particularly a Good harmony & understanding amongst all the officers as well as sailors & to asist the English officers (who knew best the methods of this place & what was necessary for the ships here) to the utmost of his power to do the ships Business & the Companys service & to avoid incouraging any parties or distinctions in the ship of English or Swedes but to unite all together as True Swedes in promoting the service we were all imploýd

103   in, and as Capt Kitching was best acquainted with the buying of provisions here for the ships Company, I had left him to keep the Account with the Compradore^{161} after consulting together what was proper for Dieting them here, I mention'd this on purpose to take it out of his power to cheat the Company either by his Knavery (which I much suspected) or Ignorance in making wrong & foolish Bargains or by putting things to Account that he never bought &c And to take care to sell nothing that belongd to the ship, because what was superfluous I would take the trouble to do that my self & therefore orderd him & Capt Kitching to take an exact account of every thing in the ship & to let me know what we could spare, I likewise recommended to him to avoid & to advise his officers & sailors to avoid much Conversation with the Dutch they might [meet] here in order to prevent all quarrelling wlth them, & in case He or they should fall in Company with any of them to be very Cautious of what they talk'd about the Company for fear of giving the Dutch any handle to raise Idle reports of us to do us a Prejudice, And knowing that he was much in love with firing of Guns I orderd him not to fire any Guns after I was gone from the ship let who will go ashore or come aboard (for the worthy Gentleman was us'd in the East sea to have Guns fir'd when he left the ship or came aboard) except on such occasions as I knew were Customary & should direct from time to time, These & many other points I mention'd in order to keep him from playing the Fool or hindring the Business of the ship &c as I much apprehended & not without reason as soon appeard. Having my Letter ready turn'd into the Swedish language I kept it by me till I should leave the ship & then give it him at parting.

Septr 8   As I saw no appearance of getting nearer Canton today with the ship, and being very Impatient of getting to Canton, I proposd to the Super-Cargos to go up in the Pinnace which was aggreed to, especially that Mr Brown hop'd to be able to guide us as far as Vampo^{162} where the Europe ships use to ly & where I

---

161 Portuguese *comprador* 'buyer', Chinese agent who maintained continuous contact with the Europeans, purchasing and attending to the equipping and victualling of the ship, both during its sojourn in China and in preparation for the return voyage. On the China coast the term *comprador* actually had two meanings: 1) chief cashier and broker of a foreign firm, and 2) ship chandler or purveyor of supplies.

162 The roadstead of Canton was at Whampoa; the shallow draught prevented the East Indiamen from sailing further upstream. The ships were therefore unripped here, and remained at anchor until they were again made ready to sail on the return voyage. All the European ships lay in the roadstead of the island of Whampoa, in the Pearl River some miles downstream from Canton.

104   hop'd to arrive before it was very late & find some old Acquaintance in some of the ships there that would not refuse us a nights Lodging, & next morning to proseade our voyage to Canton. About sun-set or 6 a clock at night we left the ship, & took a China man along with us (being one of the Hoppo[163] officers that had come on board at Boca Tigris) believing he would be useful to us in finding out our way. But unluckily for us About half an hour after we had parted from the ship, The weather chang'd all of a sudden into squalls of winds & Rain & Thunder & Lightning & withall so dark that we could not see our way, However by Mr Brown's Direction we Row'd close along shoar and I believe might have done well enough had not the China man set us wrong several times & brought us into Creeks where we often stuck upon the Ground, About 8 a clock at night descrying a Light at some distance we suppos'd it belong'd to one of the Europe ships at Vampo & we therefore made for it as well as we could, & coming near it would have spoke with it being a China Junk But our Hoppo man would not suffer us making a noise & signs to bear off for he was a Ladroen or Pirate (which are very common in this River) At last after a good deal of trouble & steering sometimes one way sometimes another we hit upon the right way & seeing several Lights which we concluded to be of the ships at Vampo we made for them, & about 10 a clock at night arriv'd at Vampo very tir'd & wet to the skin. As we wanted very much a little refreshment & much more a nights lodging we went alongst the side of the Banksaals[164] (or places where the ships keep some people to watch their ships stores) to see if we could light on any of the English of our Acquaintance, so calling at one of them (which happen'd to belong to the Linn, a ship where Mr Brown had been Chief mate some Voyages & was to have commanded this very voyage had not some

105   misunderstanding & Party Interest amongst the Directors of the English Company disappointed him even after he was appointed Captain) where Mr Brown was well known, The sentry being surpriz'd at seeing a Boat there at such a time of

---

[163] The *Hoppo* (Chinese *Haibu*) was the local collector-general or chief inspector of customs and excise. This imperial commissioner of the Kwangtung Customs had his headquarters at Canton. Since Europeans were charged a tax for their sojourn in China, calculated according to the size of the ship, it was the Hoppo who came down, amid great pomp and ceremony, to measure every ship. The occasion was marked by the exchange of gifts between the Hoppo and the supercargoes.

[164] As soon as a ship coming from Europe had dropped anchor, it was unloaded, unripped, cleaned up and repaired or made seaworthy again. Cargo, ballast, guns and sails were taken ashore and stored in the *bank(e)shall* ("hall on the bank"). This was a kind of warehouse which served both as an emporium and as a workshop. Every East India Company had a *bankshall* at its disposal, arranged through the good offices of a *comprador* (see note 161). They were constructed of bamboo and mats shortly after the arrival of the ships. The European vessel that arrived first at Whampoa during the season was allotted the best location for its *bankshall*. The size was about 35.5–41.5 metres long and 10.5–12 metres wide. In the main it would be divided up into a large storage space and two rooms: one for the mate or *bankshall* captain, and the other for the seamen who mounted guard there. The foreshore where the *bankshall* was situated was in time provided with wharfage constructed from the ballast stones which the Company vessels brought with them. The space allotted to the companies seems not to have been particularly large. (Lewis 1991, p. 154.)

night, call'd to know what ships Boat, we answerd in English the King Frederick, upon which the fellow told us to put off or else he would fire upon us, for he was very sure there was no such ship as the King Frederick in the River, And though Mr Brown spoke to him & told him who he was he would not believe him, & would not call the officer of the watch as we desird, which made Mr Brown venture to step ashore and then the poor fellow knowing him receivd him with great submission & went immediately & wak'd the officer, who very Civilly told us what ships were there & who were aboard of them, Amongst other news he surpriz'd me with the very disaggreeable news of the Death of an Intimate friend & old Acquaintance of mine whom I had a great Respect for, I mean Mr George Arbuthnott[165] Chief SuperCargo of the 4 English ships bound for China, who had dy'd aboard of the Linn in sight of the Islands not far from Macao, where he was buried, which gave me great Concern. As we were not willing to trouble any of the English ships & that all my Acquaintance in the Country ships[166] were up at Canton, we were at a Loss what to do to find some place to shelter us from the

---

[165] Cf. Morse (1966–69), 1, p. 208. The name of Mr. Arbuthnot's ship was the *Lynn*.

[166] Ships used in the so-called country trade. Europeans, whether in service of East India companies or not, were involved in a particular trade from port to port in the Far East. This country trade could be part of the official company trade, as would later on be the case with the Swedish Company, run by the residents; but mostly the country trade was managed by individuals without actual links with the companies. In either case, however, the country trade supported the Company trade, providing necessary return cargoes. The Swedes tried to develop a country trade of their own, combined with the Company expeditions. During the second charter (1746–66) the Company sent three ships to Surat, where it was engaged in trade, mainly to exchange European products for piastres rather than to collect a complete return cargo. It should be noted that during those expeditions Surat was not the only port of call. If the Swedes remained there for about five months, afterwards they left Surat to call at various other places on the Western Ghats, the west coast of India, the Portugese factories of Damão and Gōa, Mangalore, Cannanore, Mahé and Calicut on the Malabar coast, and finally Quilon on the Travancore coast. These halts took at most a total of six weeks and had to be accomplished with the help of the monsoon. The season between monsoons had to be used to cross the Bay of Bengal to the Straits of Malacca, south of Ceylon (Sri Lanka); the Swedes sailed to Kedah on the Malay Peninsula. After calling at Kedah, Malacca or other harbours, the Swedish Surat expeditions were always prolonged to Canton. The Swedish Company was in fact making a new experiment: a sort of "country trade" combined with a China voyage. A large part of the outward cargo (from Sweden) was sold in return for silver, which in turn was used for the trade with China. Copper, steel, lead and iron were sold, as well as dyestuffs and ivory, originating from the Far East and imported to Sweden during previous expeditions, but then re-exported to the Far East. Sandalwood and olibanum were purchased during the "country trade", besides cotton, saltpetre and spices. Some of these purchases were re-sold on the coast of Malabar for cash. This trade was continued along the coast of Malacca. Tin and spices were bought there, eventually to be sold in Canton. The object of the port-to-port trading was to procure as much silver as possible in the Far East itself, instead of collecting it in Spain, and to arrive ultimately in Canton in the same situation as the direct China-bound vessels. Even so, there is no doubt that the end result of such voyages was not very advantageous. The Surat voyage was longer in terms of time, which increased costs. Moreover, at every port of call permits had to be paid for with new dues and tributes to the local princes. Finally, as demonstrated by the first expeditions of the Swedish Company, it is plain that the presence of newcomers such as the Swedes was unwelcome.

One very interesting aspect of the country trade was that the 10% levelled on goods to be exported to Europe was not imposed in the country trade, since these goods were supposed to be sold in the Far East. That this 10% could be avoided when coupled to the country trade is quite evident: see Campbell's note in *Diary* p. 207.

Rain all night, till spying the Hoppo house (or one of the China Custom-houses) near us we row'd for it & went ashoar, They receiv'd us Civilly and gave us Tea (according to the Chinese Custom) and not having any place to lodge us in, they spoke to the People of a Large China Boat lying there to take us in which they did & where we made a shift to ly upon the Boards & Chests all night. The China men could not tell what to make of us staring much at our Colours, of which they had never seen any such before.[167]

Sept[r] 8   In the morning we bid farewell to our Boat & Hoppo house, and made the best of our way for Canton. While we were going up

106   we consulted what merchants House or Hang[168] (as they call it) we should go to, as is necessary on the first Arrival till one can get a House of their own, M[r] Morford propos'd Suqua[169] (He had his reasons which I discover'd afterwards) to whom I had no objection, as being a Top merchant, except that I presumd he had the English Business this year which would make him more Careless of serving us; I inclin'd to go to Pinkys as being an old friend and whom I believ'd the Honestest merchant there, & had also sent a man on purpose to Macao to invite us to his House, But it was objected that he had no Hang to the water-side & that it was necessary to go to some Body that had one there in order to put up our Pinnace & have our people about us, I therefore propos'd Tinqua[170] who had

---

[167] A testimony that the *Fredericus R.S.* was actually the first Swedish vessel to reach China.

[168] *Hong* or *Hang*, Chinese merchant house. At first European merchants had to rely on personal relationships with individual Chinese merchants. Only in 1759 was the *Co-hang* established in Canton, a sort of syndicate of Chinese merchants whose members were ready to help each other for mutual solidarity, so that the risk of untrustworthy clients was largely eliminated. These guarantees against financial risks disappeared again as early as 1771. From then on the Europeans were dependent, just as before, upon individual merchants.

[169] *Suqua*, before 1716 known successively as *Kimco* and *Cumshaw* (Cheong 1991, pp. 218, 229), has been identified by Gui (1994) as *Chen Shouguan* in Chinese. He was active in Canton shortly after the turn of the century (Cheong 1991, p. 218; Morse 1966–69, 1, p. 156), moved to Amoy (Xiamen) in the 1720's (*ibid.* p. 176) but soon returned to Canton. In 1729 he was appointed "Chief Merchant", and a year later the English supercargoes characterized him as being "for many years past [...] reputed the most considerable Merchant in Canton, and can dispatch any number of Ships in good time, for he is in great Circumstances, and generally allowed to be an able and skillfull Merchant, but He will always endeavour to make a hard Bargain" (*ibid.* p. 198).

After having bargained and contracted with Suqua for various goods Campbell notes on 16 Sept. (*Diary* p. 127) that Suqua had been imprisoned and charged with having had close connections with the former Hoppo, who had also been arrested. (For Campbell's unsuccessful efforts to obtain his release see *Diary* p. 141 ff.) After some years in prison Suqua apparently managed to regain his former position as an important Hong merchant, and Campbell records dealings with him in his journal of the expedition in 1738–39. Because the English found Suqua dishonest, he was sometimes forced to act under the cover name of *Chetqua* or *Kettqua* (Morse 1966–69, 1, p. 257 ff.).

[170] *Tinqua*, identified by Gui (1994) in Chinese sources as *Chen Tingguan*, is known as a wealthy and important merchant from 1726 onwards. He was chosen to be what was later called "security merchant" for the Swedish ship and is mentioned by Campbell as "the merchant that answerd for us" (*Diary* p. 187). This function included the duty of letting the Europeans rent premises in his Hong, if they did not have a factory building of their own. He also acted as an intermediary between the Hoppo and the foreigners, e.g. in securing audiences, in arranging to have the ship

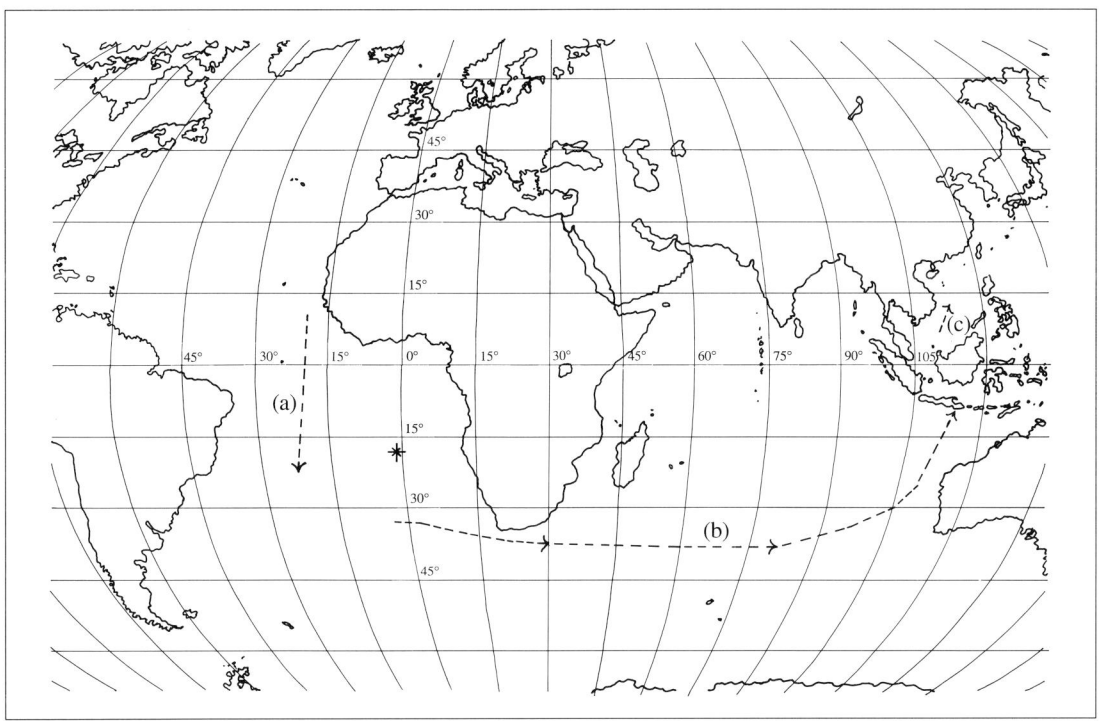

Route of the *Fredericus Rex Sueciæ* (1732–33) on her way to China, according to
Utdrag af 20 loggböcker … (UUB. L 183). The point * in the South Atlantic
is the only precise position of the homebound ship known.

a Hang by the water-side and a Good naturd man & ready to serve Europeans in
case of any difficulty & a man I had done Business with when there some years ago
with my Brother & who had serv'd us very well, This was aggreed to, & happen'd
not ill for us, for he provd of Good service to us as will be seen in its place, & the
two others above mention'd were both clapt up in Prison a few days after our
Arrival. So we went directly to Tinquas where we arriv'd about noon and were
very well receiv'd. And thus through the blessing of Good we put an End to one
very troublesome part of our voyage and arrivd at Canton safe & in Good health,
which was matter of no small Joy to us all.

For my part I well foresaw I could not pretend to have much pleasure even here,
(which a Chief SuperCargo seldom has time for) arriving so late & being earnest
to get away soon & if possible before any other ship which would require the
greater application & dispatch, But my Chief Care was the trouble I apprehended

measured upon arrival, and in obtaining permission to leave (the "Grand Chop") (Pritchard 1929
p. 114 ff.; Morse 1966–69, 1, pp. 247, 279; Gui 1994; cf. *Diary* pp. 109, 147, 163 ff., 188 f.).

to meet with from the Captain & others of the ship, For having the Chief Command & not daring trust the Captain with the management even in my

107   Absence made me easily perceive that I must have all the plague & trouble which I should have been without, had he been good for any thing, And indeed he took care to give me as much as he could by falling into his old Knavish designs almost as soon as my Back was turn'd from the ship, which He & his friends carryd much greater lengths than I could have expected. However I comforted my self with the hopes of some respite at least from his Bad Company, and the injoyment of some better at Canton to help to drive him & what had pass'd out of my thoughts.

Whampoa, roadstead of Canton. 18th century oil painting on canvas.
Gothenburg City Museum.

Notes on the voyage of the *Fredericus Rex Sueciæ* to Canton and back,
from *Utdrag af 20 loggböcker* ... (UUB. L 183).   →

Månad	D̊	Latitud	Longitud fr Teneriffa	Longit: från	NordDist: från	Compassens Missvisning	Fredericus Rex Sveciæ, Capt: Geo: H: Trolle Chef Å:
1731.							
Novb:	21.						Gick Seg: fr: Stockholm, kom till Gborg 11. Januarii 1732.
Februar: 1732	25	afseglade från Gborg. d: 9 Mars passe:		Duynkerk och d: 29. Mars			till ankars i Cadico. d: 13 Aprill Seglade därifrån.
Maij	1.	10: 6 X	356: 42			4: 6A NW	i Cadix lossade på Compade adras kongens flagg. 5: Skp:
	13.	0: 36 N				1: 42	man kom här ombord.
Juny	3.	32: 65	12: 12. 0			2: 58 NW	
Maij	27.	23: 10	351: 25			2: 11 NO	Juny 3: L: 32: 52. Long: 12: 12. Var: 2: 58 NW
Juny	8.	35: 22	28: 30			11: 61 NW	5: 33: 20 18: 40 7: 52
	10.	35: 40	34: 54			14: 23	14: 36: 48 45: 5 19: 27
	12.	35: 32	39: 43			16: 17	hade 85 f̶: grund på Caps bank
	24.	37: 3	77: 21			25: 30	Julij 1: 37: 44 95: 21 20: 13
	28.	37: 2	90: 34			22: 12	37: 52 96: 8 20: 16
Julij	3.	37: 38	97: 22	Longituden till P. Paul		20: 6 19: 30	Sag P. Paul i OSO
	7.	33: 44	113: 41			16: 4 17: 12	Julij 10: 29: 42 121: 28 10: 40
	3.	32: 32	116: 30			12: 25	16: 21: 4 136: 9 7: 14
	12.	26: 25	125: 9.			8: 46	
	24.	8: 44	136: 7			3: 36	Sags Land af Java d: 30. kom i N. Sunda
Aug:	14.	7: 11N	126: 57			2: 55	
	17.	11: 16	131: 56				Sags Pulo Sapate i NNW d: 26 Sag Chena.
Septb:	3.	Sags Land af China och d: 8 Septb: ankr: i Wampo; dar låg					2 Hollenske. 6 Enge: och 1 Fransk: Skepp: af de Eng:
Decem:	31.	Lyftade anckar o. Warpade fr: Wampo					var 2 country Skepp:
Janua: 1733	5.	1733 kom Directeuren Campbell o. Supercarg: ombs: Seglade					Septb: 25: kom till Ohuidukt Skepp
	28.	Ankrade på Batavia Redd					Octob: 1. borjade at lasta in
Mars	21.	SO: windarne borjade d: 16 i 12: 30 S: o d: gingo O: om SO i 17: 30					
Aprill	27.	Jinge 70 f̶: g̶r̶: O: om Caps				20: 31 NW	
	30.	hade 110 f̶: fin grå Sand på Banken				16: 42 16: 14	
Maij	23.	17: 255	16: 6 0:			10: 19	
	24.	16: 10.				8: 42	
	25.	16: 0	S. Helena i SSW i 5: 20			8: 45	Passerade S. Helena
Juny	8.					2: 4 2: 14 NO	i Sigte af Ferdinando, hwarest ankrades på Uk:
	16.	0: 0	Passerade Linien				grå Sand, och togs in watn
	17.	0: 52 N				1: 26 NW	
July	21.	42: 11				10: 21	
Aug:	14.	Sags land af Norrige d: 22 Sags Skagen och den 27. Augusti kom hem till Götteborg —					
Janua:	23.	Under Land af Wantam som bar SO; Sago 4 Skepp: gjorde klart till defension, och stodo 15 K. Siduing					
	24.	p: m: ankrade under Sumatra. De 4 Skeppen under Segel jämte 3 andra, som ankrade ½ mihl aktar om Skepp:					
	25.	Off: Comendeuren skot ett skarpt skott, då Flagg: och Wimpel					ströks: a: m: he 7: hemtades Capot: ombord, och d:
		Hollenske Skeppen Sände Sitt folk ombord, förgäfves sökande, och togo brättningen på sine Skepp					
	27.	Till Segels under Convoy af ett Skepp och en Brigg fr: Batavia, deraf ankrade d: 28. d: 29. bef Skep: frit					
Febr:	6.	Till Segels N: Hirdnan Capt: Rundinchen convoyade Skept: hit det Kallte hwaraf det blef taget					
	15.	blef Skeppet berott: fandondt: och Hollen: bottagna; Skildes från Hirdnan den 16:					
Aug:	9.	Sag Orcades d: 11. Sago Fairhill, och råkade Ostindiske skep:					
	14.	Sago Nazel d: 15 ankade på grund i Marstrand, man kom af; Seglade dädan d: 20:					
	22.	Sago Skagen och ankrade i Marstrand d: 27. kom till Gborg					

93

As there is kept here a Generall Diary[172] by all the Super-Cargos jointly, of the most material transactions that pass'd while we were here, which gives a daily Account of our Business & other things that happen'd here, I shall have the less to take notice of, but shall Content my self to relate such passages as are not mention'd in that, & which came often to my knowlege after those were wrote down, and all such matters as relate to the ship which came more particularly under my management & Direction, And for the rest I must refer to the foresaid Joint Diary, as well as Book of Contracts[173].

Sept[r] 8   After Dinner, we receiv'd visits from the Gentlemen of the French, Dutch & other Factorys[174] (all except from the English) as also from most of the China merchants of this place.

– 9   Not being yet able to wait upon the Hoppo (or Overseer or Chief Director of the Customs of this Province) we went to return the visits made us the day before by the Europeans & China merchants & tryd among the latter to sound the market or Prices of sundry Goods without coming to any Resolution.

---

[171] While the ship's company remained on board or took turns at mounting guard over the *bankshall*, the supercargoes took up residence in the factory for the duration of the stay in China. Every company rented a factory in the neighbourhood of the city of Canton, which functioned more or less as the office for their company's commercial affairs. It was at the factory that Chinese and European trading partners met each other.

[172] Campbell's mention of a general diary kept by all the supercargoes jointly serves to confirm that the present journal was written by Campbell for his own purposes.

[173] The book of contracts recorded the trading contracts between the Swedish Company, represented by its supercargoes, and the Chinese merchants.

[174] Every company rented a factory in the vicinity of Canton. The factory buildings were arranged entirely according to the Chinese building plan. The proprietors allowed Europeans gradually to introduce "amenities" and, more particularly, security measures to the buildings. Window-glass would be filled in place of mother-of-pearl frames so as to let in more light. Wooden sides were replaced by solid walls, while the roof-coverings of mats were exchanged for gypsum. Cellar vaults would be constructed inside the factory to accommodate the silver chests. There were cellars and emporia for stocking the goods awaiting transport by sampan out to the Company ships. In the factory itself the goods were inspected, inventoried and often also packaged. There were also spacious, sumptuous rooms and chambers for the accommodation of the supercargoes. In the early days the supercargoes would move into the factory for as long as their ship was lying at anchor. Later on they left permanent factory staff behind, who were permitted to stay on there as long as ships of their company were expected during the season. In the off-season, however, these factory personnel were obliged by the Chinese authorities to remove themselves to Portuguese Macao. Permanent personnel were not appointed by the Swedish Company until the termination of the second charter. These residents then had the task of following the prices of goods, and also their speculative value. At the same time they were to supply information concerning the annual consumption of imported products. They were supposed to keep themselves thoroughly informed of the needs of the Chinese market and also of the prospective supply and demand situation.

– 10   Tinqua went with [us] this morning to pay our Compliments to the Hoppo, we told him by our Interpreter (or Linguist[175]) that we had come very far off by orders of the King of Sweden to indeavour to settle a Good Corrospondence & Trade with China, & that we hop'd that he would please to give us all necessary protection & asistance, which would incourage the Company his Swedish Majesty had establish'd in his Dominions to carry on this Trade to send ships every year to this Country, He receiv'd us very Civilly & having made us sit down in Chairs plac'd there for us (as is Customary with Europeans) offerd us Tea, & told us he was very glad we were come, & assurd us that

109   we should injoy all necessary Protection & all the Privileges that any European nation injoy'd here, He wish'd us a Good Trade & a great deal of money, & made us a present of a couple of pieces of silk, which was a piece of Civility not practis'd by former Hoppos. He had done the same, it seems, by all the European & Country SuperCargos. We thank'd him & withdrew

Sept.[r] 11   Tinqua having inform'd us that the Hoppo had order'd his Pay de Casas[176] (as the Portuguese & others term them here, being a sort of stewards or Head Officers of the Household of the Mandarins[177] or Great Men) to go down to day to measure the ship, we went down Early aboard to receive them in Company with Tinqua, They came about {&} noon, & by their Measure (for which vide Journal   [178]) she was above a 3[d] Rate but under a 2[d]. We treated them as well as we could & saluted them with 8 Guns at their going away, They went aboard another ship & return'd to us, but did not stay long with us, These Gentlemen were not very fond of our firing Guns so beggd me not to fire any more which request I very willingly complyd with, hating it full as much as they.

– 12   We could not as yet bring the merchants to fall[179] their prices, being glad to flatter themselves with the hopes of more ships arriving, & taking it off their hands, which notion some of the Europeans themselves incourage them as the French by telling they expect another French ship, & the Dutch by talking [of] one from Zealand which they had reason to expect long ago having left Europe as I believe in the month of January but they have as yet heard nothing of her. And now there is little reason to expect any since the Easterly winds seem to be set in and will in all appearance continue so these 6 months which will make it impossible

---

[175] Local interpreter, assisting the supercargoes in their contacts with the Chinese merchants. (Lewis 1991, p. 154.)

[176] From Portuguese *pai* 'father' and *casa* 'house, household, residence'.

[177] Civil or military Chinese servants. The term *mandarin* as used by the Europeans originates from the Portuguese, representing a transcription from Sanskrit *mantrin*, which means 'counsellor'. In Chinese, the term *kuan-fo* was used. Mandarins were divided into nine ranks; the lower ranks could climb in the hierarchy by passing examinations. (Lewis 1991, p. 160 f.)

[178] Campbell's blank.

[179] *Fall* (trans. verb) 'to lower' (a price etc.; now obsolete).

for any ships to get hither more from the Westward this year. The English having made their Contracts long ago don't trouble themselves whether more ships arrive or not, But the Dutch being wiser in their own Conceit than all others think better to stay being assur'd as they pretend that they will buy

110   cheaper some months hence, without reflecting upon the time they lose by it, and the risk of getting the worst Tea after all others are provided, Besides the Chinese know as well as themselves what Commodities they want & understand very well how to manage such strange Ignorant Creatures as they seem to be, none of all the 6 SuperCargos having ever been before but the Chief who was Captain of one of their ships one voyage to this place. But I hear the true reason of their not having yet made any Contract is their not being able to agree among themselves, for as they all want to make money by any means good or bad, without Regard to their owners, one wants to buy of one merchant & another of another, in order to make some private Bargain for themselves, I can't help wishing them to continue long in these sentiments. The English Super-Cargos I hear have contracted as I am informd at 16 or 17 Tales[180] a pecul[181] for their Bohea Tea[182] & the French at 17 & 18 Tales pr D⁰ though we know the price to be much lower, But these Gentlemen have likely their own Reasons, as buying of Gold so much the Cheaper for themselves or such like fine reasons, as has been too much practis'd by European SuperCargos here.

Upon our Arrival at Canton I set about immediately getting a Compradore for the ship (or a Person to provide the ships Company with Provisions while she is at Vampo) & to aggree for a piece of Ground to build a Banksaal to unload the ships stores into, & having found one Antonio & aggreed with him for 90 Tales to build it (which is cheaper than any ship here has it for) I have sent him aboard & order'd him to set immediately about it that we may not lose any time.

Sept\[r\] 13\[th\]   Last night I receivd a Letter from C. Kitching from the ship (now lying at Vampo

---

[180] *Tael*, a Chinese monetary unit (originally a unit of weight). 1 tael silver = 10 mas = 100 candareens = 1,000 cash. 1 tael = at least 4 1/2 *daler silvermynt* (Swedish currency).

[181] *Picul* (Malay-Javanese *pikul* 'a man's load'), a measure of weight used in China and the East generally, equal to 100 catties, i.e. about 133 1/2 lbs. avoirdupois or 60.5 kg.

[182] Tea was one of the most important products in the return cargoes, especially for the Swedish Company. There were many varieties. In the category of black teas we find Bohea, Congou, Souchong, and Pekoe. The green teas were Bing, Singlo, Hyson, Hyson Shin, and Tonkay – to restrict ourselves to the most common varieties. Black and green teas are differentiated from one another more by the manner in which the tea leaves were dried than by their own natural properties. In broad terms, green teas originated from the province of An-hwei, while black teas were harvested in the province of Fukien. The different varieties were determined simply by the different seasons in which the tea leaves were harvested. Black Bohea tea was to account for the bulk of Swedish tea shipments during the Company's entire existence. Bohea was picked in the early summer and sold at a moderate price, all the lower if the types were coarse or the tea no longer as fresh. Bohea was itself once subdivided into three classes. It was a delicate task for the supercargoes to determine whether the Bohea corresponded to the quality ordered.

about a couple of leagues from this place) complaining that Styrman Lund had refus'd to obey Him & Mr Baron & hinderd the People from doing their work as they had orderd them, & had grossly abus'd them by most scurillous language &c

111   & that they complaind to the Captain who did not think fit to give them any manner of satisfaction pretending he would first speak to me, Provok'd to find that I must be never free from plague & vexation from such villains, whether I was ashore or aboard, I wrote to the Captain by the same messenger letting him know that I was surpriz'd to hear that Lund should begin so soon after I had left the ship to his Extravagance & to be guilty of open mutiny against his superiour officers, & yet more that He whose Duty it was to quell such Crimes should be present & see it & take no notice of it nor to put Lund in Arrest immediately &c for which I refer to their Letters & mine.

This being an Affair of Consequence & fit to be put an immediate Check I resolv'd to go aboard this morning, & as I was just ready to go up comes the worthy Captain his mouth full of Lies to Excuse himself from what I allegd against him in my Letter which he had receivd, But as I never believ'd one word he sayd but on the Contrary did not doubt but he had been the first Actor in this himself and stirr'd up Lund to what he had done I told him since he did not think fit to punish such Actions I would go & see what I could do & immediately got into the China Boat with Mr Brown to go aboard, He seeing this came along with us. Amongst other ridiculous nonsense he told me He could not pretend to put Lund in Arrest without those officers giving him a memorial in writing desiring it, as if their complaining to him by word of mouth & his own seeing a part of it were not sufficient reasons, But he did all he could not to see it for assoon as he observ'd it begin he retird off the Deck instead of preventing it. We got on board before Dinner and assoon as we had din'd I examin'd into the Affair by calling several witnesses that had been present & saw what pass'd, & confirm'd every word the officers had alleg'd against him & that he had even threatend to beat them &c I then call'd Lund & ask'd him how he could have the Impudence to abuse his superiour officers in such a mutinous manner

112   or to hinder the men from doing what work they had been commanded, to which he had no reply to make. I dismiss'd him & then ask'd the Captain what he thought of the matter now & what he thought should be done with such a fellow, that I knew no other way but to call immediately a Court Martial and have him punish'd as the Laws of Sweden in such Cases requir'd, This was what the Captain did not want pretending he could not hold a Court Martial not having officers enough for it, And I reflecting that as Kitching & Baron could not sit at such a Court in their own Cause and that except Styrman Breemer all the rest of the officers were more likely to be of the Captain's or Lunds side than of the side of Justice, I thought better drop that for the present, In the mean put him immediately in Arrest in his Cabbin with 2 sentrys upon him till I should see what Course would be proper to take with him, which I saw immediately done. After having perform'd this Act of Justice & told the Captain a little of my mind, I went back to Canton with Mr Brown where we arriv'd the same Evening.

Septr 14   Having intelligence that the ship we had seen on the [5th]^183 lying at Anchor was really an Ostend ship & the SuperCargos were already at Macao or on the way coming up, I was desirous at once to make a Contract before the China men should have the news or at least before the Super-Cargos arriv'd at Canton, for being a large ship and as I heard a Rich stock I apprehended the merchants would immediately raise the price of Tea, we had before tryd most of the merchants and they talkd of 15 & 14 Tales pr pecul the lowest price, And Considering that Suqua had no dealings this year with English or Dutch and had a good deal of Tea upon his hands, I thought he was as likely a man as any to break the price & sell as Cheap as any Body, so I resolv'd once more to try him, Just as I was

113   going out, Hunqua (a top merchant sprung up since I was here & whom I had never seen before, but known to Mr Brown when he was here last) call'd young or fat Hunqua^184 to distinguish him from Tan-Hunqua^185, came to pay us a Visit & incouragd me to go to Suqua (from whom he was very likely sent) who he sayd would sell as Cheap as any Body. I accordingly went to talk with him, usd many reasons with him to serve us Cheap, as being the first time & that he might be assurd that he who serv'd this new Company cheapest & gave the best Goods this time would be preferd on all other Occasions &c I brought him down after a good deal of reasoning pro & Con to 13 Tales for Bohea & 10 Tales for Green but could not get him lower, so I left him telling him that we could not pretend to give that price, though I was very well satisfyd that he had offer'd it for that. I returnd Home immediately to acquaint the SuperCargos where I had been & what Suqua had profferd to sell Tea for, & ask'd their opinion, As they all knew that this was the lowest price Any merchant had yet offerd to sell for (the cheapest others came to being 14 T.^186 a pecul Bohea & 12 for Green) and much cheaper than any that had been sold this year, They readily aggreed to my proposal of going all together & try to beat him lower if not to strike a Contract with him at those prices (before the Ostend Super-Cargos should arrive which happening we could not tell but he might alter his mind) if not for the whole at least for a part of what

---

^183 Campbell left a blank for the date, which he had evidently forgotten.
^184 Campbell describes *(Young) Hunqua* as "the fairest merchant we met with here this year" (*Diary* p. 116 f.). He was apparently the only merchant with whom Campbell managed to keep on good terms to the end and who paid him the courtesy of going on board with him upon his departure (*Diary* p. 189).
^185 According to Morse (1966–69), 1, p. 183, *Ton Hungqua (Hungqua, Honqua)* is first mentioned in 1727 in the East India Company Chronicles ("the best man upon the place next to Suqua"). He was in fact Suqua's rival and the man behind the downfall of the Hoppo on 26 Sept. 1732 and the imprisonment of Suqua. (For Campbell's lengthy account of the causes of these events see *Diary* pp. 169–171; cf. also Morse 1966–69, 1, pp. 202 ff., 211.)
^186 From here onwards Campbell often uses the abbreviation *T.* for *Tales*, i.e. *taels* (cf. note 180).

we had Occasion for. We accordingly went all to Suqua and did all we could to lower the price, but to no purpose, so Contracted for a part of Bohea at 13 T. pr pecul & Green for 10 T pr D^O he to pay for the Chests & all Charges, after which vide Joint Diary & Contract Book.

Amongst other Arguments I us'd with the merchants to perswade them to sell Cheaper to us than to other Super-Cargos here I told every one of them at first as well when I was with them alone as in Company with our other Super-Cargos, that the price payd by other Super-Cargos was no Rule to us (for that was ever in their mouths, that the English gave them so much & the French

114
gave them so much & the Dutch had offerd so much &c) because I knew very well the underhand methods practis'd other years by Some of those Gentlemen, which made them give a greater price for the Goods they bought for their Companys & masters, but that we were upon a quite different footing intending to accept of no Presents from them nor had no Gold to buy at a low price for our own private Accounts &c They all frankly confessd that other years such ways had been us'd with them, but that this year truly the SuperCargos were very honest &c But however I found this they did not much like, and one of them very plainly told me, while I was talking to him in that strain, that truly he did not like Honest Super-Cargos because there was nothing to be got by them, The meaning of this when Super-Cargos act honestly & for their owners Interest they will not be impos'd upon by the merchants either in the price or in the Quality of the Goods which they are always sure to suffer themselves to be if the merchants make them amends another way, which they are always glad to Do as being much greater gainers than by fair dealing. However I stuck to my Argument in order to prevent the merchants having any such thoughts of us & to hinder them from offering any of us a temptation to act in such a base manner, and chose the rather to talk so to them in presence of all our Super-Cargos in order to prevent them offering any of us, as well as them from Accepting any such thing, for I must confess I had some fears of one of us (notwithstanding of what I had once hinted to him and his fair promises to me) who had been here before & who I knew had been concern'd in such sort of vile practices, And though I was in hopes He would not this time run into such measures after such declarations as I had often made; yet the temptation was too sweet for a Person bred & accustom'd to such ways, as will be seen in its due place & which I had not known if it had

115
not been for an Affair that happen'd in our Dealings of which he was the Chief Occasion of himself. But to leave this Case to another time, I will faithfully relate a Circumstance that happend about this time to my self, in order to show our Gentlemen at Home (especially such as are not acquainted with the ways practisd here by Europeans) what risks they run in trusting their Affairs in Bad peoples hands, and how Easy it is for those that are trusted especially a Chief Super-Cargo, to cheat & abuse them, enough of which I saw this year at Canton. The

Circumstance I mean is this, Amongst other merchants I visited & sounded about the price of Teas was Beau-Keyqua[187], who of late years has grown the greatest merchant & much by such a practice as I have hinted, Though I did not expect to do much good with him as being intirely in with the English whose business he did this year, as well as with the Chief of the Dutch whose business he expected to do as being much his Friend, yet I was resolvd not to neglect trying him as well as the rest so that before we concluded any Contract I also went to see him for a second time, He no doubt expecting that I was come with an Intent to do Business with him receiv'd me very Civilly, carry'd me to a dark inner Room, shut windows & Doors so that we were in no danger of being overheard or interrupted, I immediately guessd what thoughts he might intertain of me as being so much accustom'd with such ways from other with whom he was better acquainted, However I began my story asking him the price of Goods & chiefly the price of Teas, He told me that he could not sell Bohea under 16 Tale a pecul & Green under 13 T. p^r D^o, I answerd him that was an Extravagant price and that there was not one merchant in Town but what offerd it me much lower than that, & then ply'd him with the same Arguments as I had done the rest, that though this new Company had sent but a small ship & a small stock this year only to try & see who were the most reasonable merchants and who would serve them best, for he might believe the Person that serv'd them best this year would be their Chief merchant another time and that as I was a Director of the Company my self I could with

116   the more reason assure him of this &c After musing a little he sayd that was very well & true, But how much Tea did we want to buy of him, I told him that would be according to the price & Goodness of it but would not explain my self as to the quantity or give any positive promise, He then thinking to strike the nail on the Head at once open'd him self more freely & sayd that If I would take all of him & give a reasonable price though not quite so much as others gave him He would make me a very handsome face (an expression they use when they intend to offer a handsome present or some way or other to make it worth our while to deal with them) I seeing his drift & not being able to keep my Temper told him roundly that he was very much deceiv'd if he took me for such a person as many of the Super-Cargos he us'd to deal with were, That I came upon no such footing, and all I wanted was to buy Cheap & Good for those that had imployd me, & wanted no handsome faces of any Body. This not being language He was us'd to at least from many Super-Cargos from Europe, stunn'd him for a while & made him very silent, at last he sayd he would give Bohea at 15 and Green at 12 p^r pecul but no

---

[187] According to Gui (1994) the name of *Beau Khiqua (Keyqua, Caiqua, Coiqua, Khoiqua)* actually refers to two Hong merchants, *Li Kaiguan* and his son *Li Guanghua*, "Beau" in Cantonese meaning "security" as in "security merchant" (cf. note 170 above). The father was appointed one of the "chief merchants" in 1729. The Swedes made no contract with him in 1732–33. Old Khiqua seems to have been succeeded by his son not later than 1736.

lower. I then told him I saw very well what sort of a man he was, & that I would take care to have no Contracts or do any Business at all with him without he would change his way, And so we parted not at all satisfy'd with one another, & without ever having a good understanding together afterwards as I had reason to discover before I left Canton.

Not being willing to put all the Business in one mans hands (as is often practis'd when any underhand work is carryd on) and desirous to see who would serve us best this year, I thought better to take some from one & some from another, especially from such merchants as had not much dealings with other Super-Cargos here, so went and aggreed to day with Tinqua Pinky & Hunqua for sundry parcels of Tea. And I must do the Justice to the Person I mentiond last, to say that he was the fairest merchant

117 we met with here this year (though some of our Gentlemen could not at all come to like him for reasons [that] will appear in time) He not only was the first that brought the price of Bohea to 13 T. p^r pecul (though he offerd to sell but little for himself & rather advis'd me to go to Suqua) and now sold Congo[188] at 18 T. though no Body else would speak under 22 T, & some much higher, as I was afterwards oblig'd my self to pay for a quantity I bought of another, But he never ask'd two prices in his Teas but told at one word the lowest he could sell it at, and as for the Quality of his Goods we never had the least trouble with him being always the best of the kind and which even such of our Gentlemen (as had no manner of inclination to show him the least favour or as they would do to others could refuse) could refuse, or if there should happen a Basket to be a little musty a top (as will happen in the best parcel of Teas that are to be had) or in short that any of us did not like, He made no scruple to order it away & call immediately for another Basket & let us chuse as we pleas'd, But this was not the method practis'd by some other merchants with us who did all they could to deceive us offering bad Teas & insisting upon our taking of them & that they had no better nor no better could be had, which put me often out of humour & go away & leave off packing sometimes till they found better. As I had no regard to one merchant more than another no further than as they serv'd us well, & that I did not know what opinion some of our Gentlemen might have of me (being very natural to suspect a Chief & often with too much reason) I lay'd it down for a Rule never to press my opinion of the Quality of Goods but chose rather to hear & follow theirs and kept my own opinion to my self till I heard theirs both as to the price & quality, except when I saw that they had a mind to favour some they lik'd to our prejudice, which I am sorry to say I had occasion to observe more than once notwithstanding of all their finesse & Art to hide (I mean chiefly one person

---

[188] *Congou tea*, black tea harvested in the month of May. By virtue of the leaves being smaller and finer, this type also turned out more expensive, since it was a tea of the finer type.

well known here) it, I then thought it was my Duty to interfere & cross their views, as will be seen before this Diary is finish'd.

The same morning & soon after our Contract for our Teas was done, arriv'd the Ostend SuperCargos, who went directly

118 to Pinkeys House where we met them about Dinner time, They were John Ley 1st SuperCargo – Van Pruyssen[189] 2^d & – – – – Coppinger[190] 3^d The first & last are Irish, the 2^d a Flemming. I had reason not to be extremely pleas'd with their being Here at this time, and found every day more & more reason to wish they had not come while I was here.

Septr 16 Being sensible that nothing could hinder our Early dispatch from this place but our silks[191], It was necessary to give orders about the making them as soon as possible, I therefore upon my coming hither went through all the merchants to try the prices, But Raw silk being very dear this year they kept them all very high, so that there was no making any Contract with them as yet, To be ready for it I had set down the different prices of every different sort, from every merchant, as he could sell them, in order to compare them together & better inable us to judge what to do, Suqua seem'd to be very indifferent about making of silks & therefore kept them high as did Mandarin Luiqua. As I knew also that Beau Keyqua had the Character of making the best silks of any Body here though dearer, yet as the difference of the Goodness would easily make amends for that if not too great, I thought of buying some of him, But there was no dealing with him, He not only kept the price up very high but also fairly told me that he could not promise

---

[189] The full name of the Flemish supercargo of the Ostend Company was *François van Pruyssen* (Huisman 1902, pp. 378, 498; Degryse 1988, pp. 74–77).

[190] Probably identical with *James Adam Coppinger*, known to have been in the service of the Ostend Company in 1727 and in that of the SEIC in 1740 and later. (Huisman 1902, pp. 378, 498; Kjellberg 1974, pp. 128, 178, 203.)

[191] Both silk fabrics and raw silk were bought in Canton and exported to Sweden. In the earlier years of the Company, the cargo of silk fabrics imported by the *Fredericus R.S.* in 1733 represented a record. This peak was not reached again until the years 1745 and 1748. However, imports of foreign silk textiles represented dangerous competition for indigenous manufacturers. The Swedish silk industry experienced a period of major development in the early 18th century. No wonder then that the foreign imports caused criticism, soon becoming a fierce indictment that eventually reached the *Riksdag*. The discussion led to a first taxation of import in 1741, but this did not satisfy the party hostile to the Company trade.
    Among silk fabrics, there were semi-finished and finished products. Most of the silk fabrics were taffetas, with variants such as armozeens and daridas. Pekings also belonged to the taffetas. There were large quantities of paduasoys and damasks. Fabrics could be flowered, striped or plain. Individual finished products are also found: silk hose, neckerchieves, nightcaps, handkerchieves, walking-stick braids, knee-strings, shoelaces and girdles. Sewing silk is noticed as well. That the *Fredericus R.S.* could import so much silk in 1733 is explained by the fact that the severe regulations on silk import were not yet in force. The truth is that the Swedish Company was to become the origin of the public debate in Sweden. Generally speaking, however, East Indian silk imports were an international problem. It should be noted that raw silk did not fall under the restriction imposed on fabrics. This permitted the Company to increase the import.

to have them ready in less than 110 days, which I saw was making a Jest of us, Since no body to ask more than 70 or 80 days at the longest, so I soon gave over thinking more of him.

Having often consulted our Super-Cargos in what Commodities we had best lay out the Companys stock in, as well as observ'd the Advices I had from Friends before I left Sweden, As the principal Articles must be Teas China ware & silks the way was to proportion the Quantity of each as would best answer the market at Home having regard also to the stowage of the ship & what she could Hold of each sort, not forgetting

119   how far the Companys stock would reach for the Purchase of them, I found the Majority of the Super-Cargos were for Teas which though I was a good deal dubious about them my self I aggreed to, to which I was also incourag'd by the opinion of one of our friends who was us'd to this Trade & knew the prices of Goods in forreign Countries very well. I wish they may answer for we have a good Quantity of them, If their Goodness will hold, & as they are Cheap, there is more room to hope the best.

We had unfortunately brought no Kentlage[192] in the ship from Sweden for Ballast, though I often mentiond it to the Captain at Stockholm, & for fear he did not understand me I got Mr Macket[193] the ship-Builder to explain what I meant to him, whether he could not apprehend the use of it, or that he was resolv'd not to have it because I had proposd it, He neglected to provide any, & often us'd to say he had enough, & when we came to examine afterwards what his Enough was it was faggots & pieces of wood which the English call Dunnige[194]. And our Ballast being all vast big stones we were obligd to throw them out as being very unfit for a ship to be loaded with Goods, and found it very hard to get good Ballast here at least enough for our purpose. For these reasons Mr Brown & the English officers (who best knew such things) were of opinion that we must buy Tutanegue[195] in order to make the ship stiff & fit to perform her voyage back

---

[192] *Kentledge,* the pigs of cast iron used as ballast to provide stability in a vessel. Heavy items of cargo stowed low in the holds of a ship as an addition to ballasting during a voyage are sometimes known as kentledge goods. (*The Oxford Companion to Ships & the Sea,* 1976, p. 446.)

[193] The Englishman *William Mackett* was master shipwright at least between 1724 and 1749 at the Terra Nova shipyard in Stockholm, where the *Fredericus R.S.* was built in 1725. (Zethelius 1955/56, pp. 68, 77; *Svenskt skeppsbyggeri …,* 1963, p. 179; cf. Introduction p. xxxiv.)

[194] *Dunnage,* loose wood or wooden blocks used in the holds of a merchant ship to secure the cargo above the floors and away from the sides to protect it from any sweating and to wedge it firmly so that it did not get thrown about by the motion of the ship at sea. (*The Oxford Companion to Ships & the Sea,* 1976, p. 276.)

[195] *Tutenag,* a metal whose ingredients was a matter of discussion at that time. There was also confusion with other metals. On the one hand it is believed to have been an alloy consisting of zinc, copper and nickel or tin; on the other, of iron, copper and zinc. Hence it often passed as "copper" and sometimes as "zinc". A third opinion is that of an alloy of tin and bismuth at the rate of two to one. Tin and bismuth in combination with antimony would give a new metal amalgam employed

which she would never be able to do without it, being nothing else here to be found fit for that purpose. This was very much against our inclination the price being extravagantly high compard with other years, so that there can be little profit expected by it, except that the other Europe ships carry little of it Home. In fine it being an absolute necessity we aggreed with Suqua to day for 100 pecul some more a pecul below the Current price that other sell it at.

We begun to day also to buy China ware[196], but find blew & white scarce, The English & others having pick'd the best, so that we shall be oblig'd to take up with their leavings

Sept[r] 17   As we cannot defer any longer making our Contracts for our silks after considering the prices of the Different merchants,

120   we resolv'd to make all our Contracts before them assoon as we could not only to save time but for fear they grew dearer as in all likelyhood we suppos'd they would, & as we found afterwards, at least I did to my no small loss, so this day we began & contracted with Hunqua &c for a Parcel vide Contract Book &c we had enough ado to bring other merchants so low as Hunqua, till I threatend to buy of others who offerd silks at such prices, they immediately concluded Hunqua to be the man I meant & were not at all pleasd with him for being the first to lower the price of every thing, & to show so bad an Example. We were oblig'd to give more for Tutanegue to day to Hunqua, for Suqua will let us have no more at the same price. Cap[t] Tully[197] tells me he cannot get none under 8.T.4.M[198] a pecul, which is a price he dare not meddle with.

---

to imitate silver. Combinations with zinc and lead existed too. All this indicates, however, that tutenag was further compounded. From our analysis of Swedish Company cargoes we know that porcelain and tutenag were loaded in proportion to other goods. It corroborates the function which both tutenag and porcelain performed with regard to stabilisation of the vessel in the water. The explanation given by Campbell serves to confirm this. (Ekeberg 1756, p. 316; Savary des Bruslons 1759–65, 4, pp. 798, 1006, 1114; Kjellberg 1974, p. 264 f.; Koninckx 1980b, pp. 237–240; Lewis 1991, p. 240; Ljungstedt 1992, p. 262.)

[196] Porcelain occupied an important place in the return cargoes of East Indiamen. The porcelain purchased by Europeans came from the province of Kiang-si. The Chinese, after many centuries of experience, had attained a high level of stylistic skill in porcelain manufacturing. Porcelain was highly prized in China itself. However, the porcelain purchased by the East India Companies seems to have been of the lowest category. The most valuable Chinese porcelain appears to have been reserved for the Imperial Court and for the mandarins, while Company porcelain must be reckoned as merely of third-rate quality. The arrival of the Europeans in Canton had generated such a heavy demand for porcelain that the number of kilns was considerably increased, leading to mass production. The blue and white porcelain, decorated with landscapes and plant motifs, was the most common type. There was also red and white chinaware.

[197] *Timothy Tullie* was a captain of country ships trading between India and the Far East. At this time he was in command of a ship from Fort St. George (*Diary* p. 143). He was an old friend of Campbell's, having been captain of a ship that sailed to Canton in 1726 with Colin and his brother Hugh as supercargoes. Tullie was eventually made a director of the English East India Company. (Gill 1961, p. 121.)

[198] I.e. 8 taels 4 mas (cf. note 180). Campbell seems to have usually added the abbreviations for *taels*

Sent a Chop[199] (or Order) from the Hoppo to day to bring our Perpetts[200] up to our factory, I would gladly have only brought the Companys part, but the officers aboard pressing to have the Ship unloaded as was necessary, I was oblig'd to send for mine too.

Sept[r] 18   The Mandarins having orderd the merchants to tell the Europeans to fire no more Guns at Vampo, by reason this is a time set apart for chusing the Law & Soldier Mandarins, and as they retire before their Examinuation for 6 weeks to their studies in a House appointed on purpose near the River, they say the noise of Guns will disturb them, The merchants well knowing that the Dutch are naturally great Lovers of fire & smoak, took occasion of the SuperCargos & Captains going yesterday aboard of their ships to acquaint them with this order, & beg of them earnestly not to fire, But like true Dutchmen they were above all orders & chose to do it the rather because forbid, so getting very Drunk grew very noisy and fird all the while they were on board at an extravagant rate. This provok'd the Xunhu[201] & fouyen[202] (the two greatest Mandarins the one a sort of Vice Roy or Governour & the first General or Commander in Chief of the Army in this Province) who took occasion of this to be very

121   angry with the Hoppo (who is the Mandarin that has the more particular Charge & Inspection of every thing relating to Trade & the merchants) whom they want to quarrell with & sent him a severe reprimand as if it had been owing to his neglect of giving proper orders or advertisement to the China merchants & Europeans The Hoppo being highly offended with the Dutch has forbid any Chinese to go near their factory. The more follies these Gentlemen (if that is not too honourable a term to call them by) commit the better, It were to be wish'd they would provoke the Government of China to forbid them their Ports, for they will ruin the Trade of this place in time, as they generally do for all others wherever they come, But such is the strong Appetite of the Chinese for money & Gain (not even less than that of the Dutch themselves if possible) that should the old Gentleman in Black with his Cloven foot appear with silver in his paw they would ask no questions or scruple to make him very welcome and even handsome face, though it should smell of the place he brought it from. It is true they have heard stories enough of their Tyranny in the East & know how near they are to them and neither love nor esteem them, but they consider the more ships the more money, more Duties to

---

and *mas* (or *Tales* and *mace* in Campbell's spelling) afterwards, writing each of them above the figure to which it refers.

[199] *Chop* or *chap*, a design stamped on goods as a trademark, especially in the Far East; also used to denote all kinds of documents delivered by the Chinese local authorities.

[200] *Perpet*, obsolete abbreviation of *perpetuana* (French *perpétouanes*), a light glossy twilled fabric of wool manufactured in England from the 16th century, which took its name from its durability. Exported to the East in the 17th and first half of the 18th centuries. (Lewis 1991, p. 188.)

[201] Chinese *Xunfu* 'governor of a province'.

[202] Chinese *Fuyuan*.

the Emperour, more plunder for the Mandarins & a higher price to the merchants for their Goods. The Chinese are quick sighted Enough & soon can see into the Genius of people, & they have observ'd such strange Creatures amongst the Captains & Super-Cargos of the Dutch that have been here that they speak of them with great Contempt, But at last it is Masqui[203] (or no matter) they bring a great many Dollers[204] & Ducatoons[205].

They never can see a more queer set of that nation than is here now, intirely Ignorant & unacquainted with the Affairs of this place, except the Chief Super-Cargo who has been here once before & being well acquainted with the Roguery practis'd amongst the merchants, would fain run away with the plunder without having the Conscience to allow the other poor fellows any share, which they observing have reason to oppose him, And he on his own part having more spirit & strength than any of them finds the most prevailing Argument to bring them over to his schemes to be the Argumentum bacilinum or a good hearty drubbing which he lays upon them sometimes very literally, And if that won't do he is always sure to make

122   them all very quiet at last by only sparing amongst them a small share of his Ill-got Gains, which no doubt he must do before he has done all his Business here, He will grow tir'd of his other Argument of Beating for 5 or 6 against one are too much and they had like yesterday when aboard ship to have play'd him a slippery trick by the help of their Captains (who are also members of the Councel) they had a plot to arrest him aboard, but he unluckily for them discoverd it & beat some of them & duck'd others & so made them very tame. But I must leave the Dutch Fools & return to our own.

The Captain has been with me to plead for his Dear friend Lund (who it seems is very tir'd of his Confinement) and beggs I would give orders for his Release or try him at a a Court Martial, As he knows as well as I that we cannot well do the latter he no doubt expects his Liberty, And as I was willing once more to try him & see if he would amend his manners, I told the Captain that I must know first if Capt Kitching & Mr Baron would be satisfyd with such satisfaction as I could think of to wit that Lund should ask them both Pardon for what was past & promise to behave better for the future towards them, that if they were satisfyd with this I would give him his Liberty but at the same time let him know that his Affair was not decided as to a Tryal but only suspended till he came Home

---

[203] Portuguese *mas* 'but', 'yet' and *que* 'what'.

[204] *Dollars*, silver dollars or piastres. Pillar dollars (representing the Pillars of Hercules in their design), ryals of eight, pieces of eight, were the so-called Spanish dollars, minted at the Royal Mint of Seville, current in the China trade for three centuries; 95 touch, of the Chinese standard. Mexico dollars were minted at the Viceroyal Mint of Mexico; 94 touch. (Morse 1966–69, 1, pp. 212, 263.)

[205] *Ducatoon*, a silver coin minted by the Mint of Venice; 96 touch; formerly current in Italy, Holland and some other European states, worth from 5 to 6 shillings sterling. (Morse 1966–69, 1, p. 68.)

& where we could bring him to a regular Tryal, This I added to keep him in the mean time in aw, The Captain assurd me that C. Kitching & Mr Baron would be satisfyd with this. But I not trusting to his Assurances I wrote to them both desiring their opinions, which they were willing to aggree as they saw there was no other Remedy, At the same time I told the Captain that Lund must write a Line to me confessing his fault & promising to amend his Conduct before I would allow him his Liberty, All this being done he was releas'd from his Arrest & sent ashoar to the Banksaal to take care of it, I refer for other particulars to their sundry Letters.

Septr 19   This morning the Perpetts were brought to the Factory, being 80 bales & 1/2 bale, containing in all 2411 pieces, of which 1206 1/2 ps [206] mine & 1204 1/2 the Companys, These were 2 of the Companys cutup to make wastecoats & Breeches for the Pinnace Crew before we came

123   ashoar. Suqua & some other of the merchants happen'd to be in the Factory when the Perpetts were open'd, so I ask'd them if they would not buy them but none of them were inclin'd to it but Suqua as I thought He ask'd me how many pieces there were I told him 1200 meaning the Companys & ask'd him 9 Tale a ps for them, He knowing we had more in all sayd he would let the Companys alone & would rather take those belonging to the Gentlemen meaning us all Super-Cargos (not knowing they were mine) I told him that it was the Companys we wanted to sell & not the others for there was time enough for them by & by after the Companys were all out of the House, But he offerd so low a price that we could not aggree with him. His saying he would rather take the Gentlemens had a meaning in it that I easily div'd into, which may serve to discover another method SuperCargos have here to get money to their owners loss, to wit He would not have scrupled to have given a high price for our private stock in hopes to make us give him a higher price for what Goods we might want for the Company or at least to receive of him merchandise worse in quality than we had aggreed for. Had I approvd of this practice I might have put some thousand tales in my pocket (as some of the merchants did not scruple to tell me afterwards) & sav'd my self a great deal of trouble, which I had after about them, for at that time provided I could give them any hopes of doing more business with them (especially after their way) they would have given me 9 Tale a ps for mine & even more if I insisted upon it, & would have favour'd them in the sale of the Companys or in the buying of the Companys Goods. But my firm resolution not so much as to offer mine to sale till the Companys were all gone & the difficulty I had to sell the Companys by reason of two of our merchants being lock'd up &c forc'd me to part with them just at my coming away for near a Tale less a ps than at last I sold the Companys for, which was not the only loss this Affair brought upon me, for

---

[206] *Pieces.*

being resolv'd not to lose a day for my own Goods I was glad to part with them to any Body for what I could get and receive very indifferent Goods for some & give higher prices than the Company gave for others, & Had not I perswaded Hunqua at last to take the greatest part of them almost at his own price I must have left them behind.

But it was time for us to consult how to get rid of the Companys part of the Perpetts there were but two ways, one which is often if not commonly practis'd was to barter them for Goods that is when

124   we made any Contract for Goods that we wanted to buy at the same time to fix the price of the perpetts & make them take them in part for money & to jumble the prices together, Another way was not to speak of our Perpetts when we bought Goods till after we had brought the Goods down to the lowest price & made our Contract for them & then oblige the merchant to take such a part of them at a reasonable profit in proportion to the Goods we bought of him, Some of our Gentlemen were for the first as being the Easiest & most Common method, But then I reflected that by this method we could never come at the true price of the Goods we bought since so much more we rais'd the price of the Perpetts so much more they would that of their Goods and perhaps get more profit in that way by us (which I knew they would easily enough come in to with that view or with the view of giving us worse Goods) than by selling our Perpetts as we could amongst them after we had settled the Contract for their Goods, And Mr Brown being of my opinion that this would be most for the Companys Interest, I immediately set about it, & perswaded Tinqua to take 200 ps, & Pinky 200, & Hunqua 200 ps, the rest I reserv'd for Suqua & other merchants that we should yet do Business with, The price I told them was 8 Tale a ps though I did not expect so much for them by a Tale at least the price having much fallen by reason of a great quantity (as I found afterwards) lying in the merchants hands that they had bought of the English & Dutch. Though this method in the end happend well for the Companys Interest having got a very good Profit upon them viz 7 Tales a ps, yet it cost me (by reason of the Accident before hinted of the Imprisoning of our merchants) an infinite deal of Trouble & vexation, and discover'd to me another thing that chagrin'd me very much to see how little asistance I was to expect in any thing from 2 of our Super-Cargos who seem'd to be pleas'd at the plague I had to get rid of them & though they would often talk of getting away the Perpetts yet would not give me the least help towards it though they saw the daily trouble I had about them & I often told them to do what they could to perswade their friends that had got of the Companys money to take some of them, But so far from helping that one of them (Mr Morford) who was very capable of asisting me in the Affairs by perswading some of his friends whom

125   he had got the Ostenders to do very good business with, as well as with us to take a share, on the Contrary his friend Mr Baron inform'd soon after leaving Canton

that one Phillis had asked several times to buy them & give either silks or Gold for them, And upon my telling him I never had heard a word of it, He answerd he wonderd at that because he had heard Phillis ask Mr Morford about it several times, I do not blame Mr Pike because it was not in his power to help not having any Acquaintance or Interest amongst the merchants, If he knew indeed that Phillis had offerd such a thing he ought to have inform'd us, but it may be he never heard no more than I of his doing so. In short the whole trouble of this lighted on Mr Brown & me which I had reason to believe some were not sorry for.

The merchants that deal with the Dutch, or answer for them as they call it here, are very angry with them because they will be oblig'd to pay the Hoppo & Mandarins some money before they will be reconcil'd to them, & when they talk to the Dutch about it they laugh at them. This is the way practis'd here when an European dos any thing contrary to the Law or the orders here establish'd, let him be Officer or sailor or what he will, The Mandarins immediately fall upon the Super-Cargos of the ship the Person belongs to & oblige them to pay a sum of money for the fault committed and sometimes when they can't perswade them to it have even carryd them out of their factory or when they can catch them and throw them into Prison till the money is pay'd, But if they cannot easily come at the Super-Cargos they have another way which is speedier & more commonly practis'd to send for the merchant who deals with them & oblige him to pay what they think fit, or keep him in Prison till they do, The merchant again must make the Super-Cargos repay him, either by fair means or else one way or other charge it him in his Accounts, for they commonly take care not to be losers on such occasions.

As Mr Morford is a great friend of Mandarin Quiqua's[207] and therefore often teazing me to go to his house to see his Goods, Though I did not much like the man yet I had no Objection to go any where where we might find Goods cheap & Good, so have contracted with him for a Good deal of China ware.

I refer to the Joint Diary &c for a great many Days Transactions.

126
Septr 25
The Xunhu & Fouyen have arrested the Hoppo, seal'd up his effects, & appointed the Quanchefou[208] (one of the Judges of the Police of the City) to act in his place till another is appointed from Court. There is a Chop or Edict pasted up about the Town in the publick places letting the People know that he is turn'd out of his

---

[207] This merchant, also called *old Quiqua* and *Cugin* (i.e. Cudgin; see below note 254) by Campbell, first appears in the English East India Chronicles in 1723 (Morse 1966–69, 1, p. 176) and at some stage seems to have been trading in Amoy (*ibid.* p. 183). Although Campbell had a very low opinion of him ("a Rogue", "a troublesome sneaking fellow"), he nevertheless bought both tea and chinaware from him.

[208] Chinese *Guanchafu*.

office, and charging him with {of} having committed many Extortions against the Forreigners as well as natives, and having cheated the Emperour in his Customs & other things relating to his Trust. Though it is scarce to be question'd but that The Hoppo has cheated & plunderd in the execution of his office (which most of the Mandarins here do when in their power) yet he has show'd on several occasions more Generosity and Good nature to strangers than those that were in this station before him were accustom'd to do, so that it is hard to tell if we better our selves by the Change. There are other private reasons (as it is said) that has made the Xunhu & Fouyen joyn in measures to ruin him, to wit that having good friends at Pekin or the Court, he did not care to show much dependance upon or pay much Court to them, But I am apt to think they have a more prevailing reason than all this (a very strong one with a China man) that is he did not think fit to allow them such a share of the plunder as perhaps they wanted or expected. However it is our business, upon the coming in of a new Hoppo, & the other being turn'd out for the reasons they allege, to make application for redress of Grievances that European Traders suffer here, & to complain of the many Impositions & Duties layd upon them (which I am assurd is not allowd by the Emperours Tariff) and some heavy ones a few years ago. I have for some time talk'd with the merchants upon this subject, but Especially about a new Duty of 10 pr C^t layd on all Goods imported or exported in the year 1726 when I was here in a ship from Fort St George[209], and which was aggreed to by the SuperCargos of the English & Ostend ships that were here then (not without some Roguish Connivance of some of those Gentlemen of which I believe one of ours knows a good deal if he would tell what he saw) though at the same time we from Fort St George & the other SuperCargos of the other Country ships, as they are calld,

127   that is from several parts of the East Indies, though teaz'd daily about it would never consent to pay it, & had the Europe Super-Cargos stood up as much for the Interest of their owners they could not have been oblig'd to pay it no more than we, and thereby would have prevented a heavy Charge that has been ever since extorted from all Europe though never from Country ships, such is the misfortune of Precedents especially in this Country. The merchants discourage me as much they can from demanding redress saying it will be all in vain, & that the Emperour knows of it & receives it &c But as I do not care to trust them I am resolvd to leave no stone unturnd to have redress, And if I don't succeed I at least discharge my Duty and will have the pleasure of declaiming against such practices & letting the Mandarins & perhaps the Emperour know that we are sensible we are abus'd. This I know will bring upon me the Ill will of most of the Europe Super-Cargos, But that I little value.

Septr 26   Two of our merchants, Suqua & Pinky are carry'd to Prison, The Crime of the first

---

[209] English fort established in Madras on the Coromandel coast, the eastern coast of India.

they say is for being concernd with the Hoppo & being his Chief Adviser in Affairs relating to Trade in order to inable him the better to commit the Extortions he has done. Pinkys Crime (as is allegd) is for having exported Copper which viz the red sort is forbid by Law. This may be an Occasion of great hindrance to our Affairs & prevent so Early a Dispatch from this place as we had reason to expect, if they are not soon again set at Liberty.

– 29 Tinqua having privately inform'd me that the Achantsi[210] (or Chief Justice or Judge in Criminal Causes) is appointed Hoppo for the Port of Canton & the Quanchefeu to have the Inspection of the out Ports, And as this new Hoppo is a particular friend of Tinquas and has already shown some more Confidence in him than in any of the rest by sending for him & promising him his favour &c we must imbrace the opportunity & see to get Tinqua to stand our friend & asist us in getting Redress. I see some of our Gentlemen dont like Tinqua at all, But it is our Business more than ever (especially that our other merchants are lock'd up) to carry

128 fair with him & keep him our friend as being the only merchant at present Capable of doing us any service with the Mandarins, And I saw he was not at all pleasd with us for buying most of our Goods of other merchants & us'd to tell me of it, I could not help telling him it was his own fault that I had showd inclination enough to do business by coming to his Hang first & by our offering to buy of him at a reasonable price, But he having refus'd to sell at the same price that I assurd him we could buy it at from another made us go to such as would serve us Cheapest, which he had no reason to take Ill, That though we had not bought much Tea of him (which is what He & All of them most desird) yet there were several Goods we should yet have occasion for And I would do what I could with the other SuperCargos to come to him to buy assoon as of any other provided he would serve us well & Cheap. Being willing to dispatch our Affairs without losing a moments time we were busy now about China ware, which was wanted for the flooring of the ship, I therefore spoke often on the subject to the Super-Cargos & that we had best do something with Tinqua for the reasons above mentioned & see if he had not some China ware we yet wanted, They did not much like the proposal (at least two of them) though Mr Brown saw well the reason of obliging Tinqua in the situation we were in at present & readily aggreed to it, However out we went this afternoon from Home to go about amongst the merchants to see what they had fit for us, Assoon as I got out of the Door I turn'd towards Tinquas which Mr Morford perceiving where I was going told me that He thought it would be better delay buying any thing or making any Contracts till we saw if the New Hoppo would take off the 10 p^r Ct, This advice I thought very unreasonable at a time we wanted to provide China for flooring the ship

---

[210] Chinese *Anchashi*.

especially after that I had often told them all that in case the 10 p^r C^t should be taken off that then we must deduct so much from the price we were to pay them and that I had spoke to the merchants about it and they were very well satisfy'd, I knowing very well if

129   I had spoke of going to Mandarin Quiquas there would be not a word of this, suspected he had other reasons for delaying buying which made me hastily add that if he wanted to delay the Companys business I assurd him I did not nor would not one moment and that I would Answer for Tinquas aggreeing to deduct the 10 p^r C^t in case it was taken off by the Hoppo which was very uncertain. What confirm'd me in this suspicion of his wanting to delay was that I had often before talk'd of making the utmost dispatch we could in buying our Goods if we could find any fit for us & amongst the rest to see about for China ware assoon as we could before the Ostenders who wanted it as well as we should get before hand with us, He always put it off, except when we were to go to his friend Mandarin Quiquas, by saying that there would be time enough to buy China ware and that there would be enough come from the Country about the latter end & better than at present, It is true that might very well be & often is the Case as I told him but at the same time that was no reason why we should not look about now & buy up what we found cheap & fit for the market & often bid him & Mr Pike who generally went in a string together, to look about the shops & Hangs & see where they could find any for our purpose, to show them that I was not wedded to any merchant more than Another & never refusd to go any where to see any sort of Goods we wanted & which they recommended, I had also some opinion that he would not have been sorry that the Ostenders should be provided before us, for which I shall assign my reasons presently. But however at present to return to the Affair in hand we went to Tinquas & look'd over sundry parcels of China ware but were some hours about coming to any aggreement by reason of Mr Morford's disputing & jangling about the difference of a Cash in the price in short every thing was too dear, which scruples I observd he never made use of at some other merchants, this held on so long that Mr Brown & I was quite asham'd seeing no reason in all this since his price was as reasonable as other peoples, which manner of

130   acting so vex'd Tinqua that he told us he found we had not come to buy but to wrangle with him & then retird from us, I seeing but too much truth in what he said was obligd to tell them that we must either buy or go away & lose no more time here in doing nothing, that as for some prices which he pretended were so dear I could not say so (not but that I was as glad as He to get things cheap but I did not like after two or 3 hours haggling & bringing a man to his lowest price & as low as other people to make unnecessary wrangling[)] & that if he did not approve of the price though I did not find the rest of his mind I would take them to my self at that price very willingly. This method was so very different from what he usd with other people he lik'd, that there I could seldom get him to speak

one word of the price, for it was my Custom always to ask Mr Brown & him what they thought such a thing worth & what they had payd other years that they were here, He did not care willingly to reply expecting very likely that I would suffer my self to be impos'd upon & offer too much, But I was upon my guard & often would not bid till I heard their opinions, Then he would say he thought we might afford to give so much, & particularly at Mandarin Quiquas I remember one of many Instances as buying some setts of China ware Tea things He told me he thought they were worth 12 Tales a sett. Mr Pike immediately took the word & without waiting till I would give my opinion offerd 12 Tales, I then seeing them play the fool told that they were too dear of 10 T. & that I would not consent to any such price, They sayd no more but this offering of theirs had like to have spoil'd our Bargain for Mand. Quiqua pretended to insist that Mr Pike had bid him 12 Tales & now I would have them for less, I told him it signifyd nothing what Mr Pike offerd for if he or any Body else should offer more than I thought a thing was worth I would not buy it, In short after threatening to go away if he would not fall his price he aggreed to sell them for 10 T. & not being able to bring him lower we aggreed.

131   Having just hinted before that I suspected Mr Morford favour'd the Ostenders[211] & perhaps more than the Company he serv'd, I must go a little back to clear up this Matter, when I knew there was an Ostend ship arriv'd I resolv'd to keep a fair understanding with them, though I was little acquainted with the Super-Cargos, as believing they would not show that shyness & distaste to us as the English & Dutch here did, But on the other hand As I know that not only in Europe but also here the English & Dutch had been very assiduous in giving out that though we carry'd Swedish Colours & had a Swedish Commission yet we either belong'd to the Ostend Company or that they were concern'd with us, which thoug[h] absolutely false yet it was necessary to give them no room or pretext to continue to intertain an opinion so prejudicial to us which I knew they would be glad to incourage (as the sequel but too clearly show'd) especially if they saw us much with one another in this place, I therefore immediately upon their Arrival discours'd our Super-Cargos & gave them my opinion on this head which they aggreed to be reasonable. The first time that we visited the Ostend Super-Cargos, we were soon acquainted (as is the Custom here with Europeans who have no quarrell together) and Mr Ley the Chief Super-Cargo was launching forth upon subjects I did not like & talking as I thought very indiscreetly before so much Company about our Affairs which made me very silent & made me resolve to enter as little as I could in familiar Conversation with such strange People, Mr Ley not knowing any thing of the Trade of this place (as indeed not one of their Super-Cargos did) and having formerly known Mr Morford he thought he would be a proper Person to asist him & put him in a right way, & so they soon enter'd

---

211 Morford had been in the service of the Ostend Company (cf. Introduction p. xxxiii).

into a strict Intimacy After the first Conversation with him I presently spoke to Mr Morford to desire him in a Civil Manner to refrain from talking upon such subjects before people as he had done which would probably be of prejudice to us &c Mr Morford told me afterwards he had done so, & told me besides that Mr Ley being sensible that He

132   was Ignorant of the Trade & manners of this place had desir'd his asistance, and that he would depend upon him &c I believing this could be no disservice to us but rather of use as Mr Morford thereby might be able to give me useful hints for our own Affairs, & not supposing he would discover to him any of ours, I answerd him that I had nothing to object to that provided he took care not to discover to him any of our Business or manner of Acting or prices of some things that we payd which some of the merchants desird us not to mention, as it was not our business to acquaint any Body with to help them to buy as Cheap as we did, since their buying dearer would be no doubt an Advantage to our Company upon our return as it would help to make them keep up their price of sales at Home & inable us to undersell all others, In short it was Every Bodys Business to buy as well as they could without meddling to help others. Mr Morford promis'd me that he would take care to discover nothing, but that he hop'd to be rather thereby useful to our own Company. The Intimacy betwixt Mr Ley & Mr Morford grew so very great, that I could not tell what to think of it, for Mr Ley every morning assoon as he was out of Bed, & most times before Mr Morford was up, the first thing he did was to come Early to Mr Morford & wake him, & then after staying some time to watch an opportunity of going out of the factory when he perceivd none of us in sight, without so much as ever once inquiring after me or paying me the least visit (in return for several I had payd him) which being a treatment so contrary to the Custom here us'd towards the Chief of a factory surpriz'd me not a little, For as I was always up by Day break & before the Factory Doors were open'd, by chance walking about I see him often at a distance coming in or going out, which Mr Brown also discoverd, his Room being opposite to Mr Morfords,though he was never favour'd with a visit no more than I, but I did not think fit to take notice of it by speaking about it, though by chance I had spyd another thing I did not know what to make of, one morning early going in to Mr Morford about some business I see Mr Dormer[212] (one of the

133   Ostend writers) sitting at his Table or Desk copying a Paper, which as I could not tell whether it was any thing relating to the Companys Affairs or not, & hearing afterwards that Mr Ley had got a Copy of the Prices of Provisions I had settled with the Factory Compradore I suppos'd might be that and therefore did not much mind it or so much as mention it to him, But as Mr Morford was the

---

[212] Kjellberg (1974), p. 128, lists a *Walter Dormer* among the foreign supercargoes and assistants employed by the SEIC in 1740, so it is not unlikely that this Ostender later joined the service of the Swedish company.

person imployd to keep the Diary of our Transactions at Canton I could not help being somewhat uneasy, for fear of his making a bad use of the trust reposd in him. He perceiving me some time pretty reserv'd took an opportunity of breaking his mind & told me he hop'd I was not Jealous of his being so Intimate with Mr Ley and of his being so much at the Ostend Factory & that it was only about private Affairs that Mr Ley took his asistance ln making him acquainted with the China merchants & helping him to buy his own private Trade, & amongst other things how glad he would be of my friendship &c & fell a crying, I being mov'd at such an odd scene told him that if his Intimacy consisted in no more than he sayd I had no fault to find with it and would not trouble my self about his being much with those Gentlemen, only that even in that it was proper to use Caution &c & that for my friendship he might be assur'd of it, provided he acted always with a regard to the Companys Interest, But at the same time I could not help wondring at Mr Leys manner of Acting with regard to me, That though it was not very proper for him & me to be seen much together yet I thought there was some little Civility due me in return for what I had payd him, & especially since he was every day almost in the Factory & sometimes twice or thrice he might have sometimes step[ped] in & ask me how I did. All this I guessd he would tell Mr Ley which no doubt he did, for very soon afterwards he call'd in one morning to see Mr Morford & knowing that I was gone on board ship he pretended to ask for me and left word with the officer that took care of the Factory that he had been there to see me, And would call in sometimes the Evening when he had business with Mr Morford and knowing I was at Home would stay & sup with us. However I can't say I was much displeasd with his & all the Ostenders Ill manners since it gave me a fair pretext to keep shy

134 & very little with him, which I could not so easily have done had they been commonly Civil to me, especially that I had two Gentlemen with me that were much their friends & hinted often of inviting them to eat with us which finding I was not much inclind to, Mr Morford (at least) almost every night went & either passd his Evening or Tiffing time, or suppd, with them at their Factory from whence he knows best in what condition he us'd to return, what surpriz'd me most was to see how Early he had got his Dose for assoon as he came from them he often went to Bed before supper came on Table, & sometimes when he came to Table he was so out of order that he was oblig'd to withdraw assoon as supper was done & leave us all at Table, but chiefly when we had any friends with us at supper as some of my former India Acquaintances or some of the English of Mr Browns Acquaintance or mine who were very serviceable on some occasions to us, and could not help taking notice of this Rudeness which I could not tell how to excuse. But as for his & other peoples Ill manners it was what should have given me little trouble had they show'd that regard in other things to the Companys Interest as became them. This and many things I observ'd in some of their Conduct afterwards made me reflect that there was one thing very necessary which had been omitted (on Account of the Absence of our SuperCargos &

Forreign officers when imploy'd by the Directours) with regard to them though observ'd with regard to all the officers we imployd in Sweden as well as with me who was bound by Oath to the Company, I mean that there was no Bond or obligation sign'd & taken from all the Super-Cargos & officers importing their Dependance upon the Directors & promising to perform their Duty & obedience to their Masters orders. For to tell the truth if they had chanc'd not to be Honest men, & could have wrested the power out of my hands, what Tie had they to hinder them from joyning with the Captain & others who would have been fond enough of any scheme of that kind, in order to ruin the voyage

135 & to carry the ship to what Port they pleasd and as they thought would turn out best to their own Advantage, And if such a thing had happen'd what Redress could the Company have had, We had no plea against them nor nothing to show under their hands that they were imployd in our service, And indeed none of them had any legal tie to bind them, Mr Brown it is true was concernd considerably in the stock himself which was a pretty good tie upon him, as to his Interest & the Companys at least a greater than any of the rest Had. But bless'd be God this was not our Case For though some of them soon flew in my face & Show'd a Contempt of my Authority & indeavour'd all they could to lessen it, though they knew I was one of the Directors and had a part in imploying them & that consequently I was one of those that they must Answer to for their Conduct on their Return, I say though notwithstanding of this they acted wrong in many Instances yet they were not capable of being wilfully Guilty of doing such mischief as is supposed possible to be done. Let that be as it will As such a Case is possible and has happen'd on some Occasions, I hope the Directours will take other measures another time, Had it been done this voyage perhaps I might have pass'd my time with more pleasure or at least with less pain.

I ought to have given an Account in our Getting in to our Factory at Canton, how that was settled, & also what different part of Business fell to every one of our shares. As to the first I orderd Mr Maul midshipman & a dozen of men from the ship to come up & guard our house, who were reliev'd from time to time by others from on board that every one might have the pleasure of seeing Canton & a little respite from the work aboard, Mr Maul being a man fit to be trusted as being very honest & active I appointed him to have the Command of the men (or Captain of the Factory as they call him here) and under him was ^213 one of the sailors & a Taylor by Trade but who had been a soldier and did his part with great diligence & Care in keeping good watch, so that all the time we were at Canton we met with no disturbance nor no breakings in of Rogues or Thieves as often happens here.

---

213 Campbell has left a blank for the name.

136 As for our selves, I took upon me to oversee every thing (as I thought was my Duty) but more particularly I kept the Cash & settled & payd all Accounts whatsoever, which gave me a good deal of trouble, as it often interrupted me from other Business &c And though I had some young Gentlemen with me who could have easd me of this, yet as I was unwilling they should be let in to our Affairs, and as the SuperCargos had other Business allotted them, I was willing to take this Charge my self, and that of running daily about amongst the merchants to keep them in mind & push them on to dispatch our Affairs. Mr Brown not having a fair hand of writing made me decline imploying him in keeping any Books, though I repented afterwards I had not given him the Cash to keep which he could have done very well & we should [have] had time enough to write over the Books fair aboard, He therefore took a great deal of the trouble of[f] my hands of running about amongst the merchants, & was very serviceable to me in my own Affairs which the Companys business scarce allow'd me any time to look after. Mr Morford as being best acquainted with the forms undertook to keep the Packing Book of China ware silks &c & the Diary, & for his Ease I made Mr Campbell (whom I imployd as writer) to keep an Account of the weight & Tare of Goods, To Mr Pike we allotted the keeping of the Accounts with the Factory Compradore (with whom I had settled the price of every thing at first & I dare say cheaper than any factory at Canton excepting those of the Country ships, who are always cheaper than the Europe ones, & of which I had a Copy from Mr Cowan of the Bombay ship to asist me) which I always Oversaw & pay'd my self, To Ease him (as I saw he was a Person did not like much Trouble) I appointed Mr Moir (whom I also imployd as writer) also to keep account with the Compradore & after he had wrote down every thing daily from him to carry it to Mr Pike to correct it & write it down in his Book, so that He had very little to do but to copy at his Leisure Mr Moirs Account, Mr Pike also kept a Book of the Account of every thing shippd which I desird Mr Morford to asist him & put him in the proper method which he did. There

137 were sundry other parts of the Companys Business which we all attended and were present at as Packing of Goods whether China ware Teas silks &c as well as the shipping them off, & particularly in examining all together the Goods we wanted to buy before we made our Contracts with them & afterwards when we receiv'd them.

This same day in the morning (as I hinted above) having spoke to Tinqua (who was sent for by the Atchantsi or new Hoppo) to ask if we might have Audience of the Hoppo by our selves without the other Europeans, because as being a new Company I would gladly be the first to pay our Compliments to him; I did not care to let him know my true design of asking to take off the 10 p^r C^t & other impositions that the Europeans had suffer'd & payd for many years, as I found that He nor none of the merchants car'd to meddle in asking such things of the Mandarins for us, He readily aggreed to this & told me upon his Return Home that he had spoke to the new Hoppo as I had desird, and that he seem'd to be very well pleasd & he believ'd would send for us very soon. Upon this I thought there was no time to lose but to indeavour if possible to get a Memorial ready in the Chinese language setting forth our Grievances &c I accordingly tryd some China men of my Acquaintance who were afraid to meddle in such a thing for fear of disobliging the Mandarins or China merchants & I durst not trust any of the Europeans with my design because I knew they would not joyn in it but rather if they came to the knowlege of it put all the obstacles they could in our way, Hearing that Mr Cowan Chief Super-Cargo & Captain of the English ship from Bombay had found some China man that us'd to draw up memorials for him, I took Mr Brown with me (who was a former Acquaintance of his) to wait upon Mr Cowan & to beg the favour to help me to his China man to draw out such a memorial for us, Mr Cowan readily approv'd of our design & sayd he would joyn with us in it, & promis'd at our desire not to mention to the English or any Body what we intended, & that he would get the petition ready out of hand (the heads of which I had wrote him down in English) & send it me. In the meantime The Hoppo reflecting on the Audience we demanded, resolv'd to see all the Europeans together at one time, so after Dinner the Linguist came to tell us that the Hoppo had orderd us & all the Europeans to wait upon him next morning. As I

138   thought by the means of Mr Cowan we had layd our scheme so well that we need not care whether we went alone or in Company I was very well pleasd with the Hoppos summons. However I went again to Mr Cowan to beg to have our memorial ready for next morning early which he faithfully promisd me. In the mean time the English & others wondring whence this order from the Hoppo to us all to wait upon him should proceed since they had not ask'd for it, set their wits to work to find out the reason of it, and soon learn'd that we had desird an Audience in the morning, and what spoild our scheme they also learn'd that we were resolv'd to give in a memorial in writing complaining of the many impositions put upon Europeans, and that Mr Cowan was the person imployd to have it done for us (which I suspected he inform'd them of himself for fear of its coming some other way to their knowlege & disobliging them) they immediately apply'd to him desiring he would stop it & disappoint us, They could not bear the thoughts of making Complaints against things that their Brother Super-Cargos had so long payd (especially the English) and in particular very much vex'd to see I had design'd to mention a thing so long forgot as a Duty of 6 p^r C^t and a sum of 1950 Tale they call here Present money which had been first pay'd & allow'd of by one of their own Directors (when SuperCargo at this Port) and a leading man in the Company at present, In fine they inveigh'd very much against this complaint, as Mr Cowan told me afterwards, & perswaded him to get no memorial drawn out for us. They carryd their Cunning even further, As they could not tell but that I might have more Irons in the fire than one & procure a memorial by some other hand, they concerted measures with the Dutch & French what they

were to do & how to blast our Design, They perswaded Monsieur de Velaer[214] Chief of the French Factory to come to me & amuse[215] me with a fine story to wit that Hearing that Mr Cowan & I were preparing a memorial for the Hoppo to ask redress of Grievances, He thought that as it was a General Concern, & what all the Europeans had reason to complain of as well as we, it would have more weight with the Mandarins if we all joyn'd together in the same Complaint This I told him I readily approv'd of & aggreed to provided all the other

139 Europeans would heartily & sincerely joyn in it, which (I added) I much doubted of, To that He answerd that he had already been with the SuperCargos of the different nations of Europe as well as those of the Country ships who had all aggreed to have a memorial drawn up in all our names to the same purport as that I intended and that as He understood the Chinese Language He had at their desire undertaken to see it drawn out in proper form & to have it ready by next morning, and was in such a haste to have it done that he refusd to stay & sup with us, alleging for Excuse that he would be oblig'd to sit up all night about this Affair. Assoon as he left me, Being resolv'd to know the meaning of this Change of Mr Cowan before I went to sleep I sent to see if Mr Cowan was at Home, my servant brought me back Answer that he was gone to sup at the English Factory where I learn'd that Monsr de Velaer supp'd also. I immediately guessd we were betrayd but did not know how to help it.

Septr 30 Next morning I got up early & went to Mr Cowan to inquire into the Affair. He told me that indeed he had spoke with the English Super-Cargos & had perswaded them with a great deal of difficulty to joyn in a Complaint of Grievances which they had at last aggreed to do by their Linguist (which was as good as nothing for these fellows generally say what they think will best please & flatter the Mandarins or what the China merchants put in their mouths without having any regard to what we desire them to say) but that would not hinder him from getting the memorial I desird, & that having been disappointed of the man he had implo, d last night to write it out He had now sent for another who would set about it immediately & he would take care to have it ready & send it me before it was time to go to the Hoppo, I was obligd to be satisfyd and had nothing to do but to trust his promises as long as I could, In the mean while the time past away & no memorial came, & our Enemies the Europeans & merchants still fearing I had some other way to obtain what I was set upon, got our Linguist to come every minut to tell us to go to the Hoppo and that he waited for us &c The fellow teaz'd me so much that I told him I would not stir till I knew all the Super-Cargos of the Europe ships as well as of the Country ships were gone before, for I was resolv'd to wait as long as I could to see

---

[214] *Pierre Duvelaër* (Dermigny 1964, 1, p. 360 f.; cf. also Morse 1966–69, 1, p. 248: *Devulaire*, p. 251: *Devulaer*, p. 273: *Duvelaer*).

[215] *Amuse* in the archaic sense of 'cheat', 'deceive', the usual meaning of the word in the 18th century (for further instances see *Diary* pp. 17[4], 198).

140   if Mr Cowan would be as good as his word, But about 9 a clock being inform'd they were all gone to the Hoppos (Mr Cowan as well as all the others) I then saw we were under a necessity to go to without any memorial & do the best we could so our Chairs being ready at the Door we went (the Super-Cargos & I) after them to the Hoppos where we found all the other Europe Gentlemen & sundry China merchants. Finding Mr Cowan there I ask'd him the reason of what had happen'd, who told me he could not help it, the China man he had imployd being afraid to draw up the memorial had disappointed him. I then ask'd Monsr de Velaer if he had got the memorial he had promisd to have ready to be presented in all our names, He answerd He had not but It would be the same thing since as He was to go in with us and understood the Chinese Language it would not be in the power of the Linguist to misrepresent what we desir'd him to say & that if he did he would speak to the Hoppo himself, upon which I desird him to press the English Dutch & all the other SuperCargos to aggree to go all in to the Hoppo together & make our Complaints in a Body, which I thought would have more weight & prevent them from making different Representations from us, Mr de Velaer approv'd of this & spoke to the English about it, But soon brought me answer that they would not aggree to it and that their merchants had advis'd them against it, which he wonder'd at, upon that I thought best try Mr Turner (the Chief SuperCargo of the English)[216] my self, which I did giving him my reasons as being for the General Interest of all of them &c But He being resolv'd on the Contrary did not at all like my propos'd which he testifyd by a sullen silence, Beau Keyqua their Chief merchant bestirr'd himself mightily to hinder our going all together and amongst the rest came to tell me it was much better that every ships or nations SuperCargos should go in by themselves with some other Impertinent stuff, which made me tell him not to trouble me with his Impertinence for I had no regard to any advice

141   that he could give me &c There being no remedy we were obligd to do as they pleasd, Every nations SuperCargos were calld in according to the time of the Arrival of the ships, those of the Europe ships first and then those of the Country ships, Monsr de Velaer was first call'd in with the French, upon coming back he told me that he had made the Linguist represent all the Grievances above mentiond & desird to be put upon the footing of the Emperours Ancient Tariff settled with European Traders which did not order many of those taxes & duties we now pay &c & that the Hoppo had promis'd that he would do what he could to grant what he desir'd. The English went next in, & then the Dutch, who on coming out told us they had the same Answer; There was another Affair Monsr de Velaer desird me to ask which I readily aggreed to & which he had desir'd viz the setting Suqua & the other merchants at Liberty in order to settle their Affairs with

---

[216] Upon the death of George Arbuthnot (cf. *Diary* p. 105) Mr. Whichcott Turner had been designated as Chief of the Council formed by the supercargoes of all the English ships on their arrival at Canton (Morse 1966–69, 1, pp. 75, 208 f.).

us &c It came now to our Turn to go in, and as I was going some of the merchants spoke to me & desir'd that we & the Ostenders would go in together saying we were all the same (which I suppose the English & Dutch had indeavourd to make them believe) & Mr Ley Chief of the Ostenders (imprudently enough as I thought) proposd the same to me, which I absolutely refus'd & before him told the merchants that since the others would not aggree to go all in a Body but seperately I would take care to go in seperately too and that I wonder'd at such a proposal since we had nothing to do with the Ostenders & were of quite a different nation, And accordingly we did go in by our selves. Being all seated, The Hoppo welcom'd us & wish'd us a good Trade, After thanking him I order'd the Linguist to tell him that the King of Sweden having establish'd a Company of merchants in his Country to trade to China had sent us to begin the said Trade and that we hoped we should meet with all due incouragement and Protection, He assurd us that we should & ask'd if the King of Sweden's Country was a great way off, and how long we had been a coming from it, I answerd that it was the

142

most Remote Country of any in Europe from China, and that no ship had come hither before from so great a distance & that we had been 8 moons (or months) on our passage from Sweden. I then told him that on our Arrival hither we had heard that there were a great many high Duties layd upon The Europeans by some former Hoppos which were not orderd by the Emperour nor appointed in his Tariff, & in particular 6 p^r Ct layd on many years ago and 10 p^r Ct about 6 years ago, & also that they pretended to exact of us a sum of 1950 Tales by way of present for the Hoppo & officers belonging to him, all which lay very heave[217] on the Europe Trade, and therefore we begg'd that he would let us know truly what we were to pay according to the Ancient Tariff, being very willing to pay what his Majesty orderd & was the settled former Custom of this Port. He answer'd that as he was but just come into the Charge of Hoppo he was not as yet sufficiently acquainted with these matters, but that he would Examine the Emperours Books & orders and if he found those things that we complaind of were Impositions as we represented them he would indeavour to get them redressd & would write to Pekin about it to have his Majestys orders. I added it would be a great satisfaction to us to have a True Tariff given us of what the Emperour requir'd that we might not always be in danger of being impos'd upon. He assurd us again that he would look into those matters and publish an Account of the Duties we ought to pay & that every Factory should have one of them sent to them. I then told him that there were some of the merchants with whom we had considerable dealings {with} in Prison as Suqua Pinky &c which was a great prejudice & hindrance to us in our Trade & dispatch of Business, and that as the other merchants were willing to be security for their appearance we hopd he would do his utmost to get them inlarg'd[218], He answerd that was an Affair he could not meddle in they

---

[217] *Sic*, for *heavy*.
[218] *Enlarge* in the archaic sense of 'to set at large', 'to release'.

being arrested by the Emperours order for Crimes that concernd his Majesty, for which they must be try'd, but that should be no prejudice to our Affairs for as they

143 had other people left in their Hangs they would carry on the business with us, I answerd that the People left in their Hangs were not acquainted with the Contracts passd between us & them nor so well to manage the business we had with them He replyd again that he would take care that we should be no sufferers but that our Affairs should go on in the same manner as if they were at Liberty. We then thank'd him for his kind Promises & withdrew. Upon coming out Beau Keyqua who seemd to be very uneasy & had a notion that I had deliverd a Petition was very Curious to know what I had done & what Answer I had receivd, But the Linguist soon satisfyd his Curiosity. The Ostenders went next in, & then Mr Cowan of the Bombay ship, & last Capt Tullie of the Fort St George ship, who sayd they all receivd the same Answer. Before I went in I found the English were not at all pleasd with their Audience, for one of the Super-Cargos told me that they did not know what they came hither for except it was to ask Suqua & Pinky out of Prison; which in truth I knew well they did not desire as they had no dealings with either of them & both they & the Dutch knew that we[219] had flatterd themselves that their imprisonment would keep us longer here than we proposd, as it in the Event did, & which I had reason to think they contributed to as much as they could, & when they heard we were ready to depart put themselves in no small pain to get the merchants to delay us & in a great hurry to get away before us, which however all their Arts & haste was not able to perform, notwithstanding they had been all here several months before us.

I call to mind something more about Mr Ley & Mr Morford to wit of several things Mr Morford told me Mr Ley had told him about the Establishment of our Company, & some other things he pretended to have known himself before he left Europe (but from what hand I cant tell) which if they had

144 been true, I was obligd to tell him that it was very Imprudent for them to talk of them. Mr Morford often tryd to bring me on this subject which I always declin'd. Another thing look'd very suspicious that Mr Morford had acquainted Mr Ley with the prices we payd for Tea & other Goods, to wit that Mr Ley in making his Contracts with the merchants not being able to bring them so low as very likely he knew we payd us'd to say he would pay as Mr Campbell payd and when they would pretend I payd so & so, He would name the true price we payd. This several of the merchants told me of being dissatisfyd that we should have told him after having promis'd the Contrary, which they allegd did them a prejudice in making their Contracts with the Ostenders or others, since their business was to

---

[219] No doubt a mistake for *they*.

get as much of them as they could, and also as disobliging some other Europeans who had payd them higher prices than we did.

Octr 2 Aggreed with Hunqua for 100 ps flowerd & stript Poissies[220], for a tryal, (according to the advices given us by some of our friends at Home) we did not care to contract for more as being dear at 7.T.2.M aps. & no body car'd to undertake them so cheap but Hunqua or to deliver them in the time we wanted them.

Our officers still complain of want of ballast and that the ship is not stiff enough notwithstanding of the 500 pecul already bought, and want 300 pecul more. But as the price still keeps up and that it will make us break our other Contracts of silks (though the merchants seem willing enough to allow that as pretending they get nothing by the price we contracted for on account of the dearness & scarcity of Raw silk this year) &c we cannot aggree to buy more but must leave them to find out what other ways they can to make the ship stiff & fit for sailing.

Octr 3^d The Dutch being at work now & buying up what Pecko Tea[221] they can get, and being hard to get much that is good, Hearing Tinqua had some which appeard very good we bough[t] 100 pecul.

145 The Dutch Super-Cargos have at last we hear made their Contracts for Tea with Beau Keyqua, which their Chief or 1st Super-Cargo Shultz[222] wanted from the beginning, but was not able to get a majority till lately, Having now found ways & mean to bring over 2 of the Super-Cargos & one of the Captains so that with his own casting voice he has the majority & so little values the others now, But they give him trouble enough, for they go & contract with other merchants for Goods so that when the Goods of the different parties are sent in to their Factory one party won't allow them to come in & the others will have theirs in, They have the same fine Game when the Goods that are come in are to be shippd off, one won't & the other will, till Schults being the stronger man has no way of deciding the dispute but by knocking his Adversaries down. In short their behaviour is so scandalous that they expose them selves to all the Town both Forreigners & natives, and the latter call them mad men or in their way of speaking, Fool-men. If the reason of the other Super-Cargos opposing the Chief & his party is a view

---

220 A kind of silk fabric. Morse (1966–69), 5, p. 20, mentions "poisees" among several varieties of wrought silk shipped in 1754, adding in a footnote: "The most careful search through many dictionaries and encyclopaedias, general, philological, and technical, has failed to elicit any information on [this fabric]. W.H. Manchée states in *Notes and Queries* of November 24, 1928: 'Poisee is probably *peau de soie*, a plain black silk.'" This explanation does not seem to agree very well with Campbell's adjectives "flowered" and "striped", however.

221 *Pekoe*, black tea, harvested in the month of April, thus quite early, in fact at the shooting stage. Good Pekoe tastes strong and is soft to the touch. According to some it should be greyish in colour; according to others, straw-yellowish, inclining towards green. Generally featured in mixed form.

222 *Jan Schul*, supercargo in the service of the Dutch Company (V.O.C.) and very probably the man behind the Dutch intervention at the Sunda (see *Diary* pp. 229, 293 f.).

to their Companys Interest, and that they know Schultz is acting some private Roguery with the merchant he imploys (as every body believes and which afterwards came to be very publick) they [are] certainly in the right to Oppose him to the utmost, but they might do it methinks in a manner more becoming & more to their masters Advantage than the methods I hear they are upon, However Schu[l]tz is certainly in the wrong as he is carrying on by a majority very knavish work, we shall see the Issue of all in the sequal of this Journal.

Octr 10th Though I knew by many Instances old Quiqua to be a Rogue, yet Mr Morford (who seems to be his good friend) has prevaild with me to call & see what he has & finding he had some China-ware to our Purpose, we bought to day of him. Some time after this He perceiving that we did not buy Teas & other things of him as he expected & thought that I was the Cause of it, not knowing how to help him self resolv'd to be reveng'd of me by saying I did not give him good weight

146 when I payd him, though I payd none but in their own presence & that they were satisfyd the weight was just, and generally had Mr Brown to help me or some on[e] or other of our SuperCargos when in the way, I being inform'd of the old fellows villainous Lies spoke to him in my room on paying him some Cash & askd him the reason of such Impudence, and that I would not always send for his friend Mr Morford when I payd him money that he might convince him the weight was just, & sent immediately for him but he was gone out, Quiqua made little answer but grinn'd & fell a chattering in Chinese to another China merchant that was with me, I hearing him repeat Mr Morford's name ask'd the other what he was talking of He told me in his presence that He had sayd Mr Morford was his very Good friend & wanted to have done good business with him, but that I did not care for him, & added that I did not like Mr Morford, I made no other reply than that I liked all Honest men & that as long as Mr Morford should continue such I would like him.

Octr 12 The officers complain greatly of the inequality of the China ware Chests[223], which makes them lose a great deal of room in flooring the Hould, which surpriz'd me

---

[223] Porcelain was originally packed in chests, but even in wooden bundles or cases. Tubs were used as well, and later on small chests too, or half-cases. Paddy or straw was scattered between the pieces of porcelain. It was a task which the Chinese undertook and in which they were exceedingly skilful. The capacity varied from chest to chest. It is impossible to put a definite figure on the number of items of porcelain per chest. The same applies to smaller boxes, the bundles and cases. There are data for the dimensions of a chest of porcelain, and perhaps some kind of standard chest did exist. At all events the porcelain chests were bigger than the tea-chests. Porcelain chests were placed in the hold first, where they also contributed to ensuring the balance of the ship. In addition they afforded protection against damp for the first layer of tea-chests. The porcelain pieces were not allowed to protrude from the chests under any circumstances. Otherwise a great deal of damage might be caused during stowage of the tea-chests. In order to prevent this, a rule was extended from one side of the chests to the other. If it was found that the horizontal line was breached, the contents of the chest concerned would have to be adjusted. Matters could also be improved by

as being all made by the same man (according to the measure sent from the ship) whom Mr Morford imployd for that purpose a servant of Suquas, and that there was always one or other of the Super-Cargos that pack'd them other business hindring me from staying long with them at that work. But measuring them in the factory (some that were still there) I found the Complaint but to be true & took better Care afterwards to see them my self before they were pack'd.

The Atchantsi or new Hoppo seems to be ready to oblige the Europeans as far as He can, for upon the English Captains desiring their merchants to speak to him to forbid Samfue[224] houses (or Brandy shops) at Vampo which incouragd the sailors in drinking and quarrelling He had publish'd an order forbidding any China [man]

147   to sell Samfue to forreigners either at Vampo or Canton. Upon my first coming I also spoke to Tinqua about another Abuse which was a Custom the Hoppo had or some of his servants to make the Compradores the Europeans imployd either for their ships or Factorys to pay them some 100 Tales others 150 by way of present for suffering them to act for us, which obligd the Compradores to lay so much a higher price on the provisions we bought of them, and which they alledgd at my first indeavouring to settle the prices with them, But as all the others had payd it (except ours) to the late Hoppo, there was no remedy till he was turn'd out & then I perswaded Tinqua to speak to this new one as being a pitiful sneaking thing for the Hoppo to get money in such a way as that, Tinqua accordingly spoke to him and as he tells me he sayd he was asham'd of it & was very glad he had told him, & immediately publish'd an Edict or Chop forbidding the Compradores to pay any thing for the Liberty to serve Forreigners. It is very like he was glad of this or any other Complaint against the late Hoppo, for it was made use of afterwards at the Hoppo's tryal, for all the Compradores that had payd him were brought to trouble for it and put in the stocks (or a piece of wood about their Legs) till they confess'd what they pay'd.

Another piece of Roguery but too often practis'd in some European Factorys here is The person that keeps Account with the Compradore obliges him to make him a Present sometimes pretty considerable & to make him amends pays him a higher price for his provisions (which he charges to his Company) or receives any sort that he pleases to give him. This little piece of Roguery we also took care to avoid in ours.

Octr 16   Pack'd with Tinqua 100 Chests[225] Bohea-Tea. We had a great deal of trouble to

---

placing this porcelain deeper down in the actual ballast. Tubs and bundles were stowed in the gaps remaining between the layers of tea-chests. These were practical modes of packing, but the risk of breakage was greater.

224 Chinese brandy, brewed on rice; not to be confused with arrack.

225 Chests varied from one type of tea to another. One spoke in terms of a whole or a half chest, or large

get it all according to our wish 1ˢᵗ leaf & head sort, and were oblig'd to refuse several sorts & many Baskets²²⁶ which were offer'd us, However Tinqua sent for many different sorts to content us, so that we got the parcel I hope very Good.

– 20 Pack'd with Suquas people 100 Chests Bohea, where we met with the same trouble as at Tinquas, before we could get it to our

148 liking.

Octʳ 22 Pack'd at Hunquas 100 Chests Bohea which is the best we have had yet & without any trouble, not one of us being able to find fault with one Basket or sort offerd us, His Chests also weigh much the heaviest of any we have yet had.

– 24 It is very Difficult to get any good China Root²²⁷, that is of the white sort fit for an Europe market, though there is enough very good of the black & Gummy sort which is more esteemd in India than the white, & which they are buying up now to carry to Fort Sᵗ George.

– 25 Pack'd at Suquas 100 Chests Bohea Tea, where his Partner & people gave us more trouble than we have met with any where as yet in pretending to impose upon us with a great variety of Bad which they offerd us but we refusd, Suqua having a vast quantity of Tea upon his hands this year & having no dealings with the Dutch nor English as other years (who often took what he was pleas'd to offer them for their own reasons) his people are very much surpriz'd to find that we pretend to refuse so Good Tea as they call it & which no other people refuse, and as Chinqua²²⁸ says much better than what he gives to the French at a higher

---

and small chests, for the same variety of tea. A check of the tares reveals that they fluctuated between 16 and 100 *skålpund*. Once the tares were known the chests could be fitted on the inside with a lead lining and then with paper. The packing most commonly used for tea was the chest with a lead inner lining, which formed the most obvious means of protecting tea against damp during the sea-voyage to Europe. With this in view, and in order to guard against deterioration, the tea cargo was stowed above the porcelain in the ship's hold. Already during stockpiling at Canton very careful steps were taken to keep the tea dry. The chests were brought indoors in the daytime. They were never allowed to rest on the bare ground, but only on a floor of paddy. The aroma of the tea could deteriorate in the ship's hold itself through the stowing of strong-smelling merchandise next to the tea-chests.

   Once the chests were ready, the tea was stamped into them by coolies. When this operation was finished, a sheet of paper and another of each were laid on top of the tea and soldered to the end of the lead lining. Next the lid was nailed on and the whole chest then wrapped once more in oiled paper. The chests were then weighed again so as to determine the gross weight. It was a general rule to reckon one pound per chest for the lead lining, paper and nails.

²²⁶ Tea could also be packed in baskets or canisters. The canister was originally made of cane and must have looked something like a large hamper.

²²⁷ *China root*, the thick fleshy root-stock of a shrubby climbing plant (*Smilax China* L.), once supposed to possess great medicinal virtues. (Lewis 1991, p. 85.)

²²⁸ Later (*Diary* p. 153) Campbell describes *Chinqua* as Suqua's book-keeper. He is evidently not identical with the merchant of the same name who appears as one of Suqua's rivals in the English East India Company Chronicles (Morse 1966–69, 1, pp. 202, 204, 209, 211).

price, in fine his Partner Tanqua a sour ill natur'd fellow told us he would give us no other, I answerd him that he might then keep it & what was already pack'd should remain upon his hands, & orderd no more to be pack'd & the Coolies to give over treading. Chinqua seeing this prevaild with him to give us enough to our liking to finish the Chests.

we have been still Continuing in hopes of the Hoppos performance of his promises to redress our Grievances, which has made me refuse to pay as yet the 1950 Tales present money which the Linguist is often teazing me for pretending all the other ships have payd it which I dont believe to be true at least in regard of the Country ships. As I am afraid it is not in the Hoppos power to redress us I am indeavouring to get a memorial in the Chinese Language in order to present to the Xunhu or Fouyen upon the same subject, but find it a hard matter to perswade any China man

149   to meddle in such a thing, so have desir'd a friend going to Maccao to see if he can perswade any of the Missionaries[229] or Europe Padres there to do it, & have given him the Heads of a Paper in order to have it put in Chinese. A propos as to the missionaries It is a great prejudice to the Europeans that they are now banish'd out of all the Provinces of China (except a few mathematicians whom the Emperour yet suffers at Pekin on Account of their knowlege in the sciences) A little before we arriv'd they were all orderd to Macao where they are in herds at the expence of the Portuguese Padres who would gladly wish that all others save themselves were banish'd even from thence too, which they live in great apprehension of. When they were allow'd to be at Canton one could always have found one or other of them to asist us especially in drawing up any paper for us that we had occasion for. My friend Pere Gigues a Frenchman went to Europe last year, who had he been here would have been very serviceable to me on this occasion.

Octr 26   We pack'd at Pinkys to day 100 Chests Bohea Tea, and with a great deal ado was able to perswade young Pinky (the old man's son) who is now Head of the House to let us have any till the Ostenders had got theirs, though we contracted with him before them, But as they have bought a much greater quantity from him than we & I believe pay a greater price he seem'd much inclin'd to give them the preference. And as I knew (by what I had seen & examind) that he has a great deal of Bad Tea was not willing they should have the best and we have their Refusals. He wanted to put me off by many frivolous excuses saying the Good Tea was not

---

[229] Because of the persecution of the Roman Catholic Church, missionaries were banished from all their stations in all parts of the Chinese Empire, but they were allowed to remain in the city of Canton. They freely and willingly gave help, advice and information to all foreign traders; in recognition of this, priests were on several occasions granted a free passage to Europe on Company ships. (Morse 1966–69, 1, p. 179; Ljungstedt 1992, p. 68 *et passim*.)

yet come, and he had no Chests yet made to pack it in, though I knew that he had promis'd to pack for the Ostenders in a day or two. I seeing Chests in his Hang showd him there was no room for that Excuse, he pretended they were made for the Ostenders & could not be given to us because already promis'd to them, I did all I could to coax him to let us pack first as he ought to do, But finding that method in vain I fairly told him that if he allow'd the Ostenders to pack one Chest before us we should not take one Catty[230] Tea of him, so that at last I

150   gain'd my point & prevaild with him even to give us the Chests he had made for the Ostenders, which provok'd them very much, though I should have been very glad rather to have had older Chests (these being all new) could he have given us such. We had a good deal of Trouble with him serving us just the same way as Suqua had done, and not being able to prevail with him by reason or wheedling was forc'd to take the same method I had done at Suquas to leave off packing till he gave us better which at last he did. But as we find he has little good we think of taking no more of him. He told me some days afterwards that the Ostenders had taken the very Tea that we refus'd which I don't at all wonder at. There is none of these Gentleman[231] understand much of China Goods, the Chieff owns he dos not pretend to understand Teas & therefore leaves it intirely to the other two, which is to be wonderd at considering that he has but a mean opinion of the seconds honesty or Capacity & the 3[d] is little acquainted with such things, I was surpriz'd to see at one Manillas what sort of Tea they were packing; But that is their Affair & let them see to it.

Oct[r] 28   Pack'd at Tinquas 100 Chests Pecko Tea, He had several sorts, but not enough of the best or that we car'd to take, This made Tinqua very uneasy having depended much upon the Goodness of his Pecko especially one sort very fine & full of the white leaf (commonly call'd the flower) which we were oblig'd to refuse, as being a little touchd with the wind (as they term it here) or Air, or musty. But he very willing to satisfy us sent all over the Town, while we were packing, in order to buy of the best where he could find it to fill our Chests with. Tinqua is an Easy man & trusts intirely to his Brother & servants (who are no honester than they should be) as to his Teas & other Goods & is much abus'd by them, as he discoverd to day & was very Angry with them all about the Pecko. However not long afterwards we learn'd that the Ostenders took the

151   same musty Tea that we refusd though Tinqua had not been at the pains to open the Baskets & put in the sun for an Airing & taken away some atop, as we advis'd him, which would have help'd to recover his Tea.

Oct[r] 31   I have an account from the ship that Jonas Andersson Sailor dy'd on the 29th.

---

230 100 catties = 1 picul (Chinese weight measure). 1 catty = 16 taels (= 0.605 kg). See also note 181 above.
231 *Sic.*

Novr 1   Old Pinky's being in Prison is a great prejudice to that House, the young man being very little acquainted with the Europe Trade & in no Credit, & there is no Body at Home fit for any thing or that can do any business, which will occasion us great delays in all appearance. He has teaz'd me for many Days for money to advance to the weavers[232] because they refuse to make the silks we contracted for without he gives them more money, so that we were oblig'd to advance him some to day or else run the risk of wanting the silks we contracted for, which we cannot afford to do as the price is now higher than what we aggreed with him for.

– 3^d The Atchantsi that was lately made Hoppo being now sent for to Court, there is another Hoppo appointed to wit a military Mandarin & Governour of the City. So that I thought it would not be amiss once more to try for a Redress of Grievances with this new man, Capt Tully promis'd to joyn with us and did not doubt but Mr Cowan would too, & a favourable opportunity offering for Mr Cowans doing so at present viz a dispute he has with Suquas house about some Goods contracted but which he has refusd as not answering muster or being to his Liking Suquas people refuse to pay the Hoppo the Duties for the Goods they bought of him & for that reason the officers of the Hoppo won't permit Mr Cowan to ship off any Goods. I therefore waited on Mr Cowan & pressd him to imbrace this opportunity of giving in a memorial to the Xunhu in which we & Capt Tully would joyn with him, but I could not prevail, because he was resolv'd to take another method, that is to force his way by sending his Goods in his own Boat with his own people Arm'd, and which he actually began to day to do, which oblig'd the Hoppo men to promise that they would

152   give him leave to ship next day, provided he would not take the way he was resolvd on, to which he consented, However this brought his Linguist into trouble (the same fellow that is our Linguist) for the Hoppo sent for him & honourd him with a Chain about his neck threatning him with the Bamboo if he did not make Mr Cowan desist from such methods. This is the way here If An European dos any thing the Mandarins don't like, They send either to the merchant (that answers or acts for that factory as there is always one merchant & other that does so for every one) or to the Linguist, and punish them first in order to oblige the Europeans to submit to reason or rather to their will & pleasure.

To day I was inform'd from aboard, That our sailors had demanded that every

---

[232] Chinese merchants had 90 days in which to get the orders made up at the weaving-mill and delivered. Half or two thirds of the purchase price had to be paid in advance upon conclusion of the contract. The remainder was settled upon delivery on board ship. The directives to the super-cargoes emphasize that in packing silk the dryness, quality, closeness of weave and thickness of fabrics must be considered. Every piece had to correspond in all respects to the approved samples. After this check had been made the fabrics were packed up, having first been rolled up and packed in oiled paper. This was best done on a day of clear, sunny weather when humidity was low. A number of bundles could be bound together in bales or filled into packing-cases.

one should have a Chest aboard, Now as we have very little room for the Goods of the Company already contracted & none to spare for Empty Chests, and as the Company had never promis'd any sailor the privilege of a Chest[233] on the Contrary had taken all the precautions they could to prevent them ever Expecting by letting them know so much at Stockholm & ordering the Captain to tell them so, And in particular those ingagd at Gottenburg were ingagd upon that very condition & even had a little more pay allow'd them rather than suffer it. But our poor fellows who had no money to buy any Goods to put in their Chests, had heard that the Dutch & Ostend sailors had that privilege many of whom us'd to sell them to the Captain & officers & even Super-Cargos for a little money (as one Chief told me himself he had done) which gave me some suspicion that the Captain & some of our officers were at the bottom of this, which is a most egregious abuse & often hinders room for the owners or Companys Goods by having the ship crowded with those private Chests, This I was resolv'd to check at once in order to prevent introducing such a bad Custom or precedent amongst us, & wrote to the Captain that he knew as well as I that they had no right to any Chest & that I never would

153   allow of it &c And added that if I knew that any sailors Chests were brought on board with Goods, as they must belong to some of the officers (a practice too Common in other ships where sailors had that privilege & which I would not suffer in ours) I would seize all for the Companys use. This put a stop to all noise on this subject for a little time

Novr 4   The Hoppo men not being so Good as their word to Mr Cowan in coming to ship his Goods, [he] did actually to day send his Goods aboard in his own Boat without their Leave, & sent one of his People with them with a Petition in the Chinese Tongue complaining of the Injustice done him in not allowing him to ship his Goods on pretence of a dispute with Suqua when he had more money in Suquas hands than would pay the Duties demanded &c This petition was deliverd at the first Hoppo House where the Boat stoppd as she went down the

---

[233] Everyone on board had the right to free transport of merchandise according to his grade or appointment. This meant permission to convey a quantity of goods in order to trade privately in the Far East. It comprised free conveyance and the allotment of a certain amount of space on board for the storage of personal merchandise. Goods bought in the Far East on private account in this way were termed *pacotille*. The space reserved in the ship for this private trade could give rise to friction on appointment to a post on board, for with a personal cabin at one's disposal – as was the case with supercargoes and officers – it was possible to stow more goods there. This stowage quickly assumed inordinate proportions and had to be restrained by order of the Company directors. Though actually an internal matter, the privilege could also have national repercussions, because a great deal was sold in this way to individuals by private persons, and the monopoly conferred upon the Company as a corporate body was no longer safeguarded. For this reason the system was abolished in 1748 and replaced by "privilege money"; infractions were punished by confiscation and stoppage of pay. The system of privilege money remained in force at least until 1766. It consisted of the allotment of a sum of money to everyone on board according to his rank or appointment, paid to him at the end of the voyage. (Koninckx 1980b, p. 325 ff.)

River, The Hoppo men sent the Petition to the Hoppo detaining the Boat till they receivd the Hoppos Answer which soon returnd with an order to let his Goods & Boats pass. This brought Suqua & him to settle their Affairs so that He had no more trouble on that score.

The Same day we pack'd at Suquas 50 Chests Bohea, & had more trouble than ever to get tolerable from them, This being the last Bohea we were to pack His Partner Tanqua & Chinqua his Book-keeper seem'd resolv'd to pass as bad upon us as they could, which they long persisted in with great obstinacy, And as we refusd to take it & they would give no better put our packing at a long stand, I tryd by all sort of ways to persuade Chinqua (for the other Tanqua he is such an obstinate fool he will hear no reason) to give us better both by threatening & wheedling him but to little purpose they thought to tire us out & make us glad to take it, But we continuing as stiff as they did obligd them at last to content us & finish our 50 Chests. The quality of Suquas Tea could not be calld bad but which we thought not at all fit to carry to Europe it being so dry that the treading of it is apt to turn it into pouder, which is owing to a Custom he has & which they Show'd us in the Hang where we were packing, of drying

154   it with Charcoal fires placd along in the middle of a room & the baskets heapd up on each Side, And asking Chinqua he told us that the French desir'd it so. I ask'd the French some time afterwards the reason of choosing such dryd Tea, who told me that they lik'd it so in France and that the drying of it with these fires gave it a higher flavour which they pretended it even retaind upon its arrival at Home. But I very much suspect another reason both for the merchants thus drying their Tea, and for the French taking of it, As to the first it is evident it makes their Tea have a higher smell especially that often coming down the Country chiefly by water it receives some wet or Damp in the Boats & turns musty or (as is calld here catches wind) so that drying it before it is deliver'd makes it pass better with the Buyer & takes off that mustiness, though I doubt much it wont long retain that flavour, & therefore that the true reason of the French receiving of it (at least this year) is to favour Suqua, for as he has ways of managing them they are easily perswaded to do what he desires of them, And to confirm this suspicion we had an Instance this afternoon while we were packing for Monsr de Velaer came in upon some business with Suquas people, Assoon as Chinqua spyd him at a distance he told his people not to bring any Tea or such as he intended for us while we were here & to stop packing or opening any Baskets that were ready for us upon the floor, Asking him afterwards the reason of this He told us that if he saw our Tea he would be angry because he did not give him the same, for he must be glad to take other sort & even worse than we refus'd. This is the more to be wonderd at since they pay this very year 17 & 18 Tales a pecul for it, which Capt Morllet[234] told me was a shame since we had much better & he was sure we did

_____

[234] The name of the French captain was _Jacques Morellet_ (Dermigny 1964, 1, p. 225).

not pay near so much, As I had occasion often to talk to Chinqua while the French were a packing I could not help observing what sort they had especially some Congo Capt Morllet gave me a handfull of and

155 told me they were taking it for Souchen[235] & payd 40 Tales for it, And I must say I should be sorry if some Congo we have at 18 Tales a pecul dos not prove better than their Souchen. Another inconvenience and risk one runs in taking of fire dryd Tea is that by this means they can pass old Tea or of the last year upon us by giving it a pretty good smell which may deceive People that are not very nice. But what will People not do or not take of a China man for his owners when the merchant knows how to make it up another way to the SuperCargo for his private advantage. At least it looks very suspicious when a Super-Cargo receives Tea which at first shows bad and pays more for the same sort or even a worse than other people do. Indeed sometimes Tea that shows well at first may not come out so well after a long voyage, which is no Bodys fault at least cannot be imputed to the Super-Cargos. But when People act without those private views they dont run those risks to be imposd upon, since they can with boldness refuse any thing they dont like, a piece of ill manners the China merchants {that} are not much accustom'd to here & which they cry out much against, and has got both Mr Brown & me the Character of being very hard.

While we were Packing Mr Ley came in with some others to see the Tea we were receiving (which is what is not reckond very handsome here without being ask'd) which not knowing how he came to learn where we were made me somewhat uneasy & believe he would not have done (after the distance he had kept from me since his Arrival) without being incouragd to it & told of it by Mr Morford, which made me ask him if he had told Mr Ley of our packing here to day, He answerd with some Concern of his being suspected that He had not, I sayd it was very well & insisted no more about it. Though we had no reason to fear showing the Goods we receivd to every Body, yet as it is not usual to do so & that I by no means ow'd Mr Ley any great Complaisance especially that he was very inquisitive & prying as much

156 our Affairs not without any intent I had reason to think to do us any service, But he seeing me look very Cool soon retird & left us.

Novr 7 They being now ready on board to receive our Green Tea[236] and the officers having wrote pressingly for it, we resolvd to send them some to day & had the

---

[235] *Souchong*, a black tea, picked even earlier than Congou. The finest variety of Congou.

[236] As in the case of black teas, the different types of green tea correspond to the seasons in which they are picked. Singlo or Sunglo corresponds to black Congou. Hyson tea corresponds to Souchong. Hyson Shin seems to have been an inferior tea. Bing, also termed Imperial or Emperor tea, had very broad leaves. Tonkay appears to be a Singlo variety of the highest quality.

Sampans or China Boats Ready at the Factory to take it in & orderd the Hoppo men to attend for that purpose, so we went early all together to Suquas to examine the different sorts he had, & having flung out some Chests & examind them as narrowly as we could did not find them much to our liking & pressd him to give us better which he sayd he could not, so that we only took 50 Chests of the best we could pick to send aboard on this occasion and recommended to them to get us better for next time we should want some, The Tea lookd & smelld well but was too dry & dusty.

– 8 Pack'd at Hawksbill Keyquas[237] 50 Chests Pecko Tea, He did all he could to content us and get us the best he could find by sending to other places for some in lieu of what Baskets we refus'd.

– 9 Receiv'd Letters from the ship acquainting me they could find room for 7 or 800 more bundles China ware. I desird the Super-Cargos every one to look out where he could best find any for I could see no where any but what we had musters of already. They complain that the last Bundles we sent were many of them broke when they came aboard.

– 10 Receiv'd 104 Chests Souchen Tea from Mandarin Quiqua, And as he is a sneaking fellow had a good deal of difficulty to settle the weight of the Chests with him, he being willing to make them as heavy as he could.

Suqua & Pinky being in prison makes it very difficult to get rid of the Perpetts that are still upon our Hands, As for

157 the 200 Old Pinky promis'd to take, the son pretends he knows nothing of his Fathers Promise and can't take them but wants more money to give to the weavers in order to provide our silks in time, And as he has neither money nor Credit I must indeavour to find another way to dispose of those 200 ps. Suquas Partner refuses to take any alleging that Suqua did not promise to take them, All I can say for Answer that though he did not promise to take the Companys yet he promisd to take mine which is the same thing, And as other merchants have taken a part It is very strange that He whom we have done more business with than any other should refuse to help the Company & take his share, At last I was oblig'd to tell him if he would not take his share of Perpetts we would take no more of his Green Tea, and thus prevaild with him to accept now of 200 ps which I sent him directly.

Novr 11 Went to Suquas to receive the rest of our Green Tea saw several sorts but not being to our liking we would not aggree to take any of them, & told him plainly that if

---

[237] This merchant is mentioned once more (*Diary* p. 175: *Hawksbill*). Evidently he is not identical with Beau Khiqua (*Diary* p. 115 and note 187).

they would not provide us better we must go to some other merchants where we could find it. He insisted upon the Contract we made with Suqua, we answerd him that no doubt we were oblig'd to fulfill our part of it (as we had all the inclination in the world to do) provided he fulfilld his part in giving us this years Tea 1st leaf & best sort, & if not we would have no more to say to him. In short he insisted this was the best in Town, that he could not nor would try to get another. I went away from thence to Hu[n]qua (who is Suquas friend) to complain of such usage desiring him to speak to his Partner & to Chinqua to make them satisfy us. Coming presently back to Suquas where I had desird the SuperCargos to stay, I missd Mr Morford, Asking what was come of him I learnd that he & Chinqua were retird together assoon as I had gone out, I went directly forward through the rooms to look for them & found them in a Room forward Looking over some fans

158 & other things, They seeing me came out & met me & Mr Morford Joynd the other Super-Cargos, I suspected Chinqua had been indeavouring to corrupt him in order to ingage him to perswade us to take his Tea & was soon Confirm'd in my suspicion, for Chinqua took me aside & sayd that Mr Morford was the only Person that knew Good Green Tea and that the other Super-Cargos no Sabe[238], This provok'd me & made me tell him that we had all Eyes & noses as well as Mr Morford & we would not suffer our selves to be imposd upon by such Arts &c And Joyning Mr Brown & Mr Pike could not help telling them what Chinqua had sayd. Chinqua perceiving after this that Mr Morford would not be able to serve him so much as he had flatterd him self made their friendship take a very different unexpected turn & helpd to discover an Affair I did not suspect not much to Mr Morfords Advantage, which will appear in the Sequel. Finding there was nothing to be done at Suquas we aggreed to go look elsewhere to find better Green Tea, I took Mr Morford along with me & went to some of the merchants but we found none to our liking.

Novr 12   I was resolv'd, as Mandarin Quiqua had good dealings with the Company, to get him to take 100 ps Perpetts, I could not prevail with him as yet to take more than 60 ps so kept the other 40 ps in reserve for him being resolvd he should take them before I payd him his Account

– 14   Not being able to perswade Suquas people to give us any better Green Tea, we contracted to day with Tinqua for some, who showd us some Chests better than we had seen any where else & at 9.T.5 M pr pecul which we orderd him to send in, but next day

– 15   upon viewing some of the Chests that came in found it did not answer muster & so Sent it back again.

---

238 *No sabe* 'don't know' (Portuguese *saber* 'to know').

Finding that all the Tea in Town was much of the same Qualitys as Suquas dry & very dusty, and that we could not help our selves, and that the stowing of the ship was delayd for want of Green Tea Chests we receivd 100 Chests to day of Suquas the best we could pick out.

159
Novr 16

Mr Brown & I having pressd Tinqua to look out for some Good Green Tea, having found some of the best we had yet seen, we got the other Gentlemen to go there who all approvd of it as much the best we had seen in Town, But he would have 14 T. a pecul for it, and Mr Morford & Mr Pike insisting to have it at 9 {T} Tales & 9.T.5.M though better worth 14 T than Suquas at 10.T I would not offer any thing though I knew he would have parted with it at 12, and therefore we could not aggree with him. Mr Brown & I were of opinion that it was well worth while to take some of it at 12 T. since we were not likely to get any other Good in Town, and had it been my own private Concern would have readily done it, But as the other Gentlemen were positive not to give more for it and that I was willing to see if possible to bring his price down to what was offerd I would not pretend to give even what we thought it worth, we both knew the Aversion they had for Tinqua and the notion they had that we wanted to oblige him preferably to others (though they had not yet seen one Instance of it in our Conduct) and though we two were sufficient to strike a bargain at any time yet I was resolvd never to do it without an unanimous Consent (except a Case of absolute necessity had requird which I hop'd to avoid) which as it happend we always had in all Contracts made, and therefore did not care to buy any thing contrary to their opinions. I knew besides that they were fishing for some handle to find fault, by going sometimes to the merchants and inquiring if Mr Brown & I had been with them and had made any Contracts with them (as one informd me himself that Mr Pike had done more than once) which I did not think worth while to take notice of, & not at all afraid but rather pleasd at their making inquiry after my Conduct, But I can't help saying it was silly enough since they well knew no Contract had ever been made without their examining the Goods first and that they had it always in their power to refuse them if they did not like them. As for my own part I was resolvd never to trust to my own opinion in such things alone, but very glad to

160

have every Bodys opinion about the Goodness of every ps of merchandise as well as the price that being the best way to have them Good & thereby to serve our Companys best.

We not thinking it proper to buy the foresaid Green Tea of Tinqua, & not being perfectly satisfyd with Suqua's provided we could get better any where I desir'd all our Gentlemen to look out & inquire where they could find any Good, Mr Morford not willing to lose so good an opportunity to play a little Game (as is the Cant stile here) went to Liunquas & came & told us that He had some Green Tea much better than Suquas, I suspecting nothing took Mr Brown with me to go & see it, He show'd us some which we did indeed find to be better, Though I was very glad to get better Tea than we had receiv'd hitherto, yet I would rather [we]²³⁹ had taken Good of Suqua than of any Body else, so before I should take the SuperCargos all together to make a Contract with Liunqua, I resolv'd to try Suquas people once more & went & told them that I was unwilling to buy Green Tea from any Body else provided they would give us as Good as we could have it else where, which I assur'd them I could have at present, They insisted still that theirs was the best in Town & that they could give us no Better, Perceiving there was no overcoming their Obstinacy I told them plainly that we must go buy Good where we could get it & so took my leave. Being unwilling to break with Suqua I thought of staying yet a day to give them time to change their mind & give us better, But Mr Morford pressing us to go to Liunquas (since we could not take any more of Suqua as not being so good) this afternoon I complyd and we all went to Liunqua, who having open'd us a Couple of Chests we aggreed it was better than Suquas, & prevaild with him to give it 5 mace²⁴⁰ a pecul cheaper & also take 100 ps [of] Perpetts (which I had design'd for Suqua) at 7 Tales a ps as other merchants did, so that we aggreed to take of him 200 Chests at 9.T.5.M p^r pl.²⁴¹ which he took care to send immediately

161   to our Factory, we started some Chests which we were surpriz'd to find (at least Mr Brown & I were) that they were not so Good as what he had shown us & as dusty as Suquas, which I took the fancy to make a Tryal of by sifting a Chest of one & a Chest of the other and weighing afterwards the dust or pouder that came from them which I found to be about 9 Catty in a Chest. Could I have suspected this I should never have aggreed to have broke our Contract with Suqua, But now we had no remedy The Tea was receiv'd and for some Amends the price was less than Suquas & the Tea much of the same Goodness, so that we thought best to keep it.

Novr 18   Suquas Partner having heard that we have taken Green Tea of Liunqua is very angry, & Chinqua tells me that instead of taking more Perpetts he will send back those he has already taken. For fear he should have the Impudence to do so I orderd our Guard to let none come in to the Factory from any Body.

– 21   Having now got a petition ready in the Chinese Tongue for the new Hoppo begging him to redress our Grievances in relation to the many Duties impos'd upon the Europe Trade by former Hoppos, I have been wheedling of Tinqua to pe[r]swade him to ask the Hoppos leave to wait upon him only to pay our Complements which is more proper from us than from any other Europeans as being the first that ever came hither from Sweden, without letting him know our true design, which all the merchants will ever oppose for fear of disobliging the

---

²³⁹ Alternatively Campbell may have inadvertently written *had* for *have*.
²⁴⁰ *Mace* or *mas*, a Chinese monetary unit (cf. note 180 above).
²⁴¹ Abbreviation for *picul*.

Mandarins who never care to quit any scheme they have once practis'd for getting of money; I am even oblig'd to conceal from some of our Super-Cargos that I have a petition ready, or to tell them the Person that has drawn it which he has also intreated me not to do, In fine I durst not trust at least one of us on Account of an extraordinary Intimacy with Mr Ley and a great

162   shyness towards me, seldom seeing him but at Dinner or when I send for him about Business. What makes it necessary to lose no time in this application is the plague we have daily with the Linguist for the 1950 Tales present money which I am willing to stave off as long as I can till I see if it is possible to have any Redress, though he pretends to say that all the Europeans have already payd it. I know the English & french payd it soon after their Arrival; And the Dutch have payd it though in a different manner from others, For the parties still keeping up amongst the Super-Cargos very hot they will not consent that it should be payd to the merchant or to the Linguist for the Hoppo's Account, believing their Chief & his party intend to play the Knaves, and therefore they did at last aggree to go together in a Body to the Hoppo & there carry their money & see if he would take it, which they accordingly did, and told the Hoppo their Errand, He ask'd how much it was & bid them leave it there, so that they return'd as great Fools as they went. I should have thought they would have at least ask'd him first to be redress'd, before they show'd him their Bags of Money, which was a Temptation a China man could not resist. But what still forebodes worse luck than all this to us is that I am inform'd Mr Cowan has also payd it, though he assur'd me many times he never would, for though he did not appear directly to pay it himself yet he has done the same thing by allowing Suqua to do it for him & to charge it him in Account.

As we have great reason to suspect all Linguists & especially ours (whom I know for a Rogue being the same that serv'd my Brother and I when I was here before) I have got a Tariff of the Emperours Ancient Duties on sundry Goods with all the new Impositions layd on since, and which they now Oblige all European ships to pay, by which

163   I find the villain has cheated us in a small Account of Galangal[242] for which I aggreed to pay the Duties on purpose to catch him, & am resolvd to show it to the Hoppo & ask him if these are the true Duties that he has chargd us.

---

[242] *Galingale* or *galangal*, an aromatic rhizome of the ginger family. The root was obtained from two different plants, the larger one from *Kæmperia galanga*, the smaller one from *Maranta galanga*. Generally used in medicine as a stomach remedy, these dried roots were also employed in the distilling of *brännvin* (Swedish aquavit), for spicing vinegar and in cookery. They were usually packed in packtuns for transport. Baskets and bags were used as well. Galingale was sometimes also stowed between the tea-chests. (Savary des Bruslons 1759–65, 3, p. 9; Flückiger & Hanbury 1878, 2, p. 442; Ljungstedt 1992, p. 251.)

Novr 25   Tinqua having spoke to the Hoppo this morning of our desire to wait upon him, He orderd us to come in the Afternoon, which we did accompanyd by our Linguist & Tinqua, He receiv'd us Civilly & welcom'd us & wishd us a Good Trade, & presented us Tea, Assoon as that was over, I pulld out of my pocket the Memorial in the China Language and desird the Linguist to tell him that there was a a Paper which contain'd some Grievances which the Europe trade labour'd under here, which I hop'd He would take in good part & give us a favourable Answer, (As for the Paper I refer to the end of this Journal where such like Papers shall be plac'd.) The Linguist to whom I gave the Petition to deliver to the Hoppo holding it in his hand not without trembling, the Hoppo orderd him to give it to a servant that stood near him who deliverd it into his Hands, Having perus'd it, He say'd that it was not in his power to Redress the Grievances there complain'd of, especially that all other ships had payd them, but that he hop'd there would be some redress next year, because the Mandarins had wrote to the Emperour on that subject, and that they could not pretend to make any Alteration without his Maj^{tys} Answer & orders. We continued to press him for some Relief and usd all the Arguments I could to perswade as having come a great way, & being the first that had come so far, and that this new Company would send more & richer ships another time, & what relief or incouragement we receiv'd now would be a great satisfaction to our King &c He was well pleasd with the last part of

164   the discourse, & desird us to send a greater quantity of Goods another time, & added that as for any Redress or Relief he could not as yet do any thing but that he soon expected another Hoppo from Pekin & that he would talk with him upon the subject & do all he could with him to make Trade Easier for Europeans. In fine we were oblig'd to rest contented with his promises, which were nothing but Air, & never cost a China man any Trouble. I then desir'd the Linguist to tell him that I had an Account now in my hand of some Duties chargd upon a small quantity of Galangal which seem'd to be very great since they amounted to the third of the Cost of the Goods, and I should be very glad to know if this Account was Just & if we ought to pay it, I offerd the Account to the Linguist to present to the Hoppo, He knowing it to be his own was extremely frighten'd & was not willing to take it from me till the Hoppo orderd him to bring it to him, The Hoppo having perus'd it sayd he believ'd the Linguist had cheated us & was very angry with him & threatend to punish him, and sent the Account to his secretary to let us know truly how much we were to pay, The Linguist had a Lie at hand to excuse himself with by saying He had not drawn out that Account himself but some merchant for him. The Hoppo then told us this was a small matter. Finding the Linguist shuffle & afraid to speak what I desird him I beggd Tinqua to tell the Hoppo that we did not value a small difference of a few Tales more or less nor did we think it worth while to complain of but to show him how much we were liable to be imposd upon by our Linguists & others, & if in so small a sum as of 21 Tales we were cheated some Tales how much more must we be in greater sums, which Tinqua did. The

European factory buildings in Canton. From left to right may be seen the Danish, Spanish, Swedish, English, and Dutch flags. Chinese 18th century oil painting on canvas (before 1784). Gothenburg City Museum.

165 secretary sent back the Account corrected before we left the Hoppos, by which we found our selves cheated in between 3 or 4 Tales. Amongst other fine Comple-ments to sooth us he told Tinqua that he believ'd we were Honest men for we had Good faces, This is a Coin a China man will readily pay people with if they like it. But one thing remarkable which he ask'd or told Tinqua, was that we were not (he believd) the SuperCargos that took 2 Tales by way of present for themselves from the China merchants for every pecul of Tea they bought of them, Tinqua answerd that the Dutch had done so & not we for we were honest men & followd no such practices. In fine seeing there was nothing more to be done here we withdrew thanking him for his fine promises, which I begun to doubt was all the redress we were to have. However he carryd on his Civility to the last for his Guards accompanyd us to the Gate and they beat up all their musick to do us honour, a Ceremony we had not met with from any other of the Hoppos.

Upon returning Home Tinqua was not at all satisfyd that I had drawn him in to go with us without letting him know that we had a memorial in the China Language, assuring me if he had suspected it he would not have accompanyd us, & sayd the Hoppo wanted much to know who was the person that had put it in Chinese for us, for neither Mandarins nor merchants like much to see such papers being afraid that the Europeans get people to help them to find out their Impositions which being once payd they never care to part with again. As yet no body but Mr Brown perfectly knew who was the Person that helpd us, though it was not long possible to conceal it especially from our own people, so that he begun to be suspected, which contributed very much to baffle a design I had layd of giving in such another memorial (which I had then ready) to the Xunhu, as will be seen

166   presently

I can't help to explain the reason of the Hoppo asking if we were the Super-Cargos that had exacted 2 tales on a pecul of Tea for dealing with them, which was this viz Schultz the Chief Super-Cargo & his party had contracted with – – – – – a China merchant for a parcel of Tea for which the merchant was to allow them by way of present two shooes of Gold [243] which amounted to about 2 Tales a pecul on the Quantity aggreed for. But those worthy Gentlemen finding afterwards that it would be more [worth] while to deal with Beau Keyqua broke their Contract with the other & refus'd to take the Tea, This put the merchant in great wrath against them, & made him tell them publickly that because Beau Keyqua had given them more money than they had aggreed to take of him they had broke their Contract with him &c And this he told every body; so that it came to the Ears of the Hoppo & Mandarins. This villainous practice of the Europe Super-Cargos (which the Country Super-Cargos are not usd to nor never charg'd with) is of the very worst Consequence & dos a great prejudice even to those that act Honestly, & a great means to prevent ever their having any Redress. It not only gives the Mandarins a very indifferent opinion of the Europe Traders, but also incourages them and the merchants too to exact what they please well knowing that they have always a method to bring the greatest part of them to submit to any thing & to rob their Companys & masters as much as they please provided they allow them some advantages to themselves to make them amends for allowing them to cheat their owners.

---

[243] Canton had been an important gold market since the inception of the European companies. Since the Chinese possessed no silver, whereas gold was abundant, the latter could be traded freely. It was true that Chinese gold was less pure than Brazilian, but at any rate it was cheap. It was even asserted that this gold could realize a 70% profit on the European market. The difference in fineness between Brazilian and Chinese gold destroyed the balance between silver and gold in China and in Europe. It is understandable that massive speculation resulted from this. Although gold did not appear frequently in Swedish cargoes or in Swedish transactions, it can be affirmed that gold was traded in an illegal manner.

167   Finding that there was nothing to be expected more of the Hoppo, our time being so short here, we resolv'd to try the last resource we had which was to apply to the Xunhu who is the first man in the Government here & most capable to help us, and as he had turn'd out the Hoppo for exacting of the merchants injustly &c we presum'd that he would be ready to hear what Complaints we had to make against Crimes of the very same nature, Mr Brown & I therefore did all we could to bring this about (I confess I did not let the other SuperCargos into the methods we were taking to accomplish this for good reasons I thought I had) and to keep our China friend true to us, made him a present of a small sum of money for what he had already done, and as {as} we had now nothing to buy for the Company I was willing to help him in my private Affairs, and though I had no great opinion of his Riches or Credit yet upon his frequent pressing me I allow'd him some of my Perpetts for which he promis'd silks in return, in which I was disappointed & thereby glad to sit with the loss of 160 Tale in Cash which he now ows me, besides taking any thing of him he had to lessen his Debt; I also promis'd him, if the Affair should succeed through his means and that the Xunhu would relieve us of those Impositions or a part of them, that we would make him a handsome Present. The poor man was very hearty in our Interest & to do him Justice did all that lay in his power, but unluckily both He and we were overreach'd by the very Persons that undertook to bring it about, as will be seen in its place.

Novr 27   Our silks come in but slowly, & the merchants pretend that the Raw silk being Dear and now a great demand for silks makes the weavers hard to deal with & to demand higher prices, Though it is true that there is now a greater demand

168   especially that the English have not only of their own but of the Companys money yet to lay out which was design'd to buy Gold with but now Gold being very high they have thought it more Advantagious to buy silks and have lately made a Contract for a parcel though at a higher price than before. But I doubt there is another reason also makes the weavers so backward & late in delivering the silks, which is that the merchant[s] don't immediately pay them the money we advance for that purpose in order to set them immediatly at work, which is the occasion of being often delayd about the silks when just ready to depart.

The Imprison'd merchants were brought to day upon their Tryal, The Crimes allegd against Suqua are that he was the principal Person to advise the Hoppo to the measures he took & to teach him the methods to oppress & exact of the merchants &c & that Suqua traded for him, and had of his money lodg'd always with him in deposit for that purpose (which is a liberty not allowd the Hoppo by the Laws here) and this they want chiefly to come at. Suqua denyd every thing, He is in Chains as well as the rest, and they say his feet have been squeez'd (a sort of Torture practis'd here to make them confess) but it is believd more for form sake than any thing else, for I am privately assurd that all his Affair is as good as already made up with the Xunhu & Fouyen, & that the only rub in the way is, about the sum they expect from him which (as they know he is rich & which perhaps is his greatest Crime) is more than he cares to give. However they must make a form of trying him, Since they complaind to the Emperour against him by name, & had particular orders from Court to arrest & try him. Pinkys Crime being the exporting of red Copper (which is here prohibited) he deny'd it, & was punish'd by strokes on the face

169   with an Instrument made of pieces of hard Leather, which they say they use here against People that are found telling Lies, He afterwards confessd that he had help'd some Siam merchants to some Copper which they exported, without specifying Red or white, which made them declare him Guilty, Had he nam'd white Copper they say they could not hurt him that being allowd to be carry'd out. As poor Pinky has not much money I am afraid he will not get so soon clear of this Affair, which puts his House in great Confusion, & is like to make us suffer in our Contract with him as well as delaying us. He teazes me every day for more money, which I have refusd till he delivers us a quantity of silks.

The original Cause of all this Trouble given the Hoppo & merchants, I am assur'd is as follows. Two or 3 years ago the English Super-Cargos having contracted with one Tan-Hunqua[244] for a parcel of Teas, they afterwards finding another merchant that would make them more handsome face (as they call it) or a greater Present broke their Contract in part & receivd a great deal of their Teas from others, Tan Hunqua having a great quantity of Tea by this management left upon his hands was extremely inragd against those Gentlemen which he discoverd to one of the Super-Cargos, more honest in[245] the rest & who for that reason was not let in to their secret, He went further & put it in writing in a Letter to the English Company which the said Super-Cargo deliver'd on his Return, & which open'd a great mystery of Iniquity to the Confusion of those Super-Cargos, & occasion'd that Company this year to send him a present of plate. He had done the same in regard to the Dutch by sending to that Company an Account of all their Roguery of their Super-Cargos that same year. This being known at Canton brought the Ill will of the Chief merchants upon him, of whom he chiefly blames Suqua who he says having the greatest Interest with the Hoppo perswaded him to forbid & hinder him from trading with Europeans any more. This

170   put Tan-Hunqua upon contriving ways to revenge himself upon the Hoppo & Suqua, which he soon found good helps to inable him to do by the means of a Clerk or secretary the Hoppo had turn'd out of his service who discoverd all those practices allegd now against him & Suqua, Thus furnishd with proper materials Tan Hunqua went directly with them to the Xunhu & Fouyen who were glad of

---

[244] For *Tan Hunqua* see note 185 above.
[245] For *than* (no doubt reflecting Campbell's pronunciation of unstressed *than* as '*n*).

any handle to humble the Hoppo, which made them write to Court to inform the Emperour of the Hoppos bad discharge of his office &c Tan Hunqua at the same time sent his Brother to Court to Complain of the particular injury done him, which he was the more provok'd to do by reason that this very year the Hoppo had arrested him in his house with positive orders for him not to trade with any Forreigners this year, This piece of Injustice being done him the very day after some of the English Super-Cargos had arriv'd at Canton before their ship got up the River made him & every body conclude that they had not a little contributed to it by putting the merchants upon perswading the Hoppo to it, And we were afterwards not a little confirm'd in this opinion by their delaying till just before the ships left Canton of delivering Tan Hunqua the present of wrought plate the English Company had sent him which they had never given him if they could have found any way to excuse themselves to their masters at Home For these sort of Gentlemen never like such discoveries of their Brethren & friends, it being a very bad precedent for merchants to run into as being likely to deprive them of what they think they have almost a Right to of getting what they can at the expence of those that imploy them. In fine these Complaints being examin'd at Court, there were soon orders sent to arrest the Hoppo & Suqua & others, & in the Placaert[246] here publishd the Crimes above mention'd were specifyd by name. The same orders from the Emperour set Tan Hunqua at Liberty & gave him & all other merchants leave to

171 Trade with Forreigners or whom else they pleas'd, which they have since made publick here by a Placaat pasted up about the Town. This last order is not very aggreeable {to the Chief merchants} to the top merchants here (as they call them) who (at least some of them) have also indeavourd to bring the Hoppo to hinder any Body to trade with the Europeans but themselves, & of whom Suqua has been always been suspected to be the Principal Actor, though in other he is the richest most knowing & most punctual merchant Here. That method was too successfully practis'd when I was here in the year 1726, which by vile practices between the Hoppo & merchants & between the last & some Europe Super-Cargos brought on that monstrous Imposition of 10 p^r C^t upon all Goods loaded on Europe ships & has been kept up ever since & which without the Emperours express orders never will be taken off I fear.[247] That is a year that all honest Europe Traders have reason to curse as well as the Contrivers & those that first submitted to such a piece of villany, of which now any Body may know the particulars since the merchants make no scruple of telling the truth & naming such as were concern'd in it. I can't help remarking on this occasion that Super-

---

246 The spellings *Placaert* and (p. 171) *Placaat* for *placard* 'a printed or written notice for public display, a poster' are probably derived from such Dutch forms as *plackaert, plakkaat* (from Old French *plackart*, Latin *placatum*). Originally used for an open letter emanating from an official authority on which its seal was fixed ('sceau plaqué'), instead of hanging from it.

247 For further details on "the Ten Per Cent", see Morse (1966–69), 1, p. 189 ff.

Cargos have good reason to be very secret in their Knavish practices, for though it is possible, though not easy, to keep the secret while they are upon the place and just acting it, yet assoon as their backs are turn'd It comes all to Light, for the other merchants getting notice of it who have had no dealings with them don't fail to publish it, and even the next year or year thereafter the very merchants that did deal in that manner with the Europe Super-Cargos will discover it if you take pains to sift them, especially if they don't see the same people here again or that they dont expect ever their return hither to trade with them, of which I have met with some Instances of some years past told me by the Persons they dealt with.

Dec^r – 2   The depos'd Hoppo has told the Judges that the imprison'd merchants are not Guilty, & that he will take all their Affair

172   upon him & answer for it to the Emperour to whom he has appeal'd, & it is believ'd will be soon order'd to go to Pekin.

Decr 3   Finding Pinky's people shuffling with us about our silks and indeavouring to put us off to the last pretending they had none, and knowing there were some in the house design'd for the Dutch, (which old Pinky before he was put in prison promis'd to give me or the first he receiv'd rather than make us wait) I insisted on having them but could not prevail till I threaten'd them that I would get a memorial ready for the Hoppo to complain of their not having kept their word with us &c which put them in fear as well as great Anger against me, However I carryd my point by it & to day they deliverd us 3 Chests of silks.

– 10   Having the memorial some time ago ready for the Xunhu the great difficulty was how to come at him to deliver it, since there was no getting in to the City without leave of the present Hoppo who is the Governour of it, & whom we knew we must expect to do all he could to hinder us from getting to his superiours to complain, I had therefore got acquainted (by the means of our friend that wrote the memorial) with a Rich man in the City one of the Farmers of the Emperours salt who had been to pay me a visit & which I promis'd to return him with a pretence of seeing his House & other Curious things he has in it as well as out of Civility due to him, assoon as he would get us leave to come into the City, The French & Ostenders had got some hint of my going to see the salt Farmer (for all the pains one can take here, there is no keeping things secret) and spoke to my Friend to have leave to go along with us, which I absolutely refus'd well knowing they would (at least the French) spoil all my design, & desird him

173   to tell them that we did not intend to go, at the same time pursued my design, & the Farmer sent us to day an Invitation to come & dine with him to morrow & there being leave for us to go in to the City which I had askd for four persons,

Decr 11   we all four went to dine with the Farmer, where we found a Collonell, whom our friend thought he had sometime before secur'd to serve us & had promis'd to get us Access to the Xunhu with whom he us'd to be every day, and having taken the memorial with me did not doubt of finding an opportunity of going from thence to the Xunhu's which my friend had told me would be very Easy. Assoon as Dinner was over I Spoke to my friend to go along with us to the Xunhu to serve for an Interpreter which he was willing to do, But the Collonell & salt Farmer disswaded him & us from it under pretence that we could not get to the Xunhu without first sending to him to get his leave & to know the time he pleas'd to order us to wait upon him, &c I then desir'd they would send now to ask that leave, but they declin'd that by pretending that there was no getting to him but in a morning, & the Collonell promis'd faithfully he would bring it about in a more handsome manner for as he was to be next morning with the Xunhu he would acquaint him with our desire & assur'd us that in a day or two we would have an Audience, This made me very much out of humour, suspecting that they did not care to help us but rather betray us as being of the Hoppos friends, which we were confirm'd in by an offer made by the Salt Farmer who promis'd if we would be satisfyd & not go to the Xunhu he would speak to the Hoppo & get him to cut off 100 Tales of the present money, I told him that was not worth our while to make all this bustle for, that all we wanted to know what[248] what were truly the just Customs & fees we were to pay & to be reliev'd from those that were impositions & not orderd by the Emperour &c But all I could say or plead signify'd nothing

175[249]   so that we were under a necessity to return Home without being able to go to the Xunhu, & wait yet a while longer for the performance of the Collonells promises who now had undertaken our Cause, In the mean time being willing to keep fair with them I ask'd them to dine with us next day.

Decr 12   The Collonell & some others came to dine with us according to Invitation, but no salt Farmer, who sent an Excuse, They stayd with us till night, and we intertain'd them as well as we could, I took the opportunity to carry the Collonell into my room with the friend that wrote the memorial & made him assure him that if this Affair met with success that he had undertaken for us I would make him a handsome present, & desir'd to know in the mean time if there was any thing we had that might be for his service He ask'd for two or three Blankets which I gave him, & parted mighty Good friends in appearance with great assurances of his part to serve us & get us leave in a day or two at furthest to wait upon the Xunhu. I had another reason to suspect some underhand dealing with us, for our friend having acquainted the Xunhu's Pay de Casa of our design He beggd very much to see our memorial & he would speak to the Xunhu about it, But not willing to

---

[248] Mistake for *was*.
[249] Error for *174*.

trust them I refus'd to part with it, but told him to give him a Copy which he could easily do having drawn it out himself, which it seems he did, & told me the Pay de Casa had read it & was satisfyd with it & even had spoke to his master who promis'd soon to give us Audience. Though all this might have been a Lie invented on purpose to amuse us (which the Chinese are very dextrous at) yet we had no remedy but oblig'd to submit to what measures they pleas'd to take or promise to take to help us.

175
Decr 14 Hearing for some time that Tinqua's Affairs were not in good order and that there were some demands upon him for money left in his hands last year, I was resolv'd to get clear of him assoon as possible, & prevail'd with him to fulfill his Contract which to do him Justice he has done the first of all our merchants having to day deliver'd us the last of the silks he contracted for, so that we are now in his Debt.

– 19 They having wrote from the ship that they had room for more China ware in Bundles, we bought some of Hawksbill.

Not finding any Green Tea in Town much to our liking we think best take no more of it, but rather take a little more Souchen, especially as Suqua has some, which we choose to buy of him rather than another to make him some amends for not taking his Singlo, & hope to get it cheap & make him take some Perpetts yet unsold for payment.

– 23 Going to Suquas to Examine & receive the Souchen we had contracted with him for the day before, we found Chinqua very much out of humour, & told us that Suquas partner would not give us Souchen nor any Tea but the Green Tea we had refus'd nor would he take any more Perpetts but would have money & that we had us'd Suqua very ill &c This provok'd me to tell him that He & Suqua & his Partner had us'd us very ill in not complying with his part of the Contract in giving us the head sort of Green Tea 1st Leaf &c as he had promis'd. In fine the whole burden of his Complaint lay upon our having taken Green Tea of Liungqua & having refus'd his, which made him fly out very much in passion, & amongst other Expressions he us'd he told us that Tanqua Suqua's Partner was resolv'd to speak to all the Gentlemen & tell what had passd, I not knowing his true meaning supposd he meant all the European Gentlemen at Canton, and therefore told him angrily that I did not value what he told them & then went away

[176] from him not at all satisfyd with Chinqua's Behaviour. Though I observ'd Chinqua look very angry at Mr Morford & mutter things I could not understand & that Mr Morford look'd very much down & sayd very little all the while of our Dispute with him yet I did not suspect the real reason of it, till a little afterwards. Being very much displeas'd with Suqua's house & yet resolv'd not to leave Canton without making things as easy as possible with them, & more especially

in Consideration of Suquas being in Prison, who I do not believe would have us'd us so had he been at Home, I desir'd Mr Brown to go along with me to Hunqua who was Suqua's friend & also had some power with Tanqua & Chinqua on that Account, in order to intreat him to show them the unreasonableness of their Conduct towards us and to perswade them to end matters with us as they had before aggreed. I represented to Hunqua also how much Chinqua had been out of humour and how foolishly he had express'd himself by threatning he would tell all the Gentlemen what had past in this Affair &c which I supposd was the other Europe SuperCargos he meant &c Hunqua smil'd and sayd we had quite mistaken Chinqua's meaning for his Real meaning was by the Gentlemen us four Super-Cargos whom Tanqua desird to speak to all together and had resolv'd to do it for some days past, which he had disswaded him from, I told him had I known that I should have been very glad to hear what he had to say to us all and that we were still desirous to hear what it was, Hunqua not very much inclind to go further say'd Masquie or no matter, that He would speak to Tanqua & Chinqua to settle all affairs as we had before aggreed with them. Mr Brown & I finding Hunqua knew something he did not care to discover made us more earnest to find it out, but was oblig'd to draw him into

177   it by some Art & management, I told him that I observ'd for some time past that Mr Morford & Chinqua were not good friends which I wonder'd at since some time ago Chinqua had spoke much to me in Mr Morford's favour & had even told me that he was the person fit to advise with about Teas for the other Super-Cargos no Sabe Tea &c Hunqua then told us the reason that Suquas House were very angry because Mr Morford had carry'd us to Liungqua to take Green Tea of him which was no better than Suqua's, This I denyd & told him that the reason of our buying of Liungqua was that the muster of Tea he show'd us was better than Suquas though indeed I could not say what he sent in afterwards answerd the muster we had seen at his house, He then reply'd that Chinqua had found out the true reason of Mr Morford having carryd us to Liungqua's, which was that Liungqua in order to get him to perswade us to buy his Green Tea had promis'd to let him have some fine Teas (Souchen if I remember right) at a low price, I think it was about half the Current price it then sold for, I then ask'd him how it came about that Mr Morford should have fallen out with Suqua's house which made him do what he allegd, He sayd that Suqua before he was put in prison had promis'd Mr Morford some Chests of Congo Tea in a present in order to make him his friend and to perswade us to serve him & help him &c but that since Suqua was in prison, Tanqua who was [a] covetous fellow pretended that he knew nothing of what Suqua had promisd Mr Morford and would not let him have it though Chinqua had spoke to him about it & desird him, and that was what Tanqua had a mind to tell us all together and what Chinqua meant by saying he would speak to all the Gentlemen, & that Tanqua the other day was so Angry that he told it all over to a Portugueze that was with him, & that Chinqua had pressd him to desist &c In short from one thing to another

178   we drew him on to mention some other things he knew of presents &c he[250] had receiv'd from Mandarin Quiqua & others, but as that was on account of carrying the Ostenders to buy of them which did not relate to us, I did not take much notice of it, nor think it worth while to mention the particulars. Assoon as I found Hunqua begin to make this Discovery I desir'd Mr Brown to remember well what he sayd, & I took paper & pencil & wrote down as thinking of other things what I heard him say which I wrote out fair when I came Home and show'd to Mr Brown to see if it was exactly what he had sayd which we well remember'd & we both sign'd it, which I thought proper in case of my decease to leave in writing to be seen by the Directours at Home in order to let them know what people were fit to be trusted with Affairs another time. At parting with Hunqua we told him that we would have Tanqua yet tell us the Affair himself, He sayd better not for it might do Suqua hurt and begg'd we would take no further notice of it for if Suqua knew he would be very Angry with him for telling us, for it was not good for Merchants to tell so fashion of one another for it disobligd them and also made the Europe SuperCargos very angry &c In short I soon found Hunqua was sorry for what he had discoverd & fearing that Tanqua would tell it over to us all together in Mr Morford's presence he went to him and (as he ownd to me afterwards) dissuaded him from mentioning one word to us about it, he gave the same advice to Chinqua, but not soon enough to prevent Chinqua telling Mr Brown & me the whole secret. For we went directly from Hunquas to Suqua's, where meeting with Chinqua we ask'd him what he meant in the morning by saying

179   that Tanqua had a mind to speak to all the Gentlemen, If he meant that he had any thing to declare to us we would gladly hear what he had to say, He then told us the truth and the same as Hunqua had done just before, viz that Mr Morford had been several times to ask of him for some Chests of fine Tea (Souchen) that Suqua had promis'd him, and had pressd him to speak to Tanqua Suqua's Partner about it which he had done, & Tanqua had refus'd to give him any saying that he had nothing to do with Suquas promises &c And that upon his giving Mr Morford this final Answer He was angry and went to Liungqua to see his Green Tea and Liungqua had promis'd hin some fine Souchen (if I remember right) at a very low price by way of present if he could bring us to buy Green Tea of him, He added besides that Mr Morford had been with him Chinqua within these few days and finding he could not get the Present Suqua had promis'd him He ask'd him if he would not let him have some silks (knowing Suqua had some in his House) and that he had no money but would give him his note to pay for them upon his coming back to Canton, or if he did not come himself he would {not} send it by the first Europe ship that should go from Europe to this Port, but that He had refus'd him by saying he had no silks, and then told us he no quiere[251] trust so fashion man for he no have Good &c I could not help telling him that

---

[250] I.e. Morford.
[251] *No quiere* 'does not wish to' (Portuguese *querer* 'to wish, want, desire').

Suqua was very much to blame to have offer'd to tempt any Body to cheat their owners especially that he had no reason to think that we were all such fools as to suffer Mr Morford to impose upon us or draw us in to receive bad Goods, which I suppose was the help that Suqua expected of him according to the Custom practis'd here by SuperCargos that were not too Honest &c whether my speaking so to him or rather Hunquas doing

180

Decr 25

it soon afterwards made him silent on this subject or not I can't tell, But He never mention'd it to us all together nor Tanqua neither, However Hunqua was as good as his word in perswading Tanqua to stand to the Aggreement we had made with him about the Souchen Tea & Perpetts at least in part, for on the 25th He aggreed to take 100 ps perpetts in lieu for Souchen & the rest in Cash, and we persuaded Hunqua to take the other 100 ps giving us Bing Tea & Heysan in return for them. N.B As to the forementiond business about Mr Morford which Mr Brown & I had sign'd on a seperate paper, I destroy'd the said paper, when [we] met with the Dutch afterwards at the Straits of Sunda. But I believe Mr Brown well remembers all these particulars & many others He & I were told afterwards by sundry merchants & some Europeans (to make us to take Care of Mr Morford) about his receiving sundry Presents from merchants, But as all those regarded the Ostenders Affairs I think needless to mention them.

This Evening Hunqua being with us we kept him to supper and after supper having indeavourd to bring him down of the price of his Bing Tea (which he had sayd he would not sell under 21 Tales) Mr Morford grew pretty ill humour'd & huff'd Hunqua pretty much, upon which Hunqua went Home, and we all going in to Mr Brown's Room, Mr Morford continued growling I could not tell for what, so that I could not help asking him what he meant He then open'd himself & told Mr Brown & me (for to us He address'd himself) that He never knew Affairs so manag'd by Super-Cargos in his Life, I took him up & told him that I believe he never knew Affairs more honestly managed in his Life, but I could tell him where he had been concern'd which were not manag'd at all after that manner, & that I knew very well that as he had been sometimes

181

concernd with Honest Super-Cargos so I knew he had also been with some Great Rogues, & I wish'd he had not learn'd some of their Roguish Tricks, Mr Brown could not keep his temper & told him roundly that he was a Knave or something to that purpose & he could prove it, I beggd Mr Brown not to fly out so much, because I had resolv'd not to let Morford know what we had discoverd before we had confronted him with Chinqua in all our presence, Mr Morford then changd his note & sayd that he did not mean as to honest acting but that I & Mr Brown always went out together & took no notice of him or Mr Pike and that Mr Pike had found fault with our so doing as well as He, I replyd that it was very hard that I must not go Abroad without giving an Account to them where I went or that whenever we went from Home we must all go in a Body together whether we had any Business to transact for the Company or not, especially that they both knew that there never was any thing bought or contracted for with any of the merchants by us, or without being all together and having all their opinions, that we had as much reason to find fault with him & Mr Pike going out together as they to find fault with us which I never did nor never would do leaving every Body to go & do what they pleasd, as every Body might have their own Business to look after, so to make him easy on that Head I told him that Mr Brown and I had concerns together in our own private Trade, and that oblig'd us often to go together to look after it, that indeed we often also went sometimes together & sometimes seperately to push the merchants to hasten the Companys Affairs, and I wish'd they had always done the same. I can't well now recollect all the Answers he made but I remember well the best of what I told him, I added that I had observ'd him very surly & growling a long while (as indeed he had been almost from the time Mr Ley arriv'd) but could not imagine the reason not

182   having to my knowlege given either [of] them any provocation to such publick & open discontent as they show'd every day & had always thought better to suffer it than to trouble my self with their unreasonable humours, that for Mr Morford in particular I supposd he expected because of his having been often here (which he had been pleasd to bring often in discourse over head & shoulders) that I must blindly follow his opinion in every thing & might therefore be angry that he could not get me into all his measures & opinions, but that I assurd him I knew very well how to manage the Companys business without ever having seen him or without any asistance from him, but that I supposd his Dear friend Mr Ley had help'd to spirit him up against me & because he had made so much use of him he thought himself a very considerable Person and that I could not do any thing without him, which I had no reason to think at all &c He then put me in mind of an Affair that had happen'd a great while ago of his indeavouring to put off buying China ware (vide [p. 129]^252) and that I had been in a violent passion with him upon that occasion without any reason, I could not help telling him he ly'd & that I was in no passion but that I was not at all satisfyd to see him delaying the Companys service for a very frivolous reason, having sayd no more to him than what is mentiond ([p. 130]^252) which I repeated to him. He pretended he never had payd more respect to any Body than he had to me &c I told him I did not know what he meant by respect, which I did not want of him, but that I knew what Civility & Good manners was and that I could give him many Instances of his being wanting in that to me, though I never regarded it nor took notice of it to him, though strangers that had been at Table with us had often observ'd it. It was the more surprizing that Mr Morford should set

183   himself up for so Great a Person with me, when I knew very well how small a

---

252 Campbell left a blank for the page number which he forgot to supply later.

European supercargoes shopping for chinaware in Canton. Two scenes from a series
of Chinese watercolours from c. 1730 illustrating porcelain manufacture.
These paintings, having probably been bought by Colin Campbell
on one of his voyages, were sold at an auction after his death
and were later acquired by Lund University Library.
(Belfrage 1992.)

figure he made with other SuperCargos he had been with & how much he had
been treated by them like a Boy and I believe never so much consulted with as he
had been with me, though they could not pretend to all that superiority that I had
at present in the Companys service. And I can't help thinking that the Ostenders
had a great hand in making him believe himself so very necessary a Person and
therefore so uppish as he had been of a long while.

One thing I had reason to wonder at [was] that Mr Morford should have grown
of late so great with Liungqua, because Liungqua had some time ago complain'd
of him to me as not being his friend and when we went to see some of his Tea at the
beginning that he thought he[253] did what he could to disswade us from looking
at it, which he pretended was owing to a dispute between them about some Gold

---

[253] I.e. Morford.

Chinese dish with décor in *famille rose* and Campbell's coat-of-arms
(motto: *Deus dabit vela*). Gothenburg City Museum.

that Cugin[254] (his Cusin) had sent by him to Europe to Mr Spendelow[255], which
Mr Spendelow told when he was here last he had never receiv'd, & that Cugin
had wrote to him from Amoy[256] to inquire after it, As I knew nothing of the
Affair & as it did not regard the Business of the Company I told Liungqua that
I would not speak to him about it nor meddle in such private disputes between
them, How they made it up afterwards I know not, for I never inquird after it.

Decr 27   Receivd a Letter from the Carpenter Brown[257] from on board, complaining of the
Captains ill treatment (which I had long observ'd & I believe for no other reason

[254] *Cudgin*, another name for *Quiqua* (see note 207 above; cf. also Gill 1961, p. 30), appears in 1721
and 1728 in the English East India Company Chronicles (Morse 1966–69, 1, pp. 167, 189, without
identifying him with Quiqua)).

[255] *Peter Spendelow*, an Englishman, served as chief supercargo on three expeditions with the Ostend
Company between 1724 and 1730, the last time on the *Apollo* (see note 340 below; Huisman 1902,
p. 378; Gill 1961, pp. 99–101, 109; Baels 1972, pp. 84, 147; Degryse 1974, pp. 307, 347).

[256] *Amoy* or *Xiamen*, port in the province of Fukien, northeast of Canton and Hong Kong, on the
Formosa Strait, where the English East India Company established a factory in 1676, the first time
the English had a footing on Chinese soil.

[257] A carpenter *William Brown* occurs in a list of English-born employees of the SEIC in 1740 (Kjellberg
1974, p. 128).

but because he knew his business far beyond any of those the Captain had hird, & that for that reason I & the officers trusted him & usd him well) and that he could not bear it longer, but beggd I would give him his discharge, As I knew the Captain was his Enemy & that we had no Body in the ship to trust to but himself to help us in case of a Leak or any Accident that might happen to the ship which requird a Carpenters help, And had always found him a very quiet modest

184   man, and always busy at his work as well as his son who was the only Good Caulker we had in the ship, I had incourag'd them all the voyage as much as I could, and resolv'd now to take this opportunity to show the Captain that he was in the wrong to use him so & that I would protect him when he was in the right, I wrote to the Captain a pretty serious Letter on that subject, as also to Capt Kitching to tell the Carpenter to be Easy and that I would take care of him, & would not suffer the Captain to use him ill &c for which refer to the said Letters & to the Carpenters to me.

Decr 31   Having given orders for the ship to fall down from Vampo (as she did to day) to the 2^d Bar[258] to be more in readiness to sail, I had aggreed with our Pilote & got a Chop (or License from the Hoppo) for him to go & carry the ship down, He went with orders to stay aboard, (as I also had order'd the Captain & officers to keep him aboard) till we came down & set sail but after he had got the ship down to the bar to day, They let him go away, Finding him at Canton I reprimanded him for quitting the ship, and as I knew the French ship was to make use of the same Pilote & talk'd every day of going as well as we, I was afraid this might hinder us especially that I knew most of the Europe gentlemen were very busy underhand to lay impediments in our way to prevent our sailing before them, and had got our Linguist of their side who did all he could to delay us, I found it necessary to keep the Pilote in the factory till we were ready to leave Canton & go to sea, with orders to the Guard not to let him out upon any Account, at the same time gave him every thing he requird as to his Diet &c as was necessary.

With a great deal of Difficulty we got clear with Pinky[259], and had not Mr Brown & I been concern'd with him in our own Trade

185   and taken of him any sort of silks he pleasd to give us & of Colours & assortments we did not at all like, we must have left him in our Debt without we would have stayd 14 days longer for the rest of the silks he contracted for with the Company,

---

[258] The word *bar* here in the special sense of 'a bank or ridge of sand, silt, etc. across the mouth of a river, which obstructs navigation'; cf. e.g. Morse 1966–69, 1, p. 263 (quotation from 1739): "… at Neep Tide I am apprehensive there will not be sufficient Water over the two Barrs, and as the Spring Tides are now coming on, I desire you'll please procure me a Chop or Sufferance from Wampoe down below the Second Barr."
[259] I.e. young Pinky, his father being still in prison.

which he sayd could not be ready sooner & that he must have more money to have them finish'd by that time, I therefore took all imaginable pains to get what we could out of his hands & when found the Company & our selves clear with him, I refus'd to wait for his silks or give him any more money, which put him in great wrath against us, & made him never more come near us not even to wish us a good voyage at our departure as is the Custom of all the merchants one deals with here. What money remain'd or Goods of the Companys we were oblig'd to lay out in Teas with Hunqua & Suqua's people, as is above related, they having no other Goods to give us at any reasonable price. This occasion'd another prejudice to Mr Brown & me & oblig'd us to buy of Hunqua what we never intended both Bing & Heysan Tea in order to make him take some of the Companys Perpetts that remain'd and were design'd for Pinky which he could not now take nor were we willing to trust him with.

We had no less plague with Suquas house about the price of the Companys Perpetts which we had told them as well as all the other merchants we would not sell them under 7 Tales a ps. Tanqua Suquas Partner held out to the very last night before we went away pretending to have them at 6.T.5.M a ps and had been often with Tinqua to spirit Him up to keep to the same price which they both did & refus'd their Ballance due them till they saw they could not help themselves & that they were oblig'd to pay the same as Hunqua did who made no scruple about it (though he complain'd they were too dear) & for which the other merchants did not the more esteem him.

There having come in a small vessell from Manilla about a month ago, I sold him some of our ships stores, as I did before to Capt Cowan & Capt Tullie, to both [of] whom I could have sold a great deal more, but the Captain would not part with them

186
always pretending that we could not spare more, though we found afterwards that we had several haulsers[260] &c on board more than we had occasion for, & which I could have sold very well, I had at leaving the ship on our Arrival at Canton left orders both with Capt Trolle & Capt Kitching to send me an exact List of all stores they thought we could spare, which they did soon after but far from being exact, for on my writing often to them to let me know if there were any more because they were demanded here they found still some more, and some of them own'd afterwards when it was too late to sell them (after our departure from Canton) that we had a great many stores on board we had better left behind than give them room in the ship.

---

[260] *Haulser*, obsolete for *hawser*, 'a large heavy rope'.

I had left at Cadiz some Iron we took from Countess Wonarofski[261], & which we thought we could have sold there, but not having time to dispose of it, I left it with Mʳ Maine who promis'd to sell it & give Account to the Company, as I inform'd them from thence, But the Captain having neglected to deliver it all to him, we found upon our Arrival at Canton some remaining which being of no service to the Chinese & all eat up with rust I was oblig'd to sell it to the Manilla ship for what I could get. For the particular Account of the ships stores sold at Canton vide ships Book.

Hearing from the Captain of the Manilla ship that they could buy every year a quantity of Iron when they came this way, which they often bought at Macao, I thought that perhaps it might be worth while to send Iron hither another time, provided I could have any security that any Good merchant at Macao would aggree a quantity & a fix'd price that we could get any thing by, I wrote to the Chief Portugueze merchant at Macao to ask him if he would make any Contract with the Company on this head, But he declin'd it, for which vide his Letter in Answer to mine. Had I brought all the Iron that was once design'd

187 to be carryd (but afterwards countermanded by some of our Friends Advice) I could have sold it all & more even to the value of 40 or 50 Tun which both the Captains of the Country ships wanted this year for Surat[262] & Bombay[263] &c and assurd me they could every year take off about that quantity and allow us a pretty good profit. However I must confess there is some hazard in this, for if these gentlemen know that we brought some on purpose to sell they would indeavour to beat down the price pretending they did not want it, And this year cannot be a Rule for other years because the dearness of Tutanegue & sugar[264] (occasiond by the English Company's two ships having bought & carryd a great deal to Madras[265] & Surat this year) made the Gentlemen of the Country ships at

---

[261] *Anna Woynarowska, née Mirowicz*, wife of Stanislaus Woynarowski, a Ukrainian colonel, nephew of the famous Cossack hetman Mazepa. After the Russian Tsar Peter the Great had defeated the Swedish king Charles XII in the battle of Poltava in 1709, Woynarowski had accompanied the king and Mazepa to Bender in Turkey. After Mazepa's death later that year he inherited his uncle's large fortune, a considerable part of which he soon turned into generous loans to Charles XII and his generals. Tsar Peter's hatred of Mazepa for his treacherous desertion to the Swedes was transferred to Woynarowski, who in 1716 was dramatically kidnapped in Hamburg by the Tsar's agents and brought to Russia, where after a long imprisonment he was exiled to Siberia. His wife spent many years in Sweden trying to effect the release of her husband and to recover his claims against the Swedish government, which with accrued interest gradually grew to huge amounts. A settlement was eventually reached, and the landed property awarded Anna Woynarowska included the Eskilstuna ironworks, from which Campbell's iron was probably acquired. – Colonel Woynarowski was never ennobled, so Campbell's use of the title of Countess is incorrect.
We are indebted to the late Dr. Adam Heymowski, Stockholm, for this identification.
[262] In the Gulf of Cambay, on the Tapti River in the north of India, by the Arabian Sea.
[263] South of Surat on the Western Ghats of India.
[264] Probably castor sugar. Very few quantities were imported by the Swedish Company.
[265] City on the Eastern Ghats of India, where an important British factory had been established.

a loss what to do with their money, & Gold being at 122 this year made them choose rather to carry a good deal of their silver back again than lay it out in Gold or Goods that were too dear or that the Markets they were going to must be over-stock'd with. However I can't help thinking that a small quantity of Iron would sell always here to the Countrys ships to some profit.

1733

January 1st The merchants were to wish us a good new year as they know the Custom is amongst us.

– 2   The Linguist having put off by his tricks (as I had reason to believe) our shipping off from day to day & neglecting to get our Grand Chop (or Leave to pass Boca Tigris &c) I sent for him to day & also for Tinqua & Hunqua, where I told him very freely what I thought of him I could not help blaming Tinqua also ({who} as he was the merchant that answerd for us and ought to help us on all occasions) for not making the Linguist do his Duty & give us more dispatch, In short after an Angry dispute I found there was nothing to be done with them till I lock'd the Linguist up in my Room & gave orders to our Guard not to let him out of the Factory that night which I told him he should not till I were assurd that he would bring the Hoppo men to ship our Goods next morning & that Tinqua would be security for him

188   which Tinqua aggreed & sent him immediately to get a Chop to ship next morning, which was accordingly done.

Janr 4   The Dutch & English hearing our Grand Chop to depart was to be out that day did all they could to prevent our having it till they had theirs and what had hinderd us from getting ours for two or 3 days was a dispute about the measurage of the ship whi[ch] the New Hoppo & Quanchefou would not aggree to as being too little though settled by the Achantsi when he was Hoppo, Hearing of this I told Tinqua that I having already payd the measurage a great while ago I would not pay them one cash more, & that He must look to it, He knowing it must fall upon him if any thing more was to be payd (we now being clear with him) us'd all his Interest with the Pay de Casas and carryd all the merchants with him to the Mandarins to save himself from this scrape, which before night was accomodated by some presents he pretended to have made, & our Chop was taken out, but the Linguist did not bring it to us thinking still to delay us, & I knowing the English & Dutch had also the same day got their Grand Chop out though not ready to sail, I went & bullyd both Tinqua & the Linguist & threatend if I had it not by next morning I would go without it, having got the Pinnace up on purpose to carry us down to the ship in case they refusd it any longer, They seeing our Resolution took care to bring it next morning.

– 5   The Grand Chop being brought us we went away from Canton on board in a

Mandarin Boat which Hunqua had prepard for us, Tinqua went also a little way with us & the Linguists Asistant to the first Custom house, Tinqua was in a very bad humour & I must say did not use us with that Civility that we might have expected at parting, He was angry that I would not bate an Ace of the price of the Perpetts nor give him more than 50 Tales for the present he had given (as he pretended much more than that) to the last Hoppos Secretary for easing us in the measurage of the ship. He had also the impudence

189   to pretend to have 14 Tales a pecul for his Bohea Tea (at settling Accounts with him) though we had aggreed with him for 13 Tales as we had done with all the other merchants, He pretended that as he answerd for us (as they call it here) & that we had done so little business with him, he had been at more expence on our Account than any of the other merchants had, & therefore took it very Ill that I would not make him some Allowance. Though I pityd him on account of his present Circumstances there being sundry demands on him which I believe he was not able to answer this year, and which I knew put him upon this attempt of getting more money for us, yet I gave a deaf Ear to all his Arguments, so that we parted very cool & dry with one another. And I must say there was not one of the merchants that we dealt with show'd us the common Civilities at parting but Hunqua alone who had servd us to the last very faithfully & to good purpose, & the only one that went on board with us. The Linguist walk'd about in the Factory while we were going off but would not go down with us according to Custom, nor indeed come near us to take leave, being afraid of a Beating which I had promis'd him for all his Rogueries, instead of a present as is usual when they serve People well & which he had often demanded of me, which his base usage made us save at this time.

Going down the River some of our young Gentlemen were in another Boat & were likd to have been attack'd by a Ladroen Boat (or a Pirate) who pursud them till we being within hearing fird some pistols we had though only loaded with pouder which quickly frightend the Rogues away.

190   Not being able to recollect the true dates when sundry things happen'd, I am oblig'd to add them here pele mele[266] as they recur to my memory.[267]

After the best part of the Company's Goods were shippd, I found several private Goods coming in every day we shipp'd that belong'd to the officers & others that took up a great deal of them such as China ware & Teas[268], at the same time they

266 French *pêle-mêle*, English *pell-mell*.
267 This sentence illustrates Campbell's uncertainty in recollecting the exact sequence of events during the voyage.
268 Campbell worried about the quantity of private goods, especially those bought by the officers for their own account, according to the right of free transport of the *pacotille*. He also feared that some

were complaining of want of room for the Goods we had already contracted for on the Company's Account, I thought it time to let them know that there must be room kept for the last, and that therefore they would lay out their money in silks & such things as requir'd less room rather than in Tea & China ware which I found them running upon, though with Art & Cunning enough, to wit one day one parcel & another day another in order to hide it the better, I therefore in order to find out what belongd to them (knowing that some of them had already exceeded the privilege allow'd them by the Company) took the following precautions, viz by giving positive orders to the Linguist not to let any Goods be mention'd in the Chop given by the Hoppo for every different shipping (as is usual here) but such as I gave him my self a list of, This was to prevent a trick daily practis'd by many of them both Super-Cargos & officers, of speaking to the Linguist without my knowlege & getting him to mention in the Chop what Goods they pleas'd, so that next day when I would dispute some of the Goods as they were shipping as not knowing who they belong'd to I could not help my self for the Hoppo men & Linguist insisted they must be sent away that day aboard as being mentiond in the Hoppo's Chop. I next order'd

191 the Captain of the Guard (as he is call'd here) or watch to bring me every day an Account of what Goods came in to the factory whether Companys or private & the names of the Persons they belong'd to. I orderd also every SuperCargo officers & others to give me in a List of what they had to ship the day before the shipping & before I gave my List to the Linguist to get a Chop. But all these precautions not being effectual enough to prevent what I intended to hinder, I resolv'd to attend closely at the shipping of every piece of Goods myself & view and compare them with the List given before I let them pass through the Hoppo's Mens hands, and when obligd to retire into my room from the place of shipping in the Factory (as I was often obligd to do upon business with the merchants) I left Mr Brown in my stead & desird him privately to call me out when he observ'd any Goods going on board that I knew nothing of, my reason for this was that they had frequently upon my withdrawing if but for half an hour sent for Goods in to the factory & prevaild with the Linguist & Hoppo men to ship them before I could come back to attend, though they had not been mentiond in the List the day before. By these methods I put them more upon their Guard & prevented such practices (though I believe too late) for the time to come.

---

confusion would arise between official and private goods, upsetting what had been settled between the Chinese and the supercargoes concerning the official Company cargo. Private goods could exceed the space allotted for them on board, while the Chinese might consider them as included in the settled deliveries. Undoubtedly this led to all sorts of underhand actions on the part of the crew, especially those who had an individual cabin on board. Campbell records one such trick practised by the mate Lund (*Diary* p. 192). Nevertheless there seems to have been plenty of space in the holds of the *Fredericus R.S.*, after the Company cargo and even the private goods had been stowed, since there was some discussion of taking goods to Europe on the account of foreigners to the Company as well (*Diary* pp. 193–195).

I had also been inform'd privately that there were some were indeavouring to ship Goods at other factorys & by their corrospondence with some of the officers on board our ship to get them taken in without my knowlege, Though I was not fully assurd of this, yet as I knew it was a practise not unknown to some, and a very bad one, I resolv'd to run no risk of such schemes, I therefore wrote aboard to the Captain & officers (which I had left in my Instructions to them first on our Arrival at Canton) & repeated those orders I had given before, to wit not to receive aboard any piece of Goods that was sent on board whether from our own factory or any other

192   place, without a note or express order with it sign'd by me as was done with all the Companys Goods, threatning that If I should afterwards learn that any such had been receiv'd I would either have them turn'd out of the ship again, or if they could not be easily come at I would have them confiscated to the Company's use.

There was one trick more playd me by Mr Baron (which he had learn'd in the service he had been in before) He had without my knowlege bought the privilege of Styrman Lund & the Priests Cabbins which he fill'd with his Goods & had them shipp'd in their name as their Goods, which gave me afterwards trouble with Lund about finding room for his own Goods, As this was a practice might be of ill Consequence by giving an opportunity to such as sold their Cabbins of obtaining leave from the Captain or other officers that bought them to put afterwards their own Goods in some other place, as I am apt to believe they did, I was not a little displeasd at Mr Baron who having a very good Privilege as well as Cabbin of his own ought to have been very well content with it & not have indeavourd to lumber the ship, when every day He & the rest of them were complaining there was no room for the Company's Goods. I therefore reprimanded him for doing so without my knowlege & told him I would not suffer such doings any more. In fine they had made such a bustle about want of room (for which there was reason too) that I chose rather to lose 160 Tales than take Tea for a Debt due me, for fear of want of a proper place for the Companys Goods.

Soon after our Arrival at Canton, As our stock was not very great and after the Calculation made and aggreed to how to lay it out, I had by Mr Brown's asistance who knew

193   those matters considerd how much the ship could hold we concluded that there would be more room than we had Goods to put in for the Company & private Trade, we thought proper to accept of a proposal made us by some Europeans to take some Chests of silks aboard on their Account they paying freight to the Company & so much to us for our Trouble This proposal being made to me I would not give an Answer till I had consulted Mr Brown, As for the rest I durst not let them know of it for fear of a discovery which would have ruin'd those Gentlemen and they earnestly begg'd in case I thought fit to accept of their

proposal to let no Body know of it (& afterwards even wanted a note under my hand to bear them harmless which I would not consent to) However not being willing to meddle in such a thing my self without the advice of at least one of the Super-Cargos I told those Gentlemen that I would do nothing in it without they gave me leave to speak to Mr Brown who as he was a person known for an honest man it would be better for them in case of my Death to have a double security, This they were sensible of & aggreed to, so we accepted of the proffer made as being so much money got to the Company, without any manner of risk or damage, and on our Return to Gottenburg there are so many pieces of silk of every 100 ps to be given the Company & Mr Brown & me & the rest to be shippd for what place those Gentlemen please to order.

Mr Ley Chief of the Ostend SuperCargos often press'd me to contrive so matters as to leave Canton in Company with their ship & go to Europe all the way together which he pretended would be more security to us in case of any bad designs in our passage against us by the Dutch, & when we were ready to depart pressd me to stay for him, & finding I did not incline to it set his friend Mr Morford upon me

195[269] to use the same Arguments that he had done before, But I absolutely refus'd it, not only for the delay that would occasion us, but much more to prevent the Dutch (in case they should meet with us) to have so fair a handle to insult us which I was sure they wanted, But these Reasons were not strong enough to convince these Gentlemen, & even afterwards when we met the Dutch Mr Morford was pleasd (& others) to bring it up that it was a great misfortune we had not waited for the Ostenders & other ships to come in Company with us. But I very little regarded his sentiments on that subject, being assurd (& more by what I learnd afterwards at Batavia) that had we been met in Company with the Ostend ship we had been infallibly ruin'd. Indeed I would have been very glad to have come in Company with the French ship whose Captain was our good friend, & I believe as far as he durst or lay in his power would have protected & asisted us against all Enemies & at least if that was more than he could do, he would have been witness of any violence offer'd us and thereby in case their designs should have been very bad, He would have been able to have discover'd it to our friends in Europe who might have procur'd afterwards some Redress, This I told our Super-Cargos & accordingly aggreed with Capt de Morllet to get ready if possible to sail with him & keep him Company at least past the Straits of Sunda, and he promisd as he made no question to sail before us that he would wait 4 or 5 days for us without Boca Tigris, upon this Account I aggreed to take a Chest & Box of silks upon freight for him to Gottenburg, which I orderd to find room for in my own Cabbin. Having done this for Capt Morllet which he it seems had told Mr Ley, Truly this Gentleman thought too

---

[269] Error for *194*.

195 I must take Goods for him, though he had a ship almost twice as large as ours & heard us every day complaining that our ship was too small for our stock & that we were afraid there would not be room for the Companys Goods by reason of being obligd to lose a great deal of room for want of Kentlage or proper Ballast, But I had great reason to suspect that Mr Morford had contrivd this plot for me (with views I could guess at) with Mr Ley, In fine he payd me a visit one Evening (of which I had not the honour but once more all the while I was at Canton) and told me he had a favour to ask which was to take some China ware on his Account to Gottenburg & he would pay me what freight I pleasd for it, Though I did not presently smell his design I told him that we were in want of room for the Companys Goods as well as for my own & that as he had room enough in his ship & had other opportunities to fill it than I had, I hop'd he would excuse me from taking such bulky Goods as that into the ship, & that if he should pay the Company freight for it (for I told him I would have nothing for my own part) it would be such a Triffle, that it was not worth their while, but if it had been a Chest of silks or so that could afford good freight I should not have been so averse to it, He reply'd that the Chest or Chests of China ware should be as small as I pleasd and that he had bought it & did not know where to put it having the ship already full and that he had got a good many of the Sailors Chests but was not able to get any more, In short he pressd me so much that I told him I was going down in a day or two to the ship in order to see what room there was left and that if I found there was room & that his Chest was not too big I would indeavour to oblige him, He left me soon after, But reflecting on this strange proposal that he must know it was more worth my while to buy China ware my self and put it in the ship than to give room for his, I begun to suspect it was some pitiful Irish plot between him & Morford,

196 I resolv'd to refuse it & so discourage him & all others from any more attempts of this sort upon me any more, I therefore went directly to him & told him how difficult it would be to me to find room for his China ware when I could not for my self nor the other SuperCargos allow such bulky Goods to be shippd at that time & beggd he would excuse me; He was not very well satisfyd but left it to me to do as I pleas'd, so we parted & never talk'd together more upon that subject. But the Frenchmans imprudence in discovering this to Mr Ley (though I forbid him & told him it was to oblige him I had taken any thing on board for his Account which I would not grant to any other & told him I had refus'd of the English) brought others upon me to wit some french of the Manilla ship who wanted the same favour, which I flatly denyd him, & afterwards told Capt Morllet what trouble he had brought me to & that had I known what had happend I should not have taken any of his Goods nor any other persons whatsoevcr, He excusd it as well as he could & blam'd Mr Ley who he sayd was a prying man & had slily look'd over a paper he had drawn up about his silks as it lay upon his table in his room &c

Had the ship been almost twice as big as it was I found that by my own Credit amongst the Europeans & China merchants I could have rais'd as much money amongst the former as I pleasd (for Gold being dear they did not know how to lay out their money) to load Goods on my own Account, & Goods I could have enough at least of Teas from the China men to have loaded the ship without one farthing money only giving them a note promising to repay them with such a profit by the first Europe ship that might go to Canton. When I thought the ship would load much more than afterwards we found it did, I had with Mr Brown layd a scheme to have fill'd her up with a Cargo for the Company, & had spoke to some of the best merchants who

197 heartily aggreed to it & desir'd no better, Mr Morford told me also that Mandarin Quiqua would willingly joyn in the same, to whom I also spoke (though I knew him to be a troublesome sneaking fellow to deal with in such matters) and he aggreed to it. But afterwards finding we had little enough room for the Companys Goods & our own privileges (which I did not like to exceed) I was oblig'd both to disappoint the China merchants & the Europeans who had offerd me more money than I knew what to do with.

A propos as to Mandarin Quiqua (an Intimate friend of Mr Ley & Mr Morford for reasons I well knew) He finding that I was under hand applying to the Mandarins for to take off the 10 p^r C^t, was very earnest to clear with us for fear that should be stopt from him, And I having been long in hopes to be able to get some relief in that affair as was promis'd us was unwilling to pay the merchants all their money till I saw what would be done for us, knowing that if they were once payd I never could have got a Cash back supposing that the Hoppo had favour'd us in this Affair, I got the other merchants easily put off but this fellow plagued me every day (which I had reason to believe he was stirrd up to by others often mentiond, by several discourses dropt from them on this subject in my Company) sending his servant to receive the Ballance due him, Being teazd sometimes not only at Home but in the very streets by some of his servants he sent after me I was oblig'd to bid them tell their master that since I found he was so troublesome I would take care that all the other merchants we had dealings with should be payd before him, & that I would send to him when that was done & that I thought proper to clear with him, This message put an end to his Impertinence.

But to relate now the Event of all our Indeavours to obtain Redress of Grievances & of getting Access to the Xunhu to complain of them, Mr Brown & I never left off trying what could be done, And when I found the Collonell & other friends we trusted

198 to had amused & cheated us, I tryd to get in to the City (in order to go to the Xunhu) by sending to offer the Guard at the Gate money only to let us pass in, which they would willingly have done but were afraid of the Hoppo who they

knew would not like it & on whom they immediately depended as being Commander of all the Guards of the Gates & who must have heard of it if such a thing had happend without his knowlege and they might have suffer'd for it. So that after all the daily pains taken by us, we found it at last impossible to have any redress or even access to the Xunhu to complain, And I am assurd that the Europeans did not contribute a little to lay impediments in the way by setting all their merchants upon the look out against us, as some inform'd me that their Super-Cargos were very much afraid of our getting to the Mandarins and of meeting with a Redress which they were resolv'd not to ask for. And I must say none was more to be blamd than Monsr de Velaer Head of the French factory, who as he perfectly understood to speak the Chinese tongue himself and by his having long liv'd here was best acquainted with their manners & ways could have obtaind leave to wait upon the Mandarins to whom he could have complaind without any Interpreter. As I knew none of the Europeans was capable to serve us in this Affair (if they had been willing) but himself & that at the beginning He show'd a very hearty desire to do it, I did all I could to be in a good understanding with him & to push him to joyn with me in a thing that would tend so much to the Interest of the Company his masters and to his own Honour as being the first & principal man of bringing about so Good an Affair &c But honour or reputation signifys nothing with such sort of people when it clashes with their Interest. In fine his own knavery & the other Europeans Advices made him change his first resolution which he had promisd me faithfully to concur in without letting English or Dutch know of it who he was sure would oppose it, & amusd me some time by

199   pretending he was oblig'd to send the memorial, (which he had got ready drawn up in Chinese, to present to the Xunhu) to the Padres at Macao to correct & put in the best stile as they knew best what was the fittest for so great a Mandarin, But finding this memorial very long of coming back from Macao (whither I believe it never was sent) and hearing of some Roguish practices of his with the merchants to the prejudice of his own Company, I conceiv'd a very bad opinion of him & resolving to trust him no more took other methods to execute my design, which however all, to my great mortification, fail'd me.

The Captain who is naturally subject to commit great Acts of folly & Impertinence, had been guilty of many since coming to Canton where he never was a whole day sober, so that I had a great deal ado to keep in any temper with him, though I studyd it as much as possible by bearing with his Rudeness, & even lending him money to buy Goods. One thing not mentiond in the former part of this Journal, which might have brought us into Trouble, was that in contradiction to the orders I had left with him in writing at parting from the ship at Vampo, he had fir'd Guns the very same day the Dutch had committed the same folly which brought the indignation of the Mandarins against them, some of the Dutch went aboard to see the ship & the Captain could not refrain from pursuing his favourite Inclination of firing to salute them; This was well known to the merchants & Tinqua told me of it, but I perswaded him to deny it to every body which he did, so that the Captains noise was drown'd by that of the Dutch, which was made greater. Another thing which might have been of worse consequence, had not I prevented the effects of it, was his running Goods of his own aboard in the Pinnace without letting me know of it & having it regularly shippd by the Hoppo, and all this to save a few stivers[270] Duty upon a parcel of Bulky Lacquer'd ware[271].

200   I had done all I could to prevent this even by telling him & others not to do it at any rate and that if they did and I should hear of it I would not forgive it nor would I use the least Interest to save their Goods or their Persons in case they should be seiz'd, But He being a Gentleman above all orders or advice would do what he pleasd, & I believe was taught this fine practice by the Dutch & Ostenders who were often Guilty of it & lost their Goods by it &c But that is not the only bad thing follows from this practice, If the Loss of their Goods were all I should not trouble my head about it, But it may prove a Loss to the Company For the Chinese when they cannot get the Goods or the Persons that run them they come upon the Company or owners of the ship & oblige us to pay a fine as they please for every thing done against their Laws & Customs, if it is but a sailor dos it, The SuperCargos or ship must pay for it. It has another bad effect, It gives the Mandarins a very great aversion to us and makes them less ready to help us on any occasion for defrauding the Emperour of his Duties, &c And indeed this year they had great reason to complain of the Dutch & some others as they did daily. I was so Cautious in my own particular (for fear of bringing the Company in to Trouble) that I would not allow some Amber Beads I had to be run ashore, though it was easy to be done in peoples Pockets, and that the Duty upon it is high. However with some trouble I got clear of this folly of the Captains, Tinqua first told me of it & that the Hoppo was extremely angry & that he did not know what to say in our behalf, soon after the Hoppo sent to me to let me know what had happen'd, & that he would not suffer such things to be acted &c. I got Tinqua to make them easy by assuring them that I had given the strictest orders I could to the Captain & all the officers against such Actions, as being very injust, & to show

201   that I had no design to incourage such deeds my self they had seen that I had

---

[270] *Stiver* (from Dutch *stuiver*; cf. Swedish *styver*), a small coin of the Low Countries, about an English penny.

[271] Varnished objects were imported to some extent by all East Indiamen. Often they were *objets d'art* of high aesthetic quality, not seldom termed 'chinoiseries'. Quite early on, the Chinese had discovered the qualities inherent in the 'lacquer tree', which flourished in the southern and central provinces of China. The semi-transparent lacquer was used as a coating on copper, brass, porcelain, tin etc., but principally on wood. Lacquered articles presented a smooth and glossy upper surface that lent itself easily to painting and engraving. The raw varnish turned black in contact with the air. Although the colour range was widened by manufacture, 'black lacquer', and consequently wooden articles varnished in this colour, are the best known. Cinnobar was one of the dyes used for colouring.

brought ashore my Amber publickly & payd the Emperours Duties for it though they knew I could have easily run it without its ever coming to their knowlege, and as for [what] the Captain had done it must have been through his Ignorance of the Laws & Customs of this Country, He having never been here before, & the things that were run were of so little value that he never would have ventur'd had he known it to be forbidden &c. In fine I promis'd to take care that no such thing should be done for the time to come having given orders to all the officers to receive nothing on board but was shipp'd by the Hoppo & order'd by me, and at last Tinqua & I appeas'd them, & I heard no more of it.

As to Mr Morford, A little before we left Canton, He came to me & told me that old Quiqua had told him that I had sayd that He was not too Good or too Honest to some of the China merchants, & that he could not help telling me what had been told him, As I was not willing to enter into a dispute with him on this subject nor thought it necessary to let him know my true thoughts of him, I only replyd to him that old Quiqua was an old Lying Rascal & that whatever I thought of himself I never would discover it or tell my thoughts of him to any China merchant. He finding me very indifferent as to giving him any further satisfaction, which he was perhaps also afraid to force me to, made no reply but retir'd very grave. After the dispute on Christmas night, I judg'd it would be necessary before leaving Canton to take all the Super-Cargos to Chinqua & to make Chinqua tell to his face what he had before told Mr Brown & me, I therefore spoke to Mr Brown that as he had chargd Morford with Knavery & sayd that he could prove it, He would be the proper to ask Chinqua before us all to declare the truth on that Head, so Going to Chinqua to take our leave which we observd Morford was not much inclind to do I was resolv'd to take that opportunity to come at the bottom of the whole Affair that he might have an occasion to let us know what

202 he had to allege in his own defence & also no room afterwards to deny it, But when we got there Mr Brown took me aside & desir'd I would not mention it because it might be of Ill consequence in case the Dutch should meet with us on our Return, this discovery might make Mr Morford desperate & being convinc'd that I from that time could have no esteem for him he might do us prejudice with the Dutch & give them some wrong Informations to hurt us & the Company, As his Reason for being silent on this head had its weight in such critical Circumstances as we were I left it to him to do as he thought best, while we were with Chinqua we observ'd Mr Morford very uneasy & desirous to quit him, I not being sure whether Mr Brown would start the subject or not stayd a little while to see, but finding he had resolv'd not to do it, we took our leaves of Chinqua without mentioning one word to him about it, and I confess I was very glad afterwards when we fell into the hands of the Dutch that we had so acted for he had it in his power when examin'd by the Governour at Batavia to have done us a good deal of prejudice, so that after that Mr Brown & I resolv'd never to let him have any room to suspect that we thought any thing more of it for fear of provoking him

without doing our selves any Good, so I resolv'd to carry Civil & free with him all the voyage, to prevent him having any suspicion of my design of keeping it in mind to inform the Company, so we all seemd to be in very good friendship together till we were stoppd by the Dutch, The day we were first in their hands though aboard our own ship, Mr Morford's Conscience accusing him no doubt, he still suspected Mr Brown had discoverd something about his Conduct and that he kept it in mind, which he discoverd at that time when he was drunk & while I was sitting writing in the state Room Mr Morford came to him in the Cabbin crying & after several things sayd about the Apprehension he was under of being brought ashore to Batavia to be examin'd & that he would be true to the

203   Company &c He then mentiond that dispute on Christmas night & beggd Mr Brown to be friends with him & to forget all that had pass'd between them that night, which he promis'd to do with an imprecation on either of them that would ever think or talk more of it, & so they shak'd hands on Mr Brown's assuring him that he had no prejudice to him & would be Good friends with him &c I expected he would have made the same address to me but he thought fit to decline it which I was very glad of being firmly resolvd (if he had spoke to me) not to make him any promises that I did not intend to keep.

Notwithstanding Styrman Lund had faithfully promisd after he was set at Liberty after his making against Capt Kitching & Mr Baron, & also repeated the same to me when I lent him some money upon his often begging, yet both at Vampo & at Canton he gave many proofs of his heart being the same & that he had mischievous designs in his head, for when drunk he would talk at a strange rate wishing the Dutch might meet with us & attack us &c & as the Captain told me he also us'd to plague him with talking of his Character and his being a Kings Lieotennant & ours being a Kings ship, and that if it should so happen that He the Captain should die He would then take the Command of the ship & let the English on board then know what he was, & a great deal more impertinence of this sort which I have now forgot. But what made me most uneasy about him was, when ever he came to Town he went always to the Dutch factory and there stayd very late from whence he came always Home to the Factory Drunk, I had learnd that he had got into Acquaintance with the first SuperCargo Schultz & others of them, and therefore spoke to him and though I knew he could nothing true that could hurt the Company yet I could not tell what lies he might put in their heads, I advis'd him to be very cautious of intertaining much familiarity or Conversation with the Dutch, He confessd that he went there sometimes and that he had found one of his Countrymen there an officer in one of the Dutch ships who had made him acquainted with Schultz

[204]   & that Schultz had been so kind as to lend him some money at a very easy rate & below the common there at that time & had order'd him to pay it to Mr Francis

Bedoire[272] at Stockholm to whom he showd me Schultz Letter, All this did not give me much pleasure not knowing for what reason Schultz should lend a man of another ship money whom he had never seen before & must know to be poor, and to take less than the Common Interest for it, Notwithstanding of this I did not yet suspect Lund had carryd his malice so far as we found afterwards he had done & will appear in the sequel of this Journal.

Some nights before I came away Schultz came to pay me a visit which surpriz'd me (not having ever had a visit from him but on our first coming when the Dutch came all together to welcome us to Canton) After some little discourse He told me that he had a favour to ask which was to carry a Letter for him to Mr Francis Bedoire, which I took & promisd to take care of, He did not think fit to tell me what it was about, nor I took no notice that I knew any thing of what had passd between him & Lund, but gave him a Letter too which I had brought from Sweden for a Swede that liv'd at the Cape of Good Hope which he promisd to deliver on his Return. As to his Letter to Bedoire, when we were stopt by the Dutch as I apprehended their seizing our papers I took more care of his interest than he deservd by destroying his Letter, fearing it might ruin him with the Company had they come to the knowlege of lending money on a forreign Bottom India, which is by them strictly forbid, & I also advis'd Lund to destroy his, or to hide it in some sure place, but he kept it & I suppose has it yet. Amongst other discourse with Mr Schultz, I ask'd him about an Affair that had happend a little before which was this. Some of the Dutch SuperCargos getting it into their heads that we had

205   no right to trade to India went to the English Factory in a very formal manner to know if the English had not receivd orders from their Company to examine our Passes &c & if they would joyn with them in doing so, The English having reply'd to them that they had receiv'd no manner of orders from the Company about us & had nothing to say to us, These wise Gentlemen thought fit to talk no more of the Affair. I being informd by a friend I had in the English Factory of this solemn Embassy from the Dutch, the very day it happend made me curious to know of Schultz the meaning of it, telling him that we had as good right to trade to the East Indies & China as any Body or any European, and that we had all the Passes & Commissions necessary from the King & nation of Sweden for that purpose, which I was not at all unwilling to show to any Person who would come as a friend to desire it, but not as being oblig'd to show it to People that pretended had a Right to inquire about them, which I knew they had no more right to do

---

[272] *François Bedoire* (1690–1742), merchant in Stockholm, son of a French immigrant engaged in the import of French wines, a business which François took over and combined with salt-trading and shipowning. Together with Henrik König and Colin Campbell, François Bedoire was one of the first directors of the Board of Trade of the Swedish Company in 1731; but he left the Board as early as 1732, being replaced by Volrath Tham. (Cf. Introduction p. xx.)

than we had to ask about theirs or to see their passes, & added that it was more extraordinary this proceeding since our Right had been declard to all Europe & that the States General[273] themselves had ownd our Right to trade here to the Swedish Envoy at the Hague long before we left Sweden. He replyd that it was very foolish of the other SuperCargos & that he had disswaded them from it & would not go to the English along with them, telling them that in a free Port as this no nation could pretend to dispute anothers right of coming there, but added It was very true they had instructions from the Company that if they met with any ships at sea under other Colours or from other parts of Europe than had been usd to trade in the East Indies they should speak with them & demand a sight of their passes, & that this was the reason of their going to the English, that he knew very well our Affair before he came out &c He complain'd much of the other SuperCargos as being Boys & fools, & that they were

206   so jealous of him that he was obligd to refrain from going to other Europe Factories they having their spies upon him which was the reason he had not come to see me befor & chose now to come in the Dark, for He sayd they had given out publickly that He had concerted with the English & French and me measures to cheat our masters at Home &c As for me they had little reason since we never had been together alone, but as for the English & French, I believe they had some Cause of suspicion, for I had met him more than once at night in private with Monsr de Velaer when I happen'd to go to him about the memorial above mentiond he had promisd to get drawn up for the Xunhu. In fine we parted. Notwithstanding of all this fair Carriage of Schultz yet I found out afterwards at Batavia that He was the very Rogue that brought that misfortune upon us by a parcel of Lies he had sent to Batavia by an Express which had arrivd not many weeks there before we pass'd.

As to the Dutch SuperCargos there never were such a set of Knaves & fools met together in one Factory as they, Every day quarrelling & running from factory to factory complaining of one another, but especially to the French, and one of them Smith came often to Mr Morford upon the same Errand. Another of them upon his being beaten by Schultz was resolvd not to go Home in the Dutch ships, but to ask me leave to go to Europe with us, Full of this design he run in by mistake to the Ostend Factory instead of ours, where finding he had gone wrong he thought better of it & never came near us. It is a pity but he had gone with us, for He was one of those that had applyd to the English against us, & had he been aboard of us at Batavia, they had hang'd him there, for among other things they were very inquisitive if we had any Hollanders

207   on board our ship, and in my hearing talkd so the first night I was ashore at

---

[273] General assembly of the Dutch Republic. In this passage Campbell affirms that the Hague Government had recognized the right of the Swedes to trade in the Far East.

Batavia, and seemd very much disposd to make Mr Pike pass for a Hollander, as having been brought up at Amsterdam & of Holland Parents as they pretended, which was false as I told them there, his Father being English &c

I have mentiond above the tricks often playd about shipping of Goods privately at Canton without the Chief Super-Cargo's knowlege, which makes me think of a method very proper to prevent it & to inable them to know exactly whether they exceed the privilege allowd them by the Company or not, which is to let no private Goods be shippd whether Super-Cargos or any others till all the Companys Goods are first shipp'd, and then all the private Trade to be view'd and shippd at one or two times, viz when all the Companys China ware are in the ship then to let that belonging to the Super-Cargos & officers go on board, & so of the Teas & silks &c for by the way commonly usd it is scarce possible to know when they exceed their privilege or when not till the Goods come Home & are taken out & put in the Companys warehouses, for by sending 2 or 3 Chests one time & 2 or 3 another time it is very hard to remember or to hinder their design of filling the ship as full as they can.

I was told another thing at Canton which I had never thought of & had it been told me sooner might have sav'd the Company & me a great deal of money, especially having so Good a friend as Capt Tully there who assurd me he would have done it for me, which was this, As the Country ships do not pay the 10 p^r Cent on Goods exported as the Europe ships do, To save this heavy Duty I had no more to do but to buy of a proper merchant whom I could trust on condition to pay the Duty ourselves, & then have them shipp'd off on board one of the Country ships from their Factory.

We had some trouble to keep the sailors also from running small

things when they went down in the Pinnace, The Hoppo officers having been this year extremely strict & troublesome us'd to search their Pockets & seize things they had about them, which I had enough ado to get again, To prevent this practice I orderd them to take nothing with them but to leave all the small things they had bought with some Body in the factory in order to have them packd up together in a Chest or two, and I would take care to have them sent on board for them with the Companys Goods, This prevented their running any more but brought the Company to an expence not known here before to wit to pay Duties for all the small things shippd for them, which was owing to our villain of a Linguist who made the Hoppo men insist upon it and charg'd it me in Account, which I shall find difficult to settle or make out whom the different parcels belong'd to, The Linguist had the impudence to charge me with Duties on the shoes & stockings I had bought for the sailors, as well as other unusual impositions, which all he could say & huff did not however perswade me to pay him.

[Pages 209–220 blank except for pagination.]

Some Memoirs relating to Batavia

The Gentlemen Deputies inform'd us of the following particulars

That they had fire Arms &c there for 50000 men.

Of European soldiers they have above 2000 men of which 1200 always in the Castle where is one Company of about 100 men all Prussians deserted from the Prussian Army. The Major who commands the Troops is much esteemd.

Of Malayans under the Generals Command they have 20000 men, They were formerly commanded by one of their own number, but he being lately suspected of having some underhand treacherous designs, he was turn'd out & banish'd to Ceylon in slavery. And now the Major of the Castle commands them.

They reckon in Batavia & the Country about above 100000 souls some very rich, & to whom the Dutch are oblig'd almost for every thing they have, They first made the sugar, the Coffy, the Arrack & now are trying silk, In short it is their Industry makes Batavia so flourishing as it is.

The Company has no settlement on the East side of Java further than Samaran[274], nor none on the Island of Bally The Emperour of Java resides at Mataran[275] where the Company has a Commander & Garrison to watch his motions. He is in Alliance with the Comp[y], which always take care that he is succeded by one that they approve of. At Bantam the Comp[y] has a Castle & Garrison, The King is prisoner in his own palace, attended by Dutch Guards always when he goes abroad which is but seldom, He is so afraid of both the Dutch & his former subjects (who hate him) that he has no body with[276] women of whom he makes secretarys of state & other ministers, one of whom he sent once Ambassadress to Batavia, but she was not receiv'd, He lives at the top of his House, where there is no getting at him but by hoisting up in a Basket, The Company has crown'd his son as successor to him, He resides also at Bantam but in another Palace than that of his Fathers, They are both esteemd very bad men, & they tell sundry ridiculous stories of them, chiefly of the Father. They assur'd me the Regency has at present in Cash at the Castle 14 millions of Gilders, of which they send yearly 4 millions to the Coast of Cormandel & Malabar to buy Goods for Europe. The Company sends yearly from Holland to Batavia 4 millions of Gilders a great part in

---

[274] *Semarang*, a port on the north coast of Java.

[275] *Mataram*, Muslim state in south central Java from the late 16th century to the 18th century, which at one time gained suzerainty over most of central and east Java (Klerck 1938, 1, pp. 178, 216). Also the name of its capital, present-day Jogjakarta.

[276] Either *with* is a slip of the pen for *but*, or Campbell intended to write *no body with him but women*.

double'kees[277] & Doigts[278], on the first they gain 25 p^{r}Ct on the latter 100 p^{r}Ct & there comes yearly out of doigts 10000 Gilders

---

[277] Adaptation or corruption of Dutch *dubbeltje*, a coin formerly worth 10 cents, or about 2*d*. English.
[278] *Doit*, a former small Dutch copper coin, worth 1/8 of a stiver, or half an English farthing.

Journal Continued being
The Voyage from Canton to Gottenburg

———————

1733

Jan^r 6th   cir 7 P.M. ships stile, we heav'd Anchor & set sail after having sent Hunqua & other friends away. The Tide & wind being against us we were soon oblig'd to come to an Anchor again.

– 8 P.M.   Next day in the Evening weigh'd again but by the Carelessness or Ignorance of the Pilote we run aground, where we stuck till break of day, then got off & set sail

–   again, As the Ground was mud we receiv'd no damage. We pass'd Boca Tigris, where we expected the Hoppo men to come & demand our Grand Chop, but no Body came to ask for it. We got to sea with a fair wind, & soon after discharg'd our Pilote.

– 20   At 4. P.M discoverd Lingen Island & at 2 A.M Pulo Taya & at 8 A.M. Monepin hill[279].

– 21   See Banca & Sumatra

– 22   Came to an Anchor in the Straits of Banca. Set sail again & at 10 A.M see Lucipara Island.

– 23   We got out of the Streights of Banca, & at 5 A.M. saw the 2 Brothers[280], we kept up to windward in order to pass the Streights of Sunda by the windward passage between Dwars in the Weg[281] & the Sumatra shore, & in a few hours after espyd 7 sail of ships, one large one at Anchor behind North Island[282], the rest at Anchor to the Leeward of said Island. This sight gave room for various[283] some taking them to be some ships bound for Batavia from other parts of India &c But I soon concluded they must be Dutch ships & that they were on purpose to intercept us, we therefore consulted with the officers what was best to be

223   done, And as we could not tell how bad their Design might be it was resolv'd if possible to get to windward of them & indeavour to pass them, not being desirous

———————

279 *Monopin*, mountain on northwest Bangka.

280 *Two Brothers*, islands north of the Straits of Sunda.

281 *Dwars in den Weg*, island between Sumatra and Java in the narrowest part of the Straits of Sunda (French *Isle du Milieu*, Malay *Pulau Sanghyang*).

282 Situated at lat. 5° 30′ S, but not really in the Straits of Sunda. Together with the islands of Princes (present-day *Panaitan*) and Meeuw (also called *Cantaye*), North was one of the calls for taking in drinking water. While North became more popular towards the end of the 1750s, the preference for Meeuw may be explained by the excellent quality of its water.

283 Here Campbell has obviously omitted a word such as *guesses* or *interpretations*.

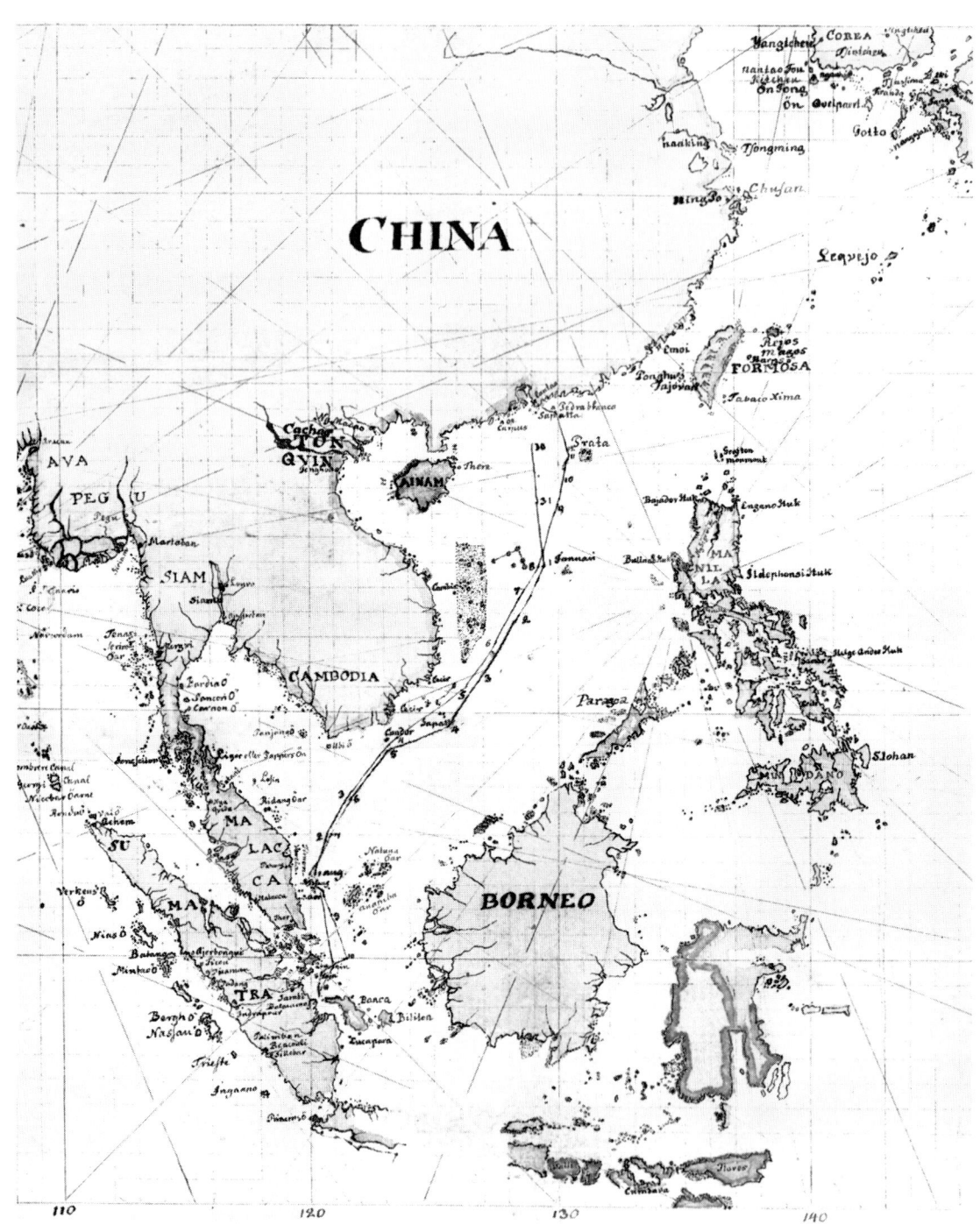

Chart of the South China Sea, with the route of the ship *Freeden* in 1748–49.
From J.F. Dalman, *Dagbok … Under Resan från Giötheborg til Canton och Hem … 1748–1749.*
(KVBS. Ms. Dalman, J.F.)

of having any Conversation with them if we could avoid it, we accordingly kept to windward as much as we could, but as we found the Current set us to Leeward & that we lost ground we thought it was best come to an Anchor to see what they intended, especially that as the wind was they could not come near us. In the mean time 6 of the ships had got up their Anchors & had set sail scattering themselves all across the straits mouth from the Sumatra to the Java shore, but falling pretty much to Leeward, the Large ship (which was the Commodore[284]) came out from behind North Island & set sail, and fir'd a Gun for the other ships to come to an Anchor which they did immediately & He also to windward of all the rest. He then made a signal for the Captains of the other ships to come aboard of him to to hold Council. They had hoisted the Dutch Colours once they got under sail. We lay as well as they at Anchor all that day & night in sight of one another at not above an English mile[285] distant. The night being dark we consulted whether it was best to ly still or indeavour to get away to the Eastward & try to pass by the Straits of Bally, some were of this opinion, some thought better to go back again to the northward to meet the English ships whom we expected to pass this way in a day or two, & then come along with them that they might be spectatours of any Act of hostility or violence that might be acted against us by which means our friends would have come to the knowlege of it, Reflecting upon the different opinions I found our officers would not attempt the Straits of Bally as being a Route they were not much acquainted with & could not answer for, another opinion propos'd of going directly to Batavia I did not think at all necessary as going so much out of our way & into their hands, And to go to the northward was not in our power the wind not permitting it, I at last concluded that it was better ly still for to pretend to get away without their seeing it either Eastward

224

or northward [was] next to impossible & could we have done it, they were much cleaner & lighter ships than we & would have soon come up with us & would have had a greater suspicion of us and therefore more apt to hurt us, we therefore kept where we were without stirring waiting to see what they wanted, In the mean time I order'd our Guns to be got clear & to get all in readiness to defend our selves in case they should attack us, being resolv'd to give them no manner of provocation which I believ'd they wanted. It was then debated whether we should get up Anchor & make for them to ask the meaning of this procedure & show them our passes, &c But as we saw they could not easily come up to us & not being certain what mischief they intended to do us, I was willing to delay time as long as we could to give time to the English ships to come in sight, and

Jan^r 24 therefore concluded best keep at an Anchor & wait for their coming up to us. Next day they heav'd Anchor & set sail making for us with all their might but were soon forc'd by Current & wind to come to an Anchor again. However they had

---

284 Normally an intermediate rank between captain and rear admiral, the term *commodore* here refers to the senior officer commanding the flotilla or squadron; also used to denote his ship.
285 One English mile = 1,609 m.

got a little nearer us. I then thought it was best to send aboard Breemer 2^{d} Mate with Copies of the Captains Passes & Commissions as well as mine, and to declare my Character as being his Maj^{tys} Envoy & representing his Person &c We put out our Pinnace in the morning & sent Breemer on board the Commodore with Copies of those papers translated into Dutch; They kept our Pinnace Mate & people & did not think fit to send us any Answer, In the Evening about sun-set they fird a Gun with shot to Leeward of us which the Captain took to be a signal to strike our Colours (as I believe it was) which he immediately orderd to be done as well as a pendant he had hoisted at main top mast head, which he said he had a right to as being a Kings Captain. In the night as it was very dark some were of opinion to run away where we could from them, being under great

225   fears that they had a design to destroy us, especially that we heard them warping with all their force against wind & Current to come at us, But they having once show'd their Colours I could not believe their design was so bad as that, but rather to carry us to Batavia & take out the forreigners & thereby make us at least lose our voyage for this year I therefore persisted in my first resolution to wait where I was & let them do their worst. Besides I thought there could not be a better time to dispute the Right of the Company to trade in these parts than this when I was on board invested with such a Character & powers

Jan^{r} 25th Next morning As the Captain was preparing the yaul[286] to go on board the Commodore with his original passes &c There came our Pinnace mannd with one of their mates & their sailors, desiring the Captain to go on board the Commodore & to carry his originals with him, which he did immediately. Assoon as he got on board there was a Grand Consultation held of all the Captains, who soon after sent an order 'aboard of us to send our Long-Boat with as many men as she could hold and to carry on board of us as many of their men in their place. Sometime afterwards there came a verbal order to take half of our people & to receive as many of theirs; They sent no more written orders, but got C. Trolle to send for such people as they wanted, naming amongst others our Chief Carpenter Brown, whom I refus'd to let go as being the only one of the ship capable of any thing. As I was preparing a Protest against the Commodore & Commanding officers of the Dutch ships, came another verbal order, to take all the people out of the ship but me & the SuperCargos & the Captain & sent particularly for Daniel Campbell writer, In the mean time came on board a sergeant with several soldiers Armd, who came directly down into the Cabbin where I was writing with an Intent to leave their Arms there, I bid them go up again & find some other place; They went up & layd them in the Captain's Cabbin. In the Afternoon the Captain Trolle came on board, with orders to hoist our own Colours & pendant as before, & a

---

[286] *Yawl*, jolly-boat (Swedish *jolle, julle*), small bark or boat, propelled by oars, used for a variety of purposes, such as going round a ship for all kinds of work outboard or purchasing fresh provisions ashore. (*The Oxford Companion to Ships & the Sea*, 1976, p. 434.)

new verbal order for Mr Pike to go on board. Soon after came Captain Backer & two of the Captains &c with a verbal order

[226]   to take out all our SuperCargos & every body else but me & the Captain, and 4 servants, two of whom they allowd to attend me & two to attend the Captain, They desird me also Civilly to go on board, that the Commodore would be glad to see me &c which I refus'd to do telling them that I knew no business I had out of my ship nor would not leave it till I was forc'd to it, so that they sayd no more on this head. The SuperCargos accordingly went (except Mr Morford who had hid himself [287]) and by them I sent my protest in Swedish, and a Letter in French to the Commodore, desiring them & Breemer who went with them to explain the protest to them. They left the Captain & me on board & about 12 of our men. Having in my protest & Letter declard my self Envoy & Minister &c of his Maj^ty to the Emperour of China &c and own'd the SuperCargos as my secretaries & others as part of my suite (having sign'd them Letters for that purpose) I demanded them back again. The Commodore was Civil to the SuperCargos & own'd he had nothing to allege against our Passes, but that he had receiv'd orders from Batavia to carry us up there, & that he could not help it, As for the Protest it being in Swedish he pretended none of them understood it, but having orderd the Super-Cargos & Breemer to explain to them in Dutch the Contents of it & of the Letter, & to insist on my being his Maj^tys Minister, He answerd He was oblig'd to obey his orders & that if the King himself had been there he must have gone also up to Batavia. The Commodore however consulted the other Captains & they came to a Resolution to send me back the SuperCargos & others I had demanded. I had desird the Captains before they left us to tell the Commodore that since I found we must go to Batavia to dispatch us thither assoon as they could. They had now sent on board of us   [288] soldiers with an Ensign (calld Adams) & sergeant & Corporal &   [288] sailors with 3 mates of which one was a Swede.[289]

Jan^r 26th In the morning we spyd two ships to northward which prov'd to be the 2 English ships we had wishd for, As they came near the Commodore fir'd a Gun to make them ly by & send aboard their Passes, which they did, & one of their Pinnaces coming on board with an officer to see me I took the opportunity to send a Letter I had ready writ to the Company to acquaint them of my misfortune, Captain Edgeton came close by us & spoke with us, & then pursud their Course.

---

[287] Morford was hiding because having formerly been in the service of the Ostend Company he might be regarded as an interloper by the Dutch.
[288] Blank left by Campbell.
[289] According to Campbell's own *Relation abrégée du Voyage* … (RAS. H & S 52; cf. also *Diary* pp. 227, 292), the *Fredericus R.S.* was taken over by 56 sailors and 36 soldiers.

(227)

Copy of the Protest against the Commodore & Captains of the Dutch ships &c

His Majesty the King of Sweden having granted to Henry Kónig & his Partners Subjects of his Majesty a Charter to Trade to the East Indies, China, & other parts on this side the Cape of Good Hope, and that the said Henry Kónig & Partners by vertue of said Charter have fitted out & sent the ship call'd Fredericus Rex Sueciæ (of which George Herman Trolle is Captain) to China &c &c

For the rest as well as other matters relating to this seizure or stop by the Dutch vide la Relation abregee du voyage given in to his Maj^{ty} in french [290]. I shall only add here what is not in that Relation. viz

I forgot to mention above on our meeting with the Dutch ships the behaviour of our SuperCargos & officers, I was the most surprizd at the terrour Mr Graham [291] was in, there was no comforting him, If we had any Pinnace he proposd to have gone away in the night towards Mew Island [292] to wait for some of the English ships or others that were soon expected that way in the strait, In short he seemd to me to have almost lost his senses, & I had enough ado to get him to bed, raving & complaining to himself of his bad fortune & bemoaning his friends that would suffer by him, &c Indeed on this occasion he did not show that Courage or presence of mind I expected of him. Mr Morford was heartily frighten'd, drank & cryd & skulk'd out of the way, Mr Pike behav'd the best to outward appearance from a meer stupidity or insensibility of danger. The Captain Trolle was furious & ragd against the Dutch & their Captains & indeed had not Captain Backer who had afterwards the Command of the ship been very Civil and had some regard

(228)

for me (as he told him) he would in all probability [have] usd him very ill.

Jan 27^r   when the English ships approachd the Dutch Commodore he fird blank at them to come to which they did & sent their boats aboard to show him their Passes. The day after we left them we were told the French & Ostender from China passd & the Commodore gave them the same complement of a Gun to make to but the frenchman refusd & made sail & struck his boltsprit athwart one of the Dutch ships & broke it, but however one of the Dutch Captains went aboard & obligd him to show his Commission, The Ostender having leave from England & Holland

---

[290] See note 289 above. This reference to Campbell's *Relation abrégée* would seem to indicate that at least this part of the *Diary* was not written until after his return to Gothenburg.

[291] *Graham* was the second supercargo (cf. Introduction p. xxxiii). Up to this point Campbell has called him *Brown*. From here on both names occur alternatingly, with a predominance of *Graham*.

[292] *Meeuw*, or *Cantaye*, island in the Sunda Straits, between the first and second corner of Java in Newbay.

for that ships voyage as also Letters to their Governours abroad in their favours they let them pass after having perusd said Licence & Letters.

When Capt Troll[e] returnd from the Commodore he brought orders to hoist the Swedish flag, he askd why they pretended to fire shot at him when he was at Anchor, they pretended it was not to strike but to oblige him to go aboard the Commodore, But that was grimace their true design was to make him strike, not doubting but we would take the first opportunity to make off in the night if we could, & by this method he thought better to secure us.

– 28   When the Dutch Captains came on board they told me they had orders to touch nothing but to seal up our Hatches & leave every thing in the Condition they found them & desird I would send one along with them to see them seald with my own seal, I desird therefore Mr Morford to accompany them, And they were all seald with their seal & mine. As for the Goods in the Cabbin & state room, As I lay there they comitted all them to my own Care.

1733
Jan^r
28

228 [bis]

Being at anchor Capt Backer came aboard and askd if I was ready to go ashoar, As I thought better not to leave the ship of my own accord, I askd if he had orders to take me out of the ship he answerd no but that Styrman van Reinse who had the command of the ship had orders to bring me ashore along with him. As I was sensible that my presence was necessary at Batavia in order to get more speedy redress & dispatch, I therefore went about noon, with them & Captain Trolle. At coming to Anchor our ship by their orders saluted the Castle of Batavia with 12 Guns, & me with 10 as I left the ship. The Commodore had seal'd up the passes that Capt Trolle had showd him & sent them by our ship to the Regency of Batavia.

The Commodore behav'd very civilly from the moment he took possession of the ship, & when he came aboard to visit me he told me he was sorry he had met with us, but he had orders to carry us to Batavia where our passes would be examind &c As I was resolvd he should not pretend ignorance I beggd him to see my originals (having only before sent the Copies to him) which he declind as saying there was no occasion, but I took them out & layd them on the Table before him, At parting he gave strict orders to his officers & people in a speech to them to take care how they behav'd and they should act with all Civility & beware of stealing or doing us any Injury for we were no Enemy but friends. Before we went in to have Audience of the Governour, there came one of his Guards to us in the hall where we were to desire our swords & Canes, this being the Custom here with every body that waits on the Governour, & as my Character was not yet declard I thought better to submit & take an opportunity to repair it afterwards so they took our swords as well as their own Captains &c And then we went in & found the Governour[293] standing in a sort of a Gallery, After a few questions as I have set down in the other Relation, he sent us to M[r] Rawenhofs Upper or first Coopman[294] to wait till the Council were assembled. At M[r] Rawenhofs there was a great deal of Company

& amongst the rest the fiscal[295], M[r] Heversman who had been Chief at Ormus[296] in Persia & lately come from thence, & was afterwards appointed one of the Deputies to conduct us back, and M[r] Armenau another of the Deputies, who was SuperCargo of an Zealand ship then in the Road bound for China, which had left Zealand about 3 months before we left Gottenburg but had met with an unlucky passage to the Cape of Good Hope where they were obligd to put in having most of their men sick or dead, and after leaving the Cape had no better fortune meeting with Calms in 40 deg. south for several days, so that in fine they fell to the westward of Java head & made for Bencoolen[297] which their want of water & provisions more inclin'd them to do, being very sickly & their Captain dead, Amongst others I found M[r] Abbesse[298] an Englishman that us'd to trade betwixt China & Batavia & whom we had seen there, He happend to be the person that brought to the Regency the first news of our being in China and a Pacquet of Lies from the Chief SuperCargo of the Dutch one Schultz who had the impudence to assure them we were Ostenders &c which was the occasion of this Accident, for two or 3 days after this Accident the squadron was fitted out to seize us, Abbesse had show'd me the Packet in China & told me that Schultz sayd it was a packet come from their factory at Japan which requir'd to be immediately dispatchd to Batavia and begd him to take it as he was going to Malacca having wrote to the Governour of Malacca to furnish him immediately with a vessel to carry him & it to Batavia, which was accordingly done, and I believe Abbess knew nothing of the Contents but believ'd as Schultz had told him, he made me an Apology for being the occasion of this Accident, but as the Dutch Captains had layd the blame on him very much I could not tell what he might have sayd or done against us, which I the more wonderd at having treated him at Canton very civilly,

---

[293] *Dirk van Cloon* (1684–1735), Governor-General of Batavia from 1732 until his death; cf. *Diary* p. 244.

[294] *Eerste koopman* or principal merchant in Batavia (Klerck 1938, 1, p. 345).

[295] In 1609 the *Heren Zeventien*, the Board of Trade of the Dutch East India Company (V.O.C.), appointed a Governor-General, remaining in Asia to take supreme authority over all settlements and possessions of the Company. The Governor-General selected the members of the Council of the Indies, a body of government over all activities and affairs. The Council also functioned as court of law, with the fiscal acting as prosecutor. (Klerck 1938, 1, pp. 213 ff., 348.) – The name of the fiscal whom Campbell met was *Wager* (*Diary* pp. 231, 244).

[296] *Ormuz*, at the entrance of the Persian Gulf.

[297] *Benkulen*, port on the south coast of Sumatra.

[298] Possibly identical with *Mr. Abbis* mentioned by Morse (1966–69, 1, p. 260) as chief of the Dutch factory at Canton in 1737.

230

I could not therefore help showing him a little resentment. Mr Armenau knew Mr Morford & Pike, they having been in Zealand alongst with him solliciting to be SuperCargos of this very ship that Armenau was SuperCargo in, which he had reported to the Governour & as he pretended had done us all the service lay in his power. I did not care to enter into much discourse with the Comp^y though many of them spoke to me in English, They were all very Civil, & chiefly Mr Rawenhof, As they conversd a good deal in Dutch (which I understood though I pretended not) I heard them talk much of Mr Pike & his Brother[299] that they were bred in Holland & that his Brother had been in the Ostend service &c In short they seemd desirous to make Mr Pike pass for a subject of Holland, which afterwards I found the Governour also hinted at to him. I had my memorial ready in french when I left the ship to deliver to the Governour & Council the first opportunity I should have, but having learn'd that he could receive no memorials out of Council, I was oblig'd to carry it with me till the first opportunity should offer to deliver it. The Commandeur by orders of the Regency carryd me in his Coach to the best Eating house in Town, where he recommended to the Host to

treat the Captain & me well & let us want for nothing that we might call for. Next morning the Commandeur payd us a visit to ask how we did. Soon after about 8 a clock I was surpriz'd to see Mr Morford & Mr Pike come in to my lodgings, They had been orderd ashore the night before (without my knowlege) to wait upon the Governour this morning, who was very civil to them & entertaind them with Coffy, ask'd them if they had a mind to come into their service, he having heard that they had been solliciting in Holland, & that he would serve them & take care all their Goods should be brought ashore, he askd Mr Pike if he was not a Dutch man &c They declind his offer of service to them, He then askd where they had been imployd & by whom in

231

the Swedish service, They answer'd by the Swedish Agent Balquerrie at Amsterdam, he then dismissd them sending them to the same house where I was, telling them they would be well intertain'd. Amongst other questions he askd if I had never been in the Ostend service & how we came to have so many forreigners on board &c to which they reply'd they never heard I was, Indeed they might have answerd very positive that they knew I never was.[300] Soon after came the Secretaire with a complement from the Governour & Council &c as in the other Relation to ask how I did &c At the same time that I deliver'd him my pass &

---

[299] *John Pike*, fourth supercargo on this first voyage to Canton, had a brother *Charles*, who after serving in the Ostend Company settled in Gothenburg as a merchant. He was a director in the Swedish East India Company from 1737 until his death in 1741. (Kjellberg 1974, pp. 126, 165; see also *Diary* pp. 273, 289, 290.)

[300] As already pointed out (Introduction p. xxi), Campbell is believed to have served in the Ostend Company, although the records of that company, which are well preserved, do not provide any evidence of this.

Letters of Credit as his Maj^{tys} Envoy & Minister plenipotentiary to the Emperour of China &c I gave him my memorial seal'd to the Governour & Council praying him to deliver it, which he did. The Secretary coming to dine with us in Company with the Fiscal Mr Heversman Mr Armenau & some others deliverd me my Passes, and told me they were well satisfyd with them &c I told him I hopd the Regency would excuse me if I had made use of any terms in my memorial that might not be aggreeable, He sayd I had no occasion to make any excuse, & that if I knew all I would not blame them so much as I had done, upon which I dropt the discourse. Besides Mr Wager the fiscal & others before mentiond who came alongst with the Secretary to Dinner, were Mr Warden bos[301] Counsellour of Justice, Mr Heversman first koopman & Mr Chacoon, I believe a son of one of that name that was formerly Governour of the Cape of Good Hope. Assoon as dinner was over the Secretary [proposd] a large bumper to the King of Sweden's health, which was accordingly drank round, In revenge I proposd that of the States General which was accordingly drank, then the Secretary proposd to the Continuance of a good friendship between his Maj^{ty} & the States General which we also drank off. In the mean time came in Mr Abbess whom the Secretary after a little raillery obligd to drink the last health. About 3 a clock the Secretary & the best part of the Company

<table>
<tr><td>Jan^r
29th</td><td style="text-align:center">232</td></tr>
</table>

took leave, and I begg'd leave of the rest to retire also to take a nap which was the more necessary as I was to wait on the Council in the Evening, and found my head not the better for the bumpers I drank a thing intirely unusual with me.[302] Mr Abbess addressd himself to me, testifying his concern that I should suspect he had any hand in the Affair that had happen'd, protesting he had not, & that if I wanted any money he would let me have it &c As I was unwilling to enter into dispute with him on this subject & was not yet perfectly satisfyd as to his conduct in this Affair, I told him that I did not know whether he had been guilty of any unfair proceeding against us or not; As for money I did not want it, And if I should want that or any thing else I would apply to the Regency for it & to no body else. While I was asleep Mr Morford wak'd me to tell me that the Captain Trolle & Mr Abbess had fallen into warm disputes on this subject & that in all appearance there would insue a quarrell betwixt them, I desird him to leave me to rest for that I did not trouble my self about their quarrells, upon my reasoning with the Secretary about taking away my sword & Cane at entring, & refusing now to submit to such a Ceremony as being unworthy of the Caracter I bore (as mentiond in the other Relation) he answerd me It was a Custom practisd not only with all their own people even Admirals as well as Captains but also with French & English whether SuperCargos or Captains &c To that I answerd that I thought

---

[301] Probably corrupt form for *van den Bos*; cf. *Diary* p. 236: *van der bos*, p. 244: *Vanden bos*.
[302] Campbell seems not to like drinking, which probably explains his repeated and somewhat exaggerated disapproval of drinking habits among crew and officers.

myself on a very different footing from any of them being invested with the Character of a Minister &c to which he replyd that though I was yet I was not an Envoy to them, I answerd that no matter to whom I was sent, for it is well known wherever one of my Character or station came there was a respect always to be payd me as representing his Maj^ty &c. My demand being granted by the Governour & Council I went to wait upon them in company with Mr Morford Mr Pike & Capt. Trolle, the Secretary introduc'd us into the Council room, where they were met sitting at a long Table & the Governour at the head upon a platform raisd a couple of feet from the ground, which was coverd with Carpet, & under a large canopy, I was brought up to the place where he sat & made my bow he rose a little up out of his Chair as did all the Council to salute me, (vide Relation) amongst other things he sayd I[303] hop'd the Commodore had usd us civilly & as well as the others that stopt us, I told him I had reason to be satisfyd with their usage, which was intirely civil

233

The Governour in speaking to me seem'd to express himself with some fear & concern, as uneasy at what had happend (as he indeed expressd himself) as appeard all the Gentlemen of the Council to be under the same Concern who had all their Eyes very intent upon me, I was beginning to hint a little at the inconveniencies &c this stop put me to, but he answering with so much Civility & excusing what had passd I did not care to continue on that subject, my chief business being to get from them assoon as I could, & thought better avoyd shocking them or putting them in any ill humour for [f]ear[304] of their contriving some means to chagrin me in my turn & perhaps delay my departure &c so we parted very friendly. I observd one who had his Eyes very intent upon me & talkd to one that sat next him (as if about me) whom I Rememberd having been Governour of Malacca when I was there Anno 1726 his name is   As he knew my Brother[305] very well I supposd he took me for him. Having made my Bow to the Governour I did the same in passing by the Council who all rose up a little wishing me a good voyage, & they very friendly took the other Gentlemen with me by the hand wishing them the same as they pass'd by. We went to pass a part of the Evening at Mr Rawenhofs, & there I fell into a pretty free discourse with the Secretary (who seem'd to be a man of good sense & who knew the world the best of any I met with there) Baron van Eimhof[306], I believe he is of Friezland or Gelderland, & as he told me his Father or uncle concluded the Treaty of Rastat[307]

---

[303] *I* is obviously a mistake for *he*.

[304] Campbell writes *hear*, an obvious slip.

[305] Colin Campbell's brother *Hugh Campbell* was a merchant who made considerable investments in the first expeditions of the Swedish East India Company. He was raised to the nobility in 1736 and made a director in the Company in 1737. Both Colin and Hugh had sailed to Canton in 1726. (Indebetou 1908, p. 126 f.; Gill 1961, p. 121; Kjellberg 1974, pp. 126, 165.)

[306] *Gustaaf Willem baron van Imhoff* (1705–50), later (1743–50) Governor-General of the Dutch Indies.

[307] In the peace treaty of *Altranstädt*, in Saxony, in 1706 August II had been forced by King Charles XII of

between Charles the 12th of Sweden & King Augustus being minister to the latter who was afterwards much dissatisfyd with said Treaty and put him in prison for it, Amongst other topicks of discourse betwixt us he told me that what had happend was not so much to be wonderd at, because of late years there had come several Interlopers[308] to the Indies under flags & Commissions of different pretences and whom they knew to be fitted out & to belong to the Ostend Company which Trade they would not suffer, and that even now they were informd the Ostend ship had left behind them in China two Gentlemen with a view no doubt of another ship coming there next year, & as this Trade had cost the Dutch very dear they had good reason to look well after it & not suffer others

who had no right to Trade to incroach upon them & therefore to examine all ships passing that way, I told him that the Swedish Company traded as legally to India as any other Company, and that we wishd there might be a stop put to all such Interlopers as he complaind of it being our Interest as well as theirs to hinder them, nor could we take it ill to have our passes examind since they did the same by English & French, and that we hop'd to meet with the same treatment at least that they did or as nations in amity & peace us'd towards one another He replyd as if they were not much concernd about our Trading saying that they were very sensible Sweden could not do much in this Trade & for his own part he wishd all Protestant Princes[309] & states might continue in a good friendship & understanding. The Secretary returnd to the Governour & came back to me with a complement from him & Council & desird to know when I proposd to go aboard my own ship that the Deputies might get themselves ready to accompany me, I told him I was ready whenever they pleasd but as I supposd they could not be ready till next morning, If the Governour would give me leave I should be glad of 2 or 3 hours stay in the morning to see the Town, He went to the Regency & returnd with an Answer immediately saying, that if I had inclination to stay & see the Town I was very welcome & that it depended upon my self, but that in case a fair wind should present in the mean time he could not answer for the ships not sailing or any Accident that might happen afterwards by such delay, which I must take upon my self, I was not at all displeasd with the answer, being very earnest to be gone not only to prevent any new difficulties that might ocur but also to save time the season being now very late for going home, Though had I been there sooner I should have been glad of a few days stay to make a better acquaintance

---

Sweden to give up the Polish crown to Stanislaw Leszczynski. Apparently Campbell is confusing this with the Treaty of Rastatt, in Baden, concluded in 1714 between Austria and France, which was one in the series of peace treaties ending the War of the Spanish Succession.

[308] At first the Dutch took the *Fredericus R.S.* to be an interloper, a disguised ship of the forbidden and abolished Ostend Company.

[309] This is probably the first time that religion is being used as an argument in the discussion concerning free trade in the Far East.

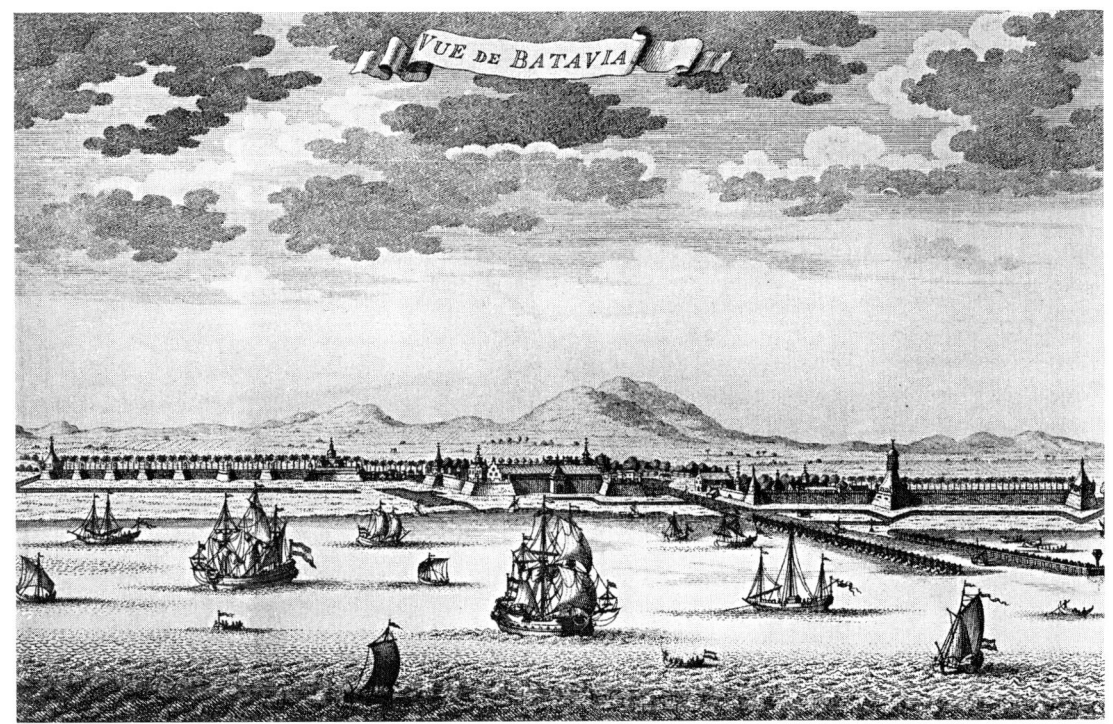

View of Batavia. From Prévost (1753).

amongst them, many of them having askd me to their Country houses & Gardens about Town, I therefore told him that I was ready to go on board as early next morning as possible or that night if the Governour thought it proper, He sayd He would therefore acquaint the Deputies & officers appointed to reconduct us to be ready to go with me early in the morning. So we parted & Mr Rawenhof, the fiscal, Mr Heversman Armenau &c carryd us home & supd with us and we passd the Evening very friendly together

<table>
<tr><td>Jan^r
30th</td><td style="text-align:center">235</td></tr>
</table>

Jan^r
30th

Early in the morning came the 3 Deputies & Captain appointed to carry us to the place where they had stopt us at North Island (as I had requird in my memorial) who were Mr Rawenhof, Mr Heversman & Armenau, Before parting I askd my Landlord what I had to pay He told me nothing, for that he had orders from the Governour & Council to take nothing, As I could not prevail with him to take any thing, I distributed some money amongst his servants, & took leave, & went to the waterside in Mr Rawenhofs Coach, & Mr Morford & Pike went with the other Deputies, At the water side the Commodore of the Marine (whose name was

Mamus[310]) waited for us with Capt Backer who was orderd with the Deputies to convey us with a sloop orderd for that purpose, They came along with us on board our ship & dind with us, The Commandeur went & orderd Boats to go fetch us wood & water which I had demanded of them, which brought us a good stock of both, The fiscal & Counsellour van der bos who had been on board 3 Dutch ships & Mr Helvetius another Counsellour of Justice[311] in the Bay who were also bound to Europe came & payd us a visit but could not stay dinner, I pressd him then to accept of a quarter of China mutton & some oranges which is highly esteemd there, & which he took very kindly, In the Evening the Deputies went on board their sloop where they invited us & pressd us to come & stay with them & pass all our time together while they should be with us, But as I was desirous to see how matters went on board our own ship, I beg'd they would excuse me under pretence of being afraid to crowd them & put them to inconveniency as the sloop being so little to accomodate them & 4 of us (including Mr Graham 2^d SuperCargo who had not been ashore at Batavia) at the same time I promisd either to be with them or they with me every day. Next morning came Commandeur Mamus on board & ordered Capt Backer to set sail immediately (not having any wind the day before). I went aboard with our Supercargos [in] the sloop to dine with our Deputies according to promise. I askd the Commandeur for an Anchor & Cable & some buoys they having lost us an Anchor in coming into the Road of Batavia for they set us upon the mud & our Rudder struck very often so that I was afraid the ship should have been lost, which put Captain Backer

– 31st

Jan^r
31st

236

& the Mate that commanded our ship in no small fright, for fear we should complain of it to the Regency, which they beg'd us not to do because it might ruin them, we promis'd not but that in Case of any Accident to the ship they must be answerable, & gave a note to Capt Trolle under their hands importing so much, Assoon as we came ashore the Commandeur told the Capt & styrman that he wonderd what they meant by bringing us upon the Ground which he plainly saw from the shore, They excusd them selves as well as they could, and as the Carpenter got our rudder to rights again & that the ship receivd no damage, I thought best not say any thing of it at Batavia. We set sail this morning but could not get far by reason of light winds & contrary Currents, & came to an Anchor in the Evening, for their orders were not to sail in the night the Road being very dangerous being full of Banks & foul ground & the Channell being very narrow between them

---

[310] Probably identical with *Gerbrand Mamus*, who is listed in *Dutch-Asiatic Shipping in the 17th and 18th Centuries* (1979–87), 2, p. 348, 3, p. 234, etc. as captain of several V.O.C. expeditions between 1718 and 1728.

[311] *& Mr Helvetius … Justice* inserted, which explains the somewhat awkward word order. – *Willem Vincent Helvetius*, born at Sluis in Zealand Flanders, later president of the Council of Justice in Batavia. He is mentioned again on p. 237 of the *Diary*.

Febr. 1st We set sail again & before noon met the Dutch squadron that had stopt us returning
from their Cruize, on which the Deputies sent imnediately [to] Batavia desiring to
have one of them[312] ships instead of the sloop to convoy us, & had their desire
granted, the Goudrian a ship of   [313] Guns &   [313] hand commanded by one

– 2 Henricks being appointed for that purpose which came the next day, & took the
Commodore & the Deputies on board & a part of our men that had been on board
the sloop & they sent some of them & all the officers on board of us as I desir'd.
I also demanded an Anchor for that they had lost to us at coming into Batavia
Road & a Cable for ours of which we were obligd to cut off   [313] fathom which
were put aboard the Goudriaan to deliver us, They were afterwards deliverd us,
and I sent them our old Cable for which they gave us a good new one. We set sail
& got near Island Onrust[314] where they have a wharf where they repair their
ships, and here keep all ships stores there is a windmill on the Island where they
saw their deals & of one side that is towards the wharf is a good fortification of
several bastions defended by a Garrison of soldiers.

– 3 Next day Mr Rawenhof proposd to go & dine with the Baas (as they call him or
head ship builder who had sent us an Invitation over night, we went and were
civilly intertaind, & returnd aboard at night

237

Besides the Baas & his people as Carpenters &c who reside on this small Island
(not a mile about) there is also an Administrateur who has the Charge of sundry
Goods & stores unloaded here by ships that come to repair, He is married to
a very pretty wellbred woman sister to one Helvetius a Counselleur of Justice of
Batavia, she is born at Sluys in Flanders & I believe descended from the famous
Doctor Helvetius[315] who first brought Antimony in practice. They have very good
houses on the Island & a pretty Church, as also some streets of little houses for the
slaves & their families on the East side of the Island which is not fortified they
keep a great number of fierce dogs chaind up which they let out upon occasion.

– 4 We went & dind again with the Baas of Onrust, where we also supp'd. The
Administrateur invited us all to dine with him next day but Mr Rawenhof refusd
him being very much displeasd at his Behaviour while in Company with us,

---

312 Either a reflection of careless speech or perhaps a slip for *the* or *their*.
313 Blank left by Campbell.
314 *Onrust*, small island off Batavia (Djakarta), where only repairs of V.O.C. ships were undertaken.
The details related by Campbell from his short visit to Onrust and its carpenters and slaves
headed by a *baas* (boss) are confirmed by other sources (*Dutch-Asiatic Shipping in the 17th and 18th
Centuries* (1979–87), 1, p. 126 f.).
315 Probably Campbell is referring to *Johan Frederik Helvetius* or *Schweitzer* (1630–1709), a physician and
alchemist of German origin, who settled in The Hague. His considerable reputation was based
both on his success as a practitioner and on his numerous books and treatises. The first in a whole
dynasty of doctors of medicine in Holland and France, he was the grandfather of Willem Vincent
Helvetius, Councillor of Justice in Batavia, and his sister. Cf. also *Diary* p. 235 and note 311.

being very Jealous of his wife & unwilling any body should talk to her, so that Rawenhof invited all the Company to dine with him except the Administrateur.

– 5   The Company that was invited came to dinner with the Baas on board the Goudriaan where we also went & returnd at night, to our own ship. As the Dutch are very fond of firing Guns, which is forbid by the Company on the penalty of paying double the value for every time they fire, yet Mr Rawenhoff could not help ordering the firing of some Patereros[316] to some healths that were drank.

– 6th   Set sail again & got a couple miles further near to a small Island call'd Amsterdam[317], where we went ashore with the Deputies in the afternoon, It is an Island about a league in Circumference a sort of a Hospital for taking care of Leprous & other sick people who have convenient apartments allotted them, It is well cultivated & inhabited by several Java-families, full of several sorts of Trees. Here we found an old Gentleman the Governour or overseer who had been formerly Burgermaster of Middleburg in Zealand & a Man of great Interest there as they told us

1735

238

and had a Daughter married to a Rich man a Burgermaster there, but his fortune declining in his old Age, he was obligd to go to Batavia or was sent thither by his Children who did not care to maintain him at Home as we were inform'd, which his bad oeconomy forc'd his relations to, He is now past 70 & has lost both memory & Judgment & is put in this station by the Regency of Batavia to subsist him honourably.

Febr 9th   Made sail & got a little way further. In the afternoon we spyd a sail from the westward, which provd to be the Susannah from Amsterdam (one Croonenburg Commander) she was the last ship that set out from Holland last year having left the Texel[318] in July, she had put into the Cape of good hope where she found some of their ships that had left Holland in May, one of them had lost 150 men by sickness, Another of their fleet had put into Saldania bay[319] near the Cape having lost 60 men by sickness. This set out from the Cape with 5 {5}[320] ships, but they soon parted & she got the start of the rest, brought no news but that the peace continued in Europe.

– 10th   dind aboard the Goudriaan, After dinner Mr Rawenhof proposd a bumper to the

---

[316] *Pedrero* (from Spanish *pedrero*), a small gun often used for firing salutes (originally for discharging stones).

[317] This island should not be confused with New Amsterdam (cf. *Diary* p. 70 and note 111).

[318] The largest and southernmost of the West Frisian Islands in Holland, roadstead for Dutch East Indiamen.

[319] *Saldanha Bay* north of Cape Town.

[320] Campbell writes *5* twice, but on separate lines; the second figure is no doubt redundant.

K[ing] of Swedens health, & now being out of sight of Batavia he thought he could take more liberty & fire away, & accordingly orderd 13 Guns to be fird to his Majtys health, I next proposd that of the States General or the Governour of Batavias health they chose the latter & fir'd the same number of Guns, then they drank our health & welfare & fird again, As they would oblige us every day to dine & pass the day with them which was no small expence to them, & now their Claret being out; I sent for 4 dozen Claret, as I had before sent them some Cote Rotie[321] & sherry, & oranges & what other things we could spare. Mr Brown & our officers being of opinion that now we were clear of all the shoals & Rocks being near Bantam that we could take care of our selves & did not want more of their piloting & asistance & that we believd their way of sailing (never sailing in the night) hinderd us, I therefore spoke to the Deputies about parting with them, They told me they had orders to carry us to North Island where we had been first stopp'd, but that he was of my opinion that it would be better for us not go thither but rather take the Leeward passage down the Straits of Sunda, and after consulting together they sayd they were

239

obligd to see us safely convoyd out of all danger, which there still was till we should come near Bantam, & then if I would take the rest of the risk upon my self they would take leave of us which I aggreed to, & from Bantam he promis'd to furnish with wood water Rice & fresh provisions, Mr Brown & our officers would willingly have parted with them sooner, which I knew to be meerly out of fear of some new hindrance or difficulty, and as I had no reason to apprehend any & that I hop'd to meet with what they promis'd from Bantam of which we stood much in need, and that if there were still danger it was much safer to trust them than our own people who did not know this part so well, I therefore thought best to follow their Advice to part off Bantam

11th   got up Anchor again, got but a little way, & came to Anchor again about noon.

12th   Got as far as Pulo Panjang[322], dind with the Deputies & went ashore upon that Island to see for wood & water but found none, It is a poor low Island having nothing but sand & shrubs, we went quite round it in our pinnace & found only one part on the E^t side where a boat could land, Here we saw some Peacocks on the small Trees by the water side which we could easily have shot. As we were soon in hopes to part I invited the Deputies & Captain of the ship to dine with us next day

---

321 *Côte-rôtie*, a red wine produced in vineyards of this name near Lyons.

322 Island northwest of Batavia; not to be confused with another island of the same name, off Bintan near Singapore (cf. *Diary* p. 97).

In the morning they sent me some Rice, Caravancas[323], a Cask of very bad old Pork, & a leaguer[324] of Arrack[325], I went on board the Goudriaan with some presents to the Deputies & Captain on Acc^t of the Charges they had been at in treating us so long, which they refusd but I insisted on their accepting of them, sent also some presents to the Secretary Baron van Eimhof he having made me a present of good Ale at leaving Batavia, I brought the Deputies on board & saluted them with 8 Guns which were returnd by the Goudriaan. Assoon as Dinner was over As I knew they lik'd firing of Guns above all things (though they are my Aversion) I proposd the General of Batavias health in a Bumper & fir'd 16 Guns, which the Goudriaan returnd, next Mr Rawenhof drank to the King of Swedens health at which we fird also 16 Guns

240

which the Goudriaan also returnd. I then proposd Mr Rawenhof & families health but he insisted on drinking first prosperity to our ship which I was obligd to do & orderd to fire 8 Guns, But the Captain notwithstanding of my orders privately told them to fire 16 for which I reprimanded him pretty smartly for not only disobeying orders but also paying as much respect to our ship as to his Maj^{ty}, He answerd a great deal of impertinent nonsense saying it was the same as the Kings health & a Confirmation of it, & told Mr Brown he represented the Kings person & therefore could not do otherwise, then fird 8 Guns to Mr Rawenhofs family, and 8 more to Hefwersman & Arminaus health, had every firing returnd by the Goudriaan. They stayd supper & at going back to their own ship I saluted them with 8 Guns more, the Goudriaan returnd it with 9. This happend to be a very noisy day & very little to my satisfaction not only hating the noise & smoak but also being always afraid of some Accident happening by the Carelessness of our people who are not very expert (I find) in this sort of business. Soon after coming on board our ship to dinner the Deputies orderd all their people out of our ship aboard theirs, & ours what were not yet come were also sent for from the Goudriaan, There stayd yet with us Capt Backer who commanded our ship &

---

[323] *Caravance, calavance* (from Spanish *garbanzo* 'chick-pea'), a name for certain varieties of pulse, e.g. *Dolichos barbadensis* and *D. sinensis*.

[324] *Leaguer* (probably from Dutch *ligger*), a holder for liquids.

[325] A drink very closely associated with the history of the Swedish Company. It is a distilled spirit: in fact that is the meaning of this Arabic word. The Chinese prepared it from rice, sugar or coconut. The method of distilling was probably copied by the Portugese in Gōa and the Dutch in Batavia. Some have erroneously concluded that arrack was imported from Gōa and Batavia into China, which seems very improbable, considering that the Chinese were great rice producers. Batavia arrack, the strongest type, was distilled from a mixture of molasses, toddy or palm wine, the latter being a liquor distilled from the juice of the coconut tree, and of rice. Although Batavia arrack was chiefly made for home consumption, some quantities may of course have been exported to China and India. The Gōa arrack was a sweeter variant, being made entirely from toddy by repeated distillation. Almost all Swedish vessels later imported large quantities of arrack, which rapidly made itself popular in Sweden. It was a requisite in the preparation of Swedish punch. Consumption of arrack in Sweden probably dates back to the homecoming of the *Fredericus R.S.* (Osbeck 1757, p. 198; Savary des Bruslons 1759–65, 1, p. 179; Lewis 1991, p. 52 f.; Ljungstedt 1992, p. 238 f.)

Styrman van Reinse being desirous to stay with us till we took our final parting from the Goudriaan, I made presents to all the Dutch mates one of whom was a Swede & promis'd to come & serve the Comp^y when he got home, I also made a present to the Ensign Adams who commanded the soldiers & had behavd very civilly. Before parting As they had now deliverd up the ship (& our men) to our own Command, they demanded a Receipt for it which I gave them, of which {is} the Copy is in the relation

After the Deputies were gone Mr Morford Mr Pike & some of our officers continued at Table over a glass of wine with Capt Backer & Styrman van reinse & I went to bed, but was soon wakd by a noise I heard upon Deck which made me go immediately up & inquire the mean

-ing of it, & found that our Styrman Lund had affronted Mr Morford & Capt Backer without any reason, upon which I reprimanded Lund & orderd him immediately to his Cabbin, & then turnd to the Captain Trolle who had been upon the Deck all the while & saw what passt without taking any notice of it, I askd how he could hear & see Gentlemen affronted in his presence especially Capt Backer a stranger who had behavd so civilly always to him & to all of us without indeavouring to prevent it or ordering that fool Lund off the Deck, He had little to say for himself but lies & ridiculous nonsense according to Custom, I desird Capt Backer to excuse it & I should take care to make Lund repent his impudence which he soon gave me room to do for notwithstanding of my ordering him to his Cabbin he did not think fit to go but went only to the main Deck where he stood cursing & swearing & damning & abusing every body, I then orderd the Captain to put him immediately in Arrest with 2 sentries at his door where he still made a great noise railing at & cursing Capt Backer & the Dutch & taking some saucy liberties with my self & every body on board

Febr. 14th dind with the Deputies who after dinner Drank & fird to the Kings Health 13 Guns which were returnd from our ship by 16 (conform to orders I left with the Captain), I then drank to the General of Batavia's health they fir'd 13 Guns, & our ship return'd but 8. Soon after our ship finding the Current favourahle went under sail which the Goudriaan observing did the same, but were both soon after oblig'd to come to an Anchor, After supper I took leave of the Deputies being resolvd to leave them next morning if wind & weather permitted, we took leave with great assurances of friendship & thanks for past Civilities of both sides. When we put off they gave us 3 huzzas[326] & fir'd 9 Guns which our ship return'd with 8 when we got on board.

---

[326] *Huzzah*, an archaic word for *hurrah*. Originally a sailor's cheer or salute (17th–18th c.), derived from the shouts that seamen make when friends come aboard or go off.

– 15   We lifted Ankar early in the morning having the Current in our

favours, we had layn almost these 2 days in sight of Bantam where is a great large Bay for ships to ride, the little Island Pulo panjang lying in the Entry, and further in another Island, ships go in between the Island of Panjang & Batavia side but they say they may go in the other side also between it & Bantam point, Mr Rawenhof had sent to the Governour of Bantam for some fresh provisions but the messenger returnd without any supply but a little fruit. But the Steerman van Reinse had been ashore on the main a shooting & had b[r]ought some fowls for us, & brought aboard a baboon or large monkey he had wounded of which he made a present, but it was an ugly fierce creature and I excusd the receiving of it, It was therefore flung over board.

febr. 16   Early in the morning with the Current in our favour we set sail, as the 5 Dutch homeward bound ships that had left Batavia with us whom we now saw under Bantam point did also, they had taken the outward passage from Batavia & got hither before us, The Deputies follow'd us a little way in the Goudriaan but seeing us resolv'd to pursue our voyage & that we had wind & Curr^t they tackd about for Bantam, Capt Backman[327] & the Steerman van reinse then took leave of us with great proffusions of friendship & thanks, we saluted them with 4 huzzas & 8 Guns at their putting off which the Goudrian returnd with 11. Assoon as they got on board we took our last farewell for which we fird 16 Guns by way of thanks for all past Civilities which I believe they could not return for want of pouder, for they had complaind two or 3 days before that it begun to be scarce. We stood on our Course & they in to Bantam, & in a few hours made up with the 5 Dutch ships & got to windward of them though they had been to windward of us all the way before, we spoke with 2 of them & wishd them a good voyage which complement they returnd us.

febr 17   At 5 p m. came to an Anchor off Bantam point. & next day made sail.

febr 18   2 p.m. anchord off North Island where the Dutch first stopt us.

Now we are parted with them, I think proper to take some notice of the Characters of some of them, & Circumstances that past that are not taken notice off before.

Mr Rawenhof is a young man betwixt 30 & 40 years of Age, was formerly a merchant at Amsterdam & had a good fortune, but was in

---

[327] Mistake for *Backer*.

England in 1720 the fatal South Sea year & got into stocks & Concerns with Sir Justus Beck[328] by whom he sayd he sufferd extremely, This obligd him to come out underCopeman a few years ago to Batavia, where they advanc'd him soon to first upperCopman, and he has since marryd there a young widow daughter to [the] late Governour of the Cape of Good Hope, He lives very hospitable there at a great expence, & is a Civil good naturd man. Mr Heversman the 2^d Deputy is a German his father kept a mathematick school at Amsterdam, He had servd formerly in the troops of Hesse Cassell[329], seems to have a great respect for the King of Sweden & told me he keeps up a Correspondence with Prince William the Kings Brother[330], He was an under officer or UnderCopeman[331] at Gombron[332] during the time of Miriveys[333] usurpation of Persia, and the Dutch Chief & some others who had gone out to wait upon one of Miriweys Generals that lay near their factory being murderd by them, he succeeded as Chief & was besiegd by those rebels by several thousand men, and defended himself so well by his Guns & a mortar he had in the factory that he did good execution upon them & oblig'd them to retire. He came last year from thence to Batavia & sets up for to go director to Japan. A sensible well bred man. Mr Arminaut 2^d SuperCargo of the Zealand ship bound for China was a broker at Amsterdam when he set up for this voyage. Capt Backer had been a long time in the service & out of Europe had been skipper two or 3 voyages to Japan, had the character of a rough cruel man on board his own ship & had killd several of his sailors by his barbarous usage, notwithstanding of this passionate temper of his he behav'd with a great deal of Civility to us on all occasions, He had often disputes with Capt Trolle which was owing to the latter who could not be commonly Civil to him nor any of the Dutch & I was obligd often to interpose to make them friends, he showing always a great regard for me. Henricks who commanded the Goudriaan was a surly illnaturd fellow had likewise murderd some of his sailors for which he was condemnd to serve some years without wages, which punishment lyes upon him at present. On this occasion I can't help taking notice of the bad treatment the poor sailors meet with aboard Dutch ships in this Country, they are very ill fed only pt rice, no bread, & some old Beef & Pork which has come from Europe & layn in the ware

---

[328] *Justus Beck*, an eminent merchant and financier of London, of Dutch extraction, was created a Baronet in 1714. He was one of the leading directors of the Royal Exchange Assurance at the time of the South Sea Bubble, which brought about his bankruptcy for liabilities amounting to £347,000. He died in 1722. (Dickson 1967, p. 158.)

[329] *Hessen-Kassel*, landgraviate in Germany. King Fredrik I of Sweden was the son of Landgrave Karl of Hessen-Kassel.

[330] When King Fredrik I inherited Hessen-Kassel in 1730, he made his brother *Wilhelm* (1682–1760) regent of the landgraviate; upon King Fredrik's death in 1751 Wilhelm succeeded him as Landgrave.

[331] Dutch *onderkoopman*, 'junior merchant' (Klerck 1938, 1, p. 345).

[332] *Gomron* or *Gamron*, former name of *Bandar (Bender) Abbas*, port in southeast Persia, north of the Strait of Ormuz. It was a major trading centre housing factories or trading stations from several European nations, including the Netherlands.

[333] *Mir Vais (Veys) Khan*, an Afghani leader of the Ghilzai tribe, who in 1709 led a successful rising against the Persian governor of Kandahar and governed the town until his death in 1715. His successors conquered most of Persia.

-houses at Batavia perhaps a year two or more, as we found by what they made us a present of, for the least offence of the world they have them severely whippd & sometimes without reason, as we often had occasion to see while we were with them, when sick they little regard them, and I believe seldom give them the necessary diet or medicines (N.B I speak of these ships that stay here in the Country & sail from one port to another of which perhaps they have near 40 here & some of them very good ships, as Backers was a ship of 40 Guns & Hindricks of 30 Guns, few of them less) The french pox[334] was very common aboard the 2 ships we had in Company, & there seemd no care to be taken of them, I saw many thrown over board without any Ceremony assoon as they died while I was with them. Indeed Most of the sailors they imploy in the Country or aboard all their ships are a mixture of all nations, of whom many are the meer scum & mob of Holland, their best people are the Norwegians & Swedes of whom they have a good many both aboard their ships officers & sailors, & ashore in several stations.

The Governour of Batavia Dirk van kloon is a man between 40 & 50 has a wife there but no Child, seems to be a plain Good man, born in India & I believe of a mulatto mother, of which he retains the complexion. He is very well esteemd here. He was formerly Governour of Pulicat on the Coast of Cormandel when M[r] Harrison[335] was Governour of Madras, but by some illwill or misinformation was turnd out by the Regency of Batavia & sent Home,where he clear'd himself to the Company, & was sent to Batavia one of the Council & in a few years about a year or less ago appointed Governour. Baron van Eimhof seemd to be the best bred man I saw amongst them, was secretary & much esteemd, & I believe knew the world better than any of them, had great influence with the Governour & Council and I believe contributed much to the Good treatment & Civility I met with there, He came but lately from Holland & is married to a rich old widow there & has one of the noblest houses in the Town, He seems to be in a fair way to rise to the greatest preferments here. The fiscal Wager, & a Counsellour of Justice Vanden bos, both civil men, as indeed they all were who were appointed (I suppose) by the Regency to keep us Company, & I could not help wondring to see so great a difference betwixt the Dutch here

& them in Holland, for I must say to their praise that they are much better bred than anywhere ever I saw in Holland (excepting the Hague) and I believe one reason of it is that of late years ever since the year 1720 a great many have come abroad who formerly had good fortunes & made some figure in the world & who had traveld into france & England in their younger Days, which that fatal year reduc'd & forc'd to come hither to repair their fortunes. I saw very few of their

---

[334] *French pox*, syphilis.
[335] *Edward Harrison*, British Governor of Madras from 1710 to 1717. (Gill 1961, p. 119.)

women, but was informd that of all ranks & both sexes they live at a great expence & love to make as much show & figure as they can in Dress, Coaches & number of servants & slaves, for Mr Rawenhof told us he had above 100 slaves male & female in his house. They drink here vast quantities of small[336] white wine (pretending that Clarets & other strong wines dont so well aggree with them on account of the heat of the Climate, In short what I could observe aboard their ships, they eat & drink all day long, & even the nights to[o], In the morning Tea or Coffy, at 10 or 11 a clock Eat fowls pigeons which they have & drink white wine & beer, besides number of drams of french Brandy or Arrack all day long, & in the afternoon Tea or Coffy &c They have so many ways to incourage drinking & dramming that one can't help laughing at their ways, sometimes 2 drams before dinner, one for a Smaachelyck maltid[337], or good Dinner, another for a good Appetite & after dinner another for a good digestion & one more for a Smaakelick pipil or a savoury pipe of Tobacco which they always smoak after dinner & often at other times of the Day. Small beer commonly calld Country beer they swill all day long, It is made of Europe beer water & sugar, & is an aggreeable liquour when made small, Coffy is also much in favour, which even their mates aboard our ship often drank in the night as well as in the day. As for sundry other things relating to Batavia & the affairs of this Island & Country I refer to another place.

when I consider the reason of the stopping of our ship by their squadron without any orders from their Masters from Holland I cannot but

condemn their rashness to commit such an Act of hostility without any orders, only on the idle Intelligence that their SuperCargo Schultz sent them from China, which they had no great room to believe if they considerd that had we been Interlopers or belonging to Ostend or any other place that had no right to trade to India such an expedition could not have escapd notice from their Comp^y at Home who no doubt would have advisd them of it and sent them the necessary Instructions. But this they did not pretend to have for they told us they did not know that there was any such ship as ours passd the Straits of Sunda nor had any news from Europe about us, It is true they might not know we had pass'd because I did not show our Colours in sight of any of their ships on purpose they should have no Intelligence for I was always apprehensive of some hindrance from them if I met with any number of them and they should know us. And as to the excuse they made that their expedition was with a view only to examine us & see if the Intelligence we[338] had from Canton was true, & that if it was not they could immediately release us, for as I told them at Batavia they could have done all this without the formality of carrying us up to Batavia which they must know must

---

[336] In the obsolete sense of 'of low alcoholic strength'.
[337] Dutch *smakelijke maaltijd* (Swedish *smaklig måltid*).
[338] Mistake for *they*.

be a great hindrance to us & be the means of losing our voyage for that year, and that they could have informd themselves in a nother manner without doing us so great a prejudice to wit by sending one of their Council or a person they could trust to examine our passes & finding them valid immediately to let us go our Course, they answerd to this that it being an Affair of some Consequence they were not willing to trust any body with it but themselves. But their orders were positive to bring us up to Batavia & that if they found our passes Good to hoist our own Colours upon our ship if not to hoist the prince of Oranges Colours[339] by which they would know at Batavia we were a lawful prize, they had besides given very strict orders (as I knew by one that Saw the Instructions) to the Commodore & Captains to take all due Care that we did not escape them & put them in mind of the escape of the Apollo[340] an ostender under Prussian Colours the year before in the straits of Malacca from 4 of their ships in which they

heavily blamd the Commodore & took notice in their Instructions that had he livd to come to Batavia he had met with a Severe punishment hinting even the loss of his life, but he dyd in his passage thither. On the other hand I must do them justice to say that once they had seen our passes they behavd with the utmost Civility & regard to us, did not meddle with any thing neither Goods nor papers nor even provisions till they applyd to me for allowance for their people aboard which could not be refusd, especially that they had the subsisting of ours aboard their ships, The Civility at Batavia was no less where they treated us very nobly & the intertainment given us there the time they dind with us cost the Regency some hundred Rixdollars[341] for we had the best of every thing as Turkeys, Capons, fine fish, fruits & all sorts of wines, in short had every thing at command we had a mind to call for, in doing which I was very sparing. Provisions of the Country are cheap here but their duties in Town makes living very dear, & fish of which they are very fond & will have quite fresh comes very dear at Batavia, though they have as much as they can catch in the Road about 2 or 3 miles from the Town, but it will keep but a few hours on account of the great heat, They told us that one dish of fish we had at Dinner cost 12 Rix Dollers. I never saw such a variety of fine fish as at Onrust where they took them up close by the shoar & kept them in well boats[342] placd there, They were all different from any in Europe

---

[339] I.e. the Dutch colours.

[340] The *Apollo* made a single voyage under the imperial flag of the Ostend Company and in 1730 was sailing under the Prussian flag, as Campbell very exactly records. She was purchased in Hamburg in 1735 by Johan Friedrich König, the Swedish East India Company's commissioner in that city. Thus the *Apollo* went into Swedish service under the name of *Tre Cronor*, as a vessel of 225 *läster*. For the Swedish Company it made only one voyage to China, in 1736. (RAS. KHH; Zethelius 1955/56, p. 98; Dermigny 1964, 1, p. 177.)

[341] *Rix-dollar* (modern Dutch *rijksdaalder*), a silver coin and money of account current in the 16th–19th centuries in Holland and other European countries and in their commerce with the East.

[342] *Well-boat*, fishing-boat with a perforated tank in the hold for keeping caught fish alive.

perfectly fresh & well tasted, and of all sorts of colours some spotted, & some streakd, blew, green red, Gold Colour &c

That stop lost us near 2 months in our voyage,[343] when we met them we were entring the straits with a fine N East wind and could have easily passd it with that gale in near 24 hours, whereas it cost us afterwards 3 weeks, besides the keeping us 3 days before we were sent to Batavia (where we stayd but about 36 hours) but it cost us 16 days to come back to North Island by reason of contrary winds & Currents, though we saild from thence to Batavia in 12 hours. Another great prejudice that stop causd us was the sickness it brought on our men

248

for while they were aboard the Dutch ships near 3 weeks they were very ill usd I mean the sailors, for the officers were well treated as they acknowlege, for they had no where to ly but upon the Deck, & for their food Rice old musty Pork & Beef & one dram of Arrack a day, and even that small quantity allowd them which was given out at so much a week was stole from them for they had no place to keep it, In short they stole their victuals Cloaths & every thing they could lay hold on & when they complaind to the Captains they had no redress, on the contrary some of them usd them the worse especially Henricks Commander of the Goudriaan of which I had an instance for they complaind to me in his presence, which as was none of my business I could not meddle in but spoke privately to the Deputies who spoke to Henricks, but instead of redress he was highly offended that his people should be taken for thiefs, though he knew the most of them were so. In short their own people were little better treated than ours, & would have all deserted from them could they have had any opportunity, & often begd of us to take them & hide them offering to sail with us for no wages, but we durst not connive at such things for fear of giving the Dutch too much reason to complain. Amongst those on board of our ship, there were several french who had deserted with a whole Company with their sergeants & Corporals from the frontiers of France, but much repented their doing so. In short they are so badly us'd & a great many of them having little hopes of ever getting home, for they disperse them & send them from one place of India to another that they may not have an opportunity to return, that I verily believe we could easily have run away with the ship while their people were aboard of us who would [have] gladly joind in such a design against their officers. Vide Relation to his Majty & That to the College of Commerce for some things omitted in this Journal

---

343 The *Fredericus R.S.* met the Dutch vessels on 23 January. If we agree that the ship had a favourable wind only from 17 March on, Campbell is right when affirming that the blockade brought the stop to nearly two months. (*Utdrag af 20 loggböcker* … UUB. L 183.)

As I was informd afterwards the Commodore of the squadron   de Vries[344] was the most reasonable man amongst them, for as no doubt they all would [have] been very glad to have seiz'd us as a prize at any rate it seems some of them even proposd it without troubling themselves about our passes, and I was told that Backer was one of the most violent of them, He sayd to some

1735[345]

of our people himself, upon the occasion of their firing a shot to take down our Colours, that if we had answerd it with shot or had not taken them in they would [have] given us a whole broadside, seeming as if they only wishd we would give them any provocation which I was resolv'd not to do except forc'd to it in our own defence.

Now to return to the Voyage.

febr. 20.   Weighd anchor from North Island, but the Currents & contrary winds forc'd us back again to the same place.

– 21
– 22   Sent the long boat ashore to Sumatra to look for water but finding it brackish they brought none of it. Next day sent ashore for water again but found none, Mr Pike would go ashore with the Boat, they found some people ashore who made signs to them to go further up into the Country which was through a wood & by a very narrow path, but they would not in which they did well, for as the people of this Coast are a very bad treacherous people, they wanted probably only to draw them out of sight of the Boat & so rob & murder them. Now for many days having a northerly Current against us & little wind we were daily imployd in casting Anchor & weighing again, at least 12 times from Bantam point where we were the 17th till we came to Princes Island[346] the 1st March

– 24   As we were so much hurryd & continually imployd what with sending our Boats for water, & letting fall & taking up Anchor again I had no time to examine yet steersman Lunds Affair, the officers being every moment imployd about the ships Affairs, but yesterday as I was going upon Deck he accosted me very rudely & in an impudent manner desir'd to be releasd, & made a dreadful noise accompanyd with volleys of oaths &c so that now we were at a little Rest and in all appearance would be obligd to stay here 2 or 3 days to take in water & fresh provisions, I was resolvd the sooner the better to take his affair under Consideration, and accordingly orderd him into the Cabbin &c for which see the particular Account of that examination. The people being very much fatigued in such hot weather

---

[344] The name of the commander of the Dutch squadron was *Herman de Vrij* (Campbell, *Relation abrégée* ... RAS. H & S 52). Campbell had evidently forgotten his first name and so left a blank for it.
[345] *Sic* (as also on pp. 238, 252).
[346] *Princes Island*, now *Panaitan*, is located in the centre of the Straits of Sunda.

I orderd them a dram extraordinary a day which is the thing in the world I found they lik'd the best.

250

March 1ˢᵗ at Anchor off Princes Island, we chose this place as much more proper than Mew bay to take water in, because it was much easier getting out of the straits from thence with such winds as we were like to have, we were told besides by the Dutch that they commonly took their water there & where they found fresh
– 2d provisions. I sent immediately the Boat for water, & next day they returnd with the Casks fill'd, sent it again but it returnd without any, sent it therefore back in the Evening to look for Some in another place which they did & found some & filld their Casks & came aboard 6 hours afterwards with it. Here the people of the Island came to us with fowls & some fruit & other things, amongst the rest they brought a little creature like a Deer which the English call Hog-deer[347] because it has the head something like a hog It has very slender legs & feet & long for its bigness, & body very small, It has long Ears & seems to be a peaceable timorous Creature, I bought in hopes to preserve it & bring it home, but it would eat nothing but Greens, & when the few we had were done we tryd it with rice & corn, but it card for nothing we had, I then thought of trying it with the leaves of the Tea after we had drank the Tea which was the only thing he would take and on which he subsisted for above a month, but at last dyd with his belly all swelld which might be probably owing to the moisture of the Tea, so that I can't tell but had I given him the leaves dry but he would have eat them & perhaps might have liv'd, though they are very tender, They must be confind for if they go loose they are so timorous and always skipping about, & their legs being so very weak & tender, they are apt to break them. We weighd but were obligd to come to an Anchor again. We found the people very civil, they are the same that use to go over with provisions to Mew Island when they see ships there, for there are now no Inhabitants on that Island since one Funnell an Englishman from Ostend in the year   [348] was ashore there & very barbarously without the least provocation set fire to the peoples houses robbd them of all they had whether provisions or stores, they did not even so much as leave them the tools & vessells they usd for their household Affairs or Agricu[l]ture &c It is by such practices as these that the Europeans have

251

got a very bad name in many parts of India & have made the natives so afraid of them & watch all opportunities to destroy them when they land. The Dutch ships when they come to any place where they have settlements or any ways under or near their power serve the people bad enough, for in the Straits of Sunda the

---

[347] *Hog-deer*, the common name of a small Indian deer, *Axis porcinus*. (Lewis 1991, p. 127.)

[348] Campbell has left a blank. Possibly the year was 1719, when an Ostend ship sailed for Canton with one N. Funnel as captain (Degryse & Parmentier 1993, p. 166).

people come off with provisions to English french or any other ships but the Dutch which they never care to go to, for they take their provisions at such price as they please & sometimes give them nothing but blows for it, we had an Instance of the difference of this now for though there were 2 Dutch lying not far from us off Angerpoint yet they passd them & came to us to sell what they had.

March 4   Weighd & in 3 hours Mew Island bore S E 1/2 S dist 2 m.

– 5   in the morning see the 5 Dutch ships that saild with us from Batavia to the N N W of us. At noon Java head bore E.S.E 1/2 S. distant 9 l. & the peak of Princes Island E.1/4 S.

– 6.   Saw the 5 Dutch ships a great way to leeward, & soon after saw but four of them, we sail much better in a wind than they do or those ships that convoyd us, which we always got to windward of when we saild together.

          From the 6th to the 17 we had variable squally weather with Rain, small winds & Calms, & in all that time have run but 430 miles

– 17th now have a fast S.E wind & run 135 miles, which continued till the 26th pretty fresh gales & then to the 29 gentle gales but same wind

– 29   same wind good moderate gale run 120 m.

– 30.   Squally weather, wind has shifted to N E^t & northerly

– 31   Same weather as yesterday & variable wind N & N westerly

April 1st variable winds & weather with Calms run but 31 m, in the morning wind came about S E & E b S.

– 2   wind N E moderate weather which continued so to the 4th when turnd about to E b S. & continued so or rather S E^t till the 12th

– 12th wind about to N E & continued so to the 16th with fair weather.

– 16   wind S W & little wind with Calms

– 20   wind & weather variable since the 16th & little wind, sometimes at S.E. some-times S.W. to day it has come to S. & b. E.

April 20th while we were in the Straits [of] Sunda the sickness which our people brought from the Dutch ships with them increasd among them, breaking out into looseness, bloody fluxes[350], pains in their breasts & fevers, of which some have died, particularly the Gunner who had a fever & looseness who was as I thought recovering, but while we were at Anchor in the [   ][351] he would absolutely go ashore which I diswaded him from as much as I could on Account of the heat he would be exposd to going so far in the sun, but he was obstinate in it that the Land would do him Good which the Captain joynd in, which I was obligd to consent to for fear if I did not let him go and he should die afterwards they might [have] reflected upon me for preventing him from going ashore & made that the cause of his death. But he very foolishly assoon as he got ashore put off his Cloaths & flung himself in the fresh water which increasd his fever & he came back very bad, & grew delirious & in a few days after died. He was a quiet sober man but very little acquainted with what belongd to his business aboard ship or any thing of sea affairs though he was cryd out for an Excellent Gunner ashore & was one of the Admiralty, but I must say that there is little regard to be made to the Characters they give people ashoar for I have not found any man belonging to the Admiralty whether officers mates Carpenters or sailors good for any thing, They are very lazy & very Ignorant all of them.[352] They begin now to be pretty healthy on board. I impute their sickness to be chiefly owing to the bad usage they had aboard the Dutch ships by which they contracted a bad habit of Body, & after leaving them they had a good deal of fatigue with constant heaving & falling of the Anchor for many Days running & it being very hot they usd when in a high sweat to run constantly to the water Jar & swill as much as they could which contributed to the Cold they catchd afterwards (as also their lying in the Air when they were warm & sweating) & turnd chiefly to Loosenesses.

---

[349] *Sic.*

[350] Dysentery was of common occurrence, quite frequently with fatal consequences. It was particularly widespread in tropical areas, but chronic and relapsed cases could occur in cooler climates as well. The disease consisted of an inflammation of the caecum, the colon and the rectum, which together form the large intestine. Abscesses form on the mucous membrane through bacilli ingested with the drinking water, causing diarrhoea in the first instance, usually with an admixture of blood, hence the name "bloody flux", and always watery. There would be twenty or more motions per day. The diarrhoea is accompanied by prolonged straining and abdominal pains. Recovery is not rapid even with good treatment. Only after fourteen days do the symptoms diminish, but it is still possible that after the termination of the illness, chronic exhaustion may supervene and also recovery may not be complete. In that case the disease continues in less severe chronic form. Dysentery is characteristic of a closed society such a ship's crew, and is very contagious. Therefore even chronic patients must be segregated. At sea, however, people are forced to live in crowded conditions, making infection almost inevitable. Medical precepts prescribed castor oil for expelling the contents of the bowel together with the bacilli. A diet of rice boiled in broth was also used as a remedy. (Allison 1943, p. 93; Goubert 1974, p. 217.)

[351] The omission occurs at the end of the line, with no space left to be filled in later.

[352] A period of service in the Swedish Navy was not always to be regarded as an advantage. Lack of training was a frequent cause for complaint in the Navy, so that the merchant service – for instance that of the Company – was more of a nursery for the Navy than the other way round.

– 22   Since the 20th the wind has continued Good & fresh in which time have run 150 leagues. It now slackens a little

– 24   wind S.E. a good gale but Cold weather. Some time ago apprehending we might be put to it for water having a long run to make before we can supply our selves & that we dont know what delays & unfavourable weather we may meet with going about the Cape in this time of the year I with the Captains & officers Approbation limited the peoples allowance (which was before what they pleasd) to a bottle a day for drinking, I did also cut off some kans[353] a day from the allowance for boiling of Rice Caravancas &c by which I hope to be able to do pretty well till

253

we can get a fresh supply. But apprehending that even these retrenchments were not sufficient & that we our selves SuperCargos as well as officers should show good example & contribute our parts to saving in so necessary an Article, I proposd to Mr Morford & Pike to retrench a little in their Punch which they love too much, for they have (with the Captain & mates) had the whole voyage every day 2 large bowls a day one at 11 in the morning for their Tiffing & another at 5 in the afternoon containing each about a Gallon or between 3 & 4 bottles, besides what they had a[t] Table half such a Bowl every day at Dinner & as much at supper, which I think a very Extravagant Custom, but which is hard to break them off, for besides all this these 2 Gentlemen above named have punch by themselves in Comp^y w^t the Chief mate Baron (who is a meer drunkard) twice or thrice a day. I therefore proposd my opinion to these Gentlemen, which they did not at all relish for Mr Morford was pleasd to say that the tiffing was chiefly for Capt Kitching who had always been us'd to Punch & could not be without it, presuming I would favour him as being the person I chiefly confided in for the navigating part, but unluckily for Morford what he sayd I knew to be false for Kitching is the most moderate man amongst them, & though he can drink he can also let it alone & to do him justice I never saw him overtaken with liquour, I wish I could say the same of these Gentlemen & their friend Baron, who seldom any of the 3 go to bed or even come to supper sober, And Kitching had already of himself spoke to me about the consumption of the water & especially in that Article of Punch, & advisd to allow less, so notwithstanding of this pretence of Morfords I immediately orderd to give but half a bowl morning & afternoon which will save above a kan or 3 bottles of water a day. I wish they would also give up Tea in the Afternoon which I am sure they have no occasion for considering the quantity of liquour they swallow all day long, but I have no other way to bring them to this but by abstaining it from my self, who have much more occasion for it than they as I never drink any Punch nor any thing else between meals. But as their chief

---

[353] One *kanna* (or pint) = 2.617 litres.

study is Eating & drinking I dont expect my example will have any influence but on Mr Graham who is very sober & never Joins in their tiffings or drinking bouts.

April 26th Wind Easterly moderate warm weather & little sea, which is the more to be wonderd at this time of the year so near the Cape for we expect to be in soundings off the Bank to morrow night, If the winds & weather continues as it has done till we pass it never people passd it with easier weather. But being upon this subject I can't help taking notice of the general mistake that people are under about getting round the Cape at this time of the year homewards bound, which is generally reckond impracticable, but our good fortune shows it possible & besides it is certain that there are Dutch ships go round the Cape all months of the year both outward & homeward bound & by what I could learn at Batavia none of them are ever obligd to return back, they sometimes indeed put in to the Cape when the weather is too bad to attempt passing it, though at the same time it is true that some English ships have been forcd to put back or have been put to great difficulties to pass it homeward bound at this time of the year, so that it may sometimes happen such Contrary winds & bad weather may hinder them, but I believe that seldom happens, & therefore it ought to be attempted at any time of the year.

– 27 We sounded but find no ground. As our officers are in great want of strong liquours, I have orderd some Arrack to steerman Breemer & some others of the most serviceable, which I hope will incourage to be brisk & active, to do them justice they are much brisker now than they were the outward voyage.

– 28 Wind still fair, by our variation to day of   ^354 we ought to be upon the Bank.

– 29 now our officers think they are past the Bank because their variation is between 16 & 17 degr, nor do we find ground with 200 fathom The wind has shifted westerly & looks as if it would blow. We see Gunnets^355 a Bird common about the Bank which makes me think we are not past it, the wind westerly but fair weather. We see two sail standing the same way as we do, but in the morning lost sight of them, I suppose they are two of the Dutch ships that came from Batavia with us & have put in to the Cape, Latitude to day at noon 36.24 by which we find there is a southerly Current which has carryd us 70 miles beyond our Reckoning. the wind is come about to S.W.

– 30th We sounded but find no ground, next morning found it with 120 fathom wind veerd about in the night to N & N W. Had not Mr Graham perswaded C. Kitching to Sound this last time we had supposd we had passd it two days

---

354 Campbell has left a blank.
355 *Sic*, for *gannets*, a heavily built marine bird of the genus *Morus* (or *Sula*). On p. 257 Campbell writes *Garnets*.

ago as Baron according to his positive way assurd Kitching & made him suppose it though contrary to his own judgment & observations which were the truest & all this because Baron was sure their variation could not be wrong, little considering how many small Circumstances may render such observations, not only owing to the Compass it self but also the person that observes, motions of the ship &c While we were with the Dutch, & had the Dutch officers on board of us, being willing to treat them as well as I could, we were put to a great expence of wine & fresh provisions, in so much that I found without great oeconomy we had not enough for half the voyage, and as some of our SuperCargos had introduc'd a very bad Custom of not only calling for wine & water between meals as often as they pleasd, but would even send for a bottle of wine sometimes on Deck & drink to the Captain & some others of our Chief Officers, this incourag'd the Captain & some of them to take the same liberties, which had I sufferd longer they would have consumd it all in a month, I therefore resolvd to put an end to this bad Custom & told our SuperCargos the small quantity of wine we had left & that I reckond at the rate of 3 bottles a day viz for Dinner & supper, we might if we had a good passage be able to make a shift to the end of the voyage; & with enough ado, I therefore thought better not to have any wine opend between meals because I found, their calling for it from time to time incourag'd the Captain & others to do the same, by which means it would be all gone in a very little time. I accordingly orderd the Steward to open no more bottles of wine between meals & only to bring 3 bottles a day to table. This very unexpectedly brought me into a dispute with Mr Pike who has no thought nor consideration of any thing but his own appetite, & resolv'd to be under no regulations or limitations though for his own good. The occasion was this, Pike out of laziness not caring to go upon Deck to tiff according to Custom by which means he had not his share of punch this morning, for they had made a rule amongst themselves on his Acc^t that no body should have a share without joyning with the rest upon Deck; finding himself therefore disappointed of his Punch, he calld my servant to give him a glass of wine, He told him that I had orderd no wine should be opend more between meals, upon which he flew in a violent passion against

my servant, & came down to me all flusterd with Complaints against him, As I resolvd to bear with the fools humours as much as I could on his Brothers Account, for I confess his own conduct made me have no regard for himself, I heard him patiently & told him my servant was not in the wrong, but that I had orderd as he had told him, & he knew very well the reason for it, but at the same time if he or the SuperCargos should on occasion wanted[356] it should not be refusd them provided they came down to the Cabbin for it & not call for it upon

---

[356] *Sic*, probably for *want it*.

Deck in sight of the Captain & officers who would think it hard if they were not allowd the same liberty, I then orderd my servant to carry him a glass of wine, but instead of accepting of it he abusd him before the Captain & all the officers and threatend to beat him if he did not obey his orders & give him what he call'd for, The fellow gave him such an Answer as he deservd & told him he had nothing to do with him nor could he obey any orders from him &c But as I heard the noise continue and Mr Pikes voice upon Deck very loud which was very indecent before the Captain & officers, I therefore went up to know what was the matter, Pike immediately in a passion told me it was very hard his orders could not be obeyd & that he could not have a glass of wine when he wanted it, and a great deal of such impertinent stuff, upon this I was resolvd at once to check this impudence of his (which I had been often troubled with before) & before all those who had heard his impertinence, I therefore told him at once that he did not seem to know himself nor me, that as to his ordering he had no power to order the least thing in the ship & that I knew no body had power to do so but my self or with my Consent, & that since I was intrusted with that power I assurd him I would use it when I found it necessary, that he saw very well I never made use of any power I had for my own profit, & for liquours he had a much greater share of them than I had, And that I could not but be surprizd to find him always giving himself airs & taking liberties that Mr Graham nor Mr Morford never did though they had as good a right if not a better than He, that as to his threatening of my servant I must let him know that I would not suffer him or any man in the ship to touch him, but that if he was saucy to him or any other Gentleman their business was to let me know of it & I would do them justice, for it was my business then to punish him

& not theirs. I added that I had not forgot his arrogant behaviour the outward voyage, & ordering things without my knowlege; & boasting behind my back that his orders were as good as mine & such impertinence, at a time when he knew the trouble I had with the Captain & some mutinous officers & others, when he & all that wishd well to the voyage ought to have done their best to have supported my authority, without which he had proofs enough that the voyage & the Companys service had been ruind long ago. But that now I found it more necessary than ever to exert the authority I had, & that if he or any other should think themselves injurd they should be very welcome to complain at Home on their Return. By this publick reprimand I showd those people, before whom he had been blustring in a high tone the moment before, how little such Conduct would avail with me & how little I could make him when I pleasd. But indeed his own behaviour had spard me that trouble, for he had thereby got in contempt almost with every Body

May 1st	Put a hook to our Lead[357] & brought up two very good fish which are common here upon the bank & resemble Haddocks. A bad wind at N W which it continued till the 4th

– 4   wind at S b E. Great Currents to the South west.

– 5   wind at S E b E moderate weather, See vast flocks of pintada[358] birds, Alcatrazes[359], silverbirds[360], littrells[361], &c but no Garnets[362]. The people are dissatisfyd with their allowance of Pork & brought some pieces on Deck to show complaining they had not their Allowance, suspecting I suppose the steward, I desird the Captain to tell them that this way of theirs was not to be sufferd to come so in a body that if they had any complaints to make they were to send their complaint in an orderly manner by the Boatswain, & it should be examind & if injustice were done them they should have redress, He accordingly reprimanded them pretty smartly, to do him justice of late he has been pretty good how long he may continue so is hard to tell, I desird him also for the peoples satisfaction to send for the future always an officer to be present to see their Allowance weigh'd & justice done them.

– 6   wind contrary again at N W & W N W a fresh gale & Cold, see two ships bound to the Eastward Crowding with all their sail, our people say they take their Colours to be English, they are outward bound, but as it is not our business with any ships at sea we continue our

258

May 7th	Course and take no notice of them. Same bad wind, A vast number or Pintado Birds follow the ship & are very voracious, the boys catch many of them with a pin baited with pork

– 8   Wind at E. After sunset see under orions Girdle a star darting up from it a long trail of rays, It is small & less than those of orions Girdle but has a long tail & must be a Comet[363], which we should have seen clearer were it not for the moon light,

---

[357] Refers to the lead weight suspended on a line used to take soundings of the depth of water.

[358] *Pintado* (Portuguese *pintado*, literally 'painted'), a species of petrel, *Daption capensis*, also called *Cape pigeon*.

[359] English *alcatras, alcatrace* (Spanish and Portuguese *alcatraz* 'pelican'), applied loosely to sea mews and allied birds.

[360] *Silver bird*, some East Indian bird.

[361] Unidentified bird. In some English dialects *titterel* is used for 'whimbrel', *Numenius phaeopus*.

[362] For *gannets*; cf. *Diary* p. 254 and note 355.

[363] Hitherto this comet had never been registered. According to the Dutch geographer Nicolaus Struyck, a comet was observed by three ships cruising in the vicinity of the Cape in May 1733: from the *Ypenroode*, the *Spiering* and the *'t Hof niet altyd Zomer*, but without precise location or description. Apparently the comet was seen just once from each of the three ships, while Campbell's *Diary* reports four observations and situates the comet in Orion, giving at the same time the position of the *Fredericus Rex Sueciæ*. The comet has now been registered at the Smithsonian

it being now the 6th day of the moon. When we first saw the Comet it was about 8 at night, in South Latitude by Account 34.23 & Long. 1.12. W^t from C. Good Hope & at noon by obs. Lat. 34.31. Long. 1.7.

– 9   Wind at S.E & fine weather & no swell. By my late regulations I find a saving of 101 kans last week, but all that wont be sufficient to inable us to push on to Gottenburg without a new supply, which I would fain do to save time. We had from Princes Islands of water in all 44 Tun in Casks or   [364] Gallons & find it is now half out. I have also savd in our own Expence by bringing the SuperCargos to drink Tea or Coffy only now & then & not every day as before, which I believe is not much to their liking, but that there is no help for.

– 11 & 12th   Same wind as before now & then shifting a little. We see still wast[365] number of Birds same as before mentiond & also some Cape hens, a bird as big as a hen & flys or flutters with its wings as a hen dos and I suppose is therefore calld so, seen no where but near the Cape. See the Comet again It has marchd a great way up since we saw it last night with its tail still darting upwards or to the Meridian, to give a clearer Idea of it I here set down its appearance at different times.

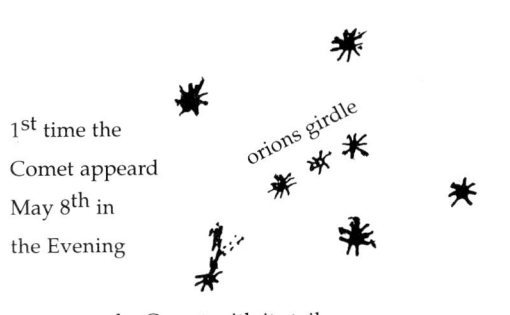

1st time the Comet appeard May 8th in the Evening

the Comet with its tail

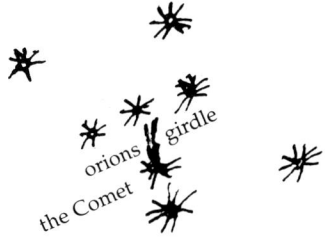

2^d time we see the Comet May 11th in the Evening

It made a sort of Mangle in this manner with the two lowermost large stars of orion & had got up near halfway between them and the Girdle
Its Course from South to North

Astrophysical Observatory (Cambridge, Mass.) as *Comet 1733 K1 (Koninckx-Vanouplines)*. (Koninckx & Vanouplines 1994, 1995; Koninckx, Vanouplines & Marsden 1995; Tullberg 1995.)
[364] Campbell has left a blank.
[365] *Sic*, for *vast*.

We could not see the Comet the 12th for Clouds nor the 13th for the bright moon-shine

May
– 14th
– 15

See the Comet again above all the stars of orions Girdle & near as high as the highest star of orion. the 15th had enough ado to see it on acc^t of the bright moons shine but could perceive a great way above the highest star of orion

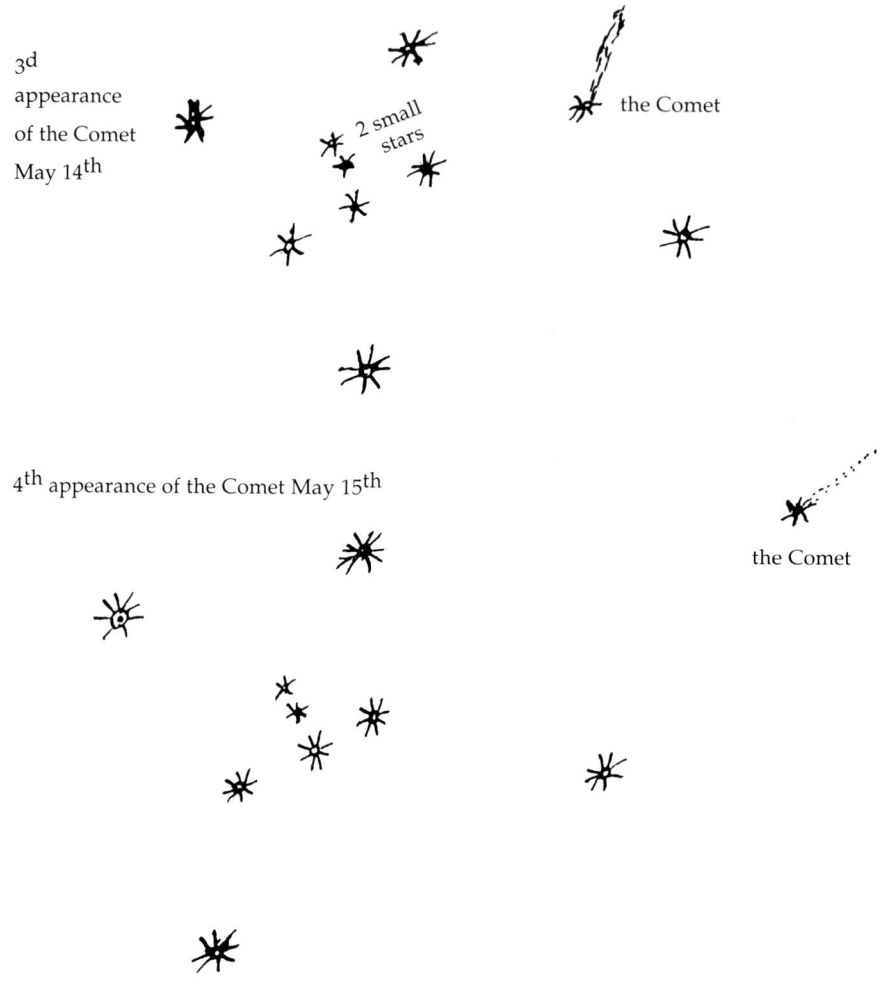

3^d
appearance
of the Comet
May 14th

2 small stars

the Comet

4th appearance of the Comet May 15th

the Comet

After the 15th we saw it no more I could have wishd for Instruments aboard to have taken its different Altitudes & distance run at different times but there was no such thing aboard

– 15.

Squally wind W. for some days wind & weather has been very variable from N to W & sometimes Calm

Scientific representation of Comet C 1733/K 1:
calculated positions during May 1733.

– 17   in the Evening had an Eclipse of the Moon, It begun at 50 m. after 5 Its greatest obscuration was at 7.27. L.M & emersion at 9.4. L.M was obscurd 10 digits. We have now the S. E. wind & I hope the settled Trade wind.

Being informd that Lieotenant Lund had a Custom to come upon the quarter Deck every night assoon as I left it & went to bed & went in

260

to the Captain as privately as he could, I was resolv'd to check this assoon as possible to prevent their caballing again against me, so got some of our people to come down & let me know the first time he walkd the Quarter deck, to night about 11 a clock being informd he was walking I went up, and he soon sneakd off, Finding the Captain there also I told him what I had heard & that I hopd he would not incourage such a fellow to come to him from time, when he knew how ill he had behavd to himself as well as to me, and especially now that I had suspended the Companys service & had positively orderd him never to come upon the Quarter decks but to his meals (for I allowd him still to Eat at the 2^d Table) that however I might bear with faults against me yet I would not overlook those committed against the voyage or the Comp^{ys} Service. He denyd that he had been in his Cabbin but that he sometimes call'd for a dram which he orderd his Boy to give him, Though I knew this to be false and that Lund not only was sometimes with him privately, but that he & the Priest were often together & kept a close intimacy with Lund as had been constantly their Custom, & that the Captain imployd a parcel of people as spys to follow me about to hear what I sayd to any of the officers &c particularly one Nyman an Idle Good for nothing Boy whom I had allowd him as an Apprentice, I upon this gave him my opinion & advice for the Good of the Comp^y & for his own Interest, without caring to enter too close into particulars, He then began to talk about people perswading him at Stockholm against the voyage by reason of some forreign officers that he was told were to come aboard &c As I had been often plagued with such discourse before, I was resolvd to put an end to this sort of discourse, & told him that he might be assurd we knew our Interest so well that we would always imploy such people as understood the India navigation, no matter whether Swedes or forreigners for we would not trust our fortunes in the hands of Ignorant people & more to the same purpose, which made him put on his sour Countenance, though without any reply. His reason no doubt for indeavouring to keep well with Lund & the Priest is because they having been long his Chief Counsellours are acquainted with all his secret caballings & have it in their power to discover his rogueries.

May 22 Peter Bartz one of our best seamen dyd, He was bruisd by a fall some time & has wasted away ever since. The people begin to fall down in the scurvy, & I am afraid it will be fatal to many of them, for we have a poor Ignorant surgeon[366] a German who was very well recommended at Stockholm, but not much the better for that, for he knows no more

261

than to bleed & shave, & make use of a pouder & pill in which all his skill I believe consists, but it is our misfortune that we have no better, for whenever any falls sick they are sure to dye, for none have yet ever recoverd under his Care nor do

---

[366] Many of the ship's doctors in the Swedish Company were foreigners, among them numerous Germans, as in the case of the *Fredericus R.S.* The situation was the same in the Navy. The fact that foreigners were engaged reflects a severe shortage of Swedish doctors, who themselves had frequently acquired their knowledge abroad. Although foreigners filled the gaps, this did not mean that their professional skill was of the highest standard, as also appears from Campbell's account. Few of them were actual doctors of medicine. There seems to be no evidence of examinations, but presumably there would have been committees capable of testing before making appointments. It was then possible to advance in due course from third and second surgeon to first surgeon, as they were generally called. Although there was no difference between the wages paid to a first surgeon and those to a doctor, one may nevertheless suspect that there was still a difference in the level of training. (*Svenska flottans historia* ... 1942–55, 2, p. 275; Koninckx 1980b, p. 315 ff.)

I expect they ever will, He is afraid ever to give a vomit or a blister or even to bleed, without I speak to him of it, and then he tells me if I please to order it he will do it.

May 24th The Pintado Birds have accompanyd us hitherto, to day being in 17 d. of Latitude we expect to see St Helena[367] to morrow. Though I did all was possible to save our water, in order to go directly Home without touching any where, yet I find we cannot expose ourselves to such a risk as the want of water of which we have now but 18 Tun left on examination, so that I have consulted with our Super-Cargos & officers which will be the fittest place & least out of our way for getting a supply, and find the Island Ferdinando noronha[368] is the only proper place as being but a few days sailing westerly out of the ordinary tract, & there Baron who has been formerly there in the Ostend ships says there is plenty of water as well as Goats & Antiscorlutick[369] plants all which we stand in need of, so have resolvd to make directly for it, & not having seen the Cape of Good Hope think best to make St Helena in order to be more sure of lighting on the Island we want

Since leaving the Bank of the Cape we had examind some Chests of Green Tea which they had carelessly put forward & had been exposd to the waves of the sea that came in at the forecastle, we found only the Chests wet & the outer lead Covers but the Tea not damagd however gave them an Airing in the sun & took of[f] the papers that were damp & put on fresh papers, & have orderd them into the Gun room where they will not be exposd to Such an Accident, They are N°s 144, 125, 227, 214, 166 & 301.

The Captain is in one of his usual growling fits & has lockd himself up pretending to be sick, which I suppose is owing to my ordering up our Guns[370] that we had

---

367 On the home voyage, Swedish East Indiamen usually anchored off St. Helena or Ascension, since these islands lay on the normal route to Europe. The Swedes generally spent a week or slightly more at St. Helena, while the call at Ascension was shorter. Calling at St. Helena or Ascension had the same purpose as in the case of Fernando de Noroñha (see note 368). Although small and insignificant, Ascension enjoyed more attention from the Swedes than St. Helena, perhaps because the British were already established on St. Helena, whereas at Ascension supplies and drinking water were free. Ascension, moreover, was an uninhabited island with large numbers of sea-turtles, which offered a rich supplement to the shrinking food supply. Both islands were also of importance for correcting navigation, after having crossed the seas without observing any landmarks. (Koninckx 1985.)

368 *Fernando de Noroñha*, island in the Atlantic Ocean, where East Indiamen called, generally only on the home voyage, in order to replenish supplies and allow recuperation of those stricken by scurvy. It was on the detour to sail around the zone of the north-east trades, towards the American shores. During the first charter (1731–46) this port of call was used only twice on the return voyage, in both cases by the *Fredericus R.S.*, the first time during the present voyage, the second time in 1739. When calling at Fernando, it was the only stop during the Atlantic passage. Calling there was a detour, "out of the ordinary tract", as Campbell tells us.

369 *Antiscorbutic*, 'of use against scurvy'.

370 All Company ships were equipped with cannon, whose number varied roughly according to the size of the vessels. The number of cannon aboard the *Fredericus R.S.* must have been around

put down in the Hould to make the ship stiff in going round the Cape, I had spoke to him several times to get them up & to get our fire Arms in order in case of meeting with ships which we may expect to do very soon, Capt Kitching also had put him in mind of it which was enough of reason for him

262

not to do it such an incorrigible spirit of Contradiction he has, and gave a fine reason for not doing of it pretending there was not room in the Gun room to fill the pouder & there was time enough to get the Guns up, However I took this opportunity of his locking himself up (which is the greatest pleasure he can do for then we can do our business with ease, but when he is out upon Deck there is nothing to be done that any Body proposes till I give a positive order to have it done & see it immediately performd) to get them up & to get Cartridges filld, & to put the ship in proper order for fighting in case of need,

May 25th Early in the morning made the Island of St Helena, About 8 a clock A.M it bore W b N 6 leagues passing about 2 leagues from the Road we see their flag on Mundens fort[371], and 5 ships in the road, of which our people say 3 appear to be french by their Colours, but I cannot see them so distinctly as to affirm it, As I did not think proper to let them know any thing of us I passd without showing any Colours. At noon the middle of the Island bore S. b W 1/2 W 4 l. Sundry white Birds came off very like a Pigeon which are very common on the Rocks her & are calld St Helena pigeons.

Amongst other wise schemes of the Captains he proposd filling the Cartridges in the great Cabbin, & then putting them in the Lockers a stern, a place the most unfit in the whole ship not only on account of having candles there every night, but also being more exposd to accidents in case of an Ingagement, by which means the ship might be blown up if any shot light there, But this being like his mad projects I had no regard to his opinion.

---

twenty, by analogy with the data known from other expeditions of the same ship. The size of the vessels and Sweden's international political stance played an important role in the armament of the ships. Moreover, in the 18th century there was still reason to fear pirates. Laden with thousands of silver piastres or with rich cargoes of Oriental products the East Indiamen formed a tempting prey. Thus there is no doubt that guns were not carried merely for maritime purposes, such as fog and convoy signals, or for firing salutes to supercargoes, harbour authorities or other vessels encountered at sea. The battleworthiness of even the best-equipped East Indiaman should not be overestimated. Its clumsiness and its sail-plan as well as its smaller crew made rapid manoeuvres difficult. A medium-sized Company ship could overmaster a brig of war or corvette. It was no match for a larger frigate, so that it could be difficult to withdraw from engaging in battle. Company ships were after all merchant ships, not warships. During the voyage cannon were sometimes moved below deck to function as ballast and placed in the holds in order to increase the speed. When there was a risk of encountering enemies, the guns were moved to their proper places at the gunports, as Campbell tells us.

[371] The English East India Company dispatched a small force of troops and others to form a settlement on St. Helena in 1659. On New Year's Day 1673, the Dutch succeeded in capturing the island, but they were ejected the following May by an English force commanded by Sir Richard Munden.

I am ashamd of our SuperCargos M[orford] & P[ike] who are eternally sotting with Baron & now seldom come to supper sober, He is such an Incorrigible sot that he cant abstain from drinking even when he goes upon watch, having catch'd him more than once both drunk & asleep, & had room enough to have suspended him from his Charge had I any body of experience to supply his room

May 28th our fool of a Captain is now really sick, & considering what a quantity of liquour he daily drinks especially drams It is much how he can hold out, But he is usd to it. Had we 10 Tun of water more we might be able to go home without touching any where for we have enough of all sorts of provisions, except flower which was very much squanderd when we had the Dutch aboard, But

263

supposing we had water enough It would not be very safe to push Home without a new supply, considering that we may have bad winds & a long passage, & that if we dont touch at Ferdinando Noronho there is no other place we can go to nearer than Shetland, except the western Islands[372] which the winds will not always permit us to make, Indeed we could make Brasil but that is more out of the way than this Island & is likewise attended with great charge & many difficulties so that there is no going thither, so that we all are unanimous in opinion, to make for ferdinando Noronho, I hope a little stay of a few days there will be also of great service to our sick people who now fall down very fast of the scurvy, Indeed the Captain wisely sayd we had water enough, though he never took the trouble to make any examination about it, and is of opinion to push Home, but his opinion being only in contradiction to every Body else I have no manner of regard for.

June 2d Mr M[orford] came with a complaint against C. Kitching, that he had abusd him upon Deck, I sent for C. Kitching, and found that M[orford] had given him the provocation, & advisd them not to fall out before the Officers & people who would be very glad to find us quarelling amongst our selves. on the whole I find that M[orford] P[ike] & Baron are in a strict confederacy together, and desirous to mortify Kitching on all occasions, and I believe for two reasons 1st because they see I have more regard for him than their Governour Baron, as he well deserves being a Careful Capable officer and has the Companys service at heart more than any of them, but another very prevailing cause of disliking him is because he has not liquour enough to joyn with them in their drinking bouts

– 3d The Ships Cook complaind of the people abusing him, the Captain calld one of them forward & beat him, Another of them went directly in my presence to the Cook room door & fell a beating of the Cook, I orderd them to bring him forward but no body caring to do it Capt Kitching to go forward & bring him up, I orderd

---

372 I.e. *the Azores.*

him immediately to be tyd to a Gun & whippd, but our Quartermasters Ekstrom & Rudbeck being appointed to do it, only playd with him on which I reprimanded them, and as he was one who had been often ingaged in quarrells before I wanted to have him heartily whipt for an example to the rest, The Captain on this occasion behavd

264

better than usual & seeing the Quartermasters not much inclind to it, he took a Rope & struck Ekstrom & made him lay on a little better I took this Occasion to put him in mind to keep a strict command over the sailors & not to connive at their Insolence (as he usd to do) but when he saw them guilty of a fault that deservd punishment to give it them directly, without waiting the formality of a complaint & Examination &c As was his Custom, & then he thought it enough to call them all upon Deck & read the Articles of war to them which they no more regarded than if he had read an old Ballad to them. But I must say for the Swedish officers there is not one of them capable of any command or keeping the sailors to their Duty, except Breemer, for they make themselves so familiar with them that they can have no authority amongst them.

June 5   Another sailor dyd of the scurvy, Tore ostanson.

– 6   Baron who pretends to see further than any Body pretend[s] to see the Island we look for, & the Peak very plain, when I can discern nothing but Clouds, but he having made Account by his reckoning we must now see it he is very much affronted that I take his Land to be Clouds which I am afraid they will prove, & that we are not so near it as we fancy ourselves. But as he insists it must be so he has made his friends believe the same so that they are all preparing to kill the Doves & Catch whole shoals of fish.

– 7   no land though clear weather, I could not help taking notice of this to the sharp sighted Gentleman Baron, who now contradicts his former Account pretending by his meridian distance we should not see it yet though he told me the other day he was sure of it, but now he makes it 2 degrees more to the Eastward than it is layd down in the map, and we are even to the Westward of what it is layd down. But I find him such a positive contradictory Coxcomb that I have very little regard to what he says, He grows every day more proud & Insolent, and I find it necessary now & then to give him a small memorandum to make him learn to know himself a little better & to make him more modest if possible.

– 8th   at 1/2 an hour past 5 in the morning see the Island Ferdinando Noronho bearing W N W 5 or 6 leagues. A 1/2 an hour past 9 cast Anchor in the bay about 1/2 a mile from the shoar the high Peak bearing E 1/2 S. dist a mile the two high rocks by the ostend watring

214

place one bearing S W 1/2 S & the other S W b S 3/4 of a mile dist. The N E^t part of the Island N E b E (about which are 5 or 6 small Islands) 2 leagues, the N Westermost part S W 1/2 W 3 miles. Sent immediately our Long boat ashoar with Baron to see for water.

June 9th P.M. our Boat is come back with the melancholy news of no water to be found in the 2 watering places where the ostenders us'd to water, which discourages every Body very much especially the sailors who are a poor fainthearted people, The Captain seems to be glad of this opportunity to find fault as if it were our fault for coming so much out of the way to a place where we can have no supply, I was oblig'd to talk to him & to tell him we had done for the best and if it should so fall out that we found no water here, (which was no bodys fault for it was not in our power either to make rain or springs,) we must stay here as short while as we can & then make to some other place, in the mean time bringing every body to a short allowance, to which I would submit my self as much as the meanest sailor & I hopd every body else would do the same. But that I still was [of] opinion there must be water in some other part of the Island for which reason I would send morning early to search every where. Though they found no water in the place where the ostenders use to water which was a sort of small stream (or rather Channell as I found afterwards) made by the Rains which now might be dry occasiond perhaps by a great drought here for some time past, yet I concluded there must be water somewhere on the Island, upon account of several high Grounds & hills especially towards this side where we rode as also because there must be great rains sometimes in this Latitude so near the Line which no doubt must make streams & Channells in more places than one. Being of this opinion I thought best to order to get every thing ready for sending our sick ashore next day that they might have as much benefit of the Land & plants there as possible for the short time they might stay. In the morning early being not a little uneasy I got up & sent long boat & pinnace one to the W^t End the other to the East point to search for water About 10 a clock in the morning Baron returnd with the Joyful news of having found water to the Eastward & he hopd enough to fill all our Casks, where

he says there is also a good place for our sick there being a good quantity of purslane[373] thereabouts, We therefore fird a Gun for a signal to Capt Kitching to come aboard, who soon returnd but found no water to the Westward but brought aboard 9 Goats, there being a vast number all that way. I orderd the people therefore to dine early in order to send the sick ashore, and assoon as they [had]

---

[373] *Purslane*, a low succulent herb, *Portulaca oleracea*, widely distributed throughout tropical and warmer temperate regions, used in salads or for pickling, and especially as a remedy against scurvy.

dind I accordingly sent them with sails to make tents for them, & orderd C Kitching & the rest who went with them to look all along if they could see any more water

June 10th C. Kitching having landed our sick of whom we have a great many & very weak some of them being all troubled with the scurvy, He told us there was an appearance of water by digging of wells, but that what was found was but very little dropping from the Rocks and as it lay at so great distance from the ship it would cost us a great deal of time to fill all our Casks. He says that there are shoals of fish & great flocks of Doves by the watering place. In the night It raind pretty heavily which is a great blessing to us, though I am afraid the sick may have sufferd by it, we sent therefore the rest of our empty Casks ashoar, which Capt Kitching brought back full in the Evening, telling us that last nights rain has made water enough

– 11th Assoon as we had dind I order[d] the boats back again with more Casks And being desirous to go see what sort of a place it was where they had found the water, I resolv'd to go ashoar with them, which I did not care to do sooner while our best officers were ashoar & only Capt Trolle, & Lund & some of their Gang aboard who would be glad to make some disturbance in my absence, I therefore had desird the Captain yesterday to tell him that he might go ashore if he pleasd to take the Air, but he did not care to go, but now He & the Priest have thought fit to desire a leave to go ashore which they had granted them & are now gone. Seeing a great number of goats upon the strand, I went early in the morning just opposite where we ride and took Mr Graham with me with some firelocks & pounder & small shot to see what we could kill, we shot 30 odd Doves which are very fine Eating but the Goats were too cunning to stay for us. I having in the mean time desird C. Kitching to go & search under the peakd hill & that part of the Bay where they had seen a Gun & something like an old fortification, where no doubt the Portugueze

267

were formerly settled & where I thought most probably would be found the true watering place. I came aboard to dinner as did Kitching with an Account that about the E^t part of the Bay just under the hill where the old fort is he had seen a plentiful stream of water. I therefore resolvd assoon as I had dind to go & see it as well as the place where our sick were

June 12th I went alongst with Mr Graham & the Captain to where the sick were where I was {to} glad to find some of them much better, there being great store of purslane there which I orderd the Doctors mate to see boild for them every day in their soupe, we sent them besides Goats & kids, being to be found all over the Island & as good as any mutton the kid not inferiour to that at Madras & the Coast of Cormandel, They had also Doves in abundance & fish as many as they pleasd to catch with hook & Line. I find it a miserable place where our sick are upon the hot sand just under a Rock which makes it intolerable hot & but one tree thereabouts to shade them, & the water Baron boasted so much of nothing but drops from the Rock, so that all we get is by digging wells in the sand, which I doubt we shall find brackish. It is also very bad to land here being a great surf as indeed is every where on the Coast, & nothing but ridges of rocks to pass over to get ashoar, & the Casks must be towd through the surf by the Pinnace, with some difficulty there being many stones & small Rocks underwater. Being not at all satisfyd with this place I soon left it & cruisd all along the Bay under the Peak & near where the Portugueze fort was, could find no place to land at on account of a great surf but just at the point where Kitching spyd the stream directly under the Portugueze fort at the bottom of the Bay, & here it is dangerous landing enough, for one must jump on smooth slippery Rocks which are washd every moment by the surf so that one has enough ado to stand upon them or to craw[l] from one to another without being in danger of being washd off every moment. Here we found a fine clear stream running down from the hills above over stones & pebbles very plentifully, and a very pleasant place shaded with tall trees which I see no where else, & resorted to by abundance of Doves, Mr Graham & I took our fuzils[374] & walkd all along the Bay to look for Goats & Doves & shot some of both sorts. Here about the middle of the Bay we found

268

another small River or stream of fine clear water like the former, so that these are the proper places for watering, being very near the ship & where the Casks can be brought near the spring. In the morning early went ashore with Mr Graham to the place where the ostenders waterd which is very hard to come at on acc^t of the surf Here we found vast number of doves upon a Grove of small low trees that is there of which we shot above 50, went to view that watering place which was quite dry, being nothing but a small channell made by the rains that pour down from a very small rising ground & I suppose is only full after very frequent rains, And it is to be wonderd that the Ostend ships were never at the pains to look for a better watering place than this. We killd a Goat & wounded severals which run up amongst the low woods or shrubs, which are so strangely intangled together that we could not pass to pursue them. The water beginning to dry up at the place where the sick are I orderd them to fill for the future all our empty casks at the spring we found last out which was accordingly done. I desird Mr Maul & other of our people ashore to go up towards the Peak where you perceive a fine green flat appearing as if it had been formerly cultivated, & also to go up to the Portugueze fort to see what they could discover there.

June 13th sent several of our people to shoot Goats & Doves for our people especially the sick. Nyman left the Company ashore & went in the night overland to the place where the sick were, we could not tell what became of him till next morning fearing he

---

374 *Fusil*, a light flintlock musket.

might have fallen over the Rocks or wanderd some where out of the way. As there is such a quantity of Goats here who come at night down to the strand a little westward to sleep till morning, and that now it was time to think of leaving this place & pursuing our voyage, I resolvd first to take in {first} as good a stock of Goats for the voyage as we could, so orderd most of our officers & people ashoar very early in the morning to catch them, I did not care to leave the ship my self, there being no body on board but the Captain & Lund & the priest {&}[375] with 3 or 4 sailors. In 2 or 3 hours they came back with 50 live Goats & 14 they had shot, They found no difficulty to catch them there being several hundreds of them, no more to do than to surround them [so] that they could not run up the rocks. Having now so good a store of fresh provisions I orderd the Boats ashoar to bring all the people on board

269

that were a washing their linnen, & to fill the rest of our Empty Casks, Assoon as that was done I sent after dinner to bring all the sick on board in order to make sail in the Evening.

June 14th Having got all our people both sick & healthy aboard we unmoord at 10 at night, & at 12 left the Island with a fresh Gale at East. I shall describe what we could find in this Island.

Island Ferdinando Noronha calld so from a Portugueze that first discoverd it, lyes in 3.50 d.m South of the line about 100 leagues from the Coast of Brasil, & meridional distance from S[t] Helena 25.18 d.m. The Road we anchord in & the only place where ships can anchor here is on the East side of the Island a sort of open Bay where is there good depth of water (as pr Draught) & capacious enough to contain 40 or 50 sail well shelterd from the W & NW winds by the high hill & Peak over the Bay. On this side where we were the land rises from the shore pretty high especially the hill where the peak is which is a great height & rises like a steeple or a sugar loaff a great way above the hill & may be seen at sea at a great distance. Here it is all coverd over with small bushes & shrubs so intangled that there is no passing through them without cutting ones way through them for which one ought to have large knives or such Instruments as they use in the West Indies for the same purpose, some of these shrubs grow pretty high & make of themselves natural Arbours which might be easily improvd to fine shady walks & Alleys, Going up to the Peak the Ground is more clear of those shrubs a little way up where it appears very green & to have been formerly tilld, and there probably were the Plantations of the Portugueze it lying so near the little hill where their fort was & much the best spot of ground on this side. There are amongst these shrubs one with prickles which raises blisters the moment you touch it as

---

[375] The words *their Gang* have been crossed out here, and probably *&* should have been deleted as well.

I felt & many others by Experience, a number of Creepers that trail all along the ground with a broad leaf like a Dock, & which also creep up the trees & help to form these Arbours, There is another Creeper has a leaf like that of the Banian tree[376] which bears a purple bell flower, There is the thistle calld　　　[377] with a large red fruit

270

like an apple growing over all the Rocks, There are several low trees not known to me, I saw also some Banian trees. Mr Graham also saw bees & honey combs upon some of the Trees. All near the shore are vast quantities of Land Crabs which we met climbing up in the Evenings to the tops of the Rocks and come down in the morning to the sea, they burough[378] in the ground in holes which they dig, It is an ugly Creature with a large Belly & not good to eat, for its belly is full of nothing but durt[379] & Earth which I believe they eat sometimes though the Claws taste well enough, our sailors however boild them & eat them daily. Vast shoals of fish all along the strand where one might with a seine catch multitudes, & as many as you will with hook & line, Sharks we saw close by the strand & Dog fish all round the ship which run away with our hooks & lines so that we could catch none, We catchd Rock fish, old wives[380], & many others whose names I know not as not frequenting our seas, there is a pretty little short fish like a Trout of a Gold Colour, & a flat fish very beautiful with blew & Gold streaks, such as what we eat at Onrust in Batavia Road, per[i]winkles & Conger Eells all which tasted very well, There are also sword fish but we catch'd none. Some of the people that were up the Peak say they saw Beans in the bloom & several sorts of Trees, & on the other side of the hill a fine low Country, whic[h] confirms me in the opinion that hereabouts the Portugueze had their settlement being just under the Cannon of the fort & in view of the ships in the Bay. Mr Maul went up to the Portugueze fort where he found 2 long Iron Guns of 12 pounders & 2 more of 6 pounders eat up with rust, At the bottom of the same hill we saw also one of 6 pounders upon a rock at the turning in to the watering place which seems to have been plac'd there on purpose with its muzzle to the sea to defend the Entry of the Bay against Boats or other small Craft, A little from the old fort more in land are the ruins of a stone rampart　　　[381] foot high which has been for a battery of Guns it lying convenient to defend the road as well as the other small bay to the Eastward where our sick were, It is in the form of a half moon & overlooks both the Bays, on the other side of the Country he saw several low lands like pasture ground with small rivers emptying themselves into the sea on the N. side of the Island. for other Remarks vide Account to the College of Commerce.

---

[376] *Banyan* or *banian*, a moraceous tree, *Ficus benghalensis*, of tropical India and the East Indies, having aerial roots that grow down into the soil forming additional trunks. (Lewis 1991, p. 59 f.)
[377] Campbell has left a blank.
[378] *Burrow*.
[379] *Dirt*.
[380] *Oldwife*, any of various fishes, especially the menhaden or the alewife.
[381] Campbell has left a blank.

June 20th The S.E Trade has kept to us since we left Ferdinando Noronha, It now begins to shift with squally dark weather

– 22   Wind at N.E.

– 23   dyd one of our sailors Swen Anderson

– 24   last 2 days Calms & little winds run but 4 m these last 24 hours. variable winds & small Gales & most at S.W. till the 26th

– 26   Still variable & winds as yesterday. the day before being St Johns day & that we were becalmd, Capt Kitching proposd to have the ship cleand on the outside,³⁸² which the Captain would not permit by reason of its being a great holy day, though at the same time to show his Devotion for the Saint he took care to get drunk before night, & has been sick ever since & now to our Comfort has lockd himself up in his Cabbin, so that now we can do the ships business without his being in the way to hinder. I therefore told C. Kitching to fall about it next morning if weather permitted without speaking to the Fool about it.

– 28th   weather being favourable, Kitching set the people to Clean & scrape the ship (it being very foul) this brought the Captain out upon Deck, but he soon returnd to his Cabbin with a very grim sour Countenance, angry no doubt that we can do anything without his asistance.

– 30th   Being informd by Mr Pike that he had not got above 11 or 12 Gallons out of a Cask of Arrack which held 23 Gallons, the ships steward pretending it had leakd out, I was resolvd to inquire a little into it, having had some reasons to suspect him before about some he had given out to the people, All I could find out was that the Cooper³⁸³ was call'd to look upon it & he had mended it finding it a little wet, which he supposd was only draind through the wood it being a new Cask, But as I could not prove the thing against the steward, I orderd his mate (who is an honest man) to look well after every thing which he promis'd. This examination has very much offended the Captain & I believe not without reason, for if the steward is guilty of any Roguery this way, the Captain must be concernd in it, what makes me the more suspect this is that he is every day drunk with punch from morning to night, and he has had none of his own Arrack left for some time past.

---

³⁸² Weather permitting, the jolly-boat was lowered and attempts made to clean the hull as far as possible from deposits.
³⁸³ The cooper and his mate were in charge of the barrels, casks and hogsheads.

July 1st Another Cause of offence to our fool of a Captain is that he sees our top sails out. He is a strange loitering wretch, is always for making little sail, He dos not care how long the voyage is, as his wages will always run on[384] & that is the only thing he has a regard to, Another cause of his shortening sail is his Cowardice for he never sees a small Cloud in the Heavens but he is quite freightend & immediately usd to call to reef our sails till I was obligd to interpose & order often the contrary, notwithstanding of having made almost now the voyage yet he has not learnd the difference between sailing in these Climates & a fast Trade wind and Sailing in the N Sea & towards Greenland which he often quotes & such places as are exposd to variable winds. His Cowardice & Ignorance is so ridiculous, that sometimes when he sees the Cats playing with the ropes he falls into a Panick fear & bawls out to reeff the sails & down top Gallant sails, &c being sure of a storm as he says because the Cat has assurd him so by playing with the Ropes, He then takes particular notice of what Ropes the Cats play with then the storm must come of Course from that quarter, therefore down with the sail that Rope goes to.

The Captain comes to tell me that the oyl for the peoples victuals is almost out, As they have had no stockfish[385] for a long time I could not conceive what he meant & askd him what it signifyd to the people whether there was oyl or not since they had no stockfish, He told me he gave it them to their Rice & Caravancas, I could not [but] be surprizd at such a new unheard of needless Expence; & askd him how he came to think of giving oyl to Rice & Caravancas, He allegd it was their Custom (though they nor he I believe had never eat Rice or Caravancas in their lives before) and that the Comp^y allowd it, I told him the Comp^y allowd oyl for stockfish when the butter was out & for nothing else, but as there was Lard[386] in the ship if they likd it they might have it, that he told me he allowd them to their Caravancas but it was not good for Rice & more such nonsense, so that I was obligd to tell him that if they did not like it with Lard they might eat their Rice dry if they pleasd. He is a strange fellow for introducing new precedents, which he dos whenever the caprice takes him till

I am obligd to force him to a little better order.

July 3^d The Captain pretends to be sick and cant drink Tea this morning, This he has done more than once, and the true reason I found to be because he likd hot punch better for assoon as I had done drinking Tea, his boy carry'd off the Tea kettle with

---

384 Since it could not be predicted how long a voyage to the East Indies would last, supercargoes, officers and crew remained in service and were paid until the ship was back in Gothenburg. The longer the voyage lasted, the more the wages were multiplied.

385 Dried cod, which was normally eaten three times a week.

386 Sources concerning solid victuals always make a distinction between salt meat and lard or salt pork. Salt pork has a higher caloric value than salt meat: 3.5 cal. per gram against 2 cal.

the water to make him Punch. To morrow being the Queens nameday I orderd a Hog to be killd for the Ships Comp^y.

– 4   hoisted our Colours at sunrise for honour of the Queens day, & at 11 a clock we met upon Deck & drank to her Majestys healths & got officers & under officers to do the same giving them a small intertainment, and a dram extraordinary for the ships Comp^y & in the evening made a Tub of punch for them. As I hate the mirth of firing Guns, & more than ever since I had so much of it with the Dutch, I thought better & for some other reasons to let that ceremony alone. Indeed I could have wishd he would as he often promisd [have] usd our people a little to firing of Guns in order to exercise them for an occasion if we should be obligd to it, but never could get him yet once to do it. The Trade wind continues very fresh, & fine cool moderate weather though the sun is just over our heads.

– 8th Having after I went to bed heard a noise upon Deck and Mr Pikes voice above all the rest, I was curious next morning to know the reason, & sent for Mr Moir whose voice I had also heard in the dispute, After some difficulty he told me that Pike without any provocation had given him ill language & amongst other expressions sayd he was a Rogue as all his Countrimen were (meaning Scotsmen) Baron having been witness too I sent for him who declard the same, This being spoke before the Captain & some of the officers in such a publick place, and designd in all appearance against me chiefly, I could not help taking notice of it in order to check his Insolence which had now grown to too great a height, owing to my suffering him so long for his Brothers sake[387], I calld him into the Cabbin with the SuperCargos & Moir & Baron, who ownd what he sayd which he denyd & then he begun to prevaricate & pretend he was talking about King James the first & I can't tell what

274
other incongrous stuff, I then told him my mind very freely, and that though I would not treat him aboard as he deservd yet I should put him in mind at a proper time & place ashoar, He pretended he did not mean me I being a Swede (a naturalizd one he meant) I told him that ridiculous distinction should not save him, and that he must be a mighty Hero to quarrell with a whole nation, that he ought to know there were other Scotsmen aboard besides me, who I did not doubt would ask him the reason for his Impudence, as I know the Scots generally to be people that wont willingly affront others without provocation yet wont easily put up an Affront. I told him likewise that he ought to have rememberd that there were at least 2 Scotsmen on board who had indeavourd to do him service & requird better requital from his hands, He sayd he knew no Scotsman he was obligd to, I then could not help putting him in mind that at his desire Mr Graham

---

[387] See note 299 above.

& [I] had let him have money in China at 10 p^r C^t less than others would have given us, He replyd to that if we did not care to give it we could have let it alone. I askd him if there was any thing he could complain of which put him into so perverse an humour, He replyd many things, that there was no respect shown him, and was ridiculous enough to quote 2 Instances one was, that my servant had once put a finer napkin on the Table for me & Mr Graham than for him, and another time he had no Tea spoon set before him for his Tea, I could not help smiling at these tokens of want of respect & told him I gave no orders to the servants to make any distinction amongst us, though I thought if any was to be made I had the best right to it but very much undervalued such Triffles, as for the Tea spoons they were all my own, & how they came to omit giving him one the day he mentiond I don't know, This is only a specimen to show what a poor wretch he is, I must say I never was so long in bad Company as I have been aboard this ship, nor never sufferd so much Impertinence, choosing rather to do so than expose forreigners to the Swedes or anywise obstruct the voyage. In the Evening he & Baron & Morford got very drunk[388] (which now is their daily practice since we left Ferdinando Noronha there being plenty of water for them) so that going up after supper I found Baron on his watch fast asleep & dead drunk, I orderd {to} Breemer to wake him I put him in mind how often I had found him in this condition & that I would suffer it no longer, But he could make no answer not being able

to speak stand or go

July 17th To morrow being the Kings Name day, I orderd a hog to be killd for the ships Comp^y. Our people are daily falling down sick of the scurvy, nor do I see any remedy for them till they come ashoar, Perceiving this distemper once got amongst them I spoke to the Captain to indeavour to perswade them to an alteration of Diet & to eat more Rice sago[389] & Caravancas & less salt Beef & Pork, but especially to give no salt victuals to any of them once they fall sick which he usd to allow before, but for those in health he dos not like coming in to my opinion, supposing perhaps I do it only to save the meat, which is extremely foolish. I order wine & sugar also for the sick or any thing else the surgeon thinks fit for them. Provided they will alter their Diet I am willing to promise to give them on their Return the value of the Beef & Pork spard by it.

– 18th kept the Kings birth day in the same manner as the Queens

---

[388] That even the supercargoes got drunk and that this, as Campbell tells us, was a daily practice since the *Fredericus R.S.* left Fernando, shows that the length of the voyage was beginning to affect everyone among the crew.

[389] *Sago* is a sort of meal obtained from the pith of the sago palm. Sago was very often part of the official home cargo of Swedish East Indiamen. (Savary des Bruslons 1759–65, 4, p. 615; Lewis 1991, p. 205.)

– 19   The Captain instead of helping me to preserve the peoples Lifes & healths, he has taken the quite contrary method & all he could contrive to destroy them, for he has made them believe that Rice & Caravancas give them the scurvy, & that salt Beef & Pork can do them no hurt but is much better for them, and though I had orderd them a dram of Arrack each man that comes on watch in the night from 8 at night to 4 in the morning yet find (out of a spirit of contradiction he has not done it) so that I was obligd to send for the steward my self & order him to do it every night, I told him & C. Kitching also to keep the people constantly imployd, for their Idleness (which the Captain has always incouragd) contributes as much to their scurvy as any thing else, & to see that they wash & sent[390] themselves daily & keep as sweet & clean as possible, for they like wallowing in Dirt. As he incourages them in every thing bad for them, so now they refuse to take their Physick telling the surgeon that they will complain to the Captain when he presses them to it, and when he gives them any thing then he bullys him for not advising with him first so that the poor fellow dos not know what [to] do with them, This I have long ago warnd the Captain of not to meddle in things he knows nothing of, but all advice to him is thrown away.

– 22   Now instead of giving one dram as I orderd he has given the night watch 2 drams out of a spirit of perverseness, so that I am every moment oblige[d] to look after every thing & redress his contradictions & Insolence.

276

July 23ᵈ   Now the Captain has perswaded the people not to eat any Rice, for to night they would not take it when it was dressd for them, and he tells me the reason is because they have neither oyl nor butter to it, he knows we have no oyl in the ship & not butter enough for [our] own Table. I could not help opening my mind to him a little on this subject & told him I knew very well that the people were not so much to blame, as some others whose business it was to act more for their Good, who had instilld such absurd notions in their mind that Rice & Caravancas gave them the Scurvy, He sayd he knew no body had given them any such impression, I assurd him I knew very well how it was & that they should answer it if it pleasd God to return us safe to Gottenburg, I desird him once more to speak to the people to allow the taking off two days of the week Beef & Pork & taking Rice Caravancas Pudding & sago in place of it, He pretended to go speak with them but brought back for an Answer that they had eat no rice yesterday & that they would not eat it to day, I saw he was playing the fool with me & was informd besides that he had sayd publickly upon Deck that we gave Rice & Caravancas to the Hogs[391] & that it was not fit for the men & would give them the Scurvy, I could not help therefore [at] table coming over the affair again &

---

[390] For *scent*.
[391] East Indiamen always embarked live animals on both the out voyage and the home voyage, to be slaughtered whenever fresh meat was wanted. (Koninckx 1980b, pp. 370–372.)

asking how any Body could be so silly as to talk so ridiculous nonsense, He took it to himself and sayd he had not sayd so, I then put him in mind of what he sayd before us all lately He turnd it off by saying that Doctors were of that opinion, I told him I could not tell what Doctors he meant for I am sure our Doctor was not of his opinion; He replyd the Doctors of Sweden were of that opinion, I could not help smiling & telling him that the Doctors did not know what Caravancas were not so much as the name nor had ever seen any of them. finding him such a Brute that instead of indeavouring to preserve the peoples health he did all he could to the contrary, meerly as far as I could see out of a spirit of contradiction to me, but as this was an Affair of consequence which gave me no small uneasiness I was resolvd to redress it as well as I could; so next morning sent for him & the officers that had been usd to such voyages to consult how to preserve those that had not yet fallen down, though they

July 24

277

seem almost all to droop, we all concluded there was no better method than to give them less meat & more Rice & Caravancas in place of it, The Doctor was of the same opinion, The Captain had not yet spoke a word, so I askd him what he thought of all this, & put him in mind of his saying that Hogs eat Rice &c & was not fit for men because it gave them the Scurvy, by the same Rule I told him they ought not to eat Beef or Pork because Cats & Dogs eat it, He denyd all that he had repeated a hundred times on this subject and sayd it was only reasoning & that the Doctours thought so, I repeated to him that the Doctours in Sweden could not be of that opinion since they did not know what Caravancas were, He then impudently replyd it was the Doctours of Denmark who were of that opinion, I then askd our Surgeon if oyl was good for them he sayd that he thought not nor vinegar, & that they usd too much of both, & help'd to thicken their blood too much, I had no further patience with our Fool of a Captain, but told him since I found that he either would not or could not perswade the people to a proper Diet, I would go my self & talk to them & see what I could do, for I found I could not trust him any more, the surgeon sayd they would gladly eat Rice provided they could get a little sugar to it, and we were also of opinion that to give them a little more punch from time [to time] might do them Good, I therefore went directly upon the Quarter Deck & assembled the ships Company on the main Deck in presence of the Captain & all our officers, I told them (in such Swedes as I was master of) that I was very sorry to see so many sick of the Scurvy amongst them, and that I had considerd how to help them & for that purpose had consulted the Surgeon & all the Gentlemen & officers that had been these voyages before, and that we were all of opinion that nothing could preserve those that were yet free of this distemper but to retrench at least two meals of a week of meat & to eat Rice & Caravancas in the room of it, which I assurd them was not proposd from any view of saving so much meat of which we had enough, but intirely for their own Good, & to convince them the more of this I promis'd them that on their safe return to Gottenburg to give them all the meat that would be so sav'd or the value

225

of it if they pleasd, And besides Each of them should now have a pound of sugar which they might take with their Rice or do what they pleasd with, at the same time acquainting them that this was

not designd by way of allowance but a free Gift I made them, and in order to incourage them the more to aggree to this, I promisd them a Tub of Punch on all those days they did not eat meat, all which would occasion a greater expence to the Company than all that could be Savd by the meat, I askd them if they wanted any thing whether Bread water &c. They seemd all extremely well satisfyd & very thankful, & sayd they did not want more bread or any thing else, I then sent the surgeon amongst [them] to inculcate what I had advisd, & He brought me for answer that they were sensible they had more meat than they could digest, & were well pleasd to abstain from it & eat it but thrice a week & all the other days Rice & Caravancas in lieu of it. For it must be confessd they eat oftener Beef & Pork than they ought to have done for their health, having one or other once every day in the week, which regulation was advis'd by our officers in China for saving of our water of which Rice & Caravancas make a very great Consumption especially their way of feeding for they must have both swimming always in water Mr Graham was more earnest than any body for this bad regulation, for the reason above mentiond & for another because it was the way in English ships to which he had been usd, But I must say the Dutch & our own Swedish regulation (being much the same) is a much better Diet against the Scurvy than the English, for they allow them a great deal of Grout Rice & Caravancas & such like which being easy of digestion & free of salt must certainly be better for their health than meat. Seeing the people so easy with my proposal to them, as to do them justice they are apt enough to follow what I recommended being perswaded I believe that what I advise is only designd for their own Good, but this I say confirmd me in the belief I had that the Captain never had spoke to them as I desird him but on the contrary had indeavourd before hand to set them against their own Good because it was my opinion, for the fellow has no manner of regard to their welfare, but would easily sacrifice that & what is more wonderful even his own Interest to his cursed perverse humour & desire of thwarting me & every forreigner aboard. He stood by all the while I was speaking to them but did not open his mouth but lookd like a Criminal going to be hangd, which would be his fate if he met with his desert. Had he done as I advisd in time many of their lives might have been savd, which he has no manner

of regard for, which with many other signs I have had makes me assurd that he is no Swede at least in his heart which is all for Denmark where he servd at sea in the late war against Sweden, though he pretends to be born in Sweden. To do the people Justice they are very submissive & tractable, & easily perswaded by reason to any thing, their greatest fault is indolence & laziness, which I believe is also much owing to their officers who have no life nor spirit themselves & don't know how to raise it in others, for we see that in the Dutch English & other services they make good officers & good seamen, They have other good qualities which is seldom seen amongst sailors of other nations that they are not at all wicked or much addicted to any vice nor quarrellsome nor mutinous.

July 25.
Anders Ambiormsen sailor dyd of the scurvy. Looking over last weeks Consumption (as I do always the first day of the week after) I found that the sick as well as those in health had their drams of Arrack continually, which I could not think very proper for some of them, which made me send for the steward to ask the reason, He told me they constantly sent to him for it & sometimes by 2 or 3 different hands to see if they could impose upon him & get more than their Allowance, And as I had orderd him to give the sick whatever the Doctor should think proper for them he had continued to give them their drams by his Direction, I then askd the Doctour how he could incourage such a wrong practice, He ownd that he did [not] believe drams were fit for them all, but that they were all usd to it, & should he have forbid it they would all cry out upon him, I advisd him to have more regard to their health than to any thing they could say against him, but to act according to his own knowlege & Conscience in a Case of that consequence. This made me also order the steward to give neither more sugar or drams to any of the sick but such as the surgeon thought it proper, being afraid that for the sake of drams & sugar, there would be more of them would perhaps pretend to be sick, & leave very few to work the ship.

Augt 1.
Swen Nilson saylour dyd of the scurvy.

– 3^d
All that I can do there is no curing the beast of a Captain of his perverse humour, now he has fallen foul of the Doctor & steward the first because he pretends to prescribe or call for any thing to

280

the sick without first consulting of him, & with the Steward because he pretends to give the Doctor what he requires for the sick though he had my orders for it, They both now complain of him, the Doctour says he generally tells him first before he demands any thing for the sick (which is more than he needs do) and then he flys in a passion & abuses him, I told them both to have no regard to his passion or humours but to do their Duty & follow my orders and that I would protect them against his insolence. The wretch seems to have a pleasure in their Death & sickness, for he never comes near me [but] when he has the news to tell me of a mans being dead, & then is sure to bring a long list of the rest that are sick to read to me, though I know it but too well as well as he dos. nothing gives him greater pleasure than to see anything fall out cross to obstruct the voyage or make me uneasy.

Augt 8	See a ship to Leeward, being willing to speak with her, I bore a little higher up & show'd our Colours, But as she showd Dutch, we went again our right course, we had seen her the day before at a distance.
– 9th	Lay by all night & next morning saw the orkney Islands.[392]
– 10	See several small ships, I fird a Gun & put up English colours to a sloop that was nearest us to come & speak with us, she hoisted English Colours, and as we were becalmd I sent Capt Kitching on board to inquire after news & to try if he could get any fresh provisions from her, He returnd in a little time & reported that she is from Dublin bound to Gottenburg.
– 11	in the morning being in sight of the Passage between orkney & Shetland see a large ship to leeward edging towards us, we showd Swedish Colours & they Ostend, being the ship from ostend that was in China while we was there & passt the Straits [of] Sunda when we were at Batavia, we spoke together they askd us news about our leaving Batavia &c find they had put in to St Helena, however we have saild much better or had better fortune than they to be here assoon, the SuperCargo Mr Ley would willingly have me go on board, but I refusd it, telling him I had no time to lose but was resolvd to make the best of my way Home, So went on our Course they saluted us with 7 Guns we returnd them 8 and in a little time afterwards it grew squally & we lost Sight of them.

our Priest who has on many occasions shown his proud rebellious temper did to day abuse very grossly Mr Ross our purser while he was taking

281

account of a sailors Effects lately dead, & pretended to hinder{d} him, He being in Drink (which he had got with Lieotennant Lund as is often their custom together) I did not think worth while to speak to him at that time but sent one of the mates Breemer to him to advise him to carry himself with more decency, & not to meddle in things that did not belong to him, He answerd very saucily to Breemer & then went upon Deck and repeated his gross language to Mr Ross, However I thought fit to take no notice of it till next morning that I hop'd he would be sober, & accordingly sent my servant to desire him to speak with me, He refusd to come, I then sent Breemer to him on the same message but to no purpose, for he sayd he had nothing to do with me and would not come to me, I did not think proper

---

[392] Just as in the case of the voyage out, in the final stage there were two possibilities of crossing the North Sea to sail to Gothenburg. The first way was to run up the Channel; the second was the northabout passage around Scotland. During the first and second charters of the Swedish Company, 22 of the 34 ships sailed through the Straits of Dover, while only twelve chose the northerly route around Scotland, taking the passage between the Orkneys and the Shetlands. The northabout route was also chosen by the Ostenders, the Dutch and the Danes, making it easier to sail to their respective home ports.

(being so near Home & the people being so sickly) to confine him as he deserv'd, but being resolv'd to make him repent his bad conduct on our return, I desird the Captain & Breemer & the steward who had seen & heard what passt to give me the report of it signd.

– 12th After dinner see a yawl from Fair Isle[393] at a good distance making all the speed she can to come up with us, As probably he has some fresh provisions & fish to sell, we were obligd to bring to that they might be able to come up with us. He brought us nothing but fish, and was very desirous of old Cloaths I gave him some money & old Cloaths & dismissd him

– 14 From fair Island between Shetland & Orkney we had a fine N W wind till to day it has shifted to E.S.E with thick hazy weather, so that we are not able to beat up against it. Our people are now so sickly that there are not above 8 well enough to handle the sails most of whom are Boys[394], so that the officers complain we cannot keep the sea nor pursue our voyage without more hands I therefore calld the SuperCargos & officers to consult what was best to be done, They were of all[395] opinion that we must put in for the first Port of Norway we can find. I therefore orderd them to bear away for the land, It being very thick & hazy could not see it though very near it so fird a Gun for a pilote to come off which they are very ready to do all alongst this Coast, I was obligd to fire thrice at last came a Boat with a Pilote who carryd us into one of the vilest Ports on the whole Coast, calld Swin óe[396] on the N side of the Naes[397] which we would fain have weatherd but could not, Here we thought to have put an unfort

282
-unate end to the voyage, had not God Almighty asisted us, and sent in with us an English ship bound from Dublin for Dram[398] on the Coast of Sweden not far from Frederickshall[399], whom we had spoke with in the morning, & he not knowing the Coast & being bound almost the same way as we askd our advice & we desird him to follow us, & took in one of the Pilotes that came on board us, our Pilote set us on a Rock in the harbour under sail, Hearing the ship strike we concluded she would be soon in pieces, But finding by the Pump that she made no water we tryd all ways we could to hall[400] her off, The other Pilotes ashoar seeing the danger we were in came off to asist us with several hands with their olderman (a great villain at the head of them) we sent also to the Dublin man to

---

393 Between the Orkneys and the Shetlands.
394 It seems that the boys, the youngest members of the crew, were mostly saved from scurvy.
395 *Sic*, for *all of*.
396 *Svinøy*, 15 km northeast of Lindesnes.
397 The *Naze* (Norwegian *nes*) of Norway (present-day Lindesnes), the southernmost point of Norway.
398 *Drammen*, town on the coast of Norway (not Sweden!), 35 km southwest of Oslo.
399 *Fredrikshald*, Norwegian town, present-day Halden, close to the Swedish border.
400 For *haul*.

beg some of his hands he sent us 12 men, & it was chiefly by their asistance that we got her off after we had almost despaird of it, There was a Bergen Galiotte[401] also in the Port the skipper of which came to asist seeming to be a Good sort of man, the Commander & superCargo of the Dublin came also to help us, but after many hours labour they were all of opinion it would be impossible to get the ship off, so that we had nothing else to do but to indeavour to save the Goods if possible, for which purpose spoke with the schipper[402] of the Bergen Galiotte offering him a good Reward to come & ly by us & take in our Goods, but he refusd it, I then applyd to the master & superCargo of the Dublin man whom I offerd 45 Guineas viz 40 to the Captain & 5 to the superCargo if they would do us that service, But they being willing to prosecute their voyage with the first opportunity were very unwilling to undertake it, though inclind to asist us, but pressing them very much I had reason to believe if we could find no other remedy they would have aggreed to it, In the mean time I sent the Captain & the Purser ashoar with the olderman who told us he had very Good ware houses ashoar where our Goods would be very safe, The rascal wanted to have them ashoar to plunder us in all probability, for the place he showd our people was half open & not fit to receive any thing, But by the blessing of God, & the indefatigable labour of the hands that came from the shoar & the 12 English from the Dublin man we by the help of several haulsers we had put out a stern got her loose after several hours fatigue which was done before the Captain came back from the shore, our next business was to haul the ship into deep water at a good distance from the Rock, which was difficult to do the wind blowing very fresh into the harbour, however we sent all our Anchors & haulsers ashoar to keep her fast

283

till better weather would allow us to cary her into a safer birth. Though this Accident had at first a dreadful appearance & gave me much more concern than our meeting with the Dutch & all the other hazards we run this voyage, yet I kept always up my spirits trusting that the Gracious Providence that had deliverd us from so many other dangers would not desert us in this, for which mercy to us we have reason to be very thankful. one misfortune on such an occasion is the Confusion & terrour every body is in, being at a loss what to do & obstructing things every moment by Contrary orders, the Captain ordering one way our officers another & Mr Graham a third, And as I could not pretend to understand my self what was best I thought it the best & safest way for us was to leave it to the Norway Pilotes on board who ought to know best the harbour & the proper

---

[401] *Gal(l)iot*, originally a small galley, rowed by sixteen or twenty oars with a single mast and sail, used in the 17th and 18th centuries to chase and capture enemy ships by boarding in wartime. During the 18th century it became the accepted term for a small Dutch trading vessel, the hull built barge fashion with a bluff, rounded bow, fitted with leeboards, and fore-and-aft rigged on a single mast, often with a sprit. (*The Oxford Companion to Ships & the Sea*, 1976, p. 336.)

[402] This spelling (cf. *skipper* 4 lines above) is probably influenced by Dutch *schipper* 'skipper', captain or master of a ship, but particularly applicable to smaller vessels.

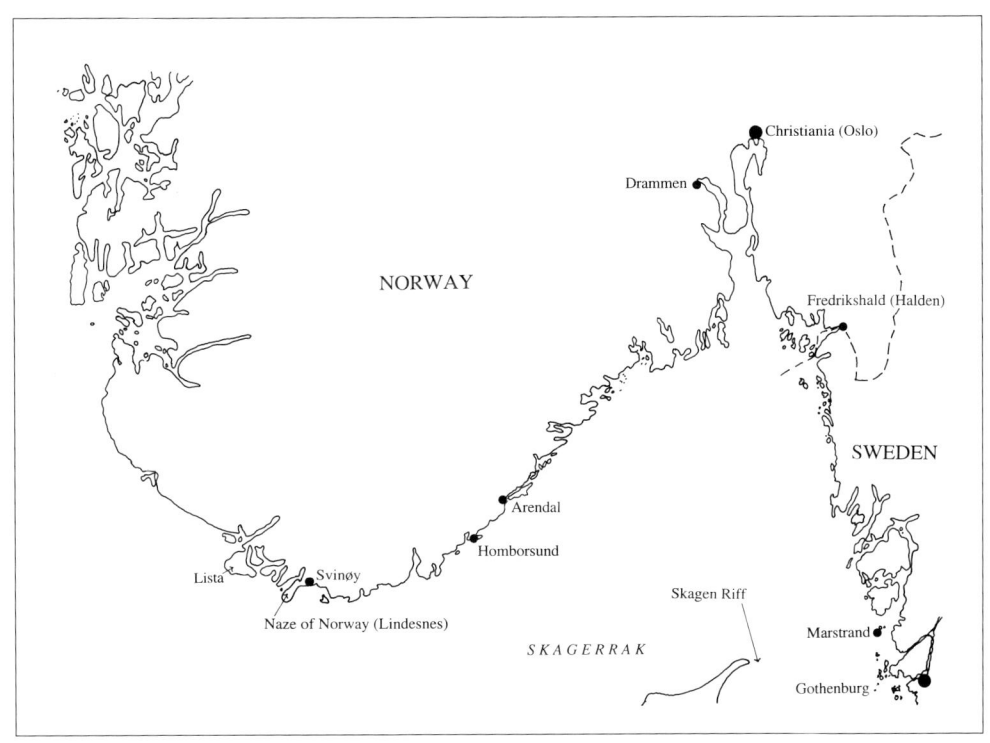

Southern Norway.

remedies for our misfortunes, (Assoon as the villain of a Pilote had set us on the rock he sneakd away in the confusion without our observing) and so I told the Captain & officers that as their opinions were all so different & I could not judge which was the rightest, I thought our safest way was to trust to the Pilotes, and this we could best answer for to the Company & to our Insurers in case of Accidents. And having reason to suspect their olderman to be a Rogue, I was resolvd he should have nothing to say but went amongst the rest that were at work & incouragd them as well as I could, and applyd especially to two of them who seemd to be the most active & knowing to do their best & let our officers know what methods they thought most proper, and I should reward them accordingly, I desird also our officers to consult them two as seeming to be the most expert. However blessd be God we escapd this disaster & I hope without damage, for the ship draws no water yet, which we have reason to wonder at considering how long she lay upon the Rock being 5 or 6 hours but did not stir all the while, and had she not been a very strong well built ship considering how heavy loaded she is she must have soon split in pieces.

– 15   Same tempestuous weather continues, so that cannot change our Birth, our officers say we cannot put to sea without 30 good hands for the few of our own that yet keep up have neither heart nor ability to do any thing, so that I orderd imnediately to look out for as many Good hands as could be got

Today our worthy priest came upon the Quarter Deck a little before

284

Dinner to desire the Captain to let him go ashoar, without taking the least notice of me though present, as he has not yet done nor made the least apology for his late Insolence & disobedience, I was resolvd therefore to mortify him & make him know himself a little better, I therefore desird the Captain to tell him that he was pleasd lately to say he had nothing to do with me, I must therefore now acquaint him that I had to do with him, & would not permit him to go ashore This put the priest in a violent passion, and he came upon the quarter Deck where I was vapouring with his hat on & his Cane in his hand ready dressd to go ashoar, and came up to me in that Insolent manner asking if I would hinder him to go ashoar, I told him he should not go that his business was to stay aboard & do his Duty especially to the sick who he knew were daily wanting him, He flew out more outragious walking about like a fellow half distracted & railing at me very impudently sometimes holding up his hand & Cane, all which I resolvd to bear on Account of his Cloath & knowing I should soon have an opportunity to do my self justice more to his cost, But he continuing in his Insolence & often asking the same question if I would not let him go ashoar, made me tell him abruptly that he should not go & that he was a fool & a madman & desird him not to trouble me more with his Impudence, But he continued in his Insolence till we went to dinner He left us for a little while to consult his friend Lund & came up again when I was at table with the Dublin Master & superCargo & the Skipper of the Bergen Galiotte, & begun his former Insolence, for which & his conduct afterwards when he went ashoar, see the particular Account I gave in at Gottenburg. I must say I never was in Company with such a parcel of fools & madmen as I have aboard, who have neither sense of their Duty, nor oaths, nor Companys nor even his Majestys orders for them to obey me, nor even their own Interest when they know it is in my power to ruine them when I get Home & call them to account for their disobedience & scandalous Conduct.

Augt 16   The Vogde[403] (as they call him, which is a sort I believe of a Judge or petty Governour of a precinct) of Lister[404], a Town some 4 or 5 Swedish miles distant came on board to see the ship whom I treated as well as I could & made him a present of some Tea, As the olderman of the Pilotes had deceivd me as well as another Imployd to get sailors for me here, for their scheme was rather to delay us & keep the ship here as long

---

[403] Swedish *fogde*, Danish *foged*, 'sheriff', 'bailiff'.
[404] *Lista* is a peninsula to the northwest of the Naze.

[as] they could for their own profit, I took this opportunity to ask the Vogde if he could not procure me some Good men at his Town that would undertake the voyage, which he very civilly promisd to do & bring them next day,

Aug^t — 17

The Vogde came again & brought 3 sailors with him, being sent by the rest to aggree with me, I accordingly aggreed with them for 14 Danish Rixdollers a head with their Victuals to Gottenburg[405]

— 18

There came 15 in all appearance brisk & sturdy fellows from Lister but would not stand to the aggreement made with the other three, but insisted on 20 RixDollers a man & went directly ashoar, upon this I orderd a Boat Ready to send with Mr Ross with a Letter to the vogde of Lister to complain to him, As he was going away [I told] some of them that had stayd aboard to have a little patience till they went ashoar to speak to their Comrades, At the same time I sent Mr Ross ashoar to get their positive answer, and if they would not aggree to lose no time but go directly to the vogde with the Letter, the 3 first who had aggreed in presence of the vogde came onboard promising to stand to their aggreement, which they hoped the others ashoar would also do, They also came on board & aggreed at same price we took their names & orderd them to be ready at a moments warning.

— 19

But the beast of a Captain had like again to have spoild all, being inragd that I was able to procure men without his asistance which he never troubled himself about,[406] fell a bullying the men I had hir'd & quarelld with the olderman ashore who to be revengd did all he could with the fellows to hinder them going the voyage, He came aboard in the Evening drunk with heavy complaints against Capt. Trolle who he sayd had abusd him & that he would not suffer it & that therefore none of the sailors should go the voyage, Though I suspected him to be a rascal, yet I was obligd to bear with him & sooth him as well as I could (to hinder this malicious design of his) and appeard very angry that Trolle should have abusd him who was as good a man (as he often told me) and beggd he would not regard what Trolle sayd, for he had nothing to do in the Affair & that I hop'd he would not to be revengd of him do me an Injury who had never done him any and assurd him the sailors should have nothing to do with the Captain but that I would take care of them & see them well treated, In short with coaxing & drink I brought him to a good

humour again & he promisd before he went away for my sake to set all things to

---

[405] The wages seem to be a forfeit until Gothenburg, including victuals. The level of compensation appears very high, compared to what the able sailors in the service of the Company earned.

[406] A further example of specific tasks of the captain which Campbell took over.

right again. But I had enough ado to keep Trolle & him from quarrelling in my presence.

Augt 20th Early in the morning orderd a Gun to be fird for the men to come on board, being ready to sail, but there not coming above 3 or 4 I found it would be necessary for me to go ashoar my self & talk with them and also coax the Olderman again at whose house they all lay being the only house here, and a sort of Inn or publick house, I therefore went very early ashore, & spoke to the sailors & promisd to treat them well & even better than I had aggreed to, & pressd them to go on board immediately [&] orderd every one of them a dram & made a present of Tea to the oldermans wife, and saw them all go off before I would leave the House. I then orderd on board all the provisions we had got here for when we came in we were almost at our last shift for wine & fowls being just spent at our putting in to this port, so now we have 20 seeming good hands besides our own people so that I hope we have nothing to fear, yesterday I was surprizd with a visit from one marshal master of a small ship belonging to Stockholm who had put in a few miles from hence in his return from St abes[407], He stayd all night with me, & having now got up Anchor & under sail I made him at parting a present of some Tea & Arrack & gave him a Letter for the Comp^y to put into a Post house near the place where his ship lay, Just as we were under sail came aboard a Danish Admiral who it seems has the command on this Coast, He went directly to Trolle whom it seems he had known when a Lieotennant in the Danish service, & told him that the Pilote that brought us in had complaind to him that we had not payd him for his Pilotage, and that we must pay him, Trolle advisd me what he sayd I told him that I thought we had more reason to demand justice & have him punishd, (than to pay him for bringing [us] in such a danger) which I thought was the Admirals duty to do for an Example & to prevent him serving other ships as he had servd us, He pretended he had already told him so but that he sayd it was the fellows mistake & the Kings orders were to pay so much & there was no remedy, Though I had right enough to dispute this had I been in a place where I could apply for right, yet being unwilling to have any disputes with a man in that station who had it in his power to do greatest Injury to other Swedish ships in case they should put in to any port under his Jurisdiction, Had the Captain pay him which I think was

287

4 Rixdollers, it being all regulated & the dues taxd in a printed list for that purpose, which he accordingly gave the Admiral, for we had not seen the Pilote since he set us upon the Rock. He soon returnd ashore and as he had taken no notice of me (though he knew who I was) I let him go without taking the least notice of him.

---

[407] Possibly identical with *St. Abbs*, on the southeast coast of Scotland, north of Berwick-upon-Tweed. The reading is uncertain ("St ubes"?).

We got out of this vile hole, which is a very narrow port & surrounded with Rocks or small Islands at the Entrance, with a fine N W wind & the finest weather we have seen for a long time so that I hope to morrow to surprize our friends at Gottenburg.

The Norway sailors being desirous to have their money advanc'd the Olderman gave me the money to pay them, 161 Dan. R. Dollers, for a bill I gave him on Mr Tham [408] merchant at Gottenburg, who as I soon learnd after my Arrival, had lately faild and at this time absconding, but the Company took up the bill & payd it.

Augt 21st The wind has shifted this morning to S.E. which make us tack about frequently to weather Schager riff [409], Lund alarmd us in the night who seeing a light of some ship took it to be that upon the Riff, and came bawling us upon Deck to tack about, we saw the Light & not being certain what it was kept off, but found afterwards it was the light of some ship.

– 22 Saw the land to westward of the Riff as well as the Riff it self, then made over for the Swedes coast with a very scrimp [410] wind, After Dinner came in sight of Wingó [411] tryd to get up with it but could not, orderd to fire Guns for Pilotes to come off, There came a boat soon off, but went directly back again, who as we found afterwards was a pilot that knew the ship & therefore went back & from thence directly to Gottenburg in hopes of getting a good reward for news which they little expected, soon afterward came off another from Wargehóla [412] whither he thought to have brought us, but we fell to Leeward & not willing to keep the sea at that time of the Evening made for the first port we could get which was Maerstrand [413], where we cast Anchor before night. I sent our Purser over land to the Comp^y with the news of our arrival & the list or Invoice of the Cargo, He arrivd at Gottenburg next morning, which [being] the forreign Post day they had the opportunity

288

to send the news to forreign parts & advertise our sale. As the affair of my being stopt & carryd to Batavia was known near 2 months ago by a Letter I sent to the

---

[408] *Volrath Tham* (1687–1737), merchant in Gothenburg, deputy judge at the Swedish Board of Trade, succeeded François Bedoire in 1732 as one of the directors of the Company (cf. Introduction p. xx). In 1733 he absconded to Norway but was permitted to return later that year.

[409] *Skagen Riff* (Danish, Swedish *Skagens rev*), a dangerous reef stretching 4 km east-northeast from the Skaw, the northernmost point of Denmark, where the Skagerrak and the Kattegat meet.

[410] A less common word for 'scant'.

[411] *Vinga*, the westernmost island in the sea approaches to Gothenburg.

[412] *Vargö Håla* (Swedish *håla* = English noun *hollow*), anchorage-ground at Vargö, an island in the Gothenburg archipelago, where ships bound for the East Indies used to wait for favourable weather (cf. note 6).

[413] *Marstrand* (see *Diary* p. 4 and note 4).

Company from the Straits of Sunda when in the Dutch hands which arrivd in England with the English ships about the middle of June, they had also all known what Character I had from his Maj^ty (which I conceald from every body when I went from Sweden) of his Envoy & Minister to the Emperour of China &c I was therefore now obligd to appear in the same & hoisted the flag at the top mast head, The Commandant of Maerstrand Collonell ⁤ [414] sent me immediately his complements & invited me to dine with him next day, The Captain officiously told the officers that I had a retinue of Gentlemen with me & he would do very well to invite them also, so that the Governour[415] sent next morning the Captain of the Train to desire me to bring what Gentlemen I pleasd with me. While we were at Supper Lund being I don't [know] how frightend at the sight of the flag I had set up begun to reflect on his past conduct & flew out into a sort of madness, He was in the steerige & calld out we were talking of him, (though his name had not been mentiond) & sayd it was not his fault, and fell a railing at the Captain, & sayd he had done his Duty but now he was punishd for his former faults, In short he was afraid I should have sent him ashoar a prisoner, this being the place where people are condenmd[416] for life to work at the fortifications as slaves when pardond for Capital Crimes, I was obligd to call to him to hold his tongue, else I must take another Course which he would have cause to repent, for had he continued I should have desird the Commandant to take him into his Custod, upon this he grew quiet. But in the night he was quite distracted with fear, & got out of his Cabbin naked, & run about crying to spare his Life, and at last hid himself in one of the mens hammocks

August 22^d As Mr Pike had not hitherto made the least acknowlegement or ask'd pardon for his late rudeness mentiond on the ⁤ [417] and that now we were to go ashore together (I having desird the SuperCargos & Captain to come along with me to the Commandants as he had desird) we could not very well be in Company together without treating him as he deservd & I had promisd him the first land we came to, & Mr Graham particularly who is of a very passionate temper meditated a severe revenge against him, which I

289

willing to prevent if possible chiefly on his Brother's Account[418], & that of all things it was not proper for me in the station I was in to be ingagd in any quarell especially just at our Return, I was resolvd to try to bring him to some Reason & better manner before we left the ship, I spoke first to Mr Graham about it &

---

[414] Campbell has left a blank. The Commandant at this time, whose name Campbell had forgotten, was *Peter Julius Starenflycht* (1698–1743).
[415] I.e. the Commandant of Marstrand.
[416] *Sic.*
[417] Campbell has left a blank.
[418] See note 299.

advis'd him not to insist upon all the Satisfaction we had a right to, nor to treat him as he well deservd there being no honour to be got by having to do with such a contemptible fool, for that reason I thought it would be better to send for him & make him ask pardon for his Rudeness, which if he refusd to do I had nothing more to say but must leave him to do as he pleasd, & that for my part I would find ways enough to do my self justice at a proper time, with some difficulty I perswaded him to aggree to this, I therefore calld Mr Pike into the Cabbin as also Mr Morford Baron & Moir who were witnesses of his Impudence, & remonstrated to him before them, that now we were going ashoar I must put him in mind of what I had promis'd, but that to prevent a greater shame falling upon him I was willing yet to give him this one opportunity of making an apology for his fault, which had he known any thing of the world or good manners he had done long ago, He begun to be in a little confusion and sayd he did not mean to affront us in what was alleg'd against him & some other wretched stuff, I told him I always supposd people meant as they spoke when the words were so plainly expressd that no favourable construction could be put upon them that his had been so very plain & spoke before sufficient witnesses that I could not but take it for one of the highest affronts that could be offerd, & that it was no doubt designd for such, and that I expected Satisfaction for it, He asked what I desir'd, I told him I thought the least thing he could do (and which he ought to have done at first) was to ask pardon of me & the other Gentlemen he had affronted, In short after much nonsense he utterd he ask'd pardon with a very bad grace of Mr Graham & me & such as he had affronted.

We went ashore & din'd with the Commandant & after dinner went to view the Castle & works, It is seated on the top of a high rock, defended by a platform of Guns all round, & in the midde on the highest part a very high Tower or Donjohn[419] vastly thick & several stories high, with large heavy Cannon all

round, but which cannot I think reach all the Inlets to the Harbour, but there were orders the Commandant told me to make a little fortificcation at the point of land that runs out to   [420] by which ships pass very near which will make this Island much stronger, & defend all the Inlets, It appears to be a small Island about an English mile about & not half a mile from the opposite land, & in some places not so far, The Criminals or slaves here, some are in Chains, others not, chiefly imployd to work at the fortifications, the worst sort have nothing but bread & water, the others (for there are of all ranks here both sea & Land officers) if they have money of their own or supply from their friends it is well, for the Governour treats each as he pleases or finds most for his Interest The town lyes by the water

---

[419] *Donjon*, 'the great tower of a castle' (the same word as *dungeon*).
[420] Campbell has left a blank.

side, where ships of 200 Tun[421] lie close by the key[422], It is but small but neat enough, and the harbour is well defended against all winds, & has 2 Entrys into it very narrow, was once a noble harbour, & could contain all the Swedish fleet & many more ships than they keep, till the year [423] that the Danes came up into the harbour with [423] ships, though there were lying here [423] men of war who instead of hindring them sunk their ships in the harbour without firing a Gun, & afterwards went ashoar to the Castle & perswaded the then Commander [423] to give up the fort without firing a Gun, And the Danes assoon as they capitulated sent the Commandant a few fans & some other womens Toys by way of mockery for his Cowardice, The Commander was afterwards beheaded, & the Captains of the men of war broke in a disgraceful manner & degraded from their quality & renderd uncapable of further service, but deservd a much severer punishment.[424] However they spoild the harbour by sinking their ships, for no big ships now can come so near the key, for they have not learnd the address to blow the ships up though under water which might be done & the harbour made good again, It cost Sweden also pretty dear for before the Danes would restore it at the peace made between the two Crowns since the present King came to the throne of Sweden they were obligd to aggree to pay the Danes the sound Duties for all their ships that pass, which I believe is but half of what other forreign ships pay, but which they did not pay formerly.

Here I learnd by some of the Custom house officers that Mr Charles Pike[425] & my Brother[426] & his wife were at Gottenburg. The Custom

291

house officers came on board, but I let them know they had nothing to say to us & gave them one of the Copies of the Companys Charter, we suppd with the Governour who & his Lady treated us very handsomely went & lay on board at night.

---

[421] It is not clear whether Campbell means the English ton or the Swedish heavy last (*svåra lästen*). 100 *svåra läster* = 239 3/4 English tons.

[422] For *quay*.

[423] Campbell has left a blank.

[424] Campbell's brief account of this incident is on the whole correct. In July 1719 the famous Danish-Norwegian admiral Peter Wessel Tordenskiold (1690–1720), who since April had been trying to blockade Gothenburg, launched a successful attack on Marstrand after having personally made a reconnaissance of the town in the disguise of a fisherman. A Swedish fleet of some 15 ships was caught in the harbour, and most of the ships were sunk by their fleeing Swedish crews. After a siege that lasted only four days, and chiefly by skilful application of cunning, Tordenskiold then managed to bring about the surrender of the castle, which at this time was considered one of the strongest in Europe. The unfortunate commandant's name, which Campbell had forgotten, was *Henrik Danckwardt*. As the garrison marched off, the Danes formed up in double line, scorning and ridiculing the capitulating officers by presenting them with various ladies' knickknacks. (Olán 1939, p. 64 ff.)

[425] See note 299.

[426] See note 305.

Augt 23^d very durty weather & bad wind with rain, stayd aboard all day

– 24. Bought some fresh provisions from one Bagge a merchant here, had a visit from the Burgermeester[427]

– 25th In the morning came from Gottenburg Mr Charles Pike one of the Directours & Mr Nils Sahlgren[428] merchant of Gottenburg.

– 26th In the morning set sail with a fair wind & arriv'd at 4 in the Afternoon with the ship by the new wharf[429], Here the Captains obstinacy set us upon the mud though I had told the Pilote to keep us clear of it but set us in good Anchoring ground which he told me he would have done but the Captain hinderd him. We passd Elfsburg fort[430] & he would salute but with 2 Guns, and when came to Anchor saluted the Town with 8 Guns. He was resolvd to continue a brute to the last & end as he had begun. The day after coming to Marstrand not knowing how long we might ly there I sent away the sick in 2 large Boats to Gottenburg with the surgeons mate with a Letter to Rear Admiral Utfalt[431] to get some place provided for them in Town, when they arrivd they were afraid to let them land having got a report amongst them that we had an Infectious distemper aboard which made the General send for the Physician of the Town to examine them who assurd him it was nothing but the scurvy, they were therefore permitted to land & lodgings provided them. Lieotennant Lund & the Priest took the opportunity to go away without asking my leave, Assoon as I heard of it I wrote to Admiral Utfalt to get Lund put in Arrest having some things of consequence to lay to his charge which he did assoon as he enterd the Gates, and had him made prisoner on the main Guard.

Before we came to Anchor Rear Admiral Utfalt came aboard in the Kings Pinnace & brought me ashoar, I waited immediately upon the Governour Baron de Ribbing[432], who (as well as all other friends) receivd me with great Civility & Joy. So that now bless'd be God I put a good end to a voyage attended with a great deal of Chagrin & uneasiness as well as Dangers, about 18 months from leaving Gottenburg, for which I desire to return my hearty thanks to God Almighty who relievd us from so many difficulties, contrary to our own

---

[427] From Dutch *burgemeester* (Swedish *borgmästare*), mayor of a town.

[428] *Niclas Sahlgren* (1701–76) was one of the prime movers in establishing the Swedish East India Company (cf. Introduction p. xx f.) and one of its directors between 1733 and 1768. He became one of the wealthiest men in Sweden, spending part of his fortune on generous donations for scientific and humanitarian purposes, including the large Gothenburg hospital which still bears his name.

[429] The so-called *New Wharf* had been established on the south side of the estuary of the Göta River in the beginning of the 18th century. The place is still called *Nya Varvet* in Swedish.

[430] *Nya Älvsborg*, fortress in the estuary of the Göta River.

[431] *Jean von Utfall* (1681–1749), chief of the Admiralty in Gothenburg.

[432] *Bengt Ribbing* (1686–1741), Governor and Commandant General of the County of Gothenburg and Bohus.

expectation as well as that of most of our friends. I arrivd sooner than any of them expected, after they had heard I was carryd to Batavia, & even 6 weeks before their China ships arrivd which had passd the Straits of Sunda while I was at Batavia, & about 2 months before the 5 ships that left Batavia with us arrivd in Holland.

I made all the haste in my Return voyage that I could, being apprehensive of a misunderstanding between the Crown of Sweden & the States General on Account of my being stopt & carryd to Batavia, for before I came his Majesty had complaind upon the Receipt of my Letter from the Straits of Sunda a Copy of which he had sent to his Envoy to produce to them, They declard their utter ignorance of the matter and that they had given no orders whether directly or indirectly to the Regency of Batavia to commit any such violence as was complaind of, being always disposd to live in a Good understanding & Amity with his Maj^{ty} &c And the Common people at Stockholm had shown great resentment (as well as the whole nation) threatning to pull down the Dutch Envoys house, and as his Secretary (who acted in the Envoys absence) told me on his return he was afraid to walk the streets or be seen abroad, the people were so much inragd against the Dutch, and measures had been proposd to seize all the Dutch ships that were then in the Port[s] of Sweden, & the Governour of Gottenburg told me he was expecting every moment orders to put it in Execution against some ships then in the Port, These violent measures my coming put a stop to, which is what I much desird.

Having wrote to my friends at Stockholm of my Arrival & presented my Duty to their Majesties, they sent me complements of Congratulation & were earnest to see me there assoon as possible, but having much to do at Gottenburg, with the unloading of the ship & other Affairs of the Comp^y I beg'd they would excuse my coming up till those affairs were over, His Maj^{ty} allowd me to stay a little while and desird in the mean time I would send him a report of the most remarkable transactions of the voyage particularly what related to my being stopt & carryd to Batavia, which I drew up in French[433] & sent accompany'd with a Letter to his Majesty. I soon after went thither post[434] my self, and immediately waited upon his Majesty who receivd me with great Goodness, and told me he was obligd as he sayd the whole nation was for my good Conduct in this expedition, & that I had behavd with prudence & resolution with which he was extremely satisfy'd. The Queen also receivd me with a great deal

---

[433] Campbell is once again referring to his *Relation abrégé …* (RAS. H & S 52).
[434] *Post* in the obsolete adverbial sense 'with post-horses', 'by post', hence 'with speed' (originating in the phrase *ride in post*, abbreviated to *ride post*, later extended to other verbs).

of affability. The King would that I should have the honour to dine with him, but excusd it at that time because the Queen was indisposd, but next night askd me to sup with their Majesties which I had the honour to do, and was treated with more regard than I had room to expect. Eating with the King is an honour, which is only allow'd to persons of such a Rank, at least that of a Collonell & such Characters as are equal to that, which I had not at present, But the King being resolv'd to show me more honour had proposd to some friends to make me a Baron of the Kingdom which I declind, He therefore would have me to accept of being Counsellour Extraordinary of the College of Commerce, which he proposd in Senate[435] in such a manner as was much to my honour, which was universally approvd by the senatours, who expressd themselves very kindly in my favour, saying they were glad of such an opportunity to aggree to what his Maj[ty] proposd for a person of my merit &c

His Maj[ty] besides orderd immediately his picture to be drawn in miniature & set all round with Brilliants & a Crown of Brill[i]ants over it, to make me a present of which not being ready at my first coming was deliverd me upon my return thither a few months afterwards, a very handsome picture & of a considerable value.[436]

The Company having thought fit still to insist on some redress from the Dutch for the injury done their Affairs by my being stopt and coming Home so late, as it might be prejudicial to our sales which must now be made the beginning of winter, I therefore gave in a memorial to his Maj[ty] in the Comp[ys] name representing the hardships & Charges that Arrest put us to at the same time acknowleging the Civilities payd me by the Regency of Batavia & their having done all they could to repair their fault &c The King orderd his Envoy at the Hague to make a representation on this head to the States, if he found it would be of any service, But as the States had declard themselves very handsomely before, and that they had no hand in it, & that they could not well punish the Government of Batavia for acting according to the informations they had receivd about us from their people in China, we thought better not to open new sores or to make any more stir about it.

I can't help taking notice of the fate of the SuperCargo Schultz who was the cause of this misfortune by his false Intelligence to the Regency

of Batavia, As he had most grossly cheated his masters the Dutch Company in

---

[435] The Swedish *riksråd* or State Council, sharing the executive power with the King. The principal State offices were dependent on this "Senate", which was exclusively reserved for the nobility.
[436] Campbell is wearing this decoration in the portrait facing the title page of the present edition.

China, so he was resolvd to continue the same practices upon his arrival, for having loaded much more Goods than the Companys privilege allowd him, he was resolv'd to have them all smuggled ashoar privately, so got a boat come off to them lying a little way out at sea, by which he sent the best parcel of his Goods, the Comp^y being informd of it, seizd a good part of the Goods, & sent the Captain of the ship & other officers who were privy to his Roguery into prison, but he luckily for himself escapd, for the Company having receivd from the other SuperCargos a full Account of all his Roguish practices as well as in China as in this last Affair were resolvd to make a publick example of him (even threatend to behead him) if they could seize him, in the mean offerd a reward to take him & publickly outlawd him & confiscated all they could find belonging to him, I was told he fled to England where he now lives in London.

I was obligd to leave Stockholm in a few weeks, after having receivd great Civilities from all the senatours & great men there, & came back to the beginning of our sales the 10th of October. And though we had no forreign buyers come there (being so late of the season) & that the Swedes were not usd to such a Trade, yet we sold our Goods very well & made a profitable voyage to the Concern'd.

I having wrote to Mr Konig at Stockholm (at my Arrival at Gottenburg) a short Account of the voyage & Conduct of the Captain, Lieotennant Lund & our Priest &c Mr Konig happen'd to read part of the Letter to one of my friends a senatour, who finding somethings in it that he was unwilling to read & which he knew I designd only for his own private information, his Excellence would know the rest of the letter by which means he discoverd the bad conduct of those people, & he mentiond it to the King, who was the more dissatisfyd as the two Chief of them were his Maj^{tys} officers one a Captain Lieotennant or ships master, & the other a Lieotennant, The King was pleasd to ask me about them, As I was not willing to ruin them I declind making any complaints telling his Maj^{ty} that now the voyage was over, I had nothing to say against any Body, But his Maj^{ty} being resolv'd to find out the whole Affair, sent orders to the Governour & Rear Admiral of Gottenburg to examine them in my presence & ask me what I had to complain of against them, which was accordingly done, But though I was not ill pleasd that some notice might be taken of

295

their bad conduct, to prevent others doing the like another time, yet I did not care to expose them too much to the Kings resentment, so that I sav'd the Captain as well as I could & desird the Governour to make a Report as little to his prejudice as he could consistent with truth since the Captain had ownd himself in the wrong which is all I wanted, As for the Priest he could deny nothing of what I allegd against him but would make no submission, but as he was a worthless wretch and a Churchman I thought better decline solliciting the punishment he deservd, & was satisfyd with the Bishops reprimanding him. But Lieotennant

Lunds case was the most difficult to manage so as to save him from ruin, for I having proofs enough to produce of his mutiny & disobedience, had it come to a tryal it might have cost him his Life, I therefore consulted the Judge of the Admiralty who is Judge Advocat in such Cases, and showd him my Case, who told me if he was brought to a Courtmartial he must be condemnd to dye, This I being resolv'd to prevent got people underhand to hint to Lund that if he would confess his fault to the Company & ask pardon of me & his superiour officers that he had disobeyd that they believd I would be satisfyd & would clear him without bringing him to a tryal, He pretended to be a little huffish & sayd he would stand his tryal I sent him word he should assoon as he pleasd, but he soon thought better of it, & waited upon the Directours & acknowlegd his fault & askd pardon of me & the officers &c He intreated very much to have his wages allowd him for the time I had suspended him, but the Company did not think proper to allow him that, since it was necessary for example sake that he should suffer for his folly in some measure, However I afterwards prevaild with them upon his great submissions & earnest intreaties to allow him half wages for that time. We dismissd the Priest after making him dance attendance for some months, and before I left Stockholm for my second voyage one of the senatours told me that he was come up & had given in a petition to the King begging a benefice on account of his having made a voyage to China with me, But as they well rememberd his Conduct during the voyage it was not thought proper to reward such a worthless fellow.

[P. 296 blank]

243

Copy Letter to Baron Gustaf van Eimhof
Secretary to the Regency of Batavia

Abord le Fred. R. Sueciae
aupres de Bantam 14me
Fevrier 1733

Monsieur

C'est avec beaucoup de regret que Je me pourrois pas rester plus long-tems a Batavia pour profiter de l'occasion d'y jouir votre aggreable Compagnie.

Messieurs les SobreCargues & moy avons a vous remercier tant pour vos honnete-tez a Batavia que pour le present de Bierre qu'il vous a plû de nous envoyer sur notre bord.

J'ay prié Monsr Rawenhoff de se charger de quelques Bagatelles pour vous livrer a Batavia & Je prens la liberté Monsieur de vous prier de les accepter comme une marque de notre reconnoissance.

Permettez moy Monsieur de vous assurer que Je suis avec beaucoup d'estime & de Consideration

Messieurs les SobreCargues	Monsieur
me prient de vous faire leurs	Votre tres h. & tres ob.
Complemens.	Serviteur

A Monsr Monsr le Baron G.v.E. Secretaire de la haute Regence a Batavia

[47 blank pages]

Indexes

(Unlike references in the footnotes, page numbers in the indexes refer to the modern pagination)

Abbreviations

Austr.   Austrian
Ch.   Chinese
Co.   Company
Dan.   Danish
Du.   Dutch
Engl.   English
Fr.   French
Ital.   Italian
Norw.   Norwegian
Span.   Spanish
Sw.   Swedish

Index of named persons

(excluding Colin Campbell and names in "Bibliographical essay")

Index of geographical names

Subject index

(Names of ships in italics)

List of Illustrations